Contract Law for Paralegals

Melinda R. Thomas

John F. Kennedy University,
School of Law

Contract Law for Paralegals

Melinda R. Thomas

John F. Kennedy University,
School of Law

WEST PUBLISHING
an imprint of Delmar Publishers

A division of International Thomson Publishing, Inc.
Minneapolis/St. Paul, Albany, NY, Bonn, Boston, Cincinatti, Detroit,
Johannesburg, London, Madrid, Melbourne, Mexico City,
New York, Paris, San Francisco, Singapore, Tokyo, Toronto,
Washington

Production Credits

Design: Merry Obrecht Sawdey / Shade Tree Designs
Copyediting: Patricia Lewis
Composition and imaging: Carlisle Communications
Cover illustration: © Joseph Nettis, Photo Researchers Inc.
Cover design: Sandra L. Triemert

West's Commitment to the Environment

In 1906, West Publishing Company began recycling materials left over from the production of books. This began a tradition of efficient and responsible use of resources. Today, 100% of our legal bound volumes are printed on acid-free, recycled paper consisting of 50% new fibers. West recycles nearly 27,700,000 pounds of scrap paper annually—the equivalent of 229,300 trees. Since the 1960s, West has devised ways to capture and recycle waste inks, solvents, oils, and vapors created in the printing process. We also recycle plastics of all kinds, wood, glass, corrugated cardboard, and batteries, and have eliminated the use of polystyrene book packaging. We at West are proud of the longevity and the scope of our commitment to the environment.

West pocket parts and advance sheets are printed on recyclable paper and can be collected and recycled with newspapers. Staples do not have to be removed. Bound volumes can be recycled after removing the cover.

Production, Prepress, Printing and Binding by West Publishing Company.

 TEXT IS PRINTED ON 10% POST CONSUMER RECYCLED PAPER

British Library Cataloguing-in-Publication Data. A catalogue record for this book is available from the British Library.

COPYRIGHT ©1997   By WEST PUBLISHING
                   An imprint of Delmar Publishers
                   A division of International, Thomson Publishing, Inc.
                   610 Opperman Drive
                   P.O. Box 64526
                   St. Paul, MN 55164-0526

Printed in the United States of America

04 03 02 01 00 99 98 97   8 7 6 5 4 3 2 1 0

Library of Congress Cataloging-in-Publication Data

Thomas, Melinda R.
     Contract law for paralegals / Melinda R. Thomas.
          p.   cm.
     Includes index.
     ISBN 0-314-20180-7 (pbk. : alk. paper)
     1. Contracts—United States.   2. Legal assistants—United States—
     —Handbooks, manuals, etc.   I. Title.
KF801.Z9T44   1997
346.73'02—dc20
[347.3062]   96-46083
                                                                     CIP

To my parents,
Elisabeth and Robert

Contents

CHAPTER 13
Third-Party Beneficiaries   271

Table of Cases

Preface

My purpose in writing this contract law textbook is to offer the paralegal student and teacher basic coverage of the law of contracts in a new and interesting format. The textbook is written in a simple style which is easily accessible to the beginner. It contains many examples, study questions, charts and assignments designed to help the student learn the major concepts necessary to the practice of today's contract law. The textbook also contains edited versions of cases with study questions, both of which are included to further comprehension of concepts and elicit class discussion. It is my hope that the simple, practical approach of the text will enable the busy paralegal student to gain solid knowledge of contract law, as well as some practice in applying this knowledge to situations that may arise on the job.

Teaching Aids and Supplements

Instructor's Manual with Testing Materials.   Written by the text author, the manual includes an overview of each chapter, teaching suggestions, suggested answers to the Review Questions and Assignments, and testing materials.

Survival Manual for Paralegals.   Written by Bradene L. Moore and Kathleen Mercer Reed, both of the University of Toledo Community and Technical College, this brief (100-page) pamphlet helps students make the most of their paralegal education. Topics include choosing courses, learning to study, and tips on taking exams.

Strategies and Tips for Paralegal Educators.   A pamphlet by Anita Tebbe of Johnson County Community College, offers specific teaching ideas to instructors to aid students in researching their educational goals.

Citation-at-a-Glance.   This card is a concise, portable reference to the basic citation rules for the most commonly cited legal sources. The rules and examples conform to *The Bluebook: A Uniform System of Citation.* Classroom quantities are available to adopters of the text.

West's **Paralegal Video Library** includes *The Drama of the Law II* and *I Never Said I Was a Lawyer,* among other videos. Available to qualified adopters.

Acknowledgments

This textbook would not have been possible without the invaluable and untiring efforts of my research assistant, Steven Feller. I am very grateful for his patience and support throughout this process and for his ever-ingenious research and computer skills. Thanks are due as well to my husband, Michael, and daughter, Eryn, for their enthusiasm and their tolerance of harried tempers and hectic deadlines. I am greatly indebted also to my colleague and dear friend, Peter Jan Honigsberg, for all his support, advice and encouragement from the beginning of this project to its end. Special thanks to my friend, Betsy Cohen - and she definitely knows why!

I'd like to thank the following reviewers for their valuable suggestions:

Joseph Annacarto
Star Technical Institute, PA

Philip A. Augustino
Erie Community College, NY

Anneta A. Buster
Johnson County Community College, KS

Angela Carson
Cleveland State Community College, TN

Teri Conaway
Pellissippi State Technical Institute, TN

Paul Guymon
William Rainey Harper College, IL

Jane S. Johnson
May Technical College, MT

Jerome M. P. Kole
Ferris State University, MI

Bill Koleszar
Denver Business College, CO

Gail Krebs
Commonwealth College, VA

Robert D. Loomis
Spokane Community College, WA

Penny Lynn
Parks Junior College, CO

Joseph D. Marcus
Prince George's Community College, MD

Karen S. McLead
Segal Institute, FL

Jill H. O'Connor
Sacred Heart University, CT

Cindy Sheaffer
Central Pennsylvania Business School

Kathleen M. Smith
The Career Institute, PA

Mary A. Whiting
Brooklyn College, NY

Joseph Woodland
Capitol Business College, WA

INTRODUCTION

A Word to the Paralegal Student

This book is designed to help students become paralegals or "legal assistants" who will work under the supervision of attorneys. Its main purpose is to help the instructor provide a law office staff, a legal department in a business, or a government agency. The author certainly would be pleased and flattered if law students or laypeople find this text helpful in increasing their own understanding of the law. But, the primary purpose of the text is to provide the basics of contract law in a format which is useful for classroom instruction.

This text provides a complete, basic contracts course for paralegals. It offers legal theory and practical training all in one volume. The text is written in "plain English." For easy reference, important terms also found in the Glossary are printed in **bold-faced type.** The text presents contract concepts in simple language accessible to non lawyers. It includes the following:

- basic contract rules and concepts
- chapter by chapter learning guides
- examples that show how the law is applied
- exercises to make contract principles easier to grasp
- short contract drafting exercises
- optional research projects
- examples of actual contract provisions
- a glossary of terms to help learn legal vocabulary
- exercises to prepare students for on-the-job tasks
- references for further study

The paralegal profession has had enormous growth in the past few years. In response to this growth, the number of paralegal programs has also grown dramatically. Currently, there are almost 900 paralegal programs operating in the United States. In all of these programs, much of the law taught in law schools is offered in paralegal courses. In spite of the enormous numbers of paralegal programs and paralegal students, relatively few textbooks have been written for the specific needs of the paralegal student. Most traditional law textbooks are casebooks, which contain excerpts from the written opinions of judges. For the most part, their length and detail makes them impractical for use in shorter paralegal courses. In addition, these casebooks contain little information about the "nuts and bolts" aspects of practicing law. Yet, a legal assistant who provides support to attorneys is likely to be very involved with these practical aspects of a law practice.

Thus, traditional law school texts do not make really satisfactory tools for paralegal education. They are too long and too theoretical. The author hopes this text provides an alternative that will help the paralegal student find his or her way through the intricacies of contract law. And if, along the way, the student discovers some of the excitement, the social policy, and the human drama behind this ancient but most modern field, so much the better!

Why Paralegals Need to Know the Law

It is sometimes assumed that paralegals are glorified clerks or secretaries, and that they do not need to know anything but the simplest legal concepts. While this may have been true years ago, today the whole legal field is changing. Paralegals acting under the supervision of attorneys are steadily replacing attorneys in many areas of law. Use of paralegals is a cost-effective way of dealing with the high price of delivering legal services. Two or three well-trained paralegals working under an attorney's supervision can deliver less expensive legal services to the client than can three or four associate attorneys working on their own.[1] Since use of well-supervised and well-trained paralegals can improve the quality and lower the cost of legal services, more and more firms are expanding the role of the paralegal.

The United States Attorney General has recently noted the increasing role of the paralegal in giving the average person access to legal services. Speaking to the American Bar Association, Attorney General Janet Reno stated "I believe it is essential that we both recognize and facilitate the work of these nonlawyer representatives. It is now time to recognize that nonlawyers can play a vital part of any solution to the problem of justice rationing."[2]

If paralegals are to continue to serve an expanded support role for attorneys, much of what they do requires the same basic knowledge of the law that attorneys have. A really complete list of tasks done by modern paralegals is too long to include here. But, in short, the paralegal does many of the jobs formerly done by law clerks or attorneys, and these jobs require legal knowledge, as well as practical skills. As a sample of some of the jobs done by modern paralegals, the student might consider the following list.

- prepare questions for client interviews with attorneys
- help interview clients
- gather information to help build a case
- draft "pleadings" such as complaints and motions
- organize evidence to support legal arguments at trial
- research legal issues
- write up the results of research
- help interview witnesses
- help prepare witnesses for trial
- review legal documents
- draft legal documents for attorney review
- summarize legal issues or arguments in legal documents
- summarize testimony of witnesses and parties

The law of contracts affects so many aspects of people's legal affairs. Thus, many of the tasks listed above will require knowledge of this area of law. While most people will not experience the criminal justice system first hand, most of us do experience contract law first hand. Our food, our homes and offices, our business transactions, our marriages, our medical care, can all be affected by contract law. The paralegal will almost inevitably encounter clients on the job whose legal concerns involve contract law.

Paralegals also should know the law because it is impossible to predict every task to be done on the job. The competent paralegal should have basic substantive knowledge so he or she can adapt it to new tasks. No paralegal program can teach students everything they need to know about the law. But, with a firm grasp of basic principles, the paralegal can branch out and adapt this knowledge to many new areas and tasks. Memorization is not really the key to effective legal practice. But, knowing basic legal concepts enables the paralegal to master new tasks more easily and thus support attorneys more efficiently.

From the paralegal point of view, the higher and broader the qualifications, the more the job market has to offer. If the paralegal has knowledge of the law, as well as familiarity with practices and procedures involved in law, there will be more flexibility and choice in positions available. A well-qualified paralegal will experience more job satisfaction because the skilled worker has a better chance of avoiding too many menial and repetitive roles.

Finally, from the attorney's point of view, there are good reasons to hire paralegals who have knowledge of basic areas of the law. Since "thinking legal" and its associated analytical and research skills are the daily bread of lawyers, it is most helpful to have a support staff trained in the same process. Few things are more frustrating to a busy attorney than having to stop and teach the support staff the very task that needs to be done.

The author hopes this textbook will enable the paralegal student to be more competent and confident on the job. If the textbook can help to build effective teamwork between paralegal and attorney, it will have accomplished an important task.

Notes

1. Arthur G. Greene, ed., "Leveraging With Legal Assistants", 1993, p. 3.
2. Quoted in "Legal Assistant Today", March/April 1994, p. 16.

PART

I

The Formation Process

CHAPTER

1

Finding Out What Law Applies to the Contract

LEARNING OBJECTIVES FOR THIS CHAPTER:
WHAT YOU SHOULD KNOW!

❐ What the phrase *common law* means.

❐ What primary and secondary authority are and how they differ.

❐ What the Uniform Commercial Code (UCC) covers.

❐ Which contracts are governed by the UCC.

❐ How the UCC defines goods.

❐ Who is a merchant under the UCC.

❐ Which contracts are governed by common law.

❐ When state or federal law applies to a contract.

❐ What purpose an applicable law provision serves.

❐ What is meant by choice of law rules.

Sources of American Contract Law

Introduction

The term *contract* probably does not have a universally accepted definition. Generally, though, when attorneys and scholars refer to a **contract,** they mean the total legal obligation that results from agreement between parties and establishes both duties and rights for those parties. Contract is a *conclusory* term. It means that a legally sufficient agreement has been reached and that neither party can back out without suffering legal consequences. Each party is under obligation to perform the duties stated in the contract.

Although modern American contract law draws elements from many cultures, its roots are found primarily in the **common law** of England, or **English common law,** which is the body of rules developed in England from ancient times until the American Revolution. These rules originally existed both in unwritten practices and beliefs and in the written opinions of judges. Among other things, the common law included rules for making contracts. Over time the American colonies adopted the common law, including its contract rules, into their own law. After the American Revolution, all areas of American law, including contract law, separated from English common law and gradually became less English and more American. Nevertheless, even today fundamental similarities still exist between the law of England and the law of the United States.

In the early years of European settlement in North America, many other legal systems competed with the English common law. French settlers in North America brought with them their version of contract law, which was based on the *civil* law of the Napoleonic Code. This version of the law is still alive and well in the state of Louisiana. Even today, Louisiana's legal system is closely connected to civil law and the Napoleonic Code.[1] Spanish and Mexican settlers had their own version of the civil law. The *community property* laws of several states, including California and Texas, still follow Spanish civil law. These laws give married women a legal share in all income and property acquired during marriage.

Furthermore, before the Europeans arrived, many Native American cultures already had established legal systems. For example, the Cherokee Nation had a complex legal system with well-developed rules covering such diverse legal issues as ownership of property, conduct of war, the institution of marriage, and international relations.[2] Nevertheless, for historical reasons, English common law had the strongest influence on the early development of American contract law.

Today, when attorneys or scholars refer to the *common law* of contracts, they may mean the American law of contracts as it developed historically from English and American law before the Revolution. The term is also used, however, to draw a distinction between law originally found in the written opinions of judges and *statutes* passed by a legislative body. This distinction can be somewhat confusing because in most states, much of the original common law has now been codified into the state statutes. Thus, saying a contract is governed by common law sometimes means it is governed by those principles that *first* existed in common law.

Yet another meaning of the common law of contracts results from a twentieth-century scholarly publication called the **Uniform Commercial Code (UCC),** which is discussed in later sections of this chapter. Although

Contract The total legal obligation that results from agreement between parties and establishes both duties and rights for those parties.

Common law The whole body of rules developed in England from ancient times and adopted in the American colonies before the American Revolution.

Uniform Commercial Code (UCC) A scholarly attempt, first published in the 1950s, to systematize and summarize several different areas of commercial law in one document.

the UCC has now been widely adopted by state statutes, these statutes govern only particular kinds of contracts. The common law no longer applies to these contracts in states that have adopted the UCC into law. Thus, today we sometimes differentiate between contracts governed by rules developed in the UCC and contracts governed by rules originally developed under the common law. Under this meaning, a *common-law contract* is one that is still governed by principles that developed historically in the common law.

Development of the Restatements of Contracts

A highly influential document called the Restatement of Contracts was issued in 1932 by a private organization. The Restatement was produced by a group of legal scholars working under the auspices of the American Law Institute. The first Restatement was updated and modified in a second edition called the Restatement (Second) of Contracts.[3] The legal scholars who wrote the Restatements saw that over the years, American contract law had developed tremendous variation among the states. They believed it would be helpful to write a standardized version of contract law. The **Restatements** are a series of volumes that attempt to standardize contract principles by describing and defining the law. The Restatements are accompanied by commentaries that discuss how the law is changing and the direction in which contract law seems to be going.

Both Restatements are often quoted by the courts, and many individual provisions of the Restatements have found their way into state statutes. This textbook makes many references to the Restatements, particularly to the Restatement (Second). Remember, however, that the Restatements were written and issued by a private group rather than by the government or the courts. Thus, Restatements are not the law itself. They are not **primary authority,** or the cases, statutes, and administrative rules, regulations, and decisions that make up the law. Instead, the Restatements are **secondary authority,** or publications that discuss the law or are used as tools to find the law. In a way, once primary authority is defined as cases, statutes, and administrative rules, regulations, and decisions, secondary authority is everything else!

Since the Restatements are secondary authority, they do not have the force of law. When a legislative body adopts portions of the Restatements into law, however, then they become primary authority because they are now statutes. The Restatements may also become primary authority if judges include provisions of the Restatements in their opinions when they decide a contract dispute. Those Restatement provisions then become part of the case law of that jurisdiction.

Although they are secondary authority, the Restatements are widely accepted as a systematic compilation of many valid principles of contract law. It must be noted, however, that the Restatements have not completely standardized the law of contracts. This is partly because legislatures and judges have tended to adopt both Restatements in piecemeal fashion rather than in their entirety.

Well-Known Legal Treatises

American contract law has also been influenced by two famous treatises. A **treatise** is a long, detailed, scholarly study of a particular area of law such as contract law, insurance law, or corporate law. Both contract law treatises were

Restatements A series of volumes on one topic, such as contract law, that attempt to standardize that topic by describing and defining the law.

Primary authority The law in its entirety, encompassing cases, statutes, and administrative rules, regulations, and decisions.

Secondary authority All publications that discuss the law or are used as tools to find the law.

Treatise A long, detailed, scholarly study of a particular area of law.

written by American law professors: *Williston on Contracts* written by Professor Samuel Williston in 1920[4] and *Corbin on Contracts* written by Professor Arthur Linton Corbin in 1950.[5] Like the Restatements, these treatises are not primary authority, so they do not have the force of law. Nevertheless, they represent some of the best existing legal scholarship, and the ideas of these authors have played a major role in the development of modern American contract law.

Development of the Uniform Commercial Code

The UCC began in 1942 as a joint project of the American Law Institute and the National Conference on Uniform State Laws.[6] A group of legal scholars from both organizations studied commercial laws and transactions in the United States as part of the process of drafting what eventually became the UCC. In drafting the UCC, the scholars were concerned with the lack of uniformity in commercial laws and attempted to systematize and summarize in one document several different areas of law, including contract law. As the text of the UCC now puts it, its underlying purpose is ". . . to simplify, clarify, and modernize the law governing commercial transactions" and ". . . to make uniform the law among the various jurisdictions." UCC § 1-102(1) (a) and (c).

Ultimately, state enactments of the UCC were not as uniform as the drafters had originally envisioned. In adopting UCC provisions, many state legislatures varied from the approved text at some points. Also, the code itself contained "optional" provisions that were adopted by some states and not by others. Nevertheless, the UCC has been highly influential. Its widespread enactment has significantly standardized the way commercial transactions are handled in the United States. Some concepts promulgated in the UCC have even made their way into the common law. Thus, contracts not strictly covered by the UCC may still be influenced by ideas developed in it.

The UCC is divided into nine major sections called Articles. An understanding of some of these Articles is crucial to a study of contract law. Article 1 is discussed in this text because it contains many provisions that apply to other Articles. Article 2, which governs contracts involving the sale of goods, a huge part of our complex economy, is also discussed thoroughly here. Article 2 has been widely adopted and has been extremely influential in the development of contract law. It has substantially changed the law that applies to contracts for goods.

A relatively new portion of the UCC, Article 2A, represents a significant development in commercial law. Article 2A covers *leases* of **personal property.** There is no universally applicable definition of personal property, but in general it includes almost any sort of property in which one can have an ownership interest and that is not classified as real estate. Both *tangible* and *intangible* property may be personal property. **Tangible property** is property that possesses some physical form; steel ingots, exercise machines, and growing crops are examples. **Intangible property** lacks a physical form, but is capable of being owned or of conferring rights; patents, copyrights, and trademarks are examples. Thus, items as varied as goods, money, stocks and bonds, machinery, store inventory, copyright interests, and livestock may be leased under Article 2A. As the Foreward to Article 2A states:

> Under present law, transactions of this type are governed partly by common law principles relating to personal property, partly by principles relating to real

Personal property
Includes almost any sort of property in which one can have an ownership interest and that is not classified as real estate. Steel rails, balloons, and cattle are examples of personal property.

Tangible property
Property that possesses some physical form. Steel ingots, exercise machines, and growing crops are examples.

Intangible property
Property that lacks a physical form, but is capable of being owned or of conferring rights. Patents, copyrights, and trademarks are examples of intangible property.

estate leases, and partly by reference to Articles 2 and 9 of the Uniform Commercial Code, dealing with Sales and Secured Transactions respectively. The legal rules and concepts derived from these sources imperfectly fit a transaction that involves personal property rather than realty, and a lease rather than either a sale or a security interest as such. A statute directly addressing the personal property lease is therefore appropriate.

A complete discussion of leases relating to personal property is beyond the scope of this text. However, the student should be aware that if a contract is a lease of *personal property* rather than real property, it may fall within the provisions of UCC Article 2A. In that case, a paralegal should check further to see if the relevant jurisdiction has adopted any of the applicable provisions of Article 2A. Even if a jurisdiction has not adopted these provisions, they may still provide some guidance about how a contract that is a lease of personal property is treated.

Assignment A transfer of some or all of a party's contract rights.

Secured transaction A particular kind of debtor-creditor relationship in which the debtor puts up collateral (security) for the loan obtained from the creditor.

Article 9 also contains some useful provisions for the study of basic contract law. Article 9 deals with *assignments* and *secured transactions*. Generally, an **assignment** is a *transfer* of some or all of a party's contract rights. A **secured transaction** is a particular kind of debtor-creditor relationship in which the debtor puts up collateral (security) for the loan obtained from the creditor. Although a thorough discussion of assignments and secured transactions under the UCC is beyond the scope of a beginning contract law text, many paralegals need some basic knowledge of Article 9 and secured transactions because such arrangements are pervasive in commercial practice. Therefore, this text includes some discussion of Article 9, primarily in Chapter 12.

The law applied to particular contract transactions has been significantly affected by the widespread adoption of the principles of the UCC. If a contract comes within the coverage of the UCC, then the principles adopted in the code apply to that contract. To resolve issues arising in contracts governed by the UCC, a court applies the relevant UCC provisions and other court decisions interpreting them. Many contract rules in the UCC are different from the historical common-law rules, but the legal process is the same in that courts interpret and apply UCC provisions to certain contracts, just as they interpret and apply common-law principles to other contracts.

The word *commercial* in the UCC's name is somewhat misleading because the UCC also applies to transactions between private parties and not just to transactions between businesses or professional buyers and sellers. If the subject matter of a contract falls under the UCC, then UCC rules generally apply whether the parties involved in the contract are companies, professionals, or private people. Unless the parties agree, however, international transactions are not governed by the UCC, even when the subject matter of the contract would normally bring it under the UCC.

The UCC has not completely supplanted the common law. First, not all American jurisdictions have adopted the UCC. Second, some jurisdictions have adopted certain provisions, but not others. Third, the drafters of the UCC did not deal with every possible aspect of commercial contracts. They chose to let common law continue to govern those aspects of commercial law the UCC did not cover. For example, Article 2 contains more than one hundred interrelated sections about contracts for buying and selling goods, yet these rules still do not cover some aspects of such contracts. To address legal problems where there are no specific relevant UCC provisions, the UCC preserves the common-law "principles of law and equity." In fact, UCC § 1-103 expressly states that the common law is preserved unless it is inconsistent with other specific provisions of the UCC.

Provisions from the UCC are cited in this text in standard form; that is, the Article number is given first, followed by the specific section number. Thus, section 103 from Article 1 is cited as § 1-103, section 207 from Article 2 is cited as § 2-207, and section 109 of Article 9 is cited as § 9-109. You can always tell which Article a provision comes from by looking at the first number in the citation.

Status of the UCC Once It Has Been Adopted by a State: State Commercial Codes

When attorneys and contract scholars discuss the UCC, they usually mean the original document with the modifications that have been made to it to date. The paralegal can find the latest text of the UCC, with a yearly update, commentary, and a table of adopting jurisdictions, in the *Uniform Laws Annotated, Master Edition* (West Publishing, 1989). Once a state legislature has adopted the UCC text into its statutes, the text becomes part of the commercial code of that state and is normally referred to and cited as a state statute. A state can adopt some or all of the UCC and can retain or change its language.

In studying contract law, the most current revision of the UCC itself is preferable to state statutes because the UCC has a standardized text and contains written commentary by the drafters. Relying on the UCC itself is more efficient and less confusing than referring to all the variations that have been adopted by the states. You should remember, however, that the UCC is not primary authority and thus is not the law.

On the job, the paralegal would normally use the version of a UCC provision adopted by the relevant state. The version of the UCC adopted by a particular state, not the original UCC, is the law in that state. When a jurisdiction has adopted the text of the UCC unchanged, the UCC commentaries can be particularly useful in interpreting provisions if the law is not clear.

Article 2 of the UCC

As noted earlier, Article 2 of the UCC has been highly influential in the development of contract law. All the states except Louisiana have adopted it into their statutes. Article 2 covers contracts for buying and selling goods. The paralegal working with contracts involving the sale of goods should be familiar with major concepts of this Article.

In particular, some understanding of what the UCC means by *goods* is needed. According to the UCC, **goods** are all things that are movable at the time the contract concerning them was made. Goods include such things as growing timber and the unborn young of animals. Even such things as minerals, oil, and gas are considered goods if they can be severed from realty without material harm to the land.

Goods All things that are movable at the time the contract concerning them is made.

The UCC specifically excludes two common movable items from being goods: (1) money used as currency (i.e., as payment for the contract, rather than as the subject matter of the contract) and (2) investment securities. The UCC definition of goods also excludes a **thing in action,** which is the right to sue for *recovery* of personal property. A contract to transfer this right to sue is not a sale of goods although the property to be recovered would ordinarily come within the definition of goods.

In applying the UCC definition of goods, you should remember that the definition of a sale contract encompasses both *present sales* of *goods already existing* and *present sales* of *goods that will exist in the future.* The UCC defines a sale generally as the passing of title (ownership) from a seller to a buyer for a price.

If a contract does not concern goods at all, common-law principles still apply. For example, contracts for services and real estate are still governed by common law. If the subject matter of a contract is employment or services of any kind or real estate, the UCC will not govern the agreement.

"Mixed" Subject Matter Contracts

Sometimes it is not immediately clear whether the UCC applies to a contract because its subject matter appears to be mixed: both goods and things that are not goods are involved. Note the issues that arise in the Example 1.1.

EXAMPLE   **1.1**

Client comes to your office and asks the attorney you work for to review a sales contract she uses with her customers. A dispute has arisen with a customer, and Client needs legal advice. Attorney asks you to review the contract, which is for the sale of machines. Client has told the attorney her company is a broker of machines used in making steel ingots. Client's company obtains the machines and then sells them to other companies that produce steel ingots. The agreement Client has shown the attorney is her company's standard contract for customers who buy the machines. Client also tells the attorney that her company installs the ingot-making machines and then services them on the buyer's premises for the life of the machines. You review the contract and find that it covers the sale, installation, and maintenance of the machines.

What law covers such a contract? Since the contract appears to involve a mixture of goods and services, is it governed by the UCC or by common law? Where the subject matter of a contract seems to involve both goods and things that are not goods, courts may use several tests to determine which law to apply. In one common test, sometimes called the **predominant factor test,** a court determines the main subject matter and purpose of the contract—its thrust—and then applies either the common law or the UCC, whichever is appropriate. Consider how the predominant factor test operates in the following examples.

Thing in action
The right to sue for recovery of personal property.

Predominant factor test A method used by courts in doubtful cases, to determine whether a contract is governed by the UCC or the common law. Depending upon whether the main subject matter and purpose of the contract—its thrust—deal with goods or things that are not goods, a court applies either the UCC or the common law, respectively.

EXAMPLE 1.2

Assume a contract involves the sale of "install-it-yourself" fencing. Seller sends a representative to Buyer when the fencing is delivered, and this representative demonstrates the correct installation by putting in the first few feet of fencing. This is a contract for sale of goods under the UCC. The fact that Seller provides an incidental service with the sale of the fencing does not change the predominant purpose of the contract, which is to sell goods.

EXAMPLE 1.3

Assume A makes a janitorial contract with B. As part of the janitorial services, B will provide paper products such as paper towels and toilet paper to A and bill A for these items once a month along with B's regular invoice for services. This is a contract for services. It comes under common law because its predominant purpose is that B will perform janitorial services for A. Providing some paper products is incidental to the main purpose of the contract.

To summarize: if the sale-of-goods aspect predominates, the contract is governed by UCC rules. If services or other subject matter that is not goods predominates, the contract is governed by common-law principles.

Returning to the contract for the sale, installation, and maintenance of machines in Example 1.1, a court could decide that the machine sales were the main subject matter and purpose of the contract. In that case, the UCC would apply because machines, being movable items of property at the time the contract was made, are clearly within the definition of goods. If the court decided instead that the main subject matter and purpose of the contract were the installation and maintenance, then the common law would apply because these are services. The decision in this case might be more difficult than in the fencing and janitorial services situations.

When a contract involves mixed subject matter and it is not clear whether the UCC or the common law should govern, a court may examine any relevant facts and circumstances surrounding the contract, including the following: (1) the intentions expressed by the parties themselves, (2) how these parties or others have treated similar contracts, (3) industry practices, (4) the type and duration of performance each party would give under the contract, and (5) other cases in which courts have dealt with similar contracts.

The determination of whether a mixed contract is governed by the UCC or by common law can vary from jurisdiction to jurisdiction. In complex situations, courts have often produced inconsistent results. Thus, paralegal students should be aware of the general concepts involved, the need to consult the specific UCC language adopted in the relevant jurisdiction, and the need to consult cases construing similar situations.[7] The following case excerpts illustrate many of the issues involved in deciding what law applies to mixed subject matter contracts. Note that the **plaintiff** in a lawsuit is the party who filed the lawsuit; the **defendant** is the party being sued. If a decision is appealed to a higher court, the party who brings the appeal is the appellant, and the other party is the appellee.

Plaintiff The party who is suing in a lawsuit; the party who has filed the complaint.
Defendant The party being sued in a lawsuit.

A CASE FOR STUDY
Snyder v. Herbert Greenbaum and Associates, Inc.
38 Md. App. 144, 380 A.2d 618 (1977)

James F. Couch, Jr. Special Judge. This is an appeal from a judgment entered in the Circuit Court for Baltimore County (Land, J.), sitting without a jury, in favor of appellee, Herbert Greenbaum and Associates, Inc., and against Alvin Snyder, Morris Sugarman, Herbert Thaler, and Harold A. Crone, individually and trading as Twin Lakes Partnership. [The court sets out three issues that form the basis of the appeal in this case and the following facts. Before deciding these issues, the court considers whether the Maryland Commercial Code should apply.]

The facts that give rise to [t]his dispute are simple. Pursuant to its plan to begin construction in 1973 of 228 garden apartments, Twin Lakes, through its management, began negotiations with the appellee, Herbert Greenbaum and Associates, Inc., to supply and install carpeting and the underlying carpet pad for the apartments. During the course of these negotiations Greenbaum estimated that appproximately 19,000 to 20,000 yards of carpeting were required for the job. Thereafter the parties entered into a contract that Greenbaum would supply the necessary carpet for the 228 apartments, and install it, for a total consideration of $87,600.00. In the contract itself no mention was made of the amount of carpeting to be installed.

Between the April, 1972 date of the contract and September, 1973, Greenbaum purchased large amounts of carpet to be used on the Twin Lakes job from several carpet wholesalers. However, no carpet was ever installed because Twin Lakes, through Alvin Snyder, canceled the contract in September, 1973. It became apparent at some point that 19,000 to 20,000 yards of carpet was an overestimation. The actual figure needed was between 17,000 and 17,500 yards.

Appellee then brought an action against the Twin Lakes Partnership for breach of contract, and was awarded a judgment for $19,407.20. It is this judgment from which this appeal stems.

Before considering the points raised by the appellants, an important threshold question must be answered: whether Md. Code (1974), Commercial Law Article, specifically Title 2, Maryland Uniform Commercial Code Sales, applies to the contract in this case, which is a mixed contract for the sale of carpet and the installation of carpet.

The leading Maryland case for determining whether the sales article applies to mixed sales and service contracts is Burton v. Artery Co., 279 Md. 94, 367 A.2d 935 (1977), which adopted the Bonebrake test (Bonebrake v. Cox, 499 F.2d 951 (8th Cir. 1974)). The test articulated is:

"Not whether they are mixed, but, granting that they are mixed, whether their predominant factor, their thrust, their purpose, reasonably stated, is the rendition of service, with goods incidentally involved (e.g., contract with artist for painting) or is a transaction of sale, with labor incidentally involved (e.g., installation of a water heater in a bathroom)." 367 A.2d at 943.

The facts in Burton are similar to the facts here. In that case, the contract was for the sale and installation of trees and shrubs. The Court of Appeals, after applying the Bonebrake test, concluded that the U.C.C. applied.

In the case sub judice, the contract involved the sale by appellee of a certain amount of carpet, and the installation of that carpet in the 228 apartments. However, this case differs from the Burton facts in that in Burton the seller/installer had grown the trees and shrubs that were the subject of the contract, whereas in this case the seller/installer purchased the carpet from a wholesaler. Further, the purchase of the carpet was made after the contract was formed, and for the sole purpose of supplying it for installation.

Despite this difference in the facts which tend to favor the service purpose of the contract, application of the Bonebrake test leads us to conclude that the primary thrust of this contract is the sale, rather than the installation, of the carpet. Therefore, the Sale Title applies to this contract. [Citations.]

Questions to Consider

1. Based on the information given in this case, how can the predominant factor test be stated?
2. Did the *Burton* court decide the UCC applied to the sale and installation of trees and shrubs? Why?
3. Why did the *Snyder* court decide the UCC applied to the sale and installation of carpets? What were the factual differences between the two cases, and how important were these facts in the outcome of the cases?
4. Do you think *Snyder* was rightly decided? Why or why not?

A CASE FOR STUDY
Ranger Construction Co., Inc. v. Dixie Floor Co., Inc.
433 F. Supp. 442 (D. South Carolina 1977)

[A construction company (Ranger) brought an action against a contractor (Dixie Floor) for alleged breach of a contract to furnish all materials and labor for the installation of resilient flooring in a building at the University of South Carolina Medical School. The plaintiff's complaint alleged the defendant contractor refused to perform the work specified in the contract for the agreed price of $52,601.00 and that as a result, the construction company was required to enter into a second contract to have the flooring installed at a substantially higher cost. They sued for the additional $22,268.00 they alleged they paid to have the carpet installed. In its answer, the contractor admitted there was a contract, but claimed the construction company wrongfully withheld payment for work completed under an entirely separate contract in North Carolina. As a result of the construction company's failure to pay on the North Carolina contract, the contractor claimed it was justified in fearing the construction company lacked willingness and ability to pay on this contract in South Carolina. Contractor claimed under these circumstances the South Carolina Commercial Code permitted them to ask for adequate assurance of performance, and, if such assurance was not received within 30 days, permitted them to consider the contract breached. In deciding whether the contractor was entitled to apply the South Carolina Commercial Code (which the construction company claimed did not apply), the court discussed applicability of the Uniform Commercial Code to mixed subject contracts.]

Hemphill, District Judge. . . . Article II of the Uniform Commercial Code is limited in its application to transactions in goods. "Goods" are defined in § 10.2-105 of the S.C. Code to mean "all things (including specially manufactured goods) which are movable at the time of identification to the contract for sale other than the money in which the price is to be paid, investment securities and things in action." The disputed contract in this action required the defendant to furnish all labor and materials necessary for the installation of resilient flooring in the plaintiff's construction project. There is no doubt that these materials, which consisted of vinyl asbestos tile, sheet vinyl, vinyl baseboards, and cement, constituted goods under the definition provided in § 10.2-105 of South Carolina's version of the Uniform Commercial Code. However, this determination is not dispositive of the issue in this case because the delivery of goods under the contract between the plaintiff and defendant was accompanied by a delivery of services by defendant. "Mixed" contracts, or contracts which involve both goods and services, are not automatically included within the scope of Article II merely because they are partially involved with the exchange of goods.

The leading case on the UCC's applicability to contracts which involve both goods and services is Bonebrake v. Cox, 499 F.2d 951 (8th Cir. 1974). In Bonebrake, the contract involved a sale and installation of bowling alley equipment between a dealer in new and used equipment and the owners of a bowling alley which had been destroyed by fire. The court found that in determining whether a mixed contract for goods and services should be covered as a "sale of goods" under the UCC,

> (t)he test for inclusion or exclusion is not whether they are mixed, but, granting that they are mixed, whether their predominant factor, their thrust, their purpose, reasonably stated, is the rendition of service, with goods incidentally involved (e.g., contract with artist for painting) or is a transaction of sale, with labor incidentally involved (e.g., installation of a water heater in a bathroom).

In Bonebrake, the plaintiff's decedent, a Mr. Simek, was engaged in the sale of new and used bowling equipment and employed a man to install the equipment incident to its sale to provide the necessary expertise for its installation. The facts of the case indicate that Mr. Simek was largely involved in the purchase and sale of bowling equipment and owned three storage facilities for such equipment within his native state of Nebraska. The Ninth Circuit characterized the contract as one for the replacement of equipment and therefore the sale of goods under the Commercial Code. It is important to note that Simek was primarily a seller of bowling equipment and apparently, from the facts of the case, installed them as a sideline and as a convenience to his customers. It is also noteworthy that the contractual language involved in Bonebrake was that of a contract of purchase and sale.

In the present case the "predominant factor, thrust, or purpose, reasonably stated" of the contract is one for the delivery of services accompanied by the acquisition and furnishing of the necessary materials. The contract involved in this lawsuit is a construction contract, not a contract for the purchase and sale of goods. It is interesting to note that throughout the contract the defendant, Dixie Floor Co., Inc., is not referred to as a materialman but rather as a subcontractor. It is apparent that the plaintiff was not contracting for the materials alone but rather was contracting for the performance of an entire segment of the prime contract. The defendant's responses to interrogatories indicated that the defendant was essentially a service corporation engaged in the installation and construction of flooring. Defendant's response to Interrogatory No.1 reveals that 75% of their business involved the contracting and installation of flooring. The answer to Interrogatory No.3 reveals that the defendant did not, at any time relevant to this action, operate as a supplier or maintain a supply house for flooring materials and supplies. The answer to Interrogatory No. 12 indicates that for this particular job the defendant planned to purchase the materials completely from an independent dealer. It is obvious from these facts that the defendant in this case is primarily a service-oriented business which deals in materials as incident to its performance of services in the construction of floors and flooring. For this reason it is only logical to conclude that the contract in dispute in this case is basically a contract for the performance of services with the sale of the goods necessary to perform those services being incidental to the service contract. Therefore, the Uniform Commercial Code would not be applicable in this case. . . . in the present case, the parties knew that it would be necessary to provide certain goods in order for the service contract to be properly carried out. The major thrust of the contract, however, was the performance of services and the contract was therefore characterized as a service contract and excluded from the scope of the Uniform Commercial Code.

In Computer Servicecenters [*Computer Servicecenters, Inc. v. Beacon Manufacturing Company,* 328 F.Supp. 653 (D.S.C. 1970), aff'd, 443 F.2d 906 (4th Cir. 1971)], this court cited three cases in support of its decision which also served to support the decision in the present case. In Epstein v. Giannattasio, 25 Conn. Sup. 109, 197 A.2d 342 (1963), a beauty salon patron who suffered dermatitis and disfigurement from loss of hair allegedly because of treatment with certain products was denied recovery on the grounds of breach of warranty since there was no "sale of goods" within the meaning of the UCC. In Stagner v. Staples, Mo.App., 427 S.W.2d 763 (1968) the applicability of the UCC to an agreement for the removal of trees and leveling of ground whereby the worker was to receive fallen timber as part of his compensation was denied. Similarly, in National Historic Shrine's Foundation, Inc. v. Dali, 4 UCC RS 71 (N.Y.S.Ct. 1967), the court held that an oral agreement by an artist to paint a picture on a television program and to donate it for sale to the public was an agreement for the rendition of services and not a contract for the sale of goods under the UCC. In all these cases, as in the present case, the contracts must be predominantly characterized as service contracts accompanied by an incidental sale of goods.

Questions to Consider

1. How would you state the predominant factor test based on this case?
2. In this case, what were the most important facts in the court's decision not to apply the UCC?
3. What difference might it make in the court's decision about whether the contractor had breached the contract with Ranger Construction if the contractor could not use the desired provisions of the South Carolina Commercial Code to justify its refusal to go forward with the contract?
4. What similarities do you see between the three cases cited at the end of the opinion and this case? Between *Bonebrake* and this case? Are there any differences? Did the court think these similarities and differences were significant? How?
5. Do you agree with the court that the UCC should not apply to this case? Why or why not?

Assignment

Which of the following contracts would probably be governed by the rules of the UCC? Explain your answers.

1. A contract identical to the contract for ingot-making machines in Example 1.1, except that your client does not sell the machines to customers, but leases the machines on condition that her company will do all installation and maintenance.
2. A contract for the purchase of U.S. dollars that are to be taken overseas and sold to Japanese currency exchange businesses.
3. A contract for the sale of whole rosebushes from a nursery, which will plant the rosebushes for the buyer.
4. A contract for the sale of all old plumbing fixtures, such as sinks, toilets, shower stalls, and bathtubs, from a housing complex that is being remodeled.
5. A contract to perform custodial services for the public schools. The service will provide its own cleaning supplies and all paper products (e.g., paper towels and toilet paper) for the schools' use. The cost of these supplies is built into the monthly service charge.

When Do Special Merchant's Provisions of the UCC Apply?

The drafters of the UCC structured the code to apply to all transactions that involve the buying and selling of goods. Thus, the UCC is meant to apply to such transactions whether the parties are professionals or laypeople. The drafters also realized, however, that professionals are usually more familiar with all aspects of buying and selling goods than laypeople are. In addition,

---

EXHIBIT 1.1

Who Is a "Merchant" Under the UCC?

1. someone who regularly deals in goods of the particular kind involved in the contract, or
2. someone who shows by the business conducted that he or she has special knowledge or skill concerning the type of *contract* involved, or
3. someone who shows by the business conducted that he or she has special knowledge or skill concerning the type of *goods* involved, or
4. someone who employs an intermediary whose occupation indicates he or she has special knowledge or skill, and this intermediary's knowledge or skill should be attributed to the employer.

UCC merchant's provisions The provisions of the UCC that apply only to experts in buying and selling goods.

Merchant Someone who regularly deals in goods of the particular kind involved in the contract, who has special knowledge related to these goods, or who employs such a person as an agent.

professional buyers and sellers often follow a number of industry-wide practices and procedures that may not be familiar to nonprofessionals. All in all, people who regularly deal in a particular kind of goods are likely to have more expertise in this area. For this reason, some provisions of the UCC apply only to people with more expertise and not to casual buyers and sellers of goods.

The provisions of the UCC that apply only to experts in buying and selling goods are known as the **merchant's provisions.** Although many situations are not clear-cut and distinguishing between a **merchant** and a casual buyer is not always easy, § 2-104 of the UCC does provide a definition, see Exhibit 1.1

Some provisions of the UCC contain subsections with these special rules for merchants. Therefore, it is important to be aware of the identity of the parties to a contract for the sale of goods. If both parties to the contract are merchants, then any relevant merchant's provisions will apply to the contract. If only one party is a merchant, the merchant's provisions may or may not apply to that party depending on the wording of the relevant provisions. If neither party is a merchant, then merchant's provisions do not apply. The UCC merchant's provisions are discussed throughout this book.

Assignment

Since special merchant's rules may apply, it is important to recognize when a contracting party is a merchant. In the following transactions, which of the parties, if any, could be classified as a merchant under the UCC and which, if any, are not merchants? Explain your answers.

1. Bob owns and operates his own small shoe store in Tinytown, USA. He regularly makes contracts with shoe suppliers all over the country.
2. Betty purchased a cheap, used car from Reliable Wrecks, Inc. She has a written contract under which Reliable financed the car for two years.
3. Bob (the shoe store owner from Question 1) goes to his daughter's soccer game where he encounters a representative from Avid Soccer Supplies, Inc., who is offering contracts to individual parents of team members under which Avid will sell shoes and uniforms at a discount price. Bob makes such a contract with Avid.

4. Georgina and Leslie, two elementary school teachers, decide to buy a used car from their neighbor Netsuko, a research chemist. The parties reach agreement, so they write and sign a short contract of sale.

5. Carmen works full-time for Jenny as a buyer. Jenny owns a large office supply company. Carmen negotiates all Jenny's contracts for purchase of office desks, chairs, and bookshelves. After negotiating with Jenny's suppliers for these items, Carmen gives the resulting written contracts to Jenny for her signature. Carmen has worked for Jenny for six months.

Does Federal or State Law Apply to a Contract?

Contracts Where Federal Law Applies

For the most part, contract law has developed as state law. Sometimes, however, federal law rather than the law of a particular state governs contract cases. An in-depth discussion of when state or federal law applies to a particular contract is beyond the scope of a basic contracts text, but a few general principles can be presented. First, if the U.S. Constitution, treaties, or presidential orders are involved in the contract, ordinarily federal law will apply. Second, federal law may also apply if the federal government or a federal agency is a party to the contract or to litigation on the contract.

Third, federal law may apply to a contract under the doctrine of **federal preemption.** Under this doctrine, when the U.S. Congress enacts legislation in a given area as a valid exercise of its authority, the states cannot enact law that contradicts the federal statute. Courts, attorneys, and legal scholars sometimes have difficulty determining when federal preemption means that federal law takes precedence over state law and applies to a contract. Generally, however, when Congress has properly exercised its authority over an area of law, neither state governments nor private parties can change this law. Under the National Fair Labor Standards Act, for example, employees may have a federally guaranteed right to a minimum wage and a maximum workday.[8] The National Fair Labor Standards Act is a valid exercise of congressional authority, and thus no state government can enact wage and hour laws that contradict the Act. If private parties make an employment contract that contradicts the Act's wages and hours guarantees, the contract is unenforceable as to any employees covered by the Act.

Questions as to whether an area of the law has been preempted by federal law can be complicated and may require research into the scope of the federal preemption doctrine to determine whether it applies to a particular case. Nevertheless, you should be alert to the possibility that federal law may preempt state law and apply to a particular contract on which you are working. The checklist in Exhibit 1.2 will help you determine whether federal law may govern some or all of the provisions of a particular contract.

Federal preemption
The right of the federal government, through the U.S. Congress, to have exclusive control over some aspects of law if Congress validly exercises its authority and enacts legislation in a given area.

Contracts Where Federal Law Does Not Apply

A huge number of contracts paralegals deal with do not involve federal law and are therefore governed by state law. Essentially, unless federal law takes precedence, the individual states and the District of Columbia have the authority to decide the law of contracts within their own borders.

EXHIBIT 1.2

The Federal Preemption Doctrine

Federal law may apply in the following situations:

- The federal government is a party to the contract.
- The federal government is a party to contract litigation.
- A federal agency is a party to the contract.
- A federal agency is a party to contract litigation.
- The contract involves a federal statute.
- The contract involves a rule or regulation of a federal administrative agency.
- The contract concerns a treaty.
- The contract relates to the U.S. Constitution.
- The contract involves presidential executive orders.

Where federal law does not apply, with some restrictions private parties normally can choose the state whose law will apply to their contracts. Basically, these restrictions prevent the parties from choosing completely unrelated law to govern their contract. There must be at least some reasonable relationship between the contract and the state whose law is to govern the contract or between the parties and that state. If the contract or the parties are related to more than one state, any of those states can be chosen. The common-law principles governing the choice of law were included in the UCC. Section 1-105, for example, contains the following provision:

> Except as otherwise provided hereafter in this section, when a transaction bears a reasonable relation to this state and also to another state or nation the parties may agree that the law either of this state or of such other state or nation shall govern their rights and duties. Failing such agreement this Act applies to transactions having an appropriate relation to this state.

Applicable law provision A contract provision in which the parties themselves state which related state law should govern the transaction.

When the contracting parties themselves can choose the state whose law will govern the transaction, they often do so by putting a specific provision into their contract. This provision, which is called an **applicable law** or governing law provision, indicates which law is to be applied. If problems arise concerning the contract, a court would normally use the law chosen by the parties to resolve the dispute. An applicable law provision might read as follows:

> The parties hereby agree this contract shall be governed and interpreted according to the laws of the State of Minnesota.

Many parties choose to have their contracts governed by the law of the state where the contract is made and will be carried out. Thus, if two parties from New York make an agreement to buy and sell a million red balloons, and the transaction is to take place wholly or primarily in New York, these contracting parties would probably prefer New York law to be used to interpret the contract and resolve any problems arising under it. (Note that New York's version of the UCC would apply because balloons are goods.) Often the parties choose the law of the state where the contract is made and carried out because they and the lawyers in their area are more familiar with that law. Furthermore, unless some other state has a significant relationship to the contract or the parties, it is unlikely any other state law could be applied.

Sometimes parties to a contract choose to have it be governed by the law of the state where the subject matter is located.

EXAMPLE 1.4

Suppose one contracting party lives in Georgia, the other in Texas, and they are making a sale contract for real estate located in Virginia. The parties may choose the law of Virginia to govern the contract because the land is located there.

In such situations, each party may fear that if the law of the other's home state governs the contract, that party may have a possible home-state advantage if there is litigation.

In many situations, the parties do not specify which state law should apply. Sometimes they forget, sometimes they assume they know which law will apply, and sometimes they assume they agree and do not think it is necessary to spell it out. If the parties do not specify which law is to govern a contract and a dispute arises, a court may have to decide what law applies. In other words, the court will make the *choice of law* for the parties. This choice is not difficult when a contract is made in one state, both parties live there, and the contract will be carried out in that state. The law of that state will govern the contract, even if the parties forgot to say so.

The choice of law can be more difficult when the law of more than one state may apply. Thus, in Example 1.4 where the Texas resident and the Georgia resident made a contract to sell land located in Virginia, all three states appear to have a real relationship to the contract. Paralegals should be aware that when the parties have not made a choice of law, and the law of more than one state may apply, specific research may be necessary to determine the law governing the agreement. Research should be initiated *before* a lawsuit is filed. Otherwise, the lawsuit may be filed in the wrong court, or the wrong law may be consulted in handling the case.

When a lawsuit has already been filed, the law of the state where the suit is filed will normally be used to determine which state's contract rules should govern the contract if this is in doubt. Consider the following example.

EXAMPLE 1.5

Assume a Wyoming resident and an Idaho resident, have a contract for the sale of steel ingots. Believing the other party has breached the contract, the Wyoming resident files a lawsuit in a Wyoming court. (In some cases, the Wyoming resident might file in a *federal* court sitting in Wyoming because the contracting parties come from different states. In other cases, the Wyoming resident might file in a Wyoming *state* court.) Further assume the contract was negotiated and signed in Michigan, but the steel ingots are being manufactured in Pennsylvania. The situation can be summarized as follows:

- The subject of the dispute is a breach of sale contract.
- The steel ingots are located and produced in *Pennsylvania.*
- The contract was negotiated and made in *Michigan.*
- The lawsuit was filed in a *Wyoming* court.
- The plaintiff lives in *Wyoming.*
- The defendant lives in *Idaho.*

If the parties' original contract does not specify which state's law applies, then the Wyoming court will make this determination before considering whether there has been a breach of contract as the plaintiff alleges. This issue could be important to the parties. For example, the plaintiff might find it easier (or harder) to show there was a breach under Wyoming law than under the law of Michigan, Pennsylvania, or Idaho. Since this is a contract for the sale of goods, different versions of the UCC adopted in each state could also become an important factor in the lawsuit.

From the facts given here, it is not clear that Wyoming law should govern the question of whether the contract was breached. Might not the Idaho defendant be able to argue just as validly that Idaho law should apply to the dispute? Perhaps the law of Pennsylvania should be applied because the performance (manufacture of steel ingots) was to take place there. Perhaps the court should apply the law of Michigan because the agreement was negotiated and finalized in that state.

The court will apply choice of law rules to decide which state's law should be used to determine if the defendant breached the contract. Since the lawsuit has already been filed in Wyoming, normally the Wyoming court will use that state's own choice of law rules to make this initial decision. Once the state is chosen, then its law will be used to determine if there really was a breach of contract as the plaintiff alleges.

Thus, as in this example, if the contracting parties themselves have not made a choice of law, the court where the lawsuit is filed generally uses it own rules to determine what law applies to the substance of the lawsuit.

Chapter Review Questions

1. What sources have contributed to the development of the American law of contracts? Describe these sources.
2. What is meant by the term *common law?*
3. What is a contract?
4. What is the difference between primary authority and secondary authority? Give examples of each.
5. What are the differences between the UCC and the commercial codes of individual states?
6. To which contracts does the UCC (or state commercial codes) apply? To which contracts does common law apply?
7. Indicate some items of personal property that would be considered goods and explain why.
8. Who is a merchant under the UCC and why does this matter?
9. When may a contract be governed by federal rather than state law?
10. Explain what the predominant factor test is and how it is used.
11. What relevance must a particular state have to a contract before the law of that state can apply to the contract?
12. What is an applicable law provision?

Key Terms

Applicable law provision, 16
Assignment, 6
Common law, 3
Contract, 3
Defendant, 9
Federal preemption, 15
Goods, 7
Intangible property, 5
Merchant, 14
Personal property, 5
Plaintiff, 9

Predominant factor test, 8
Primary authority, 4
Restatements, 4
Secondary authority, 4
Secured transaction, 6
Tangible property, 5
Thing in action, 8
Treatise, 4
UCC merchant's provisions, 14
Uniform Commercial Code (UCC), 3

Notes

1. David M. Walker, *The Oxford Companion to Law,* p. 235 (1980).
2. John Phillip Reid, *A Law of Blood: The Primitive Law of the Cherokee Nation* (1970).
3. Restatement Second of Contracts (American Law Institute, 1981).
4. Samuel Williston, *Williston on Contracts* (1920).
5. Arthur Linton Corbin, *Corbin on Contracts* (1950).
6. *West's Selected Commercial Statutes,* pp. 19–20 (1993).
7. "UCC-Mixed Contracts for Sale of Goods," 5 ALR4th 501 and "The Goods/Services Dichotomy & the UCC: Unweaving the Tangled Web," 59 *Notre Dame Law Review* 717 (1984).
8. 29 USCA § 206 (1978).

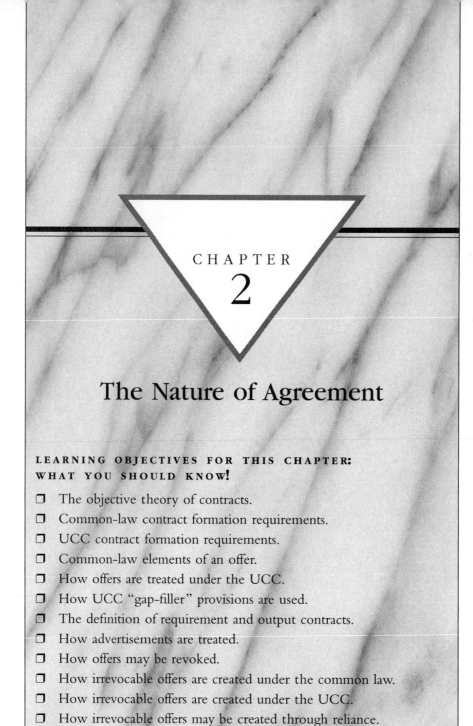

CHAPTER

2

The Nature of Agreement

**LEARNING OBJECTIVES FOR THIS CHAPTER:
WHAT YOU SHOULD KNOW!**

- ❒ The objective theory of contracts.
- ❒ Common-law contract formation requirements.
- ❒ UCC contract formation requirements.
- ❒ Common-law elements of an offer.
- ❒ How offers are treated under the UCC.
- ❒ How UCC "gap-filler" provisions are used.
- ❒ The definition of requirement and output contracts.
- ❒ How advertisements are treated.
- ❒ How offers may be revoked.
- ❒ How irrevocable offers are created under the common law.
- ❒ How irrevocable offers are created under the UCC.
- ❒ How irrevocable offers may be created through reliance.

The "Objective" Theory of Contracts

To a great degree, contract formation is based on what parties say and do. Usually, contract law does not take into account the secret workings of the mind or people's unspoken motivations. Contract law tends to be based on how a "reasonable" person would be likely to interpret what is said and done between the parties. This is considered an "objective" view of human behavior. Yet we often speak of the "intentions" of contracting parties. Ordinarily, intentions mean inner or private motives not necessarily known to others. These are thought to be more "subjective" in nature. How, then, can contract formation occur if it involves two opposites? The so-called **objective theory of contracts** is an attempt to reconcile the subjective, or personal, aspects of contract making with the objective, or external, aspects.

The objective theory of contracts is based on the realization that it would be impossible to require contracting parties to read each other's minds. It is also based on the realization that it would be impractical to require them to fully disclose their thinking to each other during negotiations. Almost all negotiating parties want to keep some information to themselves. Thus, the theory does not require people to read each other's inner thoughts. Instead, it requires that each participant behave like a "reasonable person" in judging the other's conduct and words. Each contracting party is entitled to judge the other by the reasonable, outward appearance of things.

The reasonable person standard is probably a composite view of what most of us would do in the particular circumstances if we were behaving rationally and carefully. If the parties to a contract are experts of some kind, then this reasonable person is a composite view of how rational, careful experts would behave under the circumstances.

Under the objective theory of contracts, courts usually assume parties had the intentions their outward behavior and words would convey to a reasonable person. However, if contracting parties do disclose actual, inner thoughts to one another, these are also part of their intentions, since reasonable people take shared thoughts and motives into account. Courts may consider any and all of the following factors in trying to establish what a reasonable person would have understood in particular circumstances:

- The identity of the parties
- The words and expressions used
- Relevant industry or trade practices
- Any prior relationship between the parties
- Any relevant conduct of the parties
- The subject matter of the contract
- Previous correspondence between the parties
- General knowledge of human behavior
- Types of communication used
- The "setting" or location for negotiations
- Relevant facts known about the negotiations
- Relevant circumstances existing before, during, and after the negotiations
- Market prices before and during the negotiations

This list is not exhaustive. Literally any relevant fact or circumstance a reasonable person would have been aware of can be used to establish whether

Objective theory of contracts The modern theory of contract making under which courts assume parties had the "intentions" their outward behavior and words would convey to a reasonable person. Each contracting party is entitled to judge the other by the reasonable, outward appearance of things.

there was a "meeting of the minds" between the parties and whether an agreement was reached.

In reading this chapter, you should bear in mind that all communications between negotiating parties are usually judged by the objective theory of contracts. Thus, a party who withholds private thoughts relevant to the negotiations or to the contract runs some risk in not disclosing those thoughts. If nondisclosure creates a situation in which a reasonable person would make an interpretation contrary to the private thoughts, the reasonable interpretation prevails. Note how the court uses the objective theory of contracts in the following case.

A CASE FOR STUDY
Lucy v. Zehmer
196 Va. 493, 84 S.E.2d 516 (1954)

Suit to compel specific performance of land purchase contract claimed by defendant vendors to have been entered into as a joke. The Circuit Court, Dinwiddie County, J. G. Jefferson, Jr., J., entered decree denying specific performance and dismissing suit and purchasers appealed. The Supreme Court of Appeals, Buchanan, J., held that evidence showed that the contract represented a serious business transaction and good faith sale and purchase of the farm, that no unusual circumstances existed in its making, and that purchasers were entitled to specific performance. Reversed and remanded.

BUCHANAN, J., delivered the opinion of the court. This suit was instituted by W. O. Lucy and J. C. Lucy, complainants, against A. H. Zehmer and Ida S. Zehmer, his wife, defendants, to have specific performance of a contract by which it was alleged the Zehmers had sold to W. O. Lucy a tract of land owned by A. H. Zehmer in Dinwiddie county containing 471.6 acres, more or less, known as the Ferguson farm, for $50,000. J. C. Lucy, the other complainant, is a brother of W. O. Lucy, to whom W. O. Lucy transferred a half interest in his alleged purchase.

The instrument sought to be enforced was written by A. H. Zehmer on December 20, 1952, in these words: "We hereby agree to sell to W. O. Lucy the Ferguson Farm complete for $50,000.00, title satisfactory to buyer," and signed by the defendants, A. H. Zehmer and Ida S. Zehmer.

The answer of A. H. Zehmer admitted that at the time mentioned W. O. Lucy offered him $50,000 cash for the farm, but that he, Zehmer, considered that the offer was made in jest; that so thinking, and both he and Lucy having had several drinks, he wrote out "the memorandum" quoted above and induced his wife to sign it; that he did not deliver the memorandum to Lucy, but that Lucy picked it up, read it, put it in his pocket, attempted to offer Zehmer $5 to bind the bargain, which Zehmer refused to accept, and realizing for the first time that Lucy was serious, Zehmer assured him that he had no intention of selling the farm and that the whole matter was a joke. Lucy left the premises insisting that he had purchased the farm.

Depositions were taken and the decree appealed from was entered holding that the complainants had failed to establish their right to specific performance, and dismissing their bill. The assignment of error is to this action of the court.

W. O. Lucy, a lumberman and farmer, thus testified in substance: He had known Zehmer for fifteen or twenty years and had been familiar with the Ferguson farm for ten years. Seven or eight years ago he had offered Zehmer $20,000 for the farm which Zehmer had accepted, but the agreement was verbal and Zehmer backed out. On the night of December 20, 1952, around eight o'clock, he took an employee to McKenney, where Zehmer lived and operated a restaurant, filling station and motor court. While there he decided to see Zehmer and again try to buy the Ferguson farm. He entered the restaurant and talked to Mrs. Zehmer until Zehmer came in. He asked Zehmer if he had sold the

Ferguson farm. Zehmer replied that he had not. Lucy said, "I bet you wouldn't take $50,000.00 for that place." Zehmer replied, "Yes, I would too; you wouldn't give fifty." Lucy said he would and told Zehmer to write up an agreement to that effect. Zehmer took a restaurant check and wrote on the back of it, "I do hereby agree to sell to W. O. Lucy the Ferguson Farm for $50,000 complete." Lucy told him he had better change it to "We" because Mrs. Zehmer would have to sign it too. Zehmer then tore up what he had written, wrote the agreement quoted above and asked Mrs. Zehmer, who was at the other end of the counter ten or twelve feet away, to sign it. Mrs. Zehmer said she would for $50,000 and signed it. Zehmer brought it back and gave it to Lucy, who offered him $5 which Zehmer refused, saying, "You don't need to give me any money, you got the agreement there signed by both of us."

The discussion leading to the signing of the agreement, said Lucy, lasted thirty or forty minutes, during which Zehmer seemed to doubt that Lucy could raise $50,000. Lucy suggested the provision for having the title examined and Zehmer made the suggestion that he would sell it "complete, everything there," and stated that all he had on the farm was three heifers.

Lucy took a partly filled bottle of whiskey into the restaurant with him for the purpose of giving Zehmer a drink if he wanted it. Zehmer did, and he and Lucy had one or two drinks together. Lucy said that while he felt the drinks he took he was not intoxicated, and from the way Zehmer handled the transaction he did not think he was either.

December 20 was on Saturday. Next day Lucy telephoned to J. C. Lucy and arranged with the latter to take a half interest in the purchase and pay half of the consideration. On Monday he engaged an attorney to examine the title. The attorney reported favorably on December 31 and on January 2 Lucy wrote Zehmer stating that the title was satisfactory, that he was ready to pay the purchase price in cash and asking when Zehmer would be ready to close the deal. Zehmer replied by letter, mailed on January 13, asserting that he had never agreed or intended to sell.

Mr. and Mrs. Zehmer were called by the complainants as adverse witnesses. Zehmer testified in substance as follows:

He bought this farm more than ten years ago for $11,000. He had twenty-five offers, more or less, to buy it, including several from Lucy, who had never offered any specific sum of money. He had given them all the same answer, that he was not interested in selling it. On this Saturday night before Christmas it looked like everybody and his brother came by there to have a drink. He took a good many drinks during the afternoon and had a pint of his own. When he entered the restaurant around eight-thirty Lucy was there and he could see that he was "pretty high." He said to Lucy, "Boy, you got some good liquor, drinking, ain't you?" Lucy then offered him a drink. "I was already high as a Georgia pine, and didn't have any more better sense than to pour another great big slug out and gulp it down, and he took one too."

After they had talked a while Lucy asked whether he still had the Ferguson farm. He replied that he had not sold it and Lucy said, "I bet you wouldn't take $50,000.00 for it." Zehmer asked him if he would give $50,000 and Lucy said yes. Zehmer replied, "You haven't got $50,000 in cash." Lucy said he did and Zehmer replied that he did not believe it. They argued "pro and con for a long time," mainly about "whether he had $50,000 in cash that he could put up right then and buy that farm."

Finally, said Zehmer, Lucy told him if he didn't believe he had $50,000, "you sign that piece of paper here and say you will take $50,000.00 for the farm." He, Zehmer, "just grabbed the back off of a guest check there" and wrote on the back of it. At that point in his testimony Zehmer asked to see what he had written to "see if I recognize my own handwriting." He examined the paper and exclaimed, "Great balls of fire, I got 'Firgerson' for Ferguson. I have got satisfactory spelled wrong. I don't recognize that writing if I would see it, wouldn't know it was mine."

After Zehmer had, as he described it, "scribbled this thing off," Lucy said, "Get your wife to sign it." Zehmer walked over to where she was and she at first refused to sign but did so after he told her that he "was just needling him [Lucy], and didn't mean a thing in the world, that I was not selling the farm." Zehmer then "took it back over there . . . and I was still looking at the dern thing. I had the drink right there by my hand, and I reached over to get a drink, and he said, 'Let me see it.' He reached and picked it up, and when I looked back again he had it in his pocket and he dropped a five dollar bill over there, and he said, 'Here is five dollars payment on it.' I said, 'Hell no, that is beer and liquor talking. I am not going to sell you the farm. I have told you that too many times before."

Mrs. Zehmer testified that when Lucy came into the restaurant he looked as if he had a drink. When Zehmer came in he took a drink out of a bottle that Lucy handed him. She went back to help the waitress who was getting things ready for next day. Lucy and Zehmer were talking but she did not pay too much attention to what they were saying. She heard Lucy ask Zehmer if he had sold the Ferguson farm, and Zehmer replied that he had not and did not want to sell it. Lucy said, "I bet you wouldn't take $50,000 cash for that farm," and Zehmer replied, "You haven't got $50,000 cash." Lucy said, "I can get it." Zehmer said he might form a company and get it, "but you haven't got $50,000.00 cash to pay me tonight." Lucy asked him if he would put it in writing that he would sell him this farm. Zehmer then wrote on the back of a pad, "I agree to sell the Ferguson Place to W. O. Lucy for $50,000.00 cash." Lucy said, "All right, get your wife to sign it." Zehmer came back to where she was standing and said, "You want to put your name to this?" She said "No," but he said in an undertone, "It is nothing but a joke," and she signed it.

She said that only one paper was written and it said: "I hereby agree to sell," but the "I" had been changed to "We". However, she said she read what she signed and was then asked, "When you read 'We hereby agree to sell to W. O. Lucy,' what did you interpret that to mean, that particular phrase?" She said she thought that was a cash sale that night; but she also said that when she read that part about "title satisfactory to buyer" she understood that if the title was good Lucy would pay $50,000 but if the title was bad he would have a right to reject it, and that was her understanding at the time she signed her name.

On examination by her own counsel she said that her husband laid this piece of paper down after it was signed; that Lucy said to let him see it, took it, folded it and put it in his wallet, then said to Zehmer, "Let me give you $5.00," but

Zehmer said, "No, this is liquor talking. I don't want to sell the farm, I have told you that I want my son to have it. This is all a joke." Lucy then said at least twice, "Zehmer, you have sold your farm," wheeled around and started for the door. He paused at the door and said, "I will bring you $50,000.00 tomorrow. No, tomorrow is Sunday. I will bring it to you Monday." She said you could tell definitely that he was drinking and she said to her husband, "You should have taken him home," but he said, "Well, I am just about as bad off as he is."

The defendants insist that the evidence was ample to support their contention that the writing sought to be enforced was prepared as a bluff or dare to force Lucy to admit that he did not have $50,000; that the whole matter was a joke; that the writing was not delivered to Lucy and no binding contract was ever made between the parties.

It is an unusual, if not bizarre, defense. When made to the writing admittedly prepared by one of the defendants and signed by both, clear evidence is required to sustain it.

In his testimony Zehmer claimed that he "was high as a Georgia pine," and that the transaction "was just a bunch of two doggoned drunks bluffing to see who could talk the biggest and say the most." That claim is inconsistent with his attempt to testify in great detail as to what was said and what was done. It is contradicted by other evidence as to the condition of both parties, and rendered of no weight by the testimony of his wife that when Lucy left the restaurant she suggested that Zehmer drive him home. The record is convincing that Zehmer was not intoxicated to the extent of being unable to comprehend the nature and consequences of the instrument he executed, and hence that instrument is not to be invalidated on that ground. . . . It was in fact conceded by defendants' counsel in oral argument that under the evidence Zehmer was not too drunk to make a valid contract.

The appearance of the contract, the fact that it was under discussion for forty minutes or more before it was signed; Lucy's objection to the first draft because it was written in the singular, and he wanted Mrs. Zehmer to sign it also; the rewriting to meet that objection and the signing by Mrs. Zehmer; the discussion of what was to be included in the sale, the provision for the examination of the title, the completeness of the instrument that was executed, the taking possession of it by Lucy with no request or suggestion by either of the defendants that he give it back, are facts which furnish persuasive evidence that the execution of the contract was a serious business transaction rather than a casual, jesting matter as defendants now contend.

If it be assumed, contrary to what we think the evidence shows, that Zehmer was jesting about selling his farm to Lucy and that the transaction was intended by him to be a joke, nevertheless the evidence shows that Lucy did not so understand it but considered it to be a serious business transaction and the contract to be binding on the Zehmers as well as on himself. The very next day he arranged with his brother to put up half the money and take a half interest in the land. The day after that he employed an attorney to examine the title. The next night, Tuesday, he was back at Zehmer's place and there Zehmer told him for the first time, Lucy said, that he wasn't going to sell and he told Zehmer, "You know you sold that place fair and square." After receiving the report from his attorney that the title was good he wrote to Zehmer that he was ready to close the deal.

Not only did Lucy actually believe, but the evidence shows he was warranted in believing, that the contract represented a serious business transaction and a good faith sale and purchase of the farm.

In the field of contracts, as generally elsewhere, "We must look to the outward expression of a person as manifesting his intention rather than to his secret and unexpressed intention. The law imputes to a person an intention corresponding to the reasonable meaning of his words and acts." First Nat. Bank v. Roanoke Oil Co., 169 Va. 99, 114, 192 S.E. 764, 770.

At no time prior to the execution of the contract had Zehmer indicated to Lucy by word or act that he was not in earnest about selling the farm. They had argued about it and discussed its terms, as Zehmer admitted, for a long time. Lucy testified that if there was any jesting it was about paying $50,000 that night. The contract and the evidence show that he was not expected to pay the money that night. Zehmer said that after the writing was signed he laid it down on the counter in front of Lucy. Lucy said Zehmer handed it to him. In any event there

had been what appeared to be a good faith offer and a good faith acceptance, followed by the execution and apparent delivery of a written contract. Both said that Lucy put the writing in his pocket and then offered Zehmer $5 to seal the bargain. Not until then, even under the defendants' evidence, was anything said or done to indicate that the matter was a joke. Both of the Zehmers testified that when Zehmer asked his wife to sign he whispered that it was a joke so Lucy wouldn't hear and that it was not intended that he should hear.

The mental assent of the parties is not requisite for the formation of a contract. If the words or other acts of one of the parties have but one reasonable meaning, his undisclosed intention is immaterial except when an unreasonable meaning which he attaches to his manifestations is known to the other party. Restatement of the Law of Contracts, Vol. I, § 71, p. 74.

"The law, therefore, judges of an agreement between two persons exclusively from those expressions of their intentions which are communicated between them." Clark on Contracts, 4 ed., § 3, p. 4.

An agreement or mutual assent is of course essential to a valid contract but the law imputes to a person an intention corresponding to the reasonable meaning of his words and acts. If his words and acts, judged by a reasonable standard, manifest an intention to agree, it is immaterial what may be the real but unexpressed state of his mind. 17 C.J.S., Contracts, § 32, p. 361; 12 Am. Jur., Contracts, § 19, p. 515.

So a person cannot set up that he was merely jesting when his conduct and words would warrant a reasonable person in believing that he intended a real agreement, 17 C.J.S., Contracts, § 47, p. 390; Clark on Contracts, 4 ed., § 27, at p. 54.

Whether the writing signed by the defendants and now sought to be enforced by the complainants was the result of a serious offer by Lucy and a serious acceptance by the defendants, or was a serious offer by Lucy and an acceptance in secret jest by the defendants, in either event it constituted a binding contract of sale between the parties.

The complainants are entitled to have specific performance of the contracts sued on. The decree appealed from is therefore reversed and the cause is remanded for the entry of a proper decree requiring the defendants to perform the contract in accordance with the prayer of the bill. Reversed and remanded.

Questions to Consider

1. From the evidence given in the record, does it reasonably appear that Mr. Zehmer was joking when he agreed to sell Ferguson Farm? What facts indicate he was or was not joking?
2. Even if Mr. Zehmer was actually joking when he agreed to sell the farm, how would his intent be interpreted under the objective theory of contracts?
3. How intoxicated were the parties according to the appellate court? What facts indicate the degree of the parties' intoxication? If Mr. Zehmer had been so intoxicated he fell down and was unable even to remember the transaction, would the opinion come out differently? Should it? Why or why not?
4. If your office represented the Zehmers and you were a paralegal preparing for trial, are there any facts that might be emphasized or used differently to make an argument that Lucy knew Mr. Zehmer was joking? Explain. How might this make a difference?

What Is a Contract?

The traditional common-law definition of a contract is that it exists where one party makes an *offer* that the other party *accepts* and, in so doing, each party promises to do something she was not previously obligated to do or to refrain from doing something she was previously entitled to do. This definition has some defects. For example, in certain kinds of situations, parties make contracts through their conduct alone. If so, it is not possible to point out a particular communication that is an offer or an acceptance of this offer. It can also be difficult to define what is meant by "giving up the right to do something" or "refraining from doing something one is otherwise entitled to do."

The truth is that no one has succeeded in developing an entirely satisfactory definition of a contract. Nevertheless, without a working definition, it is difficult to determine whether a contract exists, or whether a particular arrangement should be enforced.

Why are we even concerned with knowing whether a contract exists? The short answer to this question is that people need consistency and reliability in both their private and their commercial lives. When people make important arrangements like buying a house or car, or ordering goods and services, they need to know they can rely on these arrangements. If the arrangements are not carried out, people may need to know that at least they can go to court and try to get compensation for the failure to fulfill what was promised. Enforceable contracts are one way that human beings have tried to make sure their arrangements are carried out. Deciding which human arrangements should be *legally* enforceable is not always easy, however. Consider the two following situations. Should a contract exist in either of these cases? Why or why not?

EXAMPLE 2.1

Teenage daughter says to Mom, "Mom, I'm such a good kid and I've gotten such good grades this year that I deserve a car. Now that I can drive, I think you should buy me my own sports car." Momentarily weakened by the rigors of raising teenage offspring, Mom responds, "OK, Honey, I'll buy you that car." Two days later Mom changes her mind and refuses to buy the car.

EXAMPLE **2.2**

To relieve the stress of dealing with her teenage kids and for general health reasons, Mom wants to join a fitness club. Mom pays $400 as a membership fee, and Manager outlines for her the privileges of membership including use of the swimming pool, weight room, and free aerobics classes. Mom agrees to pay the monthly dues of $65 per month by the fifteenth of each month. She signs the "Membership Agreement," and Manager agrees to mail her a copy within the next two weeks. A week later, Mom receives notification that the club is no longer admitting new members. The club refuses to admit Mom and refunds her $400.

Questions to Consider

1. Assuming for the moment that she has legal capacity to sue, should teenage daughter have a cause of action against Mom for breach of contract? Can you find an offer or an acceptance here? How would a reasonable person in each party's position have interpreted the other's words and actions?
2. Did each party in Example 2.1 either promise to do something she was not previously obligated to do or promise to refrain from doing something she was otherwise entitled to do?
3. Should Mom have a cause of action against the fitness club for breach of contract? Can you find an offer or an acceptance here? How would a reasonable person in each party's position have interpreted the other's words and actions?
4. Did each party in Example 2.2 promise to do something it was not previously obligated to do or to refrain from doing something it was otherwise entitled to do?
5. How would you describe any differences between the fact patterns that might make them *legally* different from each other?

Most people think Mom in Example 2.2 has a better chance of legally enforcing the fitness club agreement than the daughter in Example 2.1 has of legally enforcing the car agreement. Why should this be? The answer to this question is one of the central concerns of contract law. Although these are simple examples, the issue remains the same throughout contract law: special characteristics distinguish a legally enforceable agreement from one that is not legally enforceable.

Essential Elements of a Contract: Common Law

After a long struggle to define the characteristics of legally enforceable agreements, common law eventually developed the three requirements or "elements" previously referred to:

- An offer
- An acceptance
- Consideration

An enforceable contract has two additional characteristics: *contractual capacity* and *legality*. The requirements of a common-law contract are covered in more detail elsewhere in this text, but a general understanding of these five terms is a good way to begin:

Offer A showing of intention to act or refrain from acting in a particular way, such that the recipient of the showing is justified in believing her acceptance will form a legally binding agreement.

Acceptance The effective assent to the offer by its recipient; also, the exercise of the power to make the contract conferred on the offeree by the offeror.

Consideration Acts or promises that involve each party's giving up the right to do something he is otherwise entitled to do or becoming obligated to do something he was not previously obligated to do.

Capacity The ability to understand one's own and the other party's rights and duties under the contract because one is old enough and mentally competent enough.

Legality In a UCC or common-law contract, this means the contract performance, purpose, and consideration exchanged by the parties are all lawful.

Contract An enforceable agreement reached through voluntary mutual consent; also, the total obligations and rights resulting from a legally enforceable mutual agreement.

- **Offer.** How a contract begins; a showing of intention to act or refrain from acting in a particular way, such that the recipient of the showing is justified in believing her acceptance will form a legally binding agreement.
- **Acceptance.** The effective assent to the offer by its recipient; also, the exercise of the power to make the contract that is conferred on the recipient of the offer by the party who made the offer.
- **Consideration.** Acts or promises that involve each party's giving up the right to do something he is otherwise entitled to do or becoming obligated to do something he was not previously obligated to do; also, the inducement to a contract.
- **Capacity.** The ability to understand one's rights and duties under the contract because one has reached the presumed age of maturity and is mentally competent.
- **Legality.** The contract performance, purpose, and consideration exchanged by the parties are all lawful.

None of these definitions is perfect or even universally accepted, but they do provide an idea of what the elements of an enforceable agreement are.

Essentially, then, a **contract** is a legally enforceable agreement reached through voluntary mutual consent. Through this mutual consent, the parties must exchange, or promise to exchange, something of value to each of them in doing or refraining from doing certain things. Since a contract is a legally enforceable agreement, neither party can unilaterally back out of it without suffering some legal consequences: each party is *bound*.

The Nature of the Offer Under Common Law

Often, though not always, contracts begin with a negotiating process during which one party makes an offer to the other party. As stated previously, one way to think of an *offer* is as the way a contract begins. This definition of an offer is useful in a practical way, but it has two drawbacks. First, the idea that contracts always begin the same way, with an identifiable offer, is often something of a fiction. In many cases, a steady stream of communications goes back and forth between the parties until at some point the parties themselves come to feel they have a deal. In that case, it is not always possible to identify a particular communication as the offer. The second drawback is that even though an offer may be the way a contract begins, saying this does not tell us specifically how to identify an offer.

The common law of contracts dealt with the problem of many communications going back and forth by essentially ignoring it. Over a period of many centuries, the law courts simply insisted that the party trying to enforce a contract be able to point to at least one communication that met the requirements of an offer. As to the problem of needing a more specific description of what an offer is, the common law developed three requirements for a valid offer. These requirements are referred to as the elements of an offer.

- It "manifests" the present contractual intent of the offeror.
- It has certain and definite terms.
- It is communicated to the offeree.

In cases where it is difficult to identify an offer, a party who believed a contract existed ultimately may not have one. Because the recipient of a valid offer is given the power to make a contract, the common-law requirement of an identifiable offer remains strict. If there is no communication that can be identified as an offer, this requirement may work a hardship on a party who thought she had a contract. Consider the following case.

A CASE FOR STUDY

Owen v. Tunison

131 Me. 42, 158 A. 926 (Supreme Judicial Court of Maine, 1932)

BARNES, J.   This case is reported to the law court, and such judgment is to be rendered as the law and the admissible evidence require.

Plaintiff charges that defendant agreed in writing to sell him the Bradley block and lot, situated in Bucksport, for a stated price in cash, that he later refused to perfect the sale, and that plaintiff, always willing and ready to pay the price, has suffered loss on account of defendant's unjust refusal to sell, and claims damages.

From the record it appears that defendant, a resident of Newark, N.J., was, in the fall of 1929, the owner of the Bradley block and lot.

With the purpose of purchasing, on October 23, 1929, plaintiff wrote the following letter:

Dear Mr. Tunison:

   Will you sell me your store property which is located on Main St. in Bucksport, Me. running from Montgomery's Drug Store on one corner to a Grocery Store on the other, for the sum of $6,000.00?

Nothing more of this letter need be quoted.

On December 5, following, plaintiff received defendant's reply, apparently written in Cannes, France, on November 12, and it reads:

   In reply to your letter of Oct. 23rd which has been forwarded to me in which you inquire about the Bradley Block, Bucksport Me.

   Because of improvements which have been added and an expenditure of several thousand dollars it would not be possible for me to sell it unless I was to receive $16,000.00 cash.

The upper floors have been converted into apartments with baths and the building put into first class condition.

Very truly yours,

   [Signed] R. G. Tunison.

Whereupon, and at once, plaintiff sent to defendant, and the latter received, in France, the following message:

   Accept your offer for Bradley block Bucksport Terms sixteen thousand cash send deed to Eastern Trust and Banking Co Bangor Maine Please acknowledge.

Four days later he was notified that defendant did not wish to sell the property, and on the 14th day of January following brought suit for damages.

Granted that damages may be due a willing buyer if the owner refuses to tender a deed of real estate, after the latter has made an offer in writing to sell to the former, and such offer has been so accepted, it remains for us to point out that defendant here is not shown to have written to plaintiff an offer to sell.

There can have been no contract for the sale of the property desired, no meeting of the minds of the owner and prospective purchaser, unless there was an offer or proposal of sale. It cannot be successfully argued that defendant made any offer or proposal of sale.

In a recent case the words, "Would not consider less than half" is held "not to be taken as an outright offer to sell for one-half." Sellers v. Warren, 116 Me. 350, 102 A. 40, 41.

Where an owner of millet seed wrote, "I want $2.25 per cwt. for this seed f. o. b. Lowell," in an action for damages for alleged breach of contract to sell at the figure quoted above, the court held: "He [defendant] does not say, 'I offer to sell to you.'" The language used is general, and such as may be used in an advertisement, or circular addressed generally to those engaged in the seed business, and is not an offer by which he may be bound, if accepted, by any or all of the persons addressed." Nebraska Seed Co. v. Harsh, 98 Neb. 89, 152 N.W. 310, 311, and cases cited in note L. R. A. 1915F, 824.

Defendant's letter of December 5 in response to an offer of $6,000 for his property may have been written with the intent to open negotiations that might lead to a sale. It was not a proposal to sell.

Judgment for defendant.

Questions to Consider

1. Do you think the would-be buyer's letter of October 23, 1929, was an offer? Why or why not?
2. If buyer's October 23 letter was an offer, was the owner's response on December 5, 1929, an acceptance? Why or why not?
3. How did the buyer choose to treat the owner's December 5 letter? Does the court agree with this treatment?
4. What effect, if any, should the price difference between "$6,000.00" and "$16,000.000" have on whether a contract was formed?
5. How does the court use earlier cases to help make its decision in this case?
6. Suppose similar communications were sent today except the parties used the Internet or fax machines. Would the result in the case be different? If so, how and why?

Common-Law Requirement 1: Present Contractual Intent

Offeror The party who makes an offer.

Offeree The party to whom the offer is made.

What do we mean when we say an offer must "manifest" or show "present contractual intent"? This requirement sounds very abstract, but it is actually an attempt to formalize a commonsense notion about the seriousness of people's motives and their readiness to become involved in a deal. To say an offer must manifest present contractual intent means that from its terms and circumstances, it must be clear that the maker of the offer (**offeror**) is immediately and sincerely ready to enter into the deal he proposes to the recipient of the offer (**offeree**). The notion is that if this "readiness" is present and the other party accepts, there is a contract. To understand what is involved, consider the following examples.

EXAMPLE 2.3

Kathy and Joe are colleagues in an office. They go out to lunch together. Kathy, who is thin, has several pieces of pizza, a salad, and chocolate cake. Joe, who is concerned about his weight, has only a large salad and a diet soda. They are laughing and chatting about the day's work when suddenly Joe says, "Kathy, I'd give you a million bucks, if you could tell me how you can eat that kind of lunch and still stay so slim!"

EXAMPLE 2.4

Larry and Lois are sales representatives for different companies. They meet for lunch and begin discussing the sale of Greyacres, a property owned by Larry's company that Lois's company has been trying to purchase. Larry and Lois enjoy each other's company and have often done business together. After a pleasant lunch, they push aside their dishes and begin to discuss the price, deed delivery date, and financing terms for the sale of Greyacres. Lois tells

Larry: "My company will purchase Greyacres for $200,000 payable in four equal cash installments on the first day of the next four months, if your company can guarantee clear title to Greyacres and delivery of the deed by next September 3."

Questions to Consider

1. How might the hypothetical reasonable person have understood Joe's remark about paying for the secret of staying thin? Why would reasonable people interpret the remark that way?
2. How might a reasonable person in Larry's position have understood Lois's remarks about buying Greyacres? Why would reasonable people interpret the remark that way?
3. Does "reasonable person" mean the same thing whether professionals or laypeople are involved in the contract?
4. What are the main *differences* between the two situations as to "readiness" to enter into a deal?

Most people would consider Joe's remark to Kathy to have been a joke rather than an "offer" to make a contract. On the other hand, Lois may have made Larry an effective offer for a contract. What makes the difference? There are, of course, some obvious differences between the two communications. Joe's communication about eating all that food and staying thin is less detailed than Lois's communication about the real estate transaction. Another difference is the context in which the remarks were made. Joe and Kathy seem to have been purely socializing. On the other hand, Larry and Lois appear to be having a "power lunch" where they talk business.

According to the traditional law of contracts, however, Joe's communication would probably not be an offer even if it were more detailed and Lois's communication probably would be an offer even if she and Larry had not previously talked business. The reason for this is the readiness idea mentioned above. Taken all in all, Lois's communication conveys the sense that her company intends to be immediately bound exactly as she stated if Larry says "we accept" on behalf of his company. Our sense of this readiness comes from many aspects of Lois's communication, including words chosen, amount of detail, setting, prior relationship of the parties, and general knowledge of human behavior. In contrast, Joe's remark seems to lack the sense that he will really pay Kathy a million dollars if she gives him the secret to staying thin.

Thus, the "manifestation of present contractual intent" requirement of an offer really refers to words and conduct that, taken together, show the offeree is presently willing to be bound by the deal she proposes, subject only to an appropriate acceptance. In negotiations where several offers are made and turned down, the parties can switch roles several times. Each party is the offeror for the offers it *makes* and the offeree for the offers it *receives*.

Assignment

Consider the following situation presented by the well-known San Francisco newspaper columnist Jon Carroll.

On a recent wilderness vacation, Mr. Carroll had to cope with the problem of hungry bears competing for his food supplies. He wrote several humorous columns in which campers' adventures with bears figured prominently. One of his readers sent in a clipping from an organization that arranges honeymoons in a "bear's winter den" in Sweden's Jamtland wilderness. Mr. Carroll's column then quoted the details provided by the organization, including a wedding dinner by the campfire, opening of wedding presents apparently lugged several hundred miles into the wilderness, sleeping in "newly mangled" sheets, and a romantic champagne breakfast. While the presentation given by Mr. Carroll was very funny, the intent of the organization seemed quite serious. At the end of his column, Mr. Carroll included the following:

OK, this is real. First reader to do this and write about it gets column space and a Leatherette keepsake. The man to contact is [name], fax [number]. The rest of us are waiting with guarded interest. [1]

Did Mr. Carroll make a valid offer for a contract? Why or why not? If this is an offer, what are its terms?

Common-Law Requirement 2: Certain and Definite Terms

The modern requirement of certain and definite terms means the offer must contain all essential information necessary to carry out the contract. This rule echoes common sense. If a contract could be made using an offer that lacked sufficient detail, then the resulting contract would lack sufficient detail. Thus, the terms of the offer itself must first be examined for certainty and definiteness. Ultimately, the terms of the whole contract must be sufficiently complete and clear to show what the parties are supposed to do, get, and give. Under the traditional common-law view, all effective offers were required to state at least the following information:

- Identification of the parties
- Subject matter of the contract
- Time and necessary terms of performance
- Price
- Quantity to be contracted for

Under modern common law, all of the terms need not be expressly stated in the offer, but may be implied. If essential terms cannot be reliably and clearly established from a combination of express and implied terms, however, the offer will fail for indefiniteness.

This insistence on completeness in the offer itself can create problems. For example, what if the parties have already begun performance although the original offer did not contain all essential terms? If one party then tries to back out of the deal, should she be allowed to do so? Often both parties have completed enough performance to reveal what the terms of the contract are even though the offer itself does not contain all the required information. Should a court say there is no contract solely on the technicality that the original offer lacked all of these details? Or should the court fill in the terms based on the subsequent conduct and performance of the parties?

Historically, judicial opinions often insisted on the presence of these essential terms in the offer. The theory was that a court should not rewrite the offer to make it complete if the parties did not do so. Modern court opinions have changed the focus. They examine whether the offer was sufficiently certain and definite by looking not just at its original terms, but also at the conduct of the parties, applicable industry practices or standards, and any relevant performance of the parties to see if these clarify the essential terms. Offers whose own terms are sufficiently certain and definite are preferred, but if essential terms can be provided by consulting such things as conduct, industry standards, and performance, modern courts tend to be more lenient where it is clear the parties reached agreement. Part performance on a contract can be particularly useful in clarifying an essential term. If some performance was given under an alleged contract, this can often be used to flesh out an insufficient offer. Modern contract law allows part performance by the parties to be used to "cure" indefiniteness in the terms of an offer or contract.

Obviously, in some situations, it is still appropriate to insist that the offer contain the traditional elements: parties, subject matter, price, quantity, and performance terms. Such situations most clearly occur where neither party has begun performance under the contract. If a court has nothing but the offer itself with which to fill in or clarify the terms of any resulting contract, then the offer must stand on its own.

The Restatement (Second) § 33 is helpful in expressing the modern position on certainty and definiteness of terms:

§ 33 Certainty

(1) Even though a manifestation of intention is intended to be understood as an offer, it cannot be accepted so as to form a contract unless the terms of the contract are reasonably certain.

(2) The terms of a contract are reasonably certain if they provide a basis for determining the existence of a breach and for giving an appropriate remedy.

(3) The fact that one or more terms of a proposed bargain are left open or uncertain may show that a manifestation of intention is not intended to be understood as an offer or as an acceptance.

Reference to an External Standard or Measure to Fill in Missing Terms

Sometimes parties to a contract deliberately leave one or more terms *open*. **Open terms** are terms for which specific information is intended to be filled in later.

Open terms Contract terms for which specific information is purposefully omitted and is intended to be filled in later.

EXAMPLE   **2.5**

Suppose Farmer agrees to sell "North Field" to Buyer at a price determined by averaging two appraisals—one by Buyer's representative and one by Farmer's representative. The parties work out their contract and agree upon the appraisers. The contract will not fail for lack of certainty and definiteness. There is an external mechanism for filling in the contract price: averaging the two appraisals.

References to external standards can be a useful tool in the commercial world, especially where the price or availability of the contract subject matter may change before the time for performance arrives, and the parties wish to take this into account. For example, in long-term contracts for jet airplane fuel, the price of fuel is often linked to the price of crude oil per barrel as published regularly in trade publications. Many national and international events can influence the price of crude oil per barrel. Thus, the parties can provide for flexible pricing in a contract by allowing the price to fluctuate according to the market. Although jet fuel is goods and such contracts now come under the UCC, this practice is an example of how parties fill in terms by using external standards. Any agreed external standards would normally be written into or referred to in the contract.

Common-Law Requirement 3: Communication to the Offeree

Knowledge of the Offer

Common law follows the rule that only the party to whom an offer is made can accept it. Futhermore, this party must do so knowingly. Thus, an offer must be conveyed to the intended recipient before it is effective and can be accepted. A party cannot accept an offer unless he knows about it, and the offer was made specifically to him. This theory makes some sense. If anyone could accept an offer simply by finding out about it secondhand, offerors would quickly lose control over their own proposals. Offerors would find themselves bound on contracts accepted by strangers or parties with whom they had no desire to become legally involved. Such arrangements would be more likely to foster litigation and discord than to bring about stability in commercial and private contractual relationships.

The idea that one must know of an offer for it to be legally accepted presents some difficulties in view of the objective theory of contracts. In principle, if an offeror makes an offer and the offeree behaves in such a way that a reasonable person would believe there was an acceptance, then there is one. In other words, the offeror would be entitled to treat the offer as accepted although, in fact, the offeree's behavior was entirely unknowing or coincidental. Fortunately, such situations are rare in the real world. Thus, the usual rule is that no one can accept an offer unless she does so knowingly.

Public Offers

If an offer is made to the public at large, such as a reward, then any member of the public can accept it.

EXAMPLE 2.6

If Dana offers a $50 reward to anyone who finds his lost cat, any member of the public who knows of the offer and finds the cat would be entitled to claim the reward. If someone finds the cat without knowing of the reward, however, and returns it from kindness rather than desire for money, usually this person cannot claim the reward!

The result in Example 2.6 seems to leave the more virtuous behavior unrewarded. However, traditional contract law was concerned to preserve "knowing" acceptances of offers.

Nontransferability of Offers

Because the offeror is viewed as having complete control over the offer, offers are regarded as personal to the party to whom they were made. Thus, if a particular party is the recipient of an offer, she normally cannot transfer the power of acceptance to someone else. Again, contract law was concerned with confining control over the offer, and the resulting contract, to the party selected by the offeror. That party can always refuse to accept the offer, but cannot pass it along to someone the offeror has not chosen.

Advertisements, Catalogs, Price Lists, and Circulars

Many different types of communications may appear to be offers. For example, advertisements that a seller mails out to prospective customers might be construed as offers. Traditionally, however, such advertisements are not offers, but invitations to negotiate. The reason probably has to do with the realities of supply and demand. If a seller's advertisements were construed as offers, then all recipients could accept, but the seller's supply of the product might be limited, making it impossible for him to fulfill all the contracts made when buyers placed their orders.

Thus, advertisements, price lists, catalogs, circulars, and the like are normally considered *invitations to make offers,* not offers. The "official" contract rationale for this result is that such communications do not manifest a present contractual intent to the reasonable person. Instead, the reasonable person would assume the seller is *soliciting* offers rather than making them.

It should be noted that some advertisements can be particularly problematic because their content is very detailed and specific, making them seem more "personal" in nature. Such detail may also mean that the terms required for a contract could be found. For an interesting case involving a detailed and specific advertisement, read the opinion below.

For some paralegals, the treatment of advertisements and the like may have limited relevance, but those working in commercial sales and related areas will find these concepts useful. For example, paralegals working for attorneys involved in commercial litigation may deal with contract formation issues arising from the use of ads, price quotations, or catalogs. The key idea to remember is that without some additional facts to show the seller meant to *make* an offer rather than to *solicit* an offer, there is no manifestation of present contractual intent, and thus no offer is made by the use of advertising materials, price lists, or catalogs. Consider the following case.

A CASE FOR STUDY

Lefkowitz v. Great Minneapolis Surplus Store

251 Minn. 188, 86 N.W.2d 689 (Supreme Court of Minnesota, 1957)

MURPHY, Justice.   This is an appeal from an order of the Municipal Court of Minneapolis denying the motion of the defendant for amended findings of fact, or, in the alternative, for a new trial. The order for judgment awarded the plaintiff the sum of $138.50 as damages for breach of contract.

This case grows out of the alleged refusal of the defendant to sell to the plaintiff a certain fur piece which it had offered for sale in a newspaper advertisement. It appears from the record that on April 6, 1956, the defendant published the following advertisement in a Minneapolis newspaper:

Saturday 9 A.M. Sharp 3 Brand New Fur Coats Worth to $100.00

First Come First Served $1 Each

On April 13, the defendant again published an advertisement in the same newspaper as follows:

Saturday 9 A.M. 2 Brand New Pastel Mink 3-Skin Scarfs
Selling for $89.50
Out they go Saturday. Each . . . $1.00
1 Black Lapin Stole Beautiful, worth $139.50 . . . $1.00
First Come First Served

The record supports the findings of the court that on each of the Saturdays following the publication of the above-described ads the plaintiff was the first to present himself at the appropriate counter in the defendant's store and on each occasion demanded the coat and the stole so advertised and indicated his readiness to pay the sale price of $1. On both occasions, the defendant refused to sell the merchandise to the plaintiff, stating on the first occasion that by a 'house rule' the offer was intended for women only and sales would not be made to men, and on the second visit that plaintiff knew defendant's house rules.

The trial court properly disallowed plaintiff's claim for the value of the fur coats since the value of these articles was speculative and uncertain. The only evidence of value was the advertisement itself to the effect that the coats were "Worth to $100.00," how much less being speculative especially in view of the price for which they were offered for sale. With reference to the offer of the defendant on April 13, 1956, to sell the "1 Black Lapin Stole . . . worth $139.50 . . ." the trial court held that the value of this article was established and granted judgment in favor of the plaintiff for that amount less the $1 quoted purchase price.

The defendant contends that a newspaper advertisement offering items of merchandise for sale at a named price is a "unilateral offer" which may be withdrawn without notice. He relies upon authorities which hold that, where an advertiser publishes in a newspaper that he has a certain quantity or quality of goods which he wants to dispose of at certain prices and on certain terms, such advertisements are not offers which become contracts as soon as any person to whose notice they may come signifies his acceptance by notifying the other that he will take a certain quantity of them. Such advertisements have been construed as an invitation for an offer of sale on the terms stated, which offer, when received, may be accepted or rejected and which therefore does not become a contract of sale until accepted by the seller; and until a contract has been so made, the seller may modify or revoke such prices or terms. [Citations.]

The defendant relies principally on Craft v. Elder & Johnston Co., 34 Ohio L.A. 603, 38 N.E.2d 416 (1941). In that case, the court discussed the legal effect of an advertisement offering for sale, as a one-day special, an electric sewing machine at a named price. The view was expressed that the advertisement was . . . "not an offer made to any specific person but was made to the public generally. Thereby it would be properly designated as a unilateral offer and not being supported by any consideration could be withdrawn at will and without notice." It is true that such an offer may be withdrawn before acceptance. Since all offers are by their nature unilateral because they are necessarily made by one party or on one side in the negotiation of a contract, the distinction made in that decision between a unilateral offer and a unilateral contract is not clear. On the facts before us we are concerned with whether the advertisement constituted an offer, and, if so, whether the plaintiff's conduct constituted an acceptance.

There are numerous authorities which hold that a particular advertisement in a newspaper or circular letter relating to a sale of articles may be construed by the court as constituting an offer, acceptance of which would complete a contract. [Citations.]

The test of whether a binding obligation may originate in advertisements addressed to the general public is "whether the facts show that some performance was promised in positive terms in return for something requested." 1 Williston, Contracts (Rev. ed.) § 27.

The authorities above cited emphasize that, where the offer is clear, definite, and explicit, and leaves nothing open for negotiation, it constitutes an offer, acceptance of which will complete the contract. The most recent case on the subject is Johnson v. Capital City Ford Co., La.App., 85 So.2d 75, in which the court pointed out that a newspaper advertisement relating to the purchase and sale of automobiles may constitute an offer, acceptance of which will consummate a contract and create an obligation in the offeror to perform according to the terms of the published offer.

Whether in any individual instance a newspaper advertisement is an offer rather than an invitation to make an offer depends on the legal intention of the parties and the surrounding circumstances. We are of the view on the facts before us that the offer by the defendant of the sale of the Lapin fur was clear, definite, and explicit, and left nothing open for negotiation. The plaintiff having successfully managed to be the first one to appear at the seller's place of business to be served, as requested by the advertisement, and having offered the stated purchase price of the article, he was entitled to performance on the part of the defendant. We think the trial court was correct in holding that there was in the conduct of the parties a sufficient mutuality of obligation to constitute a contract of sale.

The defendant contends that the offer was modified by a "house rule" to the effect that only women were qualified to receive the bargains advertised. The advertisement contained no such restriction. This objection may be disposed of briefly by stating that, while an advertiser has the right at any time before acceptance to modify his offer, he does not have the right, after acceptance, to impose new or arbitrary conditions not contained in the published offer.

Affirmed.

Questions to Consider

1. Does the court agree with the defendant department store that its ad was not an offer? Why or why not?
2. Rewrite the store's ad so it would clearly *not* be an offer. What are the differences between your rewrite and the ad the store ran?
3. Based on this case, can you formulate a general rule for when newspaper ads will be construed as offers?

Termination of the Common-Law Offer

For an acceptance to be effective, the offer must be "live"; that is, the acceptance can occur only if there is a valid offer outstanding at the time the acceptance is made. Thus, we must be able to determine whether an offer is still open and what kinds of events terminate an offer.

Generally, eight kinds of events or actions can terminate an offer. When any of these events occurs, the offer "dies," and exercise of the acceptance *after that time* does not create a contract. The following are the events or actions that terminate an offer:

1. *The time specified in the offer elapses.* Sometimes offerors themselves place time limits on an offer.

   EXAMPLE 2.7 Seller offers to sell Blackacre to Buyer and indicates how long he intends the offer to remain open: "this offer good until 5:00 P.M. Friday." In this case, the offeree would not be able to make an effective acceptance after 5:00 P.M. on Friday.

2. *No time is specified in the offer, and reasonable time elapses.* In many offers, the offeror does not specify a termination date. Nevertheless, unless one intends offers to remain alive indefinitely, they should have a termination time. Common law developed the theory that offers that do not specify a termination time will terminate within a "reasonable" time. This idea is probably consistent with most reasonable human expectations. Few rational people would expect an offeror to leave an offer open more or less permanently.

"Reasonable time" is a relative term. What is reasonable time depends on many factors and circumstances of the bargain. Thus, an offer for real property might last longer than an offer for perishable tomatoes sitting in the hot sun or an electronic offer for the sale of securities on a stock exchange. Generally, the following factors can all affect what constitutes "reasonable" time for a particular offer to last:

- The subject matter of the contract
- The identity of the parties
- Market conditions
- Market prices
- Weather conditions
- Previous dealings of the parties
- Industry practices
- The words of the parties
- The conduct of the parties

3. *The offeror or the offeree dies.* This rule has been criticized, but common law takes the view that if either the offeror or the offeree dies while the offer is outstanding (before acceptance), it is terminated. A related rule is that mental incapacity of either party will also terminate the offer if the incapacity occurs before acceptance is given.

Revocation Conduct or words (or a combination of the two) on the part of the offeror indicating the offer has been withdrawn. A revocation terminates the offer and can occur any time before an effective acceptance.

4. *The offeror revokes the offer.* Probably, the most obvious way an offer terminates is for the offeror to "take it back," or revoke it. An offer may be revoked by the offeror at any time prior to an effective acceptance. This **revocation** may come about directly or indirectly. The offer is directly revoked if the offeror communicates revocation to the offeree. The offer is indirectly revoked if a *reliable* third party communicates revocation to the offeree. Suppose, for example, an offeree finds out from the offeror's husband's that the offer was revoked. The husband is probably a reliable source of information provided he can be expected to be informed about the offer and his wife's intentions. If the third party is not a reliable source of information, the offeree need not regard the offer as indirectly revoked. The rationale for allowing indirect revocation of offers is that if one learns from a reliable source that the offer is revoked, one should reasonably assume the offeror no longer wishes to make the contract.

Rejection Conduct or words (or a combination of the two) on the part of the offeree indicating a refusal of the offer. A rejection terminates the offer.

5. *The offeree rejects the offer.* If the offeree rejects the offer outright, this rejection terminates the offer. If the offeree decides rejection was a mistake and later tries to accept, this acceptance is ineffective. A true **rejection** by the offeree terminates the offer absolutely. The only avenue now available to the offeree who suddenly changes her mind is to make a new offer that is the same or similar to the original offer. Rejections of an offer can be outright, or they can be accompanied by a counteroffer, as discussed next.

6. *The offeree makes a counteroffer.* If the offeree does not explicitly reject the offer, but instead makes a counteroffer, the making of the counteroffer automatically terminates the offer, even without an explicit rejection. A true counteroffer has the same effect on an outstanding offer that a rejection has. Common law requires the acceptance to be the "mirror

image" of the offer. The mirror image rule is further discussed in Chapter 3 of this text. Under common law, an acceptance that deviates from the offer terminates the offer and becomes a counteroffer.

EXAMPLE 2.8   Suppose A has made an offer to B to sell catering services at "$8 per hour plus food and beverage costs." If B responds, "I'll take the services but only at $7 per hour," B has made a counteroffer. This counteroffer is not the mirror image of the offer and has the same effect as a rejection. The original offer from A is terminated.

(a) *Reservations distinguished from a counteroffer.* In some situations, B might make a counteroffer but "reserve" the offer. In this case, the counteroffer will not terminate the offer.

EXAMPLE 2.9   Suppose B responds to A's offer of catering services at $8 per hour with the words "I still want to consider your offer, but also would be interested to know if you can make it $7 per hour." This request for modification of the offer, or for a better deal, is not a rejection. Here B still intends to keep A's offer open and to have a chance to accept if A cannot be persuaded to sell for $7.

(b) *Inquiries, grumbling, and attempts at clarification distinguished from a counteroffer.* True counteroffers must be distinguished from inquiries concerning the offer, attempts at clarifying the offer, or complaints about the offer. None of these responses is considered a counteroffer and thus does not terminate the offer.

EXAMPLE 2.10   Suppose B did not understand whether A meant to follow the industry custom of providing cleanup services with the catering services. To clarify this point without making a counteroffer, B could say: "I'm interested in the deal as you stated it, but please let me know if cleanup services come with the catering." A reasonable person would understand this to be an attempt at clarification and not a counteroffer.

Also, mere complaints about the terms of an offer (called "grumbling acceptances") are not a counteroffer and thus will not terminate the offer.

7. *Essential subject matter is destroyed or an essential person dies.* An offer is terminated if something or someone essential for performance of the contract is destroyed. This idea seems to be based on common sense. If the contract could not be carried out because of the loss of this subject matter or person, then there is no point in allowing the contract to be made.

8. *A supervening illegality occurs.* If the proposed contract would be illegal because of some problem or legal change arising after the offer is made, this has the effect of terminating the offer.

EXAMPLE 2.11   Suppose Contractor has made an offer to Owner "to build a steel processing plant for a fixed price, in Middletown on Elm Street." When Contractor makes the offer, Elm Street is zoned for industrial use. Then, City Council passes an ordinance designating Elm Street as a "historic site" and prohibiting any new uses of property located there. If the proposed plant is a new use, then Contractor's offer has been affected by a supervening illegality and would be terminated. Common sense and good policy indicate the soundness of this rule. There is no point in allowing contracts to be made when they have become illegal to carry out.

Termination of the Offer Distinguished from Discharge of the Contract

It is important to note that most of the events that can terminate offers have a different legal effect if they occur *after acceptance is given.* For example, death of the offeror or destruction of the subject matter terminates the offer if it is still outstanding and no acceptance has been made when the event occurs. Suppose, however, that the event occurs *after* the acceptance is given. In this case, the legal effect is to *discharge performance* under the contract. Contract discharge is discussed further in Chapter 7. You should note the effect of the *timing* of the events listed above. If they occur before acceptance, they prevent the contract from ever being formed because they terminate the offer. If they occur after acceptance, they may discharge the duty to perform the contract.

Creation of Irrevocable Offers under Common Law: Firm Offers and Option Contracts

All ordinary offers at common law are viewed as revocable; that is, the maker of the offer is free to revoke it anytime prior to acceptance. The law of contracts developed the vocabulary of the **firm offer,** but this terminology is misleading. A so-called firm offer at common law is essentially one in which the offeror makes assurances that the offer will stay open, such as "This offer is guaranteed to last until next Wednesday." What makes the term *firm offer* misleading is that all the events listed in the previous section can terminate even a so-called firm offer any time prior to acceptance. Thus, any ordinary offer at common law is viewed as revocable even if the offeror gives "firm" assurances to keep it open.

At times, however, negotiating parties wish to make an offer irrevocable.

Common-law firm offer An offer in which the offeror makes assurances that the offer will remain open, such as "This offer is guaranteed to last until next Wednesday."

EXAMPLE   **2.12**

Suppose Seller has offered to sell Greenacres to Buyer for $500,000 and Buyer needs time to arrange financing. If Buyer does not want to risk losing the chance to acquire Greenacres, she needs a way to guarantee the offer will stay open while she obtains financing. The common law recognizes an offer as irrevocable when (1) the offeree gives the offeror something of value to hold open the offer, and (2) the offeror accepts this value for the purpose of holding open the offer. This is referred to as giving "consideration" to hold open the offer. Thus, in this case if Buyer gives Seller $2,000 to hold open the offer for two weeks, Seller must do so if he accepts the $2,000.

Option contract A preliminary contract made expressly for the purpose of holding open an offer. Options can also be structured to allow one party the "option" to renew an existing contract at a certain time.

At common law, where the offeree pays the offeror to make an offer irrevocable, the arrangement is called an *option* or *option contract.* An **option contract** can be considered a preliminary contract made expressly for the purpose of holding open an offer. Options can also be structured to allow one party the "option" to renew an existing contract at a certain time.

Option contracts are really the only irrevocable offers at common law. The so-called firm offer is still fully revocable so long as the offeree has not exercised the power of acceptance. Thus, in a way, no such thing as a true "firm offer" exists at common law. If an offeree wishes to be certain of keeping an offer firm (open), he must give, and the offeror must accept, something of value such as money or another asset. Then the offeror is bound to keep open the offer for the agreed period. Option contracts are often used in real estate sales, where an offer to purchase may be signed and paid for prior to the contract. This allows the would-be buyer to keep open the offer for a stated period of time and requires the would-be seller not to sell the property during this option period.

Rejections Within the Option Period

Although not all courts have agreed, many courts give the offeree the right to reject during the option period and then change her mind. Thus, under common law, the option holder usually can reject the offer during the option period without terminating it. Unless this rejection misled and damaged the offeror in some way, the offeree is free to make a later acceptance so long as it is within the option period.

Other Distinctions of Options

Some of the events that terminate revocable offers do not terminate options. Option contracts are not automatically terminated by the death of the offeror, and they can usually be transferred to another party without terminating the offer. In that case, the transferee becomes the option holder and has the right to exercise the option within the original period. Although there is not much authority on the issue, apparently making a counteroffer does not terminate an option contract if the counteroffer is made within the option period.

Creation of an Irrevocable Offer Through Reliance Under the Common Law

The Restatement (Second) § 87 (2) mentions an additional way that offers can sometimes become irrevocable:

> An offer which the offeror should reasonably expect to induce action or forbearance of a substantial character on the part of the offeree before acceptance and which does induce such action or forbearance is binding as an option contract to the extent necessary to avoid injustice.

Section 87 is interpreted to mean that *reliance* may make an offer irrevocable. **Reliance** occurs when a party changes position in response to a promise, or promises, made to him. This is what the Restatement drafters meant by the phrase "to induce action or forbearance." Promises made in the form of an offer sometimes cause the offeree to *rely* on the offer, and this reliance may harm the offeree. If the offer is made in a way that misleads the offeree into taking action based on a reasonable belief that the offer was irrevocable—that the contract was a sure thing—this reliance may cause the offer to become irrevocable. Such situations sometimes occur as a result of the negotiation process. Consider the following example.

Reliance A change in position that occurs when one party is induced to action or forbearance of action because of information contained in a promise.

EXAMPLE **2.13**

Heartless Bank wishes to hire Consultant to act as an independent investment counselor. On Monday, Cynthia, Vice-President of Heartless, meets with Consultant and tells him she will award him the contract if he can put together a "package" by next Monday. Cynthia tells Consultant the package must contain all of the information Heartless needs and the names of forty investment funds that fall into various categories of risk and rate of return on investment.

Cynthia tells Consultant he is the preferred choice for the contract. Several times she assures him he has the deal, provided he can come up with the requested information by next Monday, so she can pass it along to the bank headquarters. Consultant assures Cynthia that he can produce the information and gives her some preliminary figures, which she approves. She tells him everything looks very good, and Consultant leaves.

By next Monday, Consultant has expended thirty hours and $2,000 putting together a package that meets Heartless Bank's needs. Consultant takes the package to Cynthia when the bank opens Monday morning. Cynthia tells him that she is very sorry, but Heartless awarded the consulting contract to another investment counselor last Friday.

Questions to Consider

1. Has Consultant suffered any financial losses? If so, what were these financial losses?
2. Were any losses more Cynthia's fault or more Consultant's fault? Why?
3. Has Cynthia (on behalf of Heartless) made an offer to Consultant? Why?
4. If a court were to find that Cynthia did make an offer to Consultant, were his losses caused by this offer? Why or why not?

Applying the language of the Restatement (Second), we might say that Heartless's offer (through Cynthia) has caused Consultant to take some action to his damage. It could be argued that Consultant expended considerable time and money by relying on Cynthia's verbal assurances, her approval of his preliminary figures, and her requests for specific information. If such actions were a reasonable response, Consultant might argue that Heartless's offer became irrevocable through his reliance.

Recovery Under an Option Created Through Reliance

If a court did find that an offer was made in Example 2.13 and that Consultant reasonably relied on it under the circumstances, Consultant might be able to sue Heartless to recover his costs. Usually, a party who relies on an offer and creates an option in this way is not considered to have obtained a contract. The reliance is used as a basis for the aggrieved party to recover time and money expended. Thus, Heartless can still award the contract to the investment consultant of its choice but may have to reimburse Consultant for $2,000 and thirty hours worked. This is the meaning of § 87 language making the offer "binding" but only to "the extent necessary to avoid injustice." Many states have adopted the Restatement (Second) view that reliance can create an option contract where common law applies. Such states generally allow recovery for time and money expended.

Essential Elements of a Contract
Under the UCC

As discussed earlier, UCC rules apply to all contracts involving the sale of goods. The UCC changed many of the common-law requirements of the formation process, and these changes are relevant for modern sale of goods contracts. The drafters of the UCC recognized that because many transactions involving goods are complex, informal, or extended over time, a single communication that the common law would characterize as an offer cannot always be identified in the parties' words and conduct. Thus, the drafters gave up insistence on a separately identifiable offer. Under UCC § 2-204(1), a contract for the sale of goods can be made "in any manner sufficient to show agreement, including conduct by both parties which recognizes the existence of such a contract." Thus, a contract for sale of goods is not necessarily invalid because there is no particular communication that can be identified as an offer.

Section 2-204(2) further provides that if an agreement amounts to a contract, it is a contract even if "the moment of its making is undetermined." Thus, a contract for the sale of goods may be made even though it is not really clear exactly *when* the agreement was reached. This UCC rule is a realistic assessment of how the negotiating process often occurs. As we have seen, even with many common-law contracts, saying we know the exact moment when the contract was made is something of a pretense.

Contracts for the sale of goods can also be made using the common-law criteria of an offer and acceptance if the parties so choose. In fact, parties negotiating UCC contracts sometimes use the process of offer and acceptance in the conventional common-law sense. The language of § 2-204 does not rule out this alternative. It simply allows a contract to be made in the situation where no particular written or spoken words can be identified as an offer. Thus, in summary, parties can form a contract under the UCC through the use of the offer and acceptance process or by conduct sufficient to show a contract has been made.

Certainty and Definiteness of Terms
Under the UCC

The UCC view of certainty and definiteness is less rigid than the common-law view. Under the UCC, the most critical issue is whether the parties have shown an intent to be presently bound, that is, whether they have reached agreement between themselves. Section 2-204(3) of the UCC provides:

> Even though one or more terms are left open a contract for sale does not fail for indefiniteness if the parties have intended to make a contract and there is a reasonably certain basis for giving an appropriate remedy.

Several other sections of the UCC give standardized ways to fill in information missing from a contract. These provisions, which are found principally in §§ 2-305 through 2-311, together with §§ 1-205 and 2-208, are referred to collectively as **gap-filler provisions.** They set out rules for courts to use to fill in terms missing from an offer or contract. The following are some examples of these UCC provisions:

Gap-filler provisions
Under the UCC, standardized ways to fill in information missing from a contract.

§ **2-305:** If a price term does not appear in a contract, the price is "a reasonable price at the time for delivery."

§ **2-307:** If the contract does not mention when payment is due, it is due upon complete delivery of the goods.

§ **2-309:** If no time for shipment or delivery is stated in the contract, then shipment or delivery of goods must be at a reasonable time.

§ **1-205:** Special trade practices may be used to give meaning to particular terms in the contract or to supplement them.

A court will not make or remake a contract for the parties by using the gap-filler provisions, but if the parties apparently did make a contract albeit with missing information, a court will use the provisions to supply terms where it is reasonable to do so. Doing this allows the court to give an appropriate remedy.

EXAMPLE **2.14**

Suppose Buyer of goods is suing Seller. Buyer alleges Seller breached their contract by failing to deliver 5,000 pounds of apples. Even if Buyer wins the lawsuit, the court could not calculate Buyer's damages without knowing what price Buyer was to pay for each pound of apples. If the contract did not expressly state the price term, the court could use UCC § 2-305, "reasonable price at the time for delivery," to supply this term.

The omission of a quantity term from a contract can be particularly problematic. Under most contract circumstances, there is no such thing as a "reasonable" quantity. Quantity is personal to the parties' individual needs and is therefore difficult for a court to estimate. Even a missing quantity term can be filled in, however, if there is a reasonable and reliable basis for doing so. For example, if the parties have done a great deal of business together and have always contracted for a standard amount, a court might fill in this amount. More often there is no reasonable and reliable basis on which a court can fill in an omitted quantity term. Hence, omission of the quantity involved often causes a contract to fail for indefiniteness.

Irrevocable Offers Under the UCC

The drafters of the UCC partially abandoned the requirement that the offeree must transfer something of value to the offeror to create an irrevocable offer. For laypeople, they preserved the common-law rule that the offeree must provide consideration to the offeror to create an irrevocable offer. For merchants, the drafters established different rules.

Section 2-205 states that a *merchant offeror* can create an irrevocable offer simply by putting the offer into writing and signing it. The *merchant offeree* can also create an option in the same way according to § 2-205. If the offeree receives an oral offer, the offeree can make it irrevocable by putting it in writing, conveying it to the offeror, and getting the offeror's signature on the writing. The signature requirement makes some sense. Without it the recipients of offers would have a kind of unilateral ability to turn a revocable offer into an irrevocable offer without the offeror's permission or intention to do so.

The written offers provided for in § 2-205 are the UCC's version of the common-law "option contract" concept. Note that § 2-205 contains one of the UCC special merchant's provisions. When a merchant creates an option contract under § 2-205, it is called a **UCC firm offer** or a **merchant's firm offer.** Remember that under the UCC, only merchants can create the kind of option that is made without transferring additional value to the offeror. Nonmerchants must create option contracts for goods by satisfying the common-law requirement of paying something to hold open the offer.

The merchant's firm offer under the UCC lasts for the time stated in the offer or for a "reasonable time" if no time is stated. However, § 2-205 provides that a merchant's firm offer cannot last longer than a maximum of three months. Apparently, the drafters intended the parties to renew the option if they wanted it to last longer than three months.

Interestingly, some states have passed statutes that adopt for common-law contracts a rule similar to that of the UCC. In such states, a statute usually provides that option contracts can be created without separate payment, if the arrangement is put into a writing signed by the party giving the option. Section 87(1)(b) of the Restatement (Second) alludes to this by stating that an offer may be binding as an option contract if it "is made irrevocable by statute." To find out whether a particular state allows creation of option contracts without separate payment for the option, a paralegal would have to research the statutes and cases of the relevant state. Does your state have such a statute?

Merchant's firm offer The UCC's version of the common-law option contract concept. When a merchant creates an option contract under § 2-205, it is called a **UCC firm offer.**

Creation of UCC Options Through Reliance

Some courts have recognized that options for sale of goods contracts can be created through reliance. Sometimes the courts have arrived at this conclusion by applying the common-law reliance concept to UCC contracts through UCC § 1-103. Section 1-103 states that common-law principles can be used to supplement UCC provisions unless specifically displaced. Courts that bring the principle of reliance into the UCC take the view that reliance has not been specifically displaced in the text of the UCC itself.

Assignment

Georgette Hyde, a regular business client of the attorney you work for, is a distributor of paper products to educational institutions. Last month she contacted one of her regular customers, Columbia State College, located in Columbia City. The purchasing agent for the college, Walter Well, requested Hyde's price list for xerox paper. Hyde sent out the price list and a blank order form. When he received the price list and order form, Well sent a fax to Hyde noting that the price of medium-quality xerox paper had increased considerably. The fax contained this language: "What is the lowest price you could quote me if we were to double our last order? Would that give us a price break?"

A day after receiving the fax, Hyde sent back her own fax. It stated: "Depending on the quantity you order and what date you want it delivered, I could probably give you the medium-quality xerox paper for $2 per ream. Generally, it takes at least 10 working days to place an order for more than 5,000 reams, and the price breaks begin at minimum orders of 5,000 reams.

Otherwise, the price would be $2.50 per ream with delivery within 5 to 7 working days."

A day after receiving Hyde's fax, Well sent back another fax. It stated: "We accept your offer of 5,000 reams of medium-quality xerox paper for $2 per ream, to be delivered within approximately 10 days of receipt of this fax."

The reason for the increased price of xerox paper is that the paper market is undergoing unexpected shortages, which are leading to still more price increases. Thus, Hyde feels that even the price quotes she faxed to the university are out of date. She does not believe she made a commitment to sell to the university and thinks Well misunderstood her faxes.

Your attorney wants you to review the file and let her know where Hyde stands. Do they have a contract? Why or why not?

Requirements and Output Contracts Under the Common Law and the UCC

Requirements and output contracts are agreements to purchase an amount based on the needs of the seller or the buyer rather than a specific amount. In a typical **requirements contract,** the buyer agrees to obtain all of a particular contract subject matter from the seller, and the seller agrees to supply it. The name *requirements* contract comes from the fact that the seller agrees to meet the buyer's requirements. An **output contract** typically means a contract in which the seller promises its supply of a certain subject matter to the buyer; that is, the buyer agrees to take all of a seller's output. Example 2.15 illustrates a typical output contract, and Example 2.16 illustrates a typical requirements contract.

> **Requirements contract** A contract in which the buyer agrees to obtain from the seller, and the seller agrees to supply, all or some percentage of a particular subject matter as needed.
>
> **Output contract** A contract in which the seller promises all or some percentage of its supply of a certain subject matter to the buyer.

EXAMPLE   2.15

Buyer owns a gourmet restaurant in Berkeley, California. Her restaurant is famous for serving organic lettuce of exceptionally high quality. To have enough lettuce available daily, Buyer must make supply contracts with several small growers. She makes such a contract with a lettuce grower. Both parties know Seller cannot produce all the lettuce Buyer needs. Nevertheless, Buyer wants as much lettuce as possible from this grower because his lettuce is excellent. From the point of view of the grower, it is probably desirable to have a ready customer for lettuce. Thus, it would be convenient for both parties to set up a contract in which the quantity is "as much organic, gourmet lettuce in top condition as grower can produce." Thus, Seller agrees to provide, and Buyer agrees to take, all the organic lettuce grown by Seller.

EXAMPLE   2.16

Suppose the lettuce grower in Example 2.15 produces very large quantities of organic lettuce—more than the restaurant owner can use at her restaurant. In this case, Buyer would be foolish to agree to take all of Seller's output, since she does not need it. Buyer may still prefer to get all of her lettuce from Seller, however, and Seller may still like to have a ready customer for some amount of the lettuce grown. Here, the parties could agree that Buyer will purchase from Seller "as much organic, gourmet lettuce in top condition as Buyer uses at restaurant." This is a requirements contract because Seller agrees to provide as much of the product as Buyer "requires" at the restaurant.

Output and requirements contracts need not always involve all of a particular seller's output or all of a particular buyer's requirements. These contracts can even state that a certain percentage of output or requirements will be purchased or sold. For example, a tool and die manufacturer could make a contract to sell 40 percent of its "output" to one of its buyers. Or a cotton buyer could agree to purchase at least half of the cotton it requires in one calendar year from a particular cotton grower.

At an earlier time when sales of goods were still governed by common law, courts treated requirements and output contracts as uncertain with regard to quantity. They were concerned that the buyer in the requirements situation might dishonestly manipulate the amount needed and not "require" any quantity. Doing this would be especially tempting to the buyer if it later turned out that the subject matter of the contract could be purchased more cheaply elsewhere. In the output situation, the courts feared the seller might dishonestly manipulate the quantity by refusing to have any "output" for the buyer to purchase. Doing this would be especially tempting for the seller if the contract later turned out to be unprofitable or the seller subsequently found a buyer who would pay more.

In spite of the traditional reservations of common-law courts, output and requirements contracts can be very convenient and practical arrangements. Consequently, the common law has been more or less forced to find a legal rationale to make such contracts enforceable. One rationale now advanced is that the quantity is not really indefinite under these arrangements because both parties have a duty to act in "good faith." Through case law or statutes, the common law developed the idea that an implied promise or "covenant" of good faith is inherent in every contract. An implied covenant of good faith is a promise implied into every contract that each party will deal with the other in honesty and good faith. In the case of requirements and output contracts, this implied promise to deal in good faith means the parties cannot dishonestly manipulate quantities under the contract without committing a breach of this implied promise. Thus, requirements and output contracts are now recognized under modern common law.

An output or requirements contract involving the sale of goods is governed by § 2-306 of the UCC. Section 2-306(1) provides:

> A term which measures the quantity by the output of the seller or the requirements of the buyer means such actual output or requirements as may occur in good faith, except that no quantity unreasonably disproportionate to any stated estimate or in the absence of a stated estimate to any normal or otherwise comparable prior output or requirements may be tendered or demanded.

The drafters seem to have assumed the general validity of output and requirements contracts based on the notion that duties of good faith and commercial fair dealing were inherent in them. The drafters not only stated this idea specifically in § 2-306(1), but they wrote a general provision requiring good faith in all contracts made under the UCC. UCC § 1-205 provides: "Every contract or duty within this Act imposes an obligation of good faith in its performance or enforcement."

Chapter Review Questions

1. What is meant by the objective theory of contracts, and what effect does it have on an offer?
2. What elements are required for formation under the common law? Under the UCC?
3. Under the common law, what requirements must be satisfied for a valid offer to be made?
4. What terms must be included in an offer for it to be considered sufficiently certain and definite under the common law? Under the UCC?
5. Must all essential terms in an offer be expressly stated under the common law? Under the UCC?
6. Who may accept an offer?
7. What events may terminate an offer?
8. How may an offer become irrevocable under the common law? Under the UCC?
9. What are examples of a requirements contract and an output contract? Write a fact pattern that illustrates each. Exchange your fact patterns with another student to see if he or she can correctly identify the type of contract involved in each fact pattern.

Key Terms

Acceptance, 28
Capacity, 28
Common-law firm offer, 40
Consideration, 28
Contract, 28
Gap-filler provisions, 43
Legality, 28
Merchant's firm offer, 45
Objective theory of contracts, 21
Offer, 21

Offeree, 30
Offeror, 30
Open terms, 33
Option contract, 40
Output contract, 40
Rejection, 38
Reliance, 41
Requirements contract, 46
Revocation, 38

Notes

1. Jon Carroll, *San Francisco Chronicle,* August 9, 1994.

CHAPTER

3

The Nature of Acceptance

Unilateral and Bilateral Modes of Acceptance

Assuming a valid offer is outstanding, the party to whom it was made is free to accept it. However, contract law has long drawn a distinction between two possible modes of acceptance called for by the offer: **bilateral acceptance** and **unilateral acceptance.** The following are examples of how an offer might call for either a bilateral or a unilateral mode of acceptance. Can you explain the differences?

Bilateral acceptance Acceptance of a contract made by giving to the offeror the requested return promise.

Unilateral acceptance Acceptance of a contract made by giving the actual performance requested by the offeror instead of giving a promise to perform.

EXAMPLE **3.1**

"Go out and cut my lawn tomorrow morning at 9:00 A.M. and then I will pay you $25. Come see me to get your money."

EXAMPLE **3.2**

"If you promise me to go out and cut my lawn tomorrow morning at 9:00 A.M., I promise to pay you $25. Come see me to get your money."

Examined closely, the offer in Example 3.1 invites the offeree to accept by performing certain acts—actually going out and cutting the lawn. This is one kind of contractual arrangement parties can make: the offeror can demand *performance itself as the method for accepting the offer.* This type of acceptance is termed *unilateral,* and we say the resulting contract is a **unilateral contract.**

Unilateral contract The type of contract resulting from an effective unilateral acceptance.

In Example 3.2, the offeror does not demand a performance as acceptance. Instead, the offeror makes clear her own promise in the offer and asks the offeree to make a return promise as the acceptance. In this case, *the acceptance is made by giving the requested return promise* to the offeror. No performance is necessary to complete the acceptance, just the promise of performance. This type of acceptance is termed *bilateral* and results in a **bilateral contract.**

Bilateral contract The type of contract resulting from the effective use of a bilateral acceptance.

The unilateral and bilateral forms of acceptance differ in several ways. First, in an offer for a unilateral contract, the offeror asks the offeree to make an acceptance by completing the performance that is the subject of the contract. In an offer for a bilateral contract, the offeror asks for a *promissory acceptance.* That is, instead of asking the offeree to perform, the offeror asks the offeree to indicate agreement by making a promise to perform. Thus, with a bilateral contract the acceptance is not actually part of the performance. With a unilateral contract, it is.

A less obvious difference between unilateral and bilateral acceptances is the time when the contract is formed. With a unilateral acceptance, performance itself is acceptance; the contract is not formed until the requested performance is completed. With a bilateral acceptance, the contract is formed at the moment the offeree's return promise is given.

The two types of acceptance exist for practical reasons. Each type reflects certain realities and certain commercial and human needs. For example, if people are making a contract for relatively simple acts that will take place soon after the offer is made, it makes sense to arrange a unilateral contract. In Example 3.1, it is probably convenient for the offeror to ask the offeree to *do what is necessary* and then get paid. Such arrangements are especially practical when the offeror has some reason to be insecure about whether the offeree will actually perform. If the offeree fails to perform in Example 3.1, the offeror has no obligation to pay and can simply find someone else to mow the lawn. In the modern marketplace, commercial dealers who work frequently with the same party can conveniently set up unilateral contracts as a standard arrangement.

EXAMPLE **3.3**

A mill that regularly needs cotton yarn for weaving could arrange with Supplier to "pay $1 per standard large spool for each lot of 100,000 spools shipped to us by the first of each calendar month from May to December this year." The Supplier/offeree can accept each contract unilaterally by simply shipping the requested spools by the first of the calendar months referred to. The mill would normally choose the shipment date based on its overall supply network: if no spools arrive from Supplier by the date chosen, the mill has time to look elsewhere for the cotton yarn it needs.

Unilateral contracts do not work well, however, where contracts involve performances that will be complex, take a long time to complete, or take place some time in the future. For example, if a developer makes a construction contract with a general contractor in Minnesota during December, weather conditions will probably prevent building from beginning until spring. If the contract involves building a shopping mall, the contractor's performance may extend over two or three years, especially since limited building can be done during the winter months. It is most unlikely that a unilateral contract would be made in this situation. Even if the developer wanted a unilateral contract, it would probably be impossible to find a general contractor who would agree to it. A general contractor would have to perform for a period of years, then wait until the mall was finished to collect full payment. Most general contractors could not pay their workers or procure materials without installment payments during construction. For this, they need the contract to be made ahead of time. Thus, the developer and contractor would exchange promises and form the contract bilaterally.

Aside from the contractor's problem of having to wait too long to get paid, the parties would have another problem in making a unilateral contract for construction of a shopping mall. Since the performance will not begin until some months after negotiation, either party could back out during the interim. If this were to happen, either party might already have invested time and money and might be damaged by the other party's backing out of the deal. Bilateral contracts are safer because they bind both parties from the time of agreement onward. A bilateral contract is formed at the moment promises are exchanged in the offer and the responding acceptance. Provided the promises are supported by legally adequate consideration, both parties are bound at this time. If either party backs out of the promises made, the contract is breached. Thus, the parties already have the protection of a contract when they expend time and money after exchanging promises.

Special Problems with Unilateral Contracts

As noted, the unilateral contract combines the acceptance with the performance. In a unilateral arrangement, the contract is not made until the offeree fully performs as the offeror requests. This may present a problem. Review the unilateral lawn-mowing contract in Example 3.1, where no contract was made until the cutter completed the job. What would happen if the offeror changed her mind after the cutter completed all of the lawn except one little corner? If performance is acceptance and acceptance is not complete until the cutter finishes, then the cutter is vulnerable: the offeror can withdraw the offer any time during performance. To do this, the offeror would simply say "I revoke" and notify the cutter to stop performing. Thus, the offeror would obtain almost the whole performance from the cutter, but owe the cutter nothing because no contract was formed. This problem exists not only for contracts where performance is to follow long in the future, as in the shopping mall contract, but also for contracts where performance is to follow quite soon and be quickly accomplished.

For many years, the common law allowed the offeror to revoke anytime before the offeree finished performance on a unilateral contract. In modern times, however, the rule has been changed to protect the offeree. In modern common law, an offer for a unilateral contract becomes irrevocable *once the offeree actually begins performance.*

Sometimes controversy can arise over whether the offeree has actually begun performance or merely engaged in preparation. When performance begins depends on all of the circumstances involved in the contract setting. For example, the cutter has not "begun performance" if all he did was take out his mower and oil it. If the offeror backs out at that point, it is an effective revocation of the offer for the unilateral contract. In contrast, if the offeror backs out after the cutter has taken his equipment to the yard and raked up leaves so as to begin mowing, a revocation is likely to be too late. Here the cutter has already begun performance. Note how the doctrine of part performance and revocation of unilateral offers is treated in the following case.

A CASE FOR STUDY

Marchiondo v. Scheck

78 N.M. 440, 432 P.2d 405 (1967)

WOOD, Judge, Court of Appeals. The issue is whether the offeror had a right to revoke his offer to enter a unilateral contract.

Defendant, in writing, offered to sell real estate to a specified prospective buyer and agreed to pay a percentage of the sales price as a commission to the broker. The offer fixed a six-day time limit for acceptance. Defendant, in writing, revoked the offer. The revocation was received by the broker on the morning of the sixth day. Later that day, the broker obtained the offeree's acceptance.

Plaintiff, the broker, claiming breach of contract, sued defendant for the commission stated in the offer. On the above facts, the trial court dismissed the complaint.

We are not concerned with the revocation of the offer as between the offeror and the prospective purchaser. With certain exceptions (see 12 C.J.S. Brokers § 95(2), pp. 223–224), the right of a broker to the agreed compensation, or damages measured thereby, is not defeated by the refusal of the principal to complete or consummate a transaction. Southwest Motel Brokers, Inc. v. Alamo Hotels, Inc., 72 N.M. 227, 382 P.2d 707 (1963).

Plaintiff's appeal concerns the revocation of his agency. As to that revocation, the issue between the offeror and his agent is not whether defendant had the power to revoke; rather, it is whether he had the right to revoke. 1 Mechem on Agency, § 568 at 405 (2d ed. 1914).

When defendant made his offer to pay a commission upon sale of the property, he offered to enter a unilateral contract; the offer was for an act to be performed, a sale. 1 Williston on Contracts, § 13 at 23 (3rd ed. 1957); Hutchinson v. Dobson-Bainbridge Realty Co., 31 Tenn. App. 490, 217 S.W.2d 6 (1946).

Many courts hold that the principal has the right to revoke the broker's agency at any time before the broker has actually procured a purchaser. See Hutchinson v. Dobson-Bainbridge Realty Co., supra, and cases therein cited. The reason given is that until there is performance, the offeror has not received that contemplated by his offer, and there is no contract. Further, the offeror may never receive the requested performance because the offeree is not obligated to perform. Until the offeror receives the requested performance, no consideration has passed from the offeree to the offeror. Thus, until the performance is received, the offeror may withdraw the offer. Williston, supra, § 60; Hutchinson v. Dobson-Bainbridge Realty Co., supra.

Defendant asserts that the trial court was correct in applying this rule. However, plaintiff contends that the rule is not applicable where there has been part performance of the offer.

Hutchinson v. Dobson-Bainbridge Realty Co., supra, states: "A greater number of courts, however, hold that part performance of the consideration may make such an offer irrevocable and that where the offeree or broker manifests his assent to the offer by entering upon performance and spending time and money in his efforts to perform, then the offer becomes irrevocable during the time stated and binding upon the principal according to its terms. . . ."

Defendant contends that the decisions giving effect to a part performance are distinguishable. He asserts that in these cases the offer was of an exclusive right to sell or of an exclusive agency. Because neither factor is present here, he asserts that the "part performance" decisions are not applicable.

Many of the decisions do seem to emphasize the exclusive aspects of the offer. . . . Such emphasis reaches its extreme conclusion in Tetrick v. Sloan, 170 Cal.App.2d 540, 339 P.2d 613 (1959), where no effect was given to the part performance because there was neither an exclusive agency, nor an exclusive right to sell.

Defendant's offer did not specifically state that it was exclusive. Under § 70-1-43, N.M.S.A.1953, it was not an exclusive agreement. It is not the exclusiveness of the offer that deprives the offeror of the right to revoke. It is the action taken by the offeree which deprives the offeror of that right. Until there is action by the offeree—a partial performance pursuant to the offer—the offeror may revoke even if his offer is of an exclusive agency or an exclusive right to sell. Levander v. Johnson, 181 Wis. 68, 193 N.W. 970 (1923).

Once partial performance is begun pursuant to the offer made, a contract results. This contract has been termed a contract with conditions or an option contract. This terminology is illustrated as follows: "If an offer for a unilateral contract is made, and part of the consideration requested in the offer is given or tendered by the offeree in response thereto, the offeror is bound by a contract, the duty of immediate performance of which is conditional on the full consideration being given or tendered within the time stated in the offer, or, if no time is stated therein, within a reasonable time." Restatement of Contracts, § 45 (1932).

Restatement (Second) of Contracts, § 45, Tent. Draft No. 1, (approved 1964, Tent. Draft No. 2, p. vii) states:

(1) Where an offer invites an offeree to accept by rendering a performance and does not invite a promissory acceptance, an option contract is created when the offeree begins the invited performance or tenders part of it.

(2) The offeror's duty of performance under any option contract so created is conditional on completion or tender of the invited performance in accordance with the terms of the offer.

Restatement (Second) of Contracts, § 45, Tent. Draft No. 1, comment (g), says: "This Section frequently applies to agency arrangements, particularly offers made to real estate brokers." See Restatement (Second) of Agency § 446, comment (b).

The reason for finding such a contract is stated in Hutchinson v. Dobson-Bainbridge Realty Co., supra, as follows: "This rule avoids hardship to the offeree, and yet does not hold the offeror beyond the terms of his promise. It is true by such terms he was to be bound only if the requested act was done; but this implies that he will let it be done, that he will keep his offer open till the offeree who has begun can finish doing it. At least this is so where the doing of it will necessarily require time and expense. In such a case it is but just to hold that the offeree's part performance furnishes the 'acceptance' and the 'consideration' for a binding subsidiary promise not to revoke the offer, or turns the offer into a presently binding contract conditional upon the offeree's full performance."

We hold that part performance by the offeree of an offer of a unilateral contract results in a contract with a condition. The condition is full performance by the offeree. Here, if plaintiff-offeree partially performed prior to receipt of defendant's revocation, such a contract was formed. Thereafter, upon performance being completed by plaintiff, upon defendant's failure to recognize the contract, liability for breach of contract would arise. Thus, defendant's right to revoke his offer depends upon whether plaintiff had partially performed before he received defendant's revocation.

What constitutes partial performance will vary from case to case since what can be done toward performance is limited by what is authorized to be done. Whether plaintiff partially performed is a question of fact to be determined by the trial court.

The trial court denied plaintiff's requested finding concerning his partial performance. It did so on the theory that partial performance was not material. In this the trial court erred.

Because of the failure to find on the issue of partial performance, the case must be remanded to the trial court. State ex rel. Reynolds v. Board of County Comm'rs., 71 N.M. 194, 376 P.2d 976 (1962). We have not considered, and express no opinion on the question of whether there is or is not substantial evidence in the record which would support a finding one way or the other on this vital issue. Compare Geeslin v. Goodno, Inc., 75 N.M. 174, 402 P.2d 156 (1965).

The cause is remanded for findings on the issue of plaintiff's partial performance of the offer prior to its revocation, and for further proceedings consistent with this opinion and the findings so made. It is so ordered.

Questions to Consider

1. Why did the court characterize the agent's contract as unilateral?
2. Based on this case, define what constitutes part performance.
3. How did the defendant assert that exclusivity of the agency relationship affected use of the part performance doctrine? Did the court agree?
4. Based on this case, formulate a rule for how part performance affects an offer for a unilateral contract.

Strangely enough, the common law has not generally required the offeree on a unilateral contract to notify the offeror of the *beginning* of performance. The offeree, however, must notify the offeror of *completion* of performance unless completion has already come to the attention of the offeror or is very likely to do so.

Ambiguous Offers: The Common Law

Ambiguous offer
An offer that does not clearly indicate whether the acceptance called for is a performance or a return promise.

Normally, the offeree must accept by the mode the offeror intended. Sometimes, however, the recipient of an offer cannot determine whether the acceptance called for is a performance or a return promise. Sometimes, too, the offer does not clearly state the desired form of acceptance, and the offeree incorrectly identifies the mode of acceptance. This is the problem of the so-called **ambiguous offer.** The original common-law rule was that an ambiguous offer should be construed as one for a bilateral contract. The rationale for this rule is that it gives more security to the offeree: he simply makes the appropriate promise, and the offeror is bound from that time on. The rule can work a hardship in some cases, however. Ignore the modern application of the UCC for the moment and consider the following situation.

EXAMPLE 3.4

Jack says to Jill, "I will pay you $1.00 per bucketful of ripe strawberries if you are willing to guarantee me at least 300 bucketfuls." Assume that previously Jack and Jill have made such deals on a unilateral basis, with Jill obtaining the berries and delivering them to Jack for payment. At the time Jack makes this promise, bucketfuls of strawberries are selling for $.95, but Jack is willing to pay slightly more to get strawberries in quantity. Based on past experience with Jack, Jill interprets this offer as one for a unilateral contract. Thus, Jill harvests the 300 bucketfuls and delivers them to Jack. He refuses to take the berries, however, because the market price of strawberries has suddenly fallen to $.60 per bucketful. He claims that his offer was for a bilateral contract and that he revoked it by purchasing cheaper strawberries elsewhere.

According to the common law, Jill should have interpreted the less-than-clear language of the offer as indicating bilateral acceptance. Because of the parties' past relationship, however, Jill not unreasonably interpreted the offer as calling for unilateral acceptance. Thus, if the traditional common-law rule is applied, Jill has made the wrong kind of acceptance and has no contract, although she was misled by unclear language and past dealings with Jack. For this reason, the modern common-law rule *for ambiguous offers* allows acceptance in either a bilateral or a unilateral manner. So long as the offeree makes a reasonable interpretation under the circumstances and accepts according to this interpretation, the acceptance may be either bilateral or unilateral.

The traditional common law recognizes one rather rare exception to the rule that if a bilateral acceptance is clearly called for, no unilateral acceptance can be effective. This exception applies in situations where the offeror has requested a *return promise,* but the offeree makes no such promise and instead *fully performs* the proposed contract while the offer remains open. If the offeree gives full performance before the offer is revoked or otherwise terminates, a contract exists even though the offer originally called for bilateral acceptance.

EXAMPLE 3.5

Suppose A says to B, "Make a promise to me within one week that you will build me the 10-by-10-foot standard storage shed for which you showed me the plans, and I promise you I'll pay the $4,000 price as we discussed." A goes out of town for a week, and B takes this opportunity to build the storage shed. When A returns one week later, the shed is competently completed according to the design and location they discussed. B bills A the $4,000. Here A was bargaining for an acceptance by return promise. However, since B has managed to give a unilateral acceptance by completing performance within the time specified for acceptance, B has a contract with A. A must pay as billed.

The Common-Law Mirror-Image Rule

The common law views the offeror as the master of the offer. Therefore the common law requires that any acceptance given be identical to the terms the offeror proposed. This is known as the *mirror-image rule*. Under the common-law **mirror-image rule,** the offeree is obligated to accept exactly the contract offered. Any changes are construed to be counteroffers and terminate the offer. As the court stated in *Gyurkey v. Babler,* 103 Idaho 663, 651 P.2d 928, 931 (1982), "acceptance of an offer must be positive, unconditional, unequivocal and unambiguous, and must not change, add to, or qualify the terms of the offer."

Under the common law, if an offeree changes the terms of the offer, this terminates the offer. Sometimes, however, the offeree needs to clarify the terms of the offer or wants to complain about it. Attempts at *clarification* or *complaints* about an offer are not viewed as failure to comply with the mirror-image rule. The rule with regard to mirror-image requirements is the same as the rule on rejection discussed in Chapter 2: if an offeree accepts an offer but tries to clarify or complain about the terms, this is not a rejection.

> **Mirror-image rule**
> The common-law rule long followed in England and the United States that an effective acceptance must be identical to the terms of the offer proposed.

EXAMPLE **3.6**

Suppose Seller offers to sell Buyer an undeveloped lot in an area where logging regularly occurs. Buyer responds that she will take the property, but asks Seller, "Does that include the timber?" In other words, Buyer apparently wants the deal enough to take the lot whether or not the offer includes the timber but would be pleased to get this bonus if that is what Seller meant. This is acceptance with an attempt at clarification of the offer, and it is still considered the mirror- image of the offer.

Suppose Seller in Example 3.6 responded to Buyer by saying, "No timber is included. My offer is for the bare land." Buyer might now respond rather negatively, "After all the business we've done together, I can't believe you wouldn't give me a better deal than that. I'll take the land, but I'm disappointed that you wouldn't throw in the timber considering what a profitable relationship we've always had." This response complies with the mirror-image rule because it is an acceptance of all the offeror's terms even though the offeree complains.

Acceptances accompanied by attempts at clarification or by grumbling are judged by the objective theory of contracts. If a reasonable person in the offeror's shoes should have understood the offeree to be making an acceptance that was the mirror image of the offer, the acceptance is effective whether or not it also includes grumbling or seeks clarification.

The common-law mirror-image rule has often proven to be impractical in a sophisticated commercial society. In modern times, many contracts are negotiated by the use of forms and multiple communications going back and forth between the parties. Frequently, the parties themselves feel they have reached a basic or "core" agreement, although there may be some differences in the ancillary terms reflected in their many communications. Normally, parties of good will and good faith can sort out these differences by relying on these qualities and by applying industry standards, reasonable implication, the profit motive, and ordinary common sense. There seems little reason to insist on rigid adherence to the mirror-image rule, and, as noted below, the UCC contains a significant exception to it.

Some Further Issues Concerning the Means or Method of Acceptance

As previously noted, the common law requires someone to accept an offer in the proper mode: bilaterally or unilaterally as the offeror indicates. Additionally, the method or "means" of acceptance must be as indicated. Thus, if two parties are dealing face to face and one party makes an offer, it must be accepted during the conversation, unless the offeror indicates other arrangements. If the two parties are on the telephone, then the offeree has until they hang up to accept, unless the offeror indicates otherwise. If the parties are negotiating by mail, then a written response must be mailed or sent by an even faster means such as a telegram. As previously noted, modern common law requires the offeree to accept in a timely fashion—while the offer is still open. This acceptance must also be in the proper mode: bilateral, unilateral, or either if that is reasonable under the circumstances.

In addition, an acceptance must be made by a means at least as speedy and reliable as that used for the offer. For example, unless the offer contains restrictions, someone who receives an offer by mail can accept by letter, by telegram, or by fax since these are all at least as reliable and speedy as a letter. This rule is usually irrelevant if the parties are dealing with each other face to face, but it can become important if the parties are not dealing face to face and one of them dispatches an acceptance that never arrives or arrives very late. If the delay or failure to arrive occurred because the offeree used a means of communication that was slow or unreliable, the offeree will not obtain the contract.

When Acceptance Is Effective: The Mailbox Rule

At one time, much negotiation in the business world was done by mail, so the common law had to deal with problems of delays in delivery. Although mail may be an offeror's preferred method of communication, the mail can go astray and be late. Even if mail delivery is prompt, the ordinary postal process usually involves some delay. Problems can occur if the offeror revokes the offer while the offeree's letter is in transit. If an acceptance letter is lost and arrives very late or not at all, the offeree may revoke believing the contract was never accepted.

Perhaps because of difficulties in delay or loss, the rule developed that an acceptance was effective at the moment of dispatch. This concept is traditionally referred to as the **mailbox rule.** According to this rule, once an acceptance is placed in transmission, it becomes effective, and the offeror no longer has the right to revoke the offer. To take advantage of the mailbox rule, an offeree must dispatch the communication by an authorized means, as previously discussed. Here, to "dispatch" means to place the communication in transmission. Remember that an authorized means of dispatch is the same means the offeror used or one that is equally fast and reliable. Under the mailbox rule, if an acceptance is dispatched by an authorized means, it is effective at the moment of dispatch.

Mailbox rule The majority rule followed in the United States that an acceptance is effective at the moment it is properly dispatched, and the offeror no longer has the right to revoke the offer.

Assignment

1. Assume you are a paralegal working for an attorney who represents Bill, a general contractor. Bill has put together a construction bid that is to be construed as an acceptance of an offer for a contract. The bid is to be mailed out of your office. What steps could you take to make a record of when the bid was mailed?
2. Which way(s) of making a record of when the bid was mailed would provide the best proof of date and time of mailing if a question later arises?

The mailbox rule creates some new problems even while it solves others. What if the offeror never receives the acceptance? The contract is made at the moment the acceptance is properly dispatched, even if the offeror does not know of it. Much confusion can result if the offeror, not knowing of the acceptance, makes another contract in the interim. The same thing can happen with a delayed transmission. For this reason, a few states (such as California) have rejected the mailbox rule. Such states view the acceptance as effective only when the offeror actually *receives* it.

The mailbox rule is generally applied only to acceptances. Other communications between parties negotiating a contract (offer, rejection, and revocation) are usually effective *only when they are received*. Most jurisdictions do not employ the mailbox rule with option contracts. If an option contract exists, the acceptance must not only be *dispatched* within the option period, it must also be received within this period.

Assignment

1. Use the state codes for your own state and look up the statutory rule on when acceptance of a common-law contract is effective. Does a different rule apply to contracts that fall under the UCC?
2. If your state does not have such a statute, use a legal encyclopedia for your state to see if such a rule has been developed in the case law.
3. Use the rule you found concerning acceptance to discuss whether the acceptance was effective in the circumstances described in questions 4, 5, and 6 below. If you were not able to locate your state's rule on acceptances, consider the following Civil Code §§ 1000 and 1001 to be the law in your state. Remember other applicable rules concerning the effectiveness of offers, rejections, and revocations.

▶ Civil Code § 1000

If a proposal prescribes any conditions concerning communication of its acceptance, the proposer is not bound unless these are conformed to. In other cases, any reasonable and usual mode may be adopted.

▶ Civil Code § 1001

Consent is deemed to be fully communicated between the parties as soon as the party accepting a proposal has put his acceptance in the course of transmission to the proposer, in conformity to § 1000.

4. Seller has made an offer to sell her land to Buyer. The offer was sent by registered mail and was complete. The offer arrived on May 1. It states that all acceptances must be made "by mail only, no telephone calls will be considered." Seller's offer also states "you have 5 days in which to accept." On May 2, Buyer sends a letter to Seller by regular mail accepting the offer as Seller stated it. There is a mix-up at the post office, and the letter does not arrive until May 10. Upon receiving this letter, Seller informs Buyer by telephone that the land was sold on May 4. Did Buyer make an effective acceptance? Why or why not?

5. Computer Consultant has made an offer to provide data processing services to Bank. The parties have transmitted all communications by faxes on their respective letterheads. None of the faxes specifies any time period for the offer to last. The parties have communicated with each other every two or three days, for about two weeks. Consultant's latest fax contained all terms for the offer and was sent and received on January 15. On January 16, Consultant herself receives an offer for a large consulting contract with Insurance Company. She accepts this offer from Insurance Company on January 19 and faxes to Bank at 1:30 P.M. the same day: "My offer to you of January 15 is revoked." Then Consultant notices that she has already received a fax from Bank at 1:00 P.M., which states "accept your offer for data processing services, as we have been discussing." Did Bank make an effective acceptance? Why or why not?

6. Suzi lives in Dallas, Texas, and on May 1 she writes to Alan in Bangor, Maine, offering to sell him her home. This offer states it will remain open for two calendar weeks. The mail takes five days to go between Dallas and Bangor. Suzi's letter gets to Alan on May 6, and he opens and reads it. He thinks about the offer for a week, and on May 13 he writes back to Suzi rejecting it. The next morning, May 14, Alan decides he made a mistake in rejecting the offer and mails another letter accepting Suzi's offer. The rejection arrives on May 19, but the acceptance goes astray and does not arrive until May 20. Has Alan made an effective acceptance? Why or why not? (Note: most authorities hold the mailbox rule does not apply in this situation.)

Use of Silence as Acceptance

Whether an offer is considered to invite acceptance in a unilateral or bilateral manner, contract law has generally disfavored use of mere silence as indicating acceptance of any kind.

EXAMPLE   3.7

Suppose Neighbor Nelly says to Neighbor Nate, "Nate, I am hereby offering to buy that vintage, mint condition Jaguar of yours for $1,000 cash. If you agree, just do and say nothing, and I'll consider we have a deal." Since it is unlikely a vintage, mint condition Jaguar would be sold for $1,000 voluntarily, Neighbor Nelly has placed Neighbor Nate in an inconvenient position. If Nate's silence could be interpreted as acceptance, he would be forced to take some affirmative action to prevent a contract from being formed.

Contract law seeks to avoid the problem of an offeror's pushing an unwilling offeree into a contract by default. The view is that one who does not solicit an offer should not be required to remain constantly vigilant or go out of the way to avoid another party's unwanted offer. Thus, the general rule is that mere silence cannot be used as acceptance.

The rule that mere silence is not acceptance also helps to avoid confusion. It is probably much easier to judge the intent of parties if they must take some affirmative action to make a contract. After all, silence could mean almost anything, particularly when viewed by hindsight in a later lawsuit. On the other hand, affirmative actions usually have some content (words, conduct, or both) that provides a better indication of what the parties meant. Mere silence can be difficult to interpret.

Exceptions to the Rule That Mere Silence Is Not Acceptance

In some situations, however, it is recognized that silence can be used as acceptance. Generally, such situations fall into four categories:

1. The party offering the contract leads the other party to reasonably believe that silence is a valid way to accept, and the offeree remains silent with the actual, personal intention of signifying acceptance with that silence.
2. The recipient of an offer improperly retains or otherwise takes control of property sent on approval. Note that this rule does not apply where legislation has changed the law to protect consumers from having to pay for unsolicited merchandise.[1]
3. The offeree has solicited an offer from the offeror, has drafted the terms of the offer herself, and has worded it so the offeror would reasonably assume the offeree's silence means the offer is accepted unless an express rejection is made.

   Such situations can occur, for example, where a buyer proposes and writes up an offer on the seller's behalf. Here the buyer usually writes up the offer in a way she thinks is acceptable to the seller. Then the buyer can simply turn over the written offer to the seller with instructions to sign and return if it is acceptable. Here it is the seller who is the offeror, and the offer is officially made when the seller communicates back to the buyer. Often the buyer writes into the offer that the seller's return communication is to be deemed accepted unless the seller is notified to the contrary by the buyer's "home office." In these circumstances the buyer has taken charge of the offer and put it together in a way she knows will be acceptable to the seller. Although the seller is the offeror, the terms of the offer have been drafted and preapproved by the buyer. If the seller signs and returns the form, but hears nothing from the buyer's home office, it would be reasonable to assume the buyer's silence is an acceptance.
4. The parties have had prior dealings with one another such that silent acceptance is reasonable under the circumstances, and both parties would expect the offeree to give silent assent to the proposed bargain. This might occur where a seller frequently makes contracts with a particular buyer by sending a standard proposed invoice. If the seller hears nothing from the buyer within a reasonable time, he deems the buyer's silence as acceptance and ships the order according to the invoice.

Implied-In-Fact Contracts

The rule that *mere silence* cannot be used as acceptance is to be distinguished from the *use of certain acts* as acceptance.

EXAMPLE **3.8**

Suppose A often has a gardener come to mow the lawn, sweep up the leaves, and clean up the yard. One day the gardener calls to find out whether A needs her services. A is out, so the gardener leaves a message on A's answering machine: "If you want me to do the usual work, just leave the gate unlocked, get the wheelbarrow from the shed, and put it out for me, as always." If the gardener goes by and finds the gate unlocked and the wheelbarrow out, A has made an acceptance, although she had said nothing. The acts specified by the gardener, leaving the gate unlocked and getting out the wheelbarrow, were acts or conduct used to signify assent to the gardener's promise. This is more than mere silence.

An arrangement such as that between the gardener and A in Example 3.8 is often referred to as an implied-in-fact acceptance. Actually, both offer and acceptance can be implied-in-fact.

EXAMPLE **3.9**

Suppose Owner of a flower shop wants to sell his flower business. Owner hires Agent to sell the business by finding a buyer who can pay at least $500,000 cash. Agent is unable to find such a buyer, but manages to put Owner together with a larger, very profitable partnership that operates a chain of flower shops. Agent helps the parties negotiate, and eventually Owner is offered a full partnership for the value of his small flower shop. He accepts. Most courts would find that there is an implied-in-fact contract between the flower shop owner and Agent for the reasonable value of Agent's services in obtaining a partnership for Owner. An offer by Owner to compensate Agent is implied-in-fact from Owner's overall conduct. The acceptance by Agent is implied-in-fact in the same way.

When offer, acceptance, or both are implied by conduct of the parties, this is usually referred to as an implied-in-fact contract. These agreements are contracts in the ordinary sense—the offer and acceptance are real. The only difference is that the parties use conduct, rather than words, to form the contract.

Formation of a Contract Under the UCC: Where Offer and Acceptance Are Not Used

As noted earlier, the UCC does not require the parties to use an offer and acceptance process to form a contract. If a contract is covered by the UCC, it may be formed by conduct of the parties sufficient to indicate they reached agreement. This approach is practical because it reflects the way people in modern, commercial society often do business, but it can lead to some confusion over the terms of the contract. If there is no separately identifiable offer or acceptance, how are the terms of the contract to be specified? Sometimes parties interpret the contract terms very differently and become embroiled in a serious dispute that may end up in litigation.

Where a contract is formed through "conduct," the parties usually have engaged in negotiations and exchanged many ideas and several documents.

The problem is to determine which of these ideas and communications have become part of the contract. In this situation, UCC § 2-207(3) provides ". . . the terms of the particular contract consist of those terms on which the writings of the parties agree, together with any supplementary terms incorporated under any other provisions of this Act." This provision means the parties can go ahead and make a contract by conduct, send many communications and proposals back and forth, and form the contract on the basis of those terms on which they agree. Inconsistent terms do not become part of the contract. Omitted terms that are consistent with terms they agree on can be filled in by using the UCC gap-filling provisions. The basic requirement of *mutual assent* to a contract is still present. Without that, there is no contract.

The Battle of the Forms: A Modern Phenomenon

The fact that both parties often use their own forms during contract negotiation has come to be called the "battle of the forms."[2] Use of preprinted forms is very common in sales of goods and has many advantages. For one thing, the drafter of the form has a chance to think over an efficient and favorable way to structure a deal before the heat of battle begins and negotiations get under way. Another advantage of preprinted forms is that commonly occurring issues can be covered ahead of time in a standard way. A disadvantage of such forms, however, is that life and business do not always go as planned. Thus, contingencies not anticipated in the forms can arise during and after negotiations.

Another disadvantage of preprinted forms is that the eventual contract may consist of a bewildering set of each party's proposals and counterproposals on both its own and the other party's forms. When this happens, each party tends to claim the contract consists of those terms most advantageous to its position. This is the reason the UCC drafters provided in § 2-207 that the contract would consist of those terms on which the writings agree plus those that can be filled in with other UCC provisions.

The parties themselves may choose to resolve the battle of the forms differently. Faced with a complex set of communications and documents that represent their agreement, one of the parties can draft its version of the final document. Then the other party can review this document, make changes, and return it to the drafter to review. This process can be repeated until the parties arrive at one document that they both agree fully states their contract. Then both parties can sign this final version.

Formation of a Contract Under the UCC: Where Offer and Acceptance Are Used

The Offer

As previously explained, the UCC permits, although it does not require, parties to use an offer and an acceptance process when forming a contract for the sale of goods. If the parties choose to use the offer and acceptance process, the requirements of a UCC offer are not as strict as those of the common law. Although the UCC does not explicitly define an offer, several sections, taken together, provide that an offer need only indicate an intent to contract and be sufficient to lead to a contract whose terms are certain and definite enough for enforcement. UCC gap-filler provisions, other communications exchanged, prior dealings, and the parties' conduct can all be used to supply information missing from the original offer.

The Acceptance

The drafters of the UCC provide more specifics about the acceptance than about the offer. The following are the basic UCC rules on acceptance:

§ 2-207
(1) A definite and seasonable expression of acceptance or a written confirmation which is sent within a reasonable time operates as an acceptance even though it states terms additional to or different from those offered or agreed upon, unless acceptance is expressly made conditional on assent to the additional or different terms.
(2) The additional terms are to be construed as proposals for addition to the contract. Between merchants such terms become part of the contract unless:
   (a) the offer expressly limits acceptance to the terms of the offer;
   (b) they materially alter it; or
   (c) notification of objection to them has already been given or is given within a reasonable time after notice of them is received.
(3) Conduct by both parties which recognizes the existence of a contract is sufficient to establish a contract for sale although the writings of the parties do not otherwise establish a contract. In such a case the terms of the particular contract consist of those terms on which the writings of the parties agree, together with any supplementary terms incorporated under any other provisions of this Act.

While § 2-207 is not a model of clarity, the gist of it is now clear. First, the drafters of § 2-207 abandoned the common-law mirror-image rule. Acceptance of an offer to buy or sell goods is effective even if it proposes terms different from the offer, so long as the offeree clearly accepted while the offer was still open. There are only two exceptions to this rule: (1) the offeror indicates no changes can be made in the offer, or (2) the offeree indicates acceptance is not effective unless the offeror agrees to the offeree's changes.

Abandonment of the mirror-image rule applies to anyone making a contract for the sale of goods. Both merchants and laypeople may form UCC contracts with an acceptance that deviates from the original offer. Under § 2-207, however, whether deviations in the acceptance become part of the contract depends on whether the parties are merchants or laypeople:

1. *If the parties to the contract are both merchants.* Any additional terms in the acceptance that were not a part of the original offer *automatically* become part of the contract unless one of three things is true:
   a. The original offer specified it could not be altered.
   b. The new terms *materially* change the offer made.
   c. The offeror has already objected to the new terms or does so within a reasonable time after learning of them.
      Notice that this system still allows each merchant to reject a deal that is not appealing. However, it also allows merchants to make a deal where they agree on basic terms, although perhaps not on collateral details.

2. *If one party to the contract is a merchant and one is a layperson or if both parties are laypeople.* A definite and seasonable acceptance of the terms of the offer will still operate as an acceptance. Any new terms proposed in the acceptance are simply construed as "proposals" for addition to the contract. The parties must negotiate further if they want the proposals to be included. Specifically, the offeror must consent to the new or different terms proposed in the acceptance, or they do not become part of the contract.

Under § 2-207 the offeror still has control over the offer since he can specify "no changes" or can object to changes in a timely manner and keep them out of the contract. At the same time, § 2-207 is practical because it also permits the parties to make the contract when they have reached essential agreement on what the offeror proposes. The offeree retains some control since she is still free not to accept at all. The offeree can also make it clear that there will be no acceptance *unless* the offeror permits the new terms to be included.

Essentially, the UCC system allows for more maneuverability and negotiation than the common-law system. The mirror-image rule means that any deviation at all from the terms of the offer is an outright rejection and no contract can result. Under the UCC, as long as there is an actual acceptance on the core or material terms, the acceptance is not required to be the mirror image of the offer.

A CASE FOR STUDY

Dorton v. Collins & Aikman Corporation

453 F.2d 1161 (6th Cir. 1972)

CELEBREZZE, Circuit Judge. This is an appeal from the District Court's denial of Defendant-Appellant's motion for a stay pending arbitration. . . . The suit arose after a series of over 55 transactions during 1968, 1969, and 1970 in which Plaintiffs-Appellees (hereinafter The Carpet Mart), carpet retailers in Kingsport, Tennessee, purchased carpets from Defendant-Appellant (hereinafter Collins & Aikman), incorporated under the laws of the State of Delaware, with its principal place of business in New York, New York, and owner of a carpet manufacturing plant (formerly the Painter Carpet Mills, Inc.) located in Dalton, Georgia. The Carpet Mart originally brought this action in a Tennessee state trial court, seeking compensatory and punitive damages in the amount of $450,000 from Collins & Aikman for the latter's alleged fraud, deceit, and misrepresentation in the sale of what were supposedly carpets manufactured from 100% Kodel polyester fiber. The Carpet Mart maintains that in May, 1970, in response to a customer complaint, it learned that not all of the carpets were manufactured from 100% Kodel polyester fiber but rather some were composed of a cheaper and inferior carpet fiber. After the cause was removed to the District Court on the basis of diversity of citizenship, Collins & Aikman moved for a stay pending arbitration, asserting that The Carpet Mart was bound to an arbitration agreement which appeared on the reverse side of Collins & Aikman's printed sales acknowledgment forms. Holding that there existed no binding arbitration agreement between the parties, the District Court denied the stay. For the reasons set forth below, we remand the case to the District Court for further findings.

We . . . find that there is no conflicts of law problem in the present case, the Uniform Commercial Code having been enacted in both Georgia and Tennessee at the time of the disputed transactions. . . .

The primary question before us on appeal is whether the District Court, in denying Collins & Aikman's motion for a stay pending arbitration, erred in holding that The Carpet Mart was not bound by the arbitration agreement appearing on the back of Collins & Aikman's acknowledgment forms. In reviewing the District Court's determination, we must look closely at the procedures which were followed in the sales transactions which gave rise to the present dispute over the arbitration agreement.

In each of the more than 55 transactions, one of the partners in The Carpet Mart, or, on some occasions, Collins & Aikman's visiting salesman, telephoned Collins & Aikman's order department in Dalton, Georgia, and ordered certain quantities of carpets listed in Collins & Aikman's catalogue. There is some dispute as to what, if any, agreements were reached through the telephone calls and through the visits by Collins & Aikman's salesman. After each oral order was placed, the price, if any, quoted by the buyer was checked against Collins & Aikman's price list, and the credit department was consulted to determine if The Carpet Mart had paid for all previous shipments. After it was found that everything was in order, Collins & Aikman's order department typed the information concerning the particular order on one of its printed acknowledgment forms. Each acknowledgment form bore one of three legends:

"Acknowledgment," "Customer Acknowledgment," or "Sales Contract."

The following provision was printed on the face of the forms bearing the "Acknowledgment" legend:

The acceptance of your order is subject to all of the terms and conditions on the face and reverse side hereof, including arbitration, all of which are accepted by buyer; it supersedes buyer's order form, if any. It shall become a contract either (a) when signed and delivered by buyer to seller and accepted in writing by seller, or (b) at Seller's option, when buyer shall have given to seller specification of assortments, delivery dates, shipping instructions, or instructions to bill and hold as to all or any part of the merchandise herein described, or when buyer has received delivery of

the whole or any part thereof, or when buyer has otherwise assented to the terms and conditions hereof.

Similarly, on the face of the forms bearing the "Customer Acknowledgment" or "Sales Contract" legends the following provision appeared:

This order is given subject to all of the terms and conditions on the face and reverse side hereof, including the provisions for arbitration and the exclusion of warranties, all of which are accepted by Buyer, supersede Buyer's order form, if any, and constitute the entire contract between Buyer and Seller. This order shall become a contract as to the entire quantity specified either (a) when signed and delivered by Buyer to Seller and accepted in writing by Seller or (b) when Buyer has received and retained this order for ten days without objection, or (c) when Buyer has accepted delivery of any part of the merchandise specified herein or has furnished to Seller specifications or assortments, delivery dates, shipping instructions, or instructions to bill and hold, or when Buyer has otherwise indicated acceptance of the terms hereof.

The small print on the reverse side of the forms provided, among other things, that all claims arising out of the contract would be submitted to arbitration in New York City. Each acknowledgment form was signed by an employee of Collins & Aikman's order department and mailed to The Carpet Mart on the day the telephone order was received or, at the latest, on the following day. The carpets were thereafter shipped to The Carpet Mart, with the interval between the mailing of the acknowledgment form and shipment of the carpets varying from a brief interval to a period of several weeks or months. Absent a delay in the mails, however, The Carpet Mart always received the acknowledgment forms prior to receiving the carpets. In all cases The Carpet Mart took delivery of and paid for the carpets without objecting to any terms contained in the acknowledgment form.

In holding that no binding arbitration agreement was created between the parties through the transactions above, the District Court relied on T.C.A. § 47-2-207 [UCC § 2-207]. . . . The

District Court found that Subsection 2-207(3) controlled the instant case, quoting the following passage from 1 W. Hawkland, A Transactional Guide to the Uniform Commercial Code § 1.090303, at 19–20 (1964):

> If the seller . . . ships the goods and the buyer accepts them, a contract is formed under subsection (3). The terms of this contract are those on which the purchase order and acknowledgment agree, and the additional terms needed for a contract are to be found throughout the U.C.C. . . . [T]he U.C.C. does not impose an arbitration term on the parties where their contract is silent on the matter. Hence, a conflict between an arbitration and a no-arbitration clause would result in the no-arbitration clause becoming effective.

Under this authority alone the District Court concluded that the arbitration clause on the back of Collins & Aikman's sales acknowledgment had not become a binding term in the 50-odd transactions with The Carpet Mart.

In reviewing this determination by the District Court, we are aware of the problems which courts have had in interpreting Section 2-207. This section of the UCC has been described as a "murky bit of prose," Southwest Engineering Co. v. Martin Tractor Co., 205 Kan. 684, 694, 473 P.2d 18, 25 (1970), as "not too happily drafted," Roto-Lith Ltd. v. F. P. Bartlett & Co., 297 F.2d 497, 500 (1st Cir. 1962), and as "one of the most important, subtle, and difficult in the entire Code, and well it may be said that the product as it finally reads is not altogether satisfactory." Duesenberg & King, Sales and Bulk Transfers under the Uniform Commercial Code, (Vol. 3, Bender's Uniform Commercial Code Service) § 3.03, at 3–12 (1969). Despite the lack of clarity in its language, Section 2-207 manifests definite objectives which are significant in the present case.

Although Comment No. 1 [to § 2-207] is itself somewhat ambiguous, it is clear that Section 2-207, and specifically Subsection 2-207(1), was intended to alter the "ribbon matching" or "mirror" rule of common law, under which the terms of an acceptance or confirmation were required to be identical to the terms of the offer or oral agreement, respectively. . . . Under the common law, an acceptance or a confirmation which contained terms additional to or different from those of the offer or oral agreement constituted a rejection of the offer or agreement and thus became a counteroffer. . . .

Under Section 2-207 the result is different. This section of the Code recognizes that in current commercial transactions, the terms of the offer and those of the acceptance will seldom be identical. Rather, under the current "battle of the forms," each party typically has a printed form drafted by his attorney and containing as many terms as could be envisioned to favor that party in his sales transactions. Whereas under common law the disparity between the fineprint terms in the parties' forms would have prevented the consummation of a contract when these forms are exchanged, Section 2-207 recognizes that in many, but not all, cases the parties do not impart such significance to the terms on the printed forms.

Thus, under [§ 2-207] a contract is recognized notwithstanding the fact that an acceptance or confirmation contains terms additional to or different from those of the offer or prior agreement, provided that the offeree's intent to accept the offer is definitely expressed . . . and provided that the offeree's acceptance is not expressly conditioned on the offeror's assent to the additional or different terms.

With the above analysis and purposes of Section 2-207 in mind, we turn to their application in the present case. We initially observe that the affidavits and the acknowledgment forms themselves raise the question of whether Collins & Aikman's forms constituted acceptances or confirmations under Section 2-207. . . . Absent the District Court's determination of whether Collins & Aikman's acknowledgment forms were acceptances or, alternatively, confirmations of prior oral agreements, we will consider the application of section 2-207 to both situations for the guidance of the District Court on remand.

Viewing Collins & Aikman's acknowledgment forms as acceptances under Subsection 2-207(1), we are initially faced with the question of whether the arbitration provision in Collins & Aikman's acknowledgment forms were in fact "additional to or different from" the terms of The Carpet Mart's oral offers. In the typical case under Section 2-207, there exist both a written purchase order and a written acknowledgment, and this determination can be readily made by comparing the two forms. In the present case, where the only written forms were Collins & Aikman's sales acknowledgments, we believe that such a comparison must be made between the oral offers and the written acceptances. Although the District Court apparently assumed that The Carpet Mart's oral orders did not include in their terms the arbitration provision which appeared in Collins & Aikman's acknowledgment forms, we believe that a specific finding on this point will be required on remand.

Assuming, for purposes of analysis, that the arbitration provision was an addition to the terms of The Carpet Mart's oral offers, we must next determine whether or not Collins & Aikman's acceptances were "expressly made conditional on assent to the additional . . . terms" therein, within the proviso of Subsection 2-207(1) . . . . Although Collins & Aikman's use of the words "subject to" suggests that the acceptances were conditional to some extent, we do not believe the acceptances were "expressly made conditional on [the buyer's] assent to the additional or different terms," as specifically required under the Subsection 2-207(1) proviso. In order to fall within this proviso, it is not enough that an acceptance is expressly conditional on additional or different terms; rather, an acceptance must be expressly conditional on the offeror's assent to those terms. Viewing the Subsection (1) proviso within the context of the rest of that Subsection and within the policies of Section 2-207 itself, we believe that it was intended to apply only to an acceptance which clearly reveals that the offeree is unwilling to proceed with the transaction unless he is assured of the offeror's assent to the additional or different terms therein. . . . That the acceptance is predicated on the offeror's assent must be "directly and distinctly stated or expressed rather than implied or left to inference." Webster's Third International Dictionary (defining "express").

Although the UCC does not provide a definition of "assent," it is significant that Collins & Aikman's printed acknowledgment forms specified at least seven types of action or inaction on the part of the buyer which— sometimes at Collins & Aikman's option— would be deemed to bind the buyer to the terms therein. These ranged from the buyer's signing and delivering the acknowledgment to the seller—which indeed could have been recognized as the buyer's assent to Collins & Aikman's terms—to the buyer's retention of the acknowledgment for ten days without objection—which could never have been recognized as the buyer's assent to the additional or different terms where acceptance is expressly conditional on that assent.

To recognize Collins & Aikman's acceptances as "expressly conditional on [the buyer's] assent to the additional . . . terms" therein, within the proviso of Subsection 2-207(1), would thus require us to ignore the specific language of that provision. Such an interpretation is not justified in view of the fact that Subsection 2-207(1) is clearly designed to give legal recognition to many contracts where the variance between the offer and acceptance would have precluded such recognition at common law.

Because Collins & Aikman's acceptances were not expressly conditional on the buyer's assent to the additional terms within the proviso of Subsection 2-207(1), a contract is recognized under Subsection (1), and the additional terms are treated as "proposals" for addition to the contract under Subsection 2-207(2). Since both Collins & Aikman and The Carpet Mart are clearly "merchants" as that term is defined in Subsection 2-104(1), the arbitration provision will be deemed to have been accepted by The Carpet Mart under Subsection 2-207(2) unless it materially altered the terms of The Carpet Mart's oral offers . . . . We believe that the question of whether the arbitration provision materially altered the oral offer under Subsection 2-207(2) (b) is one which can be resolved only by the District Court on further findings of fact in the present case. If the arbitration provision did in fact materially alter The Carpet Mart's offer, it could not become a part of the contract "unless expressly agreed to" by The Carpet Mart.

We therefore conclude that if on remand the District Court finds that Collins & Aikman's acknowledgments were in fact acceptances and that the arbitration provision was additional to the terms of The Carpet Mart's oral orders, contracts will be recognized under Subsection 2-207(1). The arbitration clause will then be viewed as a "proposal" under Subsection 2-207(2) which will be deemed to have been accepted by The Carpet Mart unless it materially altered the oral offers.

If the District Court finds that Collins & Aikman's acknowledgment forms were not acceptances but rather were confirmations of prior oral agreements between the parties, an application of Section 2-207 similar to that above will be required. Subsection 2-207(1) will require an initial determination of whether the arbitration provision in the confirmations was "additional to or different from" the terms orally agreed upon. Assuming that the District Court finds that the arbitration provision was not a term of the oral agreements between the parties, the arbitration clause will be treated as a "proposal" for addition to the contract under Subsection 2-207(2), as was the case when Collins & Aikman's acknowledgments were viewed as acceptances above. The provision for arbitration will be deemed to have been accepted by The Carpet Mart unless the District Court finds that it materially altered the prior oral agreements, in which case The Carpet Mart could not become bound thereby absent an express agreement to that effect.

As a result of the above application of Section 2-207 to the limited facts before us in the present case, we find it necessary to remand the case to the District Court for the following findings: (1) whether oral agreements were reached between the parties prior to the sending of Collins & Aikman's acknowledgment forms; if there were no such oral agreements, (2) whether the arbitration provision appearing in Collins & Aikman's "acceptances" was additional to the terms of The Carpet Mart's oral

offers; and, if so, (3) whether the arbitration provision materially altered the terms of The Carpet Mart's oral offers. Alternatively, if the District Court does find that oral agreements were reached between the parties before Collins & Aikman's acknowledgment forms were sent in each instance, it will be necessary for the District Court to make the following findings: (1) whether the prior oral agreements embodied the arbitration provision appearing in Collins & Aikman's "confirmations"; and, if not, (2) whether the arbitration provision materially altered the prior oral agreements. Regardless of whether the District Court finds Collins & Aikman's acknowledgment forms to have been acceptances or confirmations, if the arbitration provision was additional to, and a material alteration of, the offers or prior oral agreements, The Carpet Mart will not be bound to that provision absent a finding that it expressly agreed to be bound thereby. Remanded.

Questions to Consider

1. Did this case involve the issue of whether a contract was made, what the terms of the contract were, or both?

2. Did the Court of Appeals treat the two parties as merchants or laypeople?

3. What difference did the status of the parties (merchants or laypeople) make in determining which terms became part of the contract?

4. How does an arbitration clause like the one in this case require the parties to resolve their disputes? Could an arbitration clause be a "material" alteration if this term were added in an acceptance? Why?

Ambiguous Offers Under the UCC

As explained earlier, an ambiguous offer is one that does not make clear whether acceptance is to be made bilaterally or unilaterally. Under the traditional common-law view that ambiguous offers must be accepted bilaterally, a reasonable offeree who accepts unilaterally could be penalized. The drafters of the UCC sought to avoid these unfair results by allowing an offeree to give either a bilateral a or unilateral form of acceptance in most cases. UCC § 2-206(1)(a) states that unless the circumstances or language of the offer clearly indicate otherwise, acceptance can be made "in any manner and by any medium reasonable in the circumstances."

Thus, where an offer of a contract for sale of goods does not indicate clearly whether acceptance must be unilateral or bilateral, the contract may be accepted *either* (1) by a return promise to ship the goods or (2) by simply shipping the goods promptly.

Shipment of Nonconforming Goods As Acceptance

Unilateral acceptance under the UCC may even be made if the offeree ships goods that are "nonconforming." **Nonconforming goods** are goods that are not what the buyer ordered but which the seller has reason to believe the buyer may accept. Ordinarily, a shipment of nonconforming goods is both an acceptance of a unilateral contract and a simultaneous breach of the contract. Section 2-206(1)(b) anticipates this problem by providing a way for the seller to avoid breaching by notifying the buyer that the substitute goods are an **accommodation** only. Unless the seller indicates otherwise, the contract price for the nonconforming goods is the price for the original goods the buyer wanted.

Where the seller ships nonconforming goods as accommodation, there is no acceptance and no breach if the offeree/buyer rejects the nonconforming goods. They are simply returned to the seller, and the buyer can look elsewhere. If the nonconforming goods are acceptable to the buyer, however, the buyer can retain them, and a unilateral contract is formed for these substitute goods. In that case, technically the parties have switched roles: the original offeror has become the offeree for the contract made through the accommodation.

Nonconforming goods Goods that do not conform to those required by the contract or that do not conform to those the offeror requested where the offer is for a unilateral contract.

Accommodation A shipment of nonconforming goods identified as a substitute for the goods ordered and sent as an acceptance under a unilateral contract.

Notification of Unilateral Acceptance

The UCC requires a party who makes a unilateral acceptance of a contract for goods to notify the offeror within a reasonable time. If this is not done, the offeror may choose to treat the offer as having lapsed before acceptance. Thus, someone who accepts a contract for the sale of goods and plans simply to ship the goods rather than make a return promise is wise to send a prompt notification of this plan. If not, she takes a risk that the offeror will be legally entitled to go elsewhere to look for a deal.

Modern Use of Implied-In-Fact Contracts in Sales of Goods

The UCC view on contract formation is consistent with the common-law recognition of implied-in-fact offers and acceptances. The rule that a contract for the sale of goods can be made by "conduct recognizing the existence of a contract" is recognition of implied-in-fact contracts. Such arrangements are common in contract sales that fall under the UCC.

Implied-in-fact arrangements are commonly used between sellers and buyers of goods who do business together regularly.

EXAMPLE 3.10

Contactor regularly uses asphalt in his construction projects and therefore needs to keep the asphalt shipments coming at regular intervals. He makes the following arrangement with his chief supplier of asphalt:
"On the first of every month, Contractor shall send a price quotation, quantity request, and shipment date to Supplier. If Supplier does not notify

Contractor within five days of receipt of this order, Contractor shall deem the contract accepted as stated."

Supplier could then either notify Contractor of his disagreement with the order or, if it is acceptable, simply ship the goods according to the agreed procedures.

Both parties might find this a convenient arrangement to keep regular shipments of asphalt coming with minimum effort. Conduct of the buyer can be used to set up a commercial relationship that amounts to a series of implied-in-fact contracts. If Supplier objects to any proposed sale within five days, Supplier need never sell asphalt under terms he does not like.

Note that such an arrangement is also consistent with the idea that silence can be acceptance where the offeree has the subjective, actual intent to accept.

Assignment

In which of the following cases has a contract been formed? If a contract has been formed, what are its terms? First, you should identify what law applies: remember that formation requirements are not the same for contracts formed under the UCC and under the common law.

1. George, a neighbor of Mieko, telephones her and says: "I propose to sell you my portable potting shed. Since we're both amateur gardeners and I know how much you like that shed, I'll let it go for $200 cash on pickup. I'll make it available to you immediately, as is; just let me know within three days."

   The next day, Mieko responds to George by leaving a message on his answering machine: "I'll take it as is, but please include hauling the shed to my yard in the $200. I can pay $100 cash now and the other $100 cash when the shed arrives at my place." Mieko hears nothing from George, and when the shed does not arrive at her place, she telephones him. He tells her he sold it right after he received her response. Mieko is disappointed and thinks she has a deal. She consults the attorney you work for. What legal advice might the attorney give to Mieko?

2. On January 5, Acme Milk Company sends a letter to Better Bottles, Inc., stating: "If you can let us have the same quality, clear glass bottles as last shipment for $1 per bottle, ship 800 bottles COD our Albany warehouse ASAP." Better Bottles does have such bottles on hand and promptly ships 800 of them to the Albany warehouse. The bottles are loaded for shipment on January 8 and arrive on the same day. However, the manager of Acme's warehouse refuses both the shipment and the bill, saying that Acme has purchased cheaper bottles elsewhere. Does Better Bottles have a deal? If so, what are the terms of the contract?

3. Harry provides housekeeping services to busy working parents. He uses a preprinted contract that covers the terms of the agreement he makes with his customers. Harry's printed contract provides he will be paid $15 per hour for four-hour blocks of time. A family can sign up for Harry to work one or two blocks of time per day, at least once a week. Harry provides all household cleaners and equipment used in housekeeping. The form also

states that Harry will bill monthly and that all bills must be paid by the 15th day of the following month. He requires a refundable "security deposit" of $200. Harry only works the "morning block" from 8:00 A.M. to 12:00 noon and the "afternoon block" from 1:00 to 5:00 P.M. Harry requires families to sign on for three months' service at a time.

Harry presents his form contract to a new customer. When the customer signs the contract and returns it by mail with the deposit, Harry begins cleaning services. He cleans during four blocks of time for the customer that month. When Harry bills for the first month, however, the check that arrives on the 14th of the month is for $200 rather than the $240 billed. Harry gets out his contract and for the first time notices that the customer had crossed out the provision saying Harry would provide all household chemicals and had written: "Customer to provide for reduced fee." The customer remains adamant that they have a contract, but Harry doesn't want to work for the family unless he uses his standard arrangement regarding the household cleaners. The attorney you work for has asked you to review this situation and help her prepare to meet with Harry. What would you tell the attorney about Harry's legal position?

4. Sarah offers to sell Bo up to 12 truckloads of "grade A" onions, which will be ready to load in 10 days, at 15 cents per pound. Sarah gives Bo her standard order form so Bo can check off the quantities he wants. The order form contains a typed description of the onions and a price. Everything else is stated in standard terms, such as the necessity for the buyer to specify a place of delivery and take care of insuring the shipment. Shipping is to be paid by Sarah and reimbursed by Bo when payment is made.

Bo responds by giving Sarah his own form, which states that he will take 11 truckloads of onions, but that Sarah will pay freight, shipping, and insurance. Bo has written on his form "definitely will take the onions, let's just get the shipping details worked out." Sarah sends Bo her own form, updated to reflect all of Bo's changes except the purchase price of 15 cents per pound. She has filled in a price of 20 cents per pound since Bo insists she pay shipping and insurance. Once again, Bo returns his own form to Sarah, stating that he will pay 18 cents per pound and keeping all other terms the same.

Sarah now begins to worry that the deal won't be concluded while the onions are in prime condition, and she notifies Bo that 20 cents is her bottom line, take it or leave it. Bo claims they have a contract for 18 cents per pound and that Sarah must pay shipping and insurance. Is he right? If so, what are the other contract terms?

Chapter Review Questions

1. What are the differences between unilateral and bilateral contracts?
2. How does a legally sufficient offer under the UCC differ from a legally sufficient offer under the common law?
3. What are the differences between acceptance under the common law and acceptance under the UCC?
4. Write a fact pattern in which the offeree effectively uses silence as acceptance. Exchange fact patterns with a classmate, and have the

classmate identify whether the contract falls under the UCC or the common law. Also, see whether your classmate agrees that the acceptance is effective.

5. Where an offeree accepts a contract for the sale of goods, what difference does it make whether the parties are laypeople or merchants?

Key Terms

Accommodation, 69	Mirror–image rule, 56
Ambiguous offer, 54	Nonconforming goods, 69
Bilateral acceptance, 50	Unilateral acceptance, 50
Bilateral contract, 50	Unilateral contract, 50
Mailbox rule, 57	

Notes

1. For example, see 39 U.S.C.A. § 3009 (West, 1980), "Mailing of unordered merchandise," which allows consumers to keep unsolicited merchandise without paying for it.

2. For an early example, see *Fairmount Glass Works v. Grunden-Martin Woodenware Co.,* 106 Ky. 659; 51 S.W. 196 (1899). For modern treatment under the UCC, see *Dorton v. Collins & Aikman Corp.,* 453 F.2d 1161 (6th Cir. 1972), which is excerpted in this text.

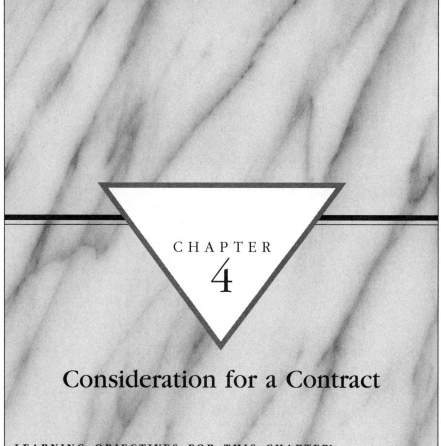

4

Consideration for a Contract

LEARNING OBJECTIVES FOR THIS CHAPTER:
WHAT YOU SHOULD KNOW!

- ❑ How to define consideration.
- ❑ Where to find consideration if the contract is bilateral.
- ❑ Where to find consideration if the contract is unilateral.
- ❑ What an illusory promise is.
- ❑ How to recognize problems with the preexisting duty rule.
- ❑ A definition of contract modification.
- ❑ When contract modifications are enforceable.
- ❑ What an "accord and satisfaction" is.
- ❑ When moral obligation is valid consideration.
- ❑ How surrender of a legal claim may be used as consideration.
- ❑ How to define and recognize nominal consideration.
- ❑ The elements and uses of promissory estoppel.
- ❑ What kind of recovery may be obtained under promissory estoppel.

The Basic Theory of Consideration

Consideration is the exchange of value, or the promise to exchange value, by the parties to a contract. This value is usually found where contracting parties agree to do something they are not already legally obligated to do, or agree not to do something they otherwise have a legal right to do. The definition of consideration is the same under common law and the UCC, and it is required for effective formation of any contract.

Unfortunately, no one has ever come up with a wholly satisfactory definition of consideration. Actually, there are several definitions that may be useful in understanding the concept. Before looking at those definitions, it is helpful to understand why the law is concerned with the requirement of consideration. The reason is that Anglo-American law does not consider every broken promise to be a legal matter. Some broken promises are considered to be too private, informal, or trivial for the law to come to the aid of the unhappy party. The problem, of course, is deciding which promises are legal matters and which are not. The doctrine of consideration is the primary way Anglo-American law differentiates between broken promises that are legal matters and those that are not.

Consideration in a Bilateral Contract

Understanding the doctrine of consideration is perhaps easiest in the case of bilateral contracts. In making a bilateral contract, the parties exchange promises with each other. The consideration is found in the promises exchanged. Thus, if Sally agrees to sell and Brett agrees to buy a forty-acre farm for $60,000, Sally's consideration is in her promise to sell the land, and Brett's is in his promise to pay money.

A bilateral contract requires each party to make at least one promise to the other. Thus, each party is the promisor for at least one promise and the promisee for at least one promise. The **promisor** is the maker of a promise. The **promisee** is the recipient of a promise. In the sale of the forty-acre farm, Sally is the promisor on the promise to sell the farm, and Brett is the promisee on this promise. On the promise to pay $60,000, Brett is the promisor and Sally is the promisee. Consider the following example.

Promisor The maker of a promise.
Promisee The recipient of a promise.

EXAMPLE **4.1**

S promises to provide maintenance services for B's office building. She makes an agreement with B that B's office building will be cleaned nightly Monday through Friday between 10:00 P.M. and midnight. S informs B that the monthly charge will be $1,000, which includes the price of all cleaning chemicals and equipment that she provides. B agrees he will pay within 15 days of the first of every calendar month by check or cash. B agrees to pay a $15 late fee for all payments not received by this date. B also promises he will keep two current copies of all necessary keys on file with S and will promptly notify S if cleaning personnel cannot be present in the building. B agrees that cleaning personnel will not be prevented from cleaning except in emergency or extraordinary circumstances. S agrees to provide necessary insurance and taxes for her employees.

Questions to Consider

1. How many promises are there in this bilateral contract?
2. Who is the promisor on each promise?
3. Who is the promisee on each promise?

Almost all contracts involve more than one promise on each side. Realistically, it is not possible to carry out most contract transactions without making several promises. Thus, consideration for a contract is often found in the totality of the promises made by each party. In most contract disputes, however, the aggrieved party is not alleging that every promise made was broken. Usually, this party is complaining only about specific promises. By focusing on who made each allegedly broken promise and who received it, one promise at a time can be examined.

The Benefit and Detriment Theories of Consideration

Although the law defines consideration as value in the promises of each party, this definition does not actually define what "value" means. Under early common law, *value* was the promise of each party to confer some benefit on the other as a result of agreeing to do something she was not previously obligated to do or agreeing not to do something she was previously entitled to do. In Example 4.1, S's promises to provide services can be viewed as promises to benefit B. B's promises to make full and timely payment, keep keys on file, and so on are viewed as promises to benefit S. This early idea about which promises should be enforceable focuses on the *benefit* given to the *recipient* of each party's set of promises. If a promisor's promises bestow benefit on the promisee, the promises are said to be enforceable because they are supported by consideration.

A more modern theory holds that value as consideration exists if a promisor agrees to *suffer a loss,* or detriment. Here, **detriment** is the loss a promisor suffers in agreeing to do something he is not already obligated to do or in agreeing not to do something he is otherwise entitled to do. Thus, under this theory, consideration can be found where a promisor's promises show that he will suffer a loss or give up something. Under this theory, S's agreement to provide services is viewed as loss or detriment to S; B's agreement to pay for those services is viewed as loss or detriment to B. Thus, each party's promises are supported by consideration.

In most contracts, both the benefit theory of consideration and the detriment theory of consideration are accurate descriptions of the value exchanged by the parties. To some extent, the main difference between the theories is that they focus on different parties. The **benefit theory of consideration** focuses on the value each *promisee* is *receiving,* while the **detriment theory of consideration** focuses on the value each *promisor* is *giving up.* The benefit and detriment theories of consideration are reminiscent of the classic joke about the eight-ounce tumbler that contains four ounces of water. The pessimist says the glass is half empty, and the optimist says it is half full. Objectively, both descriptions are true. The same can be said of most promises that contracting parties view as valuable. This value can often be described as *either* detriment or benefit.

Detriment The loss a promisor suffers in agreeing to do something she is not already obligated to do or in agreeing not to do something she is otherwise entitled to do.

Benefit theory of consideration The theory of consideration that requires each party's promises to bestow some benefit on the other.

Detriment theory of consideration The more modern theory of consideration that requires contractual promises to represent a detriment or loss to each promisor.

The benefit theory of consideration is still in use. Nevertheless, in modern times consideration is more often viewed as detriment to each party as promisor, rather than as benefit to each party as promisee. States have adopted primarily either the benefit or the detriment theory. Some degree of disagreement and confusion exists over which theory should be used in particular cases. Since consideration issues usually require state-specific research, the paralegal should be familiar with how consideration may be viewed as benefit to the promisee or as detriment to the promisor. If you understand these ideas, you can work within the definition chosen by a particular jurisdiction or applicable in a particular case.

The Bargained-for-Exchange Element of Consideration

Examined more closely, both the benefit and the detriment theories of consideration contain an additional idea aside from value. Under either theory, the detriment or benefit must be induced, at least in part, by the corresponding detriment or benefit of the other party. This is the idea that consideration or value in a contract involves mutual exchange: each party's promises are the price for the promises of the other party. **Bargained-for-exchange,** as this idea is called, focuses on *mutuality of exchange* rather than on whether the exchanged value represents loss or gain to a particular party.

Bargained-for-exchange The requirement of consideration that focuses on *mutuality of exchange* rather than on whether the exchanged value represents loss or gain to a particular party.

Consideration in a Unilateral Contract

In the case of unilateral contracts, the concept of consideration requires some adjustment. In a unilateral contract, instead of asking for a return promise, the promisor asks the promisee to perform. Thus, in a unilateral contract, *the promisor's* consideration must be found in his promises. However, the *promisee's* consideration is found right in the performance. In a unilateral contract, the promisee's performance ultimately is many things: the acceptance, the consideration, and the performance all rolled into one. If the performance is complete, but defective, it can even be a breach!

EXAMPLE 4.2

If Home Owner asks Painter to paint her kitchen pale yellow and then collect $500 for it, Painter's performance of the work is acceptance of a unilateral contract and is also consideration for and performance of the contract. If Painter happens to paint the whole kitchen pale pink, performance is also a breach. Note that consideration may be found here under either a benefit or a detriment theory.

Assignment

For each of the following hypotheticals, explain (1) whether a bilateral or unilateral contract is involved; (2) whether consideration is present; (3) if so, what the consideration is; (4) whether consideration would be present under the detriment and benefit theories; and (5) whether the bargained-for-exchange requirement is satisfied.

▶ Hypothetical 1

On August 1, A and B agree A will deliver 1,000 red frisbees to B on September 1. The price B is to pay is 79¢ per frisbee.

▶ Hypothetical 2

B requests that A ship to her 1,000 blue frisbees on September 1, and then bill her 79 ¢ per frisbee, payable within 30 days. A ships the blue frisbees and bills B as asked.

▶ Hypothetical 3

S agrees to convey to B the property known as "Greyacres." B will pay to S $45,000 down and then within two weeks will pay the remaining $55,000 for the total purchase price of $100,000. S promises to convey "good and clear title," and B promises to pay only in cash or cashier's check.

Adequacy and Equality of Consideration

The law has been remarkably unconcerned with whether the consideration on each side of the contract represents equal value. In other words, consideration for a promise can be found even where one party gets a better deal than the other. So long as the parties involved are mutually induced to make the deal, consideration can be found. If one party receives a contract performance worth more or less than the one the other party receives, consideration can still be found. Thus, consideration on each side can be *legally adequate* without being *equal*.

For the most part, the law has also been unconcerned with objective valuation of contract consideration.

EXAMPLE   **4.3**

S offers to sell to B her used computer and printer for $800 although the market value of these items is only $500. B agrees to pay $800 because she particularly likes this brand of computer and has very limited time to shop the used electronics market. The parties' promises are supported by consideration, although from an objective point of view S's computer and printer are overpriced.

Consideration for a contract need not meet a reasonable person standard. In other words, consideration for a particular contract is not legally inadequate even if reasonable people would not value it the same as the contracting parties do. If the parties are satisfied by the value involved and it induces them into the contract, then consideration is present.

The law's refusal to be concerned with equality or objectivity of value may come from the commitment to freedom of contract and a laissez-faire economy. In any event, the law allows the contracting parties to decide how much they are willing to gain or lose in a transaction. With few exceptions, if the contracting parties are content with the relative values involved, so is the law.

Problematic Promises: Is There Consideration?

Although equality and objective value are not requirements of consideration, the law does place some limits on what constitutes legally adequate consideration. Traditionally, several kinds of promises do not constitute consideration. Some of the legal issues in this area are esoteric, and the paralegal is not likely to encounter them often. Others, however, arise frequently in litigation or other aspects of the paralegal's job. The following categories of promises do not constitute valid consideration:

- Promises that do not really bind the promisor
- Promises meant only to confer gifts
- Promises made because of mere moral pressure on the promisor
- Promises to perform what a party was already obligated to do
- Promises where the consideration on one side is so small it is worthless

A final category of problematic promises may constitute consideration under some circumstances but not under others:

- promises that involve giving up a legal right or claim

Promises That Do Not Constitute Valid Consideration

Promises That Do Not Really Bind the Promisor

Illusory promise
The traditional term for a promise that does not bind the promisor. Such promises are found where the promisor has not really obligated herself to perform the contract.

Traditionally, a promise that does not bind the promisor is known as an illusory promise. An **illusory promise** is found where the promisor has not really obligated himself to perform the contract.

EXAMPLE **4.4**

Farmer and Produce Market make a deal in which Farmer promises to deliver two tons of peaches and Market agrees to pay $1,000 per ton "if we feel like it." Each party has made a promise, but Market's promise to pay only if they feel like it does not offer Farmer much reliability or security in the deal. If Market does not feel like paying, Farmer will get nothing when the time for performance comes. This is a promise in form only because ultimately Market is not bound to pay anything unless they want to.

The example of Market's promise to pay if "we feel like it" is helpful in gaining an initial understanding of the problems of illusory promises, but in reality, contracting parties are rarely so blatant in expressing their intent not to be bound. Usually, intent not to be bound is stated more subtly, and the illusory promise may be hidden. Consider the following example:

EXAMPLE 4.5

Farmer who was to sell peaches to Produce Market decides to sell zucchini instead. Market agrees. Instead of making an outright promise to deliver one ton of zucchini, Farmer says she will deliver the zucchini "by April 1 if the yield is adequate from my zucchini fields." In return for the April 1 delivery, Market agrees to a price of $1,500 per ton.

On the face of it, both parties have made promises supported by consideration. Market is promising to pay, and Farmer is promising to supply zucchini if the fields have an adequate yield. Examined more closely, however, Farmer's promise may not have bound Farmer to do anything for Market when the time for performance comes. What does Farmer really mean by "if the yield is adequate"? What is an adequate yield and who is to judge this? Suppose Farmer finds another buyer who will pay more than Market. To avoid performance to Market, Farmer could simply claim the yield was inadequate even though it was an excellent crop. Farmer might also delay the harvest until after the April 1 delivery date. After that date, Farmer would be able to sell to a buyer who could pay more than Market.

Although better disguised here than in the peaches contract, the same problem exists: one party's promises may not really obligate performance unless he personally chooses to perform when the time comes. Nevertheless, such risky promises as the promise to deliver "if the yield is adequate" often have much commercial utility. For example, they can protect an honest farmer from obligation to perform if the zucchini crop really is too small to fulfill the contract. In that case, it may be preferable for both parties to estimate the possibilities and risks, deal with each other honestly, and be able to make such a contract.

Probably because such promises have legitimate uses, contract law eventually developed a theory to allow otherwise illusory promises to be used as consideration: a *promise of good faith* is now implied into them. This means the law implies into Farmer's promise to perform "if the yield is adequate" another promise: that she will not dishonestly manipulate the yield so as to avoid performance.

All modern contracts are considered to contain a covenant of good faith. **Covenant** simply means "promise." Common-law contracts now contain a covenant of good faith because case law or statutes have placed it there. Contracts covered by the UCC contain a covenant of good faith because the drafters specifically included such a promise, and virtually all states have adopted it in their commercial codes. Section 1-203 of the UCC states: "an obligation of good faith exists for every contract or duty falling within the UCC." Under both the UCC and the common law, if a promise of good faith can be implied into an otherwise illusory promise and give the promisee reasonable assurance of performance, the promise is good consideration.

It should be noted that not even a requirement of good faith rescues a promise such as "if I feel like it" from illusoriness. Presumably, even a good faith exercise of the promisor's feelings may result in not "feeling like it." There is really no limit to the amount of control the promisor has over his promise. On the other hand, requiring a promise to be made in good faith does place some limits on a promise such as "if the yield is adequate." Here,

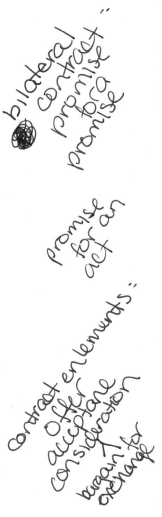

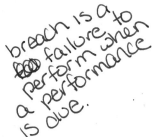

Covenant The old English and American word for a promise. An implied covenant of good faith is in all modern contracts.

good faith would require Farmer to assess the adequacy of the yield in a reasonably objective way.

The law also seeks to save otherwise illusory promises if the promisor has an independent motive to perform. For example, a farmer who cannot stay in business unless her fields produce substantial crops has her own reasons for not decreasing the yield. She wants high productivity so she can turn a profit and continue in the farming business. The need to make money to stay in business is an "independent" reason to perform on the promise. If a party has an independent reason to perform an otherwise illusory promise, most courts view the promise as good consideration.

If a promise does not bind the promisor, it is illusory unless it can be made more certain through the implied duty of good faith or the existence of an independent reason to perform. An illusory promise is not good consideration, and one who makes such a promise cannot enforce the contract even though the other party's promise is, in fact, supported by consideration. Thus, if the party trying to enforce the contract cannot show his promise bound him to perform, enforcement is denied to him. Denial of enforcement to a party whose own promises are not supported by consideration probably comes from the mutuality requirement of consideration. *Each party* must have suffered detriment or given benefit. A party who does not participate in the mutual exchange of value is denied enforcement even though the other party gave consideration.

Assignment

Discuss whether the following involve illusory promises. Explain why or why not.

- A promise by a commercial orange grove owner to sell to Juice Co. "all oranges picked this season that are not salable as whole fruit."
- A promise by a homeowner and amateur farmer to sell to Juice Co. "all oranges picked this season that are not salable as whole fruit."
- A promise by Real Estate Agent to sell Homeowner's house for a commission of 6.5 percent on any kind of sale and a promise to bring prospective "all-cash buyers" to see Homeowner's house, "if possible."

Promises Meant Only to Confer Gifts

Donative promise
A promise to make a gift.

If the promisor intends to make a gift to someone rather than to enter into a contract, the promisee does not give consideration. A promise to make a gift is sometimes called a **donative promise.** With a donative promise, the promisor agrees to do something she was not previously obligated to do or agrees not to do something she was previously entitled to do. The promisee, however, does not do either. As previously noted, consideration must go both ways if there is to be a legally enforceable contract. Thus, promises to make gifts are not contracts.

EXAMPLE 4.6

Suppose Amos buys a new computer and tells his neighbor, Max, that he will donate his old computer to Max for use by Max's third-grade class. Amos is promising to give up his computer. Max is not promising to give up anything. Although Amos may obtain some sort of tax benefit if he goes through with this transaction, this benefit does not come from Max. Clearly, Max is not giving anything as inducement for Amos's promise of the computer. Thus, although one could characterize Amos's promise as being supported by consideration in the traditional sense, Max has not even made a promise. Even if the law were to insist that Max promise something such as "I promise to use the computer in the classroom," this has no real value to Amos except perhaps personal satisfaction. Amos has offered to make a gift to Max, not make a contract with him: there is no mutual exchange of value.

A problem may occur if the promisor revokes the gift promise. If Amos changes his mind and decides not to give his old computer to Max, this would be a revocation of the gift promise. In that case Max, the promisee, may want to enforce the gift promise. The law does not require the promisor to perform a donative promise, however, because the promisee has not made a promise supported by consideration. This is true under either the benefit or the detriment theory of consideration. Thus, unless the doctrine of promissory estoppel applies (discussed later in the chapter), Max would not be able to enforce Amos's donative promise if Amos changed his mind and revoked the promise.

Promises Made Because of Mere Moral Pressure on the Promisor

Consider the moral obligations of the promisor in the following case.

A CASE FOR STUDY
Mills v. Wyman
3 Pick. 207 (Mass. Sup. Jud. Ct. 1825)

This was an action of assumpsit brought to recover a compensation for the board, nursing, etc., of Levi Wyman, son of the defendant, from the 5th to the 20th of February, 1821. The plaintiff then lived at Hartfort, in Connecticut; the defendant at Shrewsbury, in this county. Levi Wyman, at the time when the services were rendered, was about 25 years of age, and had long ceased to be a member of his father's family. He was on his return from a voyage at sea, and being suddenly taken sick at Hartford, and being poor and in distress, was relieved by the plaintiff in the manner and to the extent above stated. On the 24th of February, after all the expense had been incurred, the defendant wrote a letter to the plaintiff, promising to pay him such expenses. There was no consideration

for this promise, except what grew out of the relation which subsisted between Levi Wyman and the defendant, and Howe, J., before whom the cause was tried in the court of common pleas, thinking this not sufficient to support the action, directed a nonsuit. To this direction the plaintiff filed exceptions.

PARKER, C.J.   General rules of law established for the protection and security of honest and fair-minded men, who may inconsiderately make promises without any equivalent, will sometimes screen men of a different character from engagements which they are bound in *foro conscientiae* to perform. This is a defect inherent in all human systems of legislation. The rule that a mere verbal promise, without any consideration, cannot be enforced by action, is universal in its application, and cannot be departed from to suit particular cases in which a refusal to perform such a promise may be disgraceful.

The promise declared on in this case appears to have been made without any legal consideration. The kindness and services towards the sick son of the defendant were not bestowed at his request. The son was in no respect under the care of the defendant. He was twenty-five years old, and had long left his father's family. On his return from a foreign country, he fell sick among strangers, and the plaintiff acted the part of the good Samaritan, giving him shelter and comfort until he died. The defendant, his father, on being informed of this event, influenced by a transient feeling of gratitude, promises in writing to pay the plaintiff for the expenses he had incurred. But he has determined to break this promise, and is willing to have his case appear on record as a strong example of particular injustice sometimes necessarily resulting from the operation of general rules.

It is said a moral obligation is a sufficient consideration to support an express promise; and some authorities lay down the rule thus broadly; but upon examination of the cases we are satisfied that the universality of the rule cannot be supported, and that there must have been some preexisting obligation, which has become inoperative by positive law, to form a basis for an effective promise. The cases of debts barred by the statute of limitations, of debts incurred by infants, of debts of bankrupts, are generally put for illustration of the rule. Express promises founded on such preexisting equitable obligations may be enforced; there is good consideration for them; they merely remove an impediment created by law to the recovery of debts honestly due, but which public policy protects the debtors from being compelled to pay. In all these cases there was originally a quid pro quo; and according to the principles of natural justice the party receiving ought to pay; but the legislature has said he shall not be coerced; then comes the promise to pay the debt that is barred, the promise of the man to pay the debt of the infant, of the discharged bankrupt to restore to his creditor what by the law he had lost. In all these cases there is a moral obligation founded upon an antecedent valuable consideration. These promises therefore have a sound legal basis. They are not promises to pay something for nothing; not naked pacts; but the voluntary revival or creation of obligation which before existed in natural law, but which had been dispensed with, not for the benefit of the party obliged solely, but principally for the public convenience. If moral obligation, in its fullest sense, is a good substratum for an express promise, it is not easy to perceive why it is not equally good to support an implied promise. What a man ought to do, generally he ought to be made to do whether he promise or refuse. But the law of society has left most of such obligations to the interior forum, as the tribunal of conscience has been aptly called. Is there not a moral obligation upon every son who has become affluent by means of the education and advantages bestowed upon him by his father, to relieve that father from pecuniary embarrassment, to promote his comfort and happiness, and even to share with him his riches, if thereby he will be made happy? And yet such a son may with impunity, leave such a father in any degree of penury above that which will expose the community in which he dwells, to the danger of being obliged to preserve him from absolute want. Is not a wealthy father under strong moral obligation to advance the interest of an obedient, well disposed son, to furnish him with the means of acquiring and maintaining a becoming rank in life, to rescue him from the horrors of debt incurred by misfortune? Yet the law will uphold him in any degree of parsimony, short of that which would reduce his son to the necessity of seeking public charity.

Without doubt there are great interests of society which justify withholding the coercive arm of the law from these duties of imperfect obligation, as they are called; imperfect, not because they are less binding upon the conscience than those which are called perfect, but because the wisdom of the social law does not impose sanctions upon them. . . . These principles are deduced from the general current of decided cases upon the subject as well as from the known maxims of the common law. The general position, that moral obligation is a sufficient consideration for an express promise, is to be limited in its application, to cases where at some time or other a good or valuable consideration has existed.

A legal obligation is always a sufficient consideration to support either an express or an implied promise; such as an infant's debt for necessaries, or a father's promise to pay for the support and education of his minor children. But when the child shall have attained to manhood, and shall have become his own agent in the world's business, the debts he incurs, whatever may be their nature, create no obligation upon the father; and it seems to follow, that his promise founded upon such a debt has no legally binding force. . . . [The court then upheld the nonsuit directed by the court of common pleas and entered costs for the defendant.]

Questions to Consider

1. Who is the "promisor" in this case and who is the "promisee"? What kind of a promise was made to the promisee?
2. Under either a benefit or a detriment theory, can the promisee show that he gave any promises or that they were supported by consideration?
3. Why does the court view Father Wyman's promise differently from a renewed promise to pay a debt that was discharged in bankruptcy?
4. Do you think the court decided the case correctly? Why?

Mills v. Wyman accurately reflects the traditional rule that a promise made merely because it is the "right thing to do" under the circumstances is not enforceable. The moral obligation of the promisor is not consideration in the traditional sense. Under modern law, however, there is an exception if the promisor has also received some economic benefit from the promisee even though the benefit was in the past. Consider the following case.

A CASE FOR STUDY
Webb v. McGowin
27 Ala. App. 82, 168 So. 196 (1935)

Action by Joe Webb against N. Floyd McGowin and Joseph F. McGowin, as executors of the estate of J. Greeley McGowin, deceased. From a judgment of nonsuit, plaintiff appeals. Reversed and remanded.

Certiorari denied by Supreme Court in Webb v. McGowin, 232 Ala. 374, 168 So. 199. **BRICKEN, PRESIDING JUDGE.** This Action is in assumpsit. The complaint as originally filed was amended. The demurrers to the complaint as amended were sustained, and because of this adverse ruling by the court the plaintiff took a nonsuit, and the assignment of errors on this appeal are predicated upon said action or ruling of the court.

A fair statement of the case presenting the questions for decision is set out in appellant's brief, which we adopt.

"On the 3d day of August, 1925, appellant while in the employ of the W. T. Smith Lumber Company, a corporation, and acting within the scope of his employment, was engaged in clearing the upper floor of mill No. 2 of the company. While so engaged he was in the act of dropping a pine block from the upper floor of the mill to the ground below; this being the usual and ordinary way of clearing the floor, and it being the duty of the plaintiff in the course of his employment to so drop it. The block weighed about 75 pounds.

"As appellant was in the act of dropping the block to the ground below, he was on the edge of the upper floor of the mill. As he started to turn the block loose so that it would drop to the ground, he saw J. Greeley McGowin, testator of the defendants, on the ground below and directly under where the block would have fallen had appellant turned it loose. Had he turned it loose it would have struck McGowin with such force as to have caused him serious bodily harm or death. Appellant could have remained safely on the upper floor of the mill by turning the block loose and allowing it to drop, but had he done this the block would have fallen on

McGowin and caused him serious injuries or death. The only safe and reasonable way to prevent this was for appellant to hold to the block and divert its direction in falling from the place where McGowin was standing and the only safe way to divert it so as to prevent its coming into contact with McGowin was for appellant to fall with it to the ground below. Appellant did this, and by holding to the block and falling with it to the ground below, he diverted the course of its fall in such way that McGowin was not injured. In thus preventing the injuries to McGowin appellant himself received serious bodily injuries, resulting in his right leg being broken, the heel of his right foot torn off and his right arm broken. He was badly crippled for life and rendered unable to do physical or mental labor.

"On September 1, 1925, in consideration of appellant having prevented him from sustaining death or serious bodily harm and in consideration of the injuries appellant had received, McGowin agreed with him to care for and maintain him for the remainder of appellant's life; it being agreed that McGowin would pay this sum to appellant for his maintenance. Under the agreement McGowin paid or caused to be paid to appellant the sum so agreed on up until McGowin's death on January 1, 1934. After his death the payments were continued to and including January 27, 1934, at which time they were discontinued. Thereupon plaintiff brought suit to recover the unpaid installments accruing up to the time of the bringing of the suit. . . ."

The action was for the unpaid installments accruing after January 27, 1934, to the time of the suit. . . . The averments of the complaint show that appellant saved McGowin from death or grievous bodily harm. This was a material benefit to him of infinitely more value than any financial aid he could have received. Receiving this benefit, McGowin became morally bound to compensate appellant for the services rendered. Recognizing his moral obligation, he expressly agreed to pay appellant as alleged in the complaint and complied with this agreement up to the time of his death; a period of more than 8 years.

Had McGowin been accidentally poisoned and a physician, without his knowledge or request, had administered an antidote, thus saving his life, a subsequent promise by McGowin to pay the physician would have been valid. Likewise, McGowin's agreement as disclosed by the complaint to compensate appellant for saving him from death or grievous bodily injury is valid and enforceable.

Where the promisee cares for, improves, and preserves the property of the promisor, though done without his request, it is sufficient consideration for the promisor's subsequent agreement to pay for the service because of the material benefit received. . . . In the business of life insurance, the value of a man's life is measured in dollars and cents according to his expectancy, the soundness of his body, and his ability to pay premiums. The same is true as to health and accident insurance.

It follows that if, as alleged in the complaint, appellant saved J. Greeley McGowin from death or grievous bodily harm, and McGowin subsequently agreed to pay him for the service rendered, it became a valid and enforceable contract.

It is well settled that a moral obligation is a sufficient consideration to support a subsequent promise to pay where the promisor has received a material benefit, although there was no original duty or liability resting on the promisor. [Citations.]

The case at bar is clearly distinguishable from that class of cases where the consideration is a mere moral obligation or conscientious duty unconnected with receipt by the promisor of benefits of a material or pecuniary nature. . . . Here the promisor received a material benefit constituting a valid consideration for his promise.

Some authorities hold that, for a moral obligation to support a subsequent promise to pay, there must have existed a prior legal or equitable obligation, which for some reason had become unenforceable, but for which the promisor was still morally bound. This rule, however, is subject to qualification in those cases where the promisor, having received a material benefit from the promisee, is morally bound to compensate him for the services rendered and in consideration of this obligation promises to pay. In such cases the subsequent promise to pay is an affirmance or ratification of the services rendered carrying with it the presumption that a previous request for the service was made. . . .

Under the decisions above cited, McGowin's express promise to pay appellant for the services rendered was an affirmance or ratification of what appellant had done raising the presumption that the services had been rendered at McGowin's request.

The averments of the complaint show that in saving McGowin from death or grievous bodily harm, appellant was crippled for life. This was part of the consideration of the contract declared on. McGowin was benefitted. Appellant was injured. Benefit to the promisor or injury to promisee is a sufficient legal consideration for the promisor's agreement to pay. . . .

Under the averments of the complaint the services rendered by appellant were not gratuitous. The agreement of McGowin to pay and the acceptance of payment by appellant conclusively shows the contrary. . . . From what has been said, we are of the opinion that the court below erred in the ruling complained of; that is to say, in sustaining the demurrer, and for this error the case is reversed and remanded.

Questions to Consider

1. Who is the promisor in this case, and what promise or promises are being sued on? To what extent was the promise performed before Joe Webb brought suit? Is this different from the situation in *Mills v. Wyman*? How?
2. Under either a detriment or a benefit theory, did the injured worker make an exchange with McGowin *after* McGowin's promise to pay?
3. How does McGowin's promise differ from that of the father in *Mills v. Wyman*? If Levi Wyman had lived and had promised to pay Mills the money for services rendered, should *Mills v. Wyman* have been decided like this case? (Note the court's idea that human life and its preservation have economic value.)
4. Do medical care and personal services have economic value? To whom do they have economic value in *Mills v. Wyman*? What difference does this make in the two decisions?

Differences between cases where moral obligation is good consideration and those where it is not are not always easy to explain. A promise is not enforceable if it is given *purely* out of moral or ethical motives and the promisor did not gain material benefit from the promisee's performance. Conversely, the modern trend is to enforce a promise given out of moral or ethical motives *if the promisor has also gained material benefit from the performance*. Where the facts of the case are sympathetic to a promisee such as Joe Webb, and the promisee has even suffered harm in rendering performance, modern courts often produce the same result as the *Webb* court. They find consideration is present on the theory that there is more than mere moral pressure on the promisor.

Promises to Perform What a Party Was Already Obligated to Do

If a party already has a legal duty to perform some act or acts, a new promise to perform those acts does not constitute valid consideration. Promises made concerning existing obligations of the promisor are considered under the preexisting duty rule. The **preexisting duty rule** is the prohibition against using as consideration a promise to do what one is already obligated to do, or a promise not to do what one is not currently entitled to do. This rule applies whether consideration is defined as benefit to the promisee or detriment to the promisor. The benefit or detriment is not valid consideration if it is already pledged to the promisee at the time the promise is made or if the promisor is not entitled to it at the time the promise is made.

Many preexisting duty rule problems occur when parties already have a contractual relationship. Consider the following example.

Preexisting duty rule The rule that if a party already has a legal duty to perform some act or acts, a new promise to perform these same acts does not constitute valid consideration.

EXAMPLE **4.7**

On February 1, two parties make a contract to buy and sell 4,000 red balloons for $1,000. The balloons are to be delivered on February 12. On February 10, Seller telephones Buyer and suddenly demands to be paid $1,200 for the 4,000 balloons. Seller tells Buyer he will not deliver the balloons unless Buyer agrees to pay $1,200 instead of $1,000. Buyer needs the balloons for Valentine's Day sales and cannot now find replacements elsewhere. Thus, Buyer agrees to pay more by making a new promise to pay $1,200. Seller makes delivery and bills Buyer $1,200. Buyer refuses to pay more than $1,000.

Questions to Consider

1. Should Seller have a successful lawsuit for the full $1,200? For the $1,000? Why or why not?
2. Is Buyer's new promise supported by consideration? Why or why not?
3. Is Seller's new promise supported by consideration? Why or why not? Has Seller actually made a new promise?

It appears that the seller's promise has a consideration problem. While the buyer has made a promise to pay more, the seller has not promised to deliver more. The seller has simply succeeded in extracting a promise of increased payment from the buyer through threat of nonperformance. It is this *second promise to pay more* that presents a problem under the preexisting duty rule. If a court were to enforce the buyer's second promise to pay $1,200, the court might be encouraging a kind of legalized extortion. The preexisting duty rule is meant to discourage situations in which one party to a contract unfairly demands increased performance or payment from the other party. In Example 4.7, the seller has made a promise that lacks consideration (a second promise to deliver the same number of balloons) and cannot enforce the buyer's promise for the higher price.

Modification and the Preexisting Duty Rule

Modification

Changes made to the terms of a contract through mutual agreement of the parties. The common law requires additional consideration for an effective modification; the UCC does not.

Situations where one party makes an unfair demand for increased payment or performance are distinguished from situations where two parties have a contract and modify it. A valid **modification** of a contract occurs where the two contracting parties *mutually agree* to change the contract, and *each party gives additional consideration* for the modification. Then, there is a contract under the modified terms. If they observe the requirements, parties are generally free to modify a contract so long as they can secure the cooperation of the other party.

Although the law permits modification of contracts, problematic modifications have arisen in connection with the preexisting duty rule. Consider the following example.

EXAMPLE **4.8**

Contractor agrees to do some excavation for Landowner for $40,000. Contractor bases his price on a variety of competent soil tests and a responsible estimate of his own costs. An unforeseen soil problem arises, however, forcing Contractor to rent extra equipment and put extra workers on the job. Now Contractor needs to increase his overall price to $50,000 to make his original profit on the job. Contractor succeeds in negotiating a "modification" of the contract to protect his profit margin. Landowner later refuses to pay the higher price of $50,000.

Questions to Consider

1. Should Contractor be able to sue successfully to enforce the modification?[1]
2. Does this example seem different from Example 4.7 where the balloon seller wanted more money to deliver the same 1,000 balloons? Why or why not?

Here, it might seem fair to enforce the landowner's promise to pay more. Since the increased work for the contractor was not foreseeable and he apparently acted according to responsible business practices and standards, why should he suffer the whole burden of the increased costs? This result seems particularly harsh if the contractor would have demanded $50,000 originally had he known of the unforeseen soil condition. Allowing the contractor to charge more at this point may be inconsistent with the preexisting duty rule, however. If the contractor is just reusing his promise to excavate, the preexisting duty rule means a second promise of the owner to pay more is unenforceable.

To reconcile such situations with the preexisting duty rule, the law has developed an exception to the rule. The contractor may be viewed as *promising more* if his original promises justifiably failed to take into account the extra equipment and workers he must use. If the soil problem was not foreseeable by a reasonable contractor under the circumstances, the landowner's second promise to pay more is enforceable. Under this view, the preexisting duty rule is not violated because the contractor is viewed as agreeing to do something he did not originally promise to do: extra excavation. Under this view, the contractor's additional consideration for the modification is the extra cost of equipment and workers. The landowner's additional consideration for the modification is the additional $10,000.

It can sometimes be difficult to differentiate between cases in which a contracting party is demanding more for nothing and those in which a party is demanding more for an unforeseeably increased performance. In such cases, courts usually consider evidence of whether the party demanding more did everything a reasonable party under the same circumstances would or should have done. If so, increased performance is deemed *unforeseeable at the time of contract formation,* and the parties can make an enforceable modification based on the theory that there is "new" consideration. The "new" consideration is found in the unforeseen circumstances that have arisen. If a party ought to have foreseen the reasons for the attempted modification, however, it is not enforceable because the preexisting duty rule applies and there is no new consideration.

The preexisting duty rule is generally followed in all states. Because of dissatisfaction and confusion, however, the rule has not always been consistently applied. Courts sometimes hold that additional consideration exists even though it is difficult to find that the promisee actually rendered increased performance or encountered unforeseen problems. Such results may occur because the law favors flexibility and consensual modification of contracts. Where the parties appeared satisfied with the terms of a modification at the time it was made, the law often supports the validity of the modification.

The confusion and dissatisfaction surrounding the preexisting duty rule have also led to the development of other exceptions. One common exception is based on a legal fiction, or mere formality. This exception is based on the idea that the preexisting duty rule does not even apply where, instead of a modification, the parties simply make an express mutual agreement to *rescind* the first contract and then simultaneously make a second, new contract that contains the changes.

The drafters of the UCC simply abandoned the preexisting duty rule where the parties seek to modify a contract. Section 2-209(1) provides:

> (1) An agreement modifying a contract within this Article needs no consideration to be binding.

Thus, the drafters of the UCC decided to allow modification of sales contracts without a requirement of additional consideration by the parties. In fact, such modifications in states that have adopted § 2-209(1) normally do not even require a writing, except in two situations. First, if the modification falls within the Statute of Frauds, it must be written. The Statute of Frauds is covered in Chapter 10. Second, a writing is necessary for modification if the original contract is in writing (for whatever reason) and it contains a provision *prohibiting* oral modifications.

A number of states, such as California, have adopted a rule similar to the UCC rule even for contracts that fall under the common law. For example, California Civil Code § 1697 (West 1985) provides: "A contract not in writing may be modified in any respect by consent of the parties, in writing, without a new consideration. . . ." Under this kind of statute, *oral* contracts can usually be modified without consideration, *as long as the modification is in writing* and signed by the parties. States that have such a statute often provide that *written* contracts can effectively be modified in two ways: (1) by a writing signed by the parties, or (2) by a showing that each party gave additional consideration for oral modification of a written contract.

Discharge of Debt and the Preexisting Duty Rule

Although the preexisting duty rule has a certain logic to it, it has been problematic in situations where the parties wish to settle a debt between them. Difficulties arise when the creditor agrees to accept an amount that is less than the full sum owed in return for allowing the debtor to discharge the entire debt.

EXAMPLE **4.9**

A owes B $5,000, which A is to pay off at 10 percent interest after two years. When the debt comes due, A is in a precarious financial position. B fears A might soon be able to go bankrupt and discharge the debt, or simply be unable to pay. In these circumstances, B might find it advantageous to let A pay off the debt with as much cash as A can obtain at the moment. If this is only $3,500 and B accepts this amount, then A will probably demand a promise from B never to sue for the additional $1,500. Is B's promise to discharge A's $5,000 debt for $3,500 enforceable, so that B can no longer demand the additional $1,500?

Traditionally, a debtor's part payment of an undisputed debt is not consideration supporting a promise by the creditor to discharge the entire amount due. As Lord Coke put it in a famous English case, "payment of a lesser sum on the day in satisfaction of a greater, cannot be any satisfaction for the whole, because it appears to the Judges that by no possibility, a lesser sum can be a satisfaction to the plaintiff for a greater sum. . ." *Pinnel's Case,* 5 Coke 117a, 77 Eng.Rep. 237 (1602).

The rule that a debtor cannot enforce a creditor's promise to discharge a larger, undisputed debt by paying a smaller amount has been widely followed in the United States. A few states, however, have refused outright to follow the rule. Even states that follow it have carved out many exceptions. The rationale for these exceptions and reluctance to follow the rule probably stem from the social utility of compromise in many creditor-debtor situations. As in Example 4.9, the creditor may feel he gains an advantage by obtaining payment of cash, or a lump sum, even if it is less than is owed. In Example 4.9, $3,500 cash *now* may enable the creditor to take advantage of some opportunity he might miss if the debtor takes longer to pay the full amount or cannot pay at all.

Dissatisfaction with the rule against settling undisputed debts for lesser sums has made many courts eager to find something on the debtor's side to characterize as consideration. For example, some courts find that if the debtor was *already entitled* to file for bankruptcy, thereby wiping out the creditor's claim altogether, but agreed instead to pay a lesser sum, the creditor's promise to discharge the full amount is enforceable. The idea is that the debtor gave up something of additional value that constitutes consideration: the right to file bankruptcy and defeat the creditor's claim altogether.

The rule against settling debts for a lesser amount is confined to undisputed or liquidated debts. A **liquidated debt** is one whose existence and amount are not in dispute. Disputed or unliquidated debts may be settled by the creditor's accepting part payment. **Unliquidated debts** are those where the parties have a valid basis for disagreement as to liability or the amount due. A common arrangement under which a debtor and creditor may discharge an unliquidated debt for a lesser sum is an accord and satisfaction. An **accord** is an offer, and an acceptance of the offer, to give a performance different from that due under the contract. The **satisfaction** is performance of the accord. Thus, an **accord and satisfaction** is the making and performance of a substitute contract. In almost any contractual arrangement, the parties can use an accord and satisfaction to mutually agree to substitute one contract performance for another. When used to settle unliquidated or disputed debts, the accord and satisfaction is often made to discharge a larger debt for a lesser amount.

Many states have now passed statutes that allow even liquidated debts to be compromised without new consideration. These statutes generally require the creditor *to expressly accept in writing* the part payment as full satisfaction of the debt. Under such statutes, no new consideration from the debtor is needed if the creditor and debtor have put their agreement into writing.

Liquidated debt A debt where the existence of liability and the amount due are not in dispute.

Unliquidated debt A debt where the parties have a legitimate disagreement as to the existence of liability or the amount due.

Accord and satisfaction An arrangement by which two contracting parties make a mutual agreement to substitute a different contract for the original one. An **accord** is an offer and acceptance of a performance different from the one due under the contract. A **satisfaction** is performance of the accord. Accord and satisfaction differs from modification in that it results in a completely new, substitute contract.

It should be noted that where the debtor agrees to pay off a debt *early* for a lesser amount, the preexisting duty rule does not present a problem. In that case, there is consideration because the creditor has use of her money earlier than she would have if the debt lasted for the duration of the original contract.

Public Obligations and the Preexisting Duty Rule

Thus far, this chapter has examined the preexisting duty rule in a private setting, that is, where two contracting parties have arranged a private transaction between them. The preexisting duty rule also affects public employees, however. Consider the situation where an on-duty police officer arrests a robbery suspect and then claims the advertised reward. Should he be able to collect? A reward directed to the public at large that is specific in its terms is an offer that can be collected by any member of the public who knows of it and who performs the acts requested with the intent to collect. In this case, a unilateral contract is said to be formed between the offeror of the reward and the offeree (the performing member of the public).

A police officer in this situation is in a position different from that of the general public. The officer is a public employee who already has a duty to apprehend criminals. This is part of a police officer's job description. Thus, when the on-duty officer arrests a criminal, the officer is doing something that he is already obligated to do. Contract law applies the preexisting duty rule here: the officer cannot enforce the reward promise. In fact, even off-duty police officers cannot claim a reward unless they are outside the jurisdiction that employs them.

The preexisting duty rule applies to other public officials as well. Performance of an act already within the scope of a public official's duties is not valid consideration. Thus, for example, a citizen cannot be held to a promise to pay a higher-than-normal fee if a member of the county planning department extracts such a promise in return for granting a legal permit.

Promises Where the Consideration on One Side Is So Small It Is Worthless

As previously noted, contract law has been largely unconcerned with equality of consideration. This means there is usually no requirement of economic equivalency when judging whether either party has provided value in a contract. In a few instances, however, gross inequality of consideration can mean that one party has not really given consideration at all. In these instances, the consideration on one side is characterized as minimal or nominal consideration. **Nominal consideration** is consideration that is extremely small in relation to the other party's. It is not really consideration at all. Promises supported only by nominal consideration are not enforceable.

Nominal consideration Consideration that is extremely small in relation to the other party's. Promises supported only by nominal consideration are not enforceable.

EXAMPLE **4.10**

Suppose Creditor knows he holds a worthless IOU from family member A. Creditor goes to family member B, who wants to save penniless A from the consequences of a bad debt. Thus, Creditor is able to extract from B a promise to pay A's IOU. In return, Creditor promises to tear up the IOU and not to collect from A. Here, most courts would permit B to escape paying A's debt because Creditor has given only nominal consideration. Since A's IOU was worthless and Creditor knew this, Creditor's promise not to collect on the note does not have real value.

A party who makes a token promise in return for the other party's promise to surrender something of real value cannot enforce the agreement if the other party backs out. Sometimes these situations involve disguised gifts; that is, the parties put their agreement in the form of a contract, but the underlying transaction is actually a gift.

EXAMPLE 4.11

S promises to sell B her $200,000 house for $100. If the donor S changes her mind and the hopeful recipient B tries to enforce the donative promise by claiming they had a contract, enforcement is denied. The party whose consideration was nonexistent or a mere token will not be allowed to enforce the other party's promise.

Promises That Involve Giving Up a Legal Claim or Right

Promises to Surrender a Valid Legal Claim

The promise to surrender a valid legal claim has long been viewed as consideration for a contract if it is bargained for by the other side. Promises that involve giving up one's legal claims are often the subject of a special kind of contract: a release. A **release** is a contract in which one or both parties agree to give up claims against the other. There are many different kinds of releases.

Paralegals involved in litigation will become familiar with a primary type of release: the release used to settle a lawsuit. A release of this sort is a contract in which one or both parties agree not to pursue their legal claims in return for some payment or settlement from the other side. Releases executed to settle litigation have a variety of names depending on the jurisdiction. "Compromise, Settlement, and Release" is one common title for such a document. If both parties to litigation have claims to give up, the document may be a "mutual release."

There is much social utility in encouraging people to settle their disputes, rather than to continue litigating. Settlement helps to cut down on congestion in the courts and saves money for taxpayers and litigants alike. It may also save time and emotional wear and tear on the parties.

> **Release** A contract in which a party voluntarily gives up some or all of his rights. Releases are a common way to discharge remaining contractual obligations through mutual agreement. Releases are also used to settle litigation.

Promises to Surrender an Invalid Legal Claim

The rule that surrendering a *valid claim* constitutes good consideration makes sense. Since a person might well pursue such a claim successfully, giving up this opportunity has value. A harder issue is what to do with claims that are *invalid*. Should someone be able to use the surrender of an *invalid claim* for consideration to obtain a release? The uniform answer is no, if the party surrendering the claim knows it is wholly invalid. In many cases, however, the issue is more complicated: a person can have a passionate belief in a claim that others view as worthless.

Viewpoints vary on the degree to which invalid claims can be used as consideration for a release. Some jurisdictions allow a claim to be used as consideration for a release if the party giving up the claim has at least a good faith belief in its validity. Other jurisdictions require more. In these jurisdictions, not only must the party giving up the claim have a good faith belief in its validity, but it must also appear that a "reasonable person" would have such a belief.

Given both the strong policy toward settlement of claims and the natural desire to protect one's own right to sue on claims that others may not view favorably, it is not surprising that many differences occur in this area. The paralegal is best advised to consult the law and the formbooks in a specific jurisdiction to make sure that settlement documents, such as releases, are enforceable.

The Promise to Surrender a Legal Right

If someone promises to *give up a legal right* in return for payment or performance from another party, this constitutes sufficient consideration. In one famous American case, *Hamer v. Sidway,* 124 N.Y. 538, 27 N.E. 256 (1891), the court upheld an uncle's promise to pay his nephew a considerable sum of money if the nephew stopped smoking, drinking, and playing cards. The court found the nephew had a legal right to smoke, drink, and play cards. Since he gave up these rights in return for his uncle's promise to pay, the nephew gave consideration and could enforce the uncle's promise. Giving up any kind of legal right in return for payment constitutes valid consideration.

Promissory Estoppel

Development of the Doctrine Under the Common Law

The problem of whether donative promises should be enforceable has been the source of much debate and litigation in contract law. As previously stated, contract law regards gifts as revocable. Unlike a contractual party, a party making a gift is free to back out if he changes his mind. If a contractual party backs out, this is generally characterized as a breach. This is not the case for a gift because there is no contract to be breached. Since the *recipient* of a gift has not given consideration to obtain the other party's promise, the recipient cannot enforce the donative promise.

In most pure gift situations, the rule concerning donative promises brings about the right result: the promisee cannot obtain a "windfall" when the donor does not wish to go through with the gift. In some gift transactions, however, insistence on free revocation of gifts can work terrible hardship. Consider the following American case decided fifteen years before the American Civil War.

A CASE FOR STUDY
Kirksey v. Kirksey
8 Ala. 131 (1845)

Assumpsit by the defendant, against the plaintiff in error. The question is presented in this court, upon a case agreed, which shows the following facts:

The plaintiff was the wife of defendant's brother, but had for some time been a widow, and had several children. In 1840, the plaintiff resided on public land, under a contract of lease, she had held over, and was comfortably settled, and would have attempted to secure the land she lived on. The defendant resided in Talladega county, some sixty or seventy miles off. On the 10th October, 1840, he wrote to her the following letter:

"Dear Sister Antillico—Much to my mortification, I heard, that brother Henry was dead, and one of his children. I know your situation is one of grief, and difficulty. You had a bad chance before, but a great deal worse now. I should like to come and see you, but cannot with convenience at present. . . . I do not know whether you have a preference on the place you live on, or not. If you had, I would advise you to obtain your preference, and sell the land and quit the country, as I understand it is very unhealthy, and I know society is very bad. If you will come down and see me, I will let you have a place to raise your family, and I have more open land than I can tend: and on the account of your situation, and that of your family, I feel like I want you and the children to do well."

Within a month or two after the receipt of this letter, the plaintiff abandoned her possession, without disposing of it, and removed with her family, to the residence of the defendant, who put her in comfortable houses, and gave her land to cultivate for two years, at the end of which time he notified her to remove, and put her in a house, not comfortable, in the woods, which he afterwards required her to leave.

A verdict being found for the plaintiff, for two hundred dollars, the above facts were agreed, and if they will sustain the action, the judgment is to be affirmed, otherwise it is to be reversed.

ORMOND, J. The inclination of my mind, is, that the loss and inconvenience, which the plaintiff sustained in breaking up, and moving to the defendant's, a distance of sixty miles, is a sufficient consideration to support the promise, to furnish her with a house, and land to cultivate, until she could raise her family. My brothers, however think, that the promise on the part of the defendant, was a mere gratuity, and that an action will not lie for its breach. The judgment of the court below must therefore be reversed, pursuant to the agreement of the parties.

Questions to Consider

1. What were the donative promises involved in the case? Who made them?
2. What action did the promisee take after the donative promises were made? Were the actions related to the donative promises? If so, were they indirectly or directly related to the donative promises?
3. Did Sister Antillico's move to her brother-in-law's area do her any personal or financial harm? If so, what was this harm? Was this harm something from which she would be likely to recover?
4. Consistently with the benefit or detriment theory, was the brother-in-law's promise supported by consideration? Did Sister Antillico make any promises and, if so, were they supported by consideration?
5. Did the court hold Sister Antillico could enforce the brother-in-law's promises? Does this result seem fair? Why or why not?

Kirksey v. Kirksey makes logical sense under traditional rules about consideration. The hardship in this case, however, is that it appears the promise of a new home, and its revocation, actually caused harm to Sister Antillico that she would not otherwise have suffered. The plight of a poor woman with several children and no man to support her was very serious in the mid-1800s. Thus, Sister Antillico might have suffered had she remained where she was on her public leasehold. However, the court does note that she was "comfortably settled" and would have tried to secure this land, had her brother-in-law not convinced her to move. Thus, Sister Antillico seems to have lost even more because she believed her brother-in-law's promise of a permanent home.

The judge who wrote the opinion in *Kirksey v. Kirksey* was so uncomfortable with the result that he even notes his disagreement with the other judges. However, the judges' vote is consistent with the traditional doctrine of consideration: loss and inconvenience in giving up her leasehold and moving are not "value" transferred to the other party. Thus, the official interpretation of the transaction between Sister Antillico and her brother-in-law is that it was a gift, not a contract. Because they were donative promises, his promises were revocable.

For some hundred years after *Kirksey v. Kirksey*, this rule remained unchanged. Losses incurred in accepting a gift did not make the gift into a contract and did not make the gift irrevocable. Eventually, in the twentieth century, contract law developed another way to view losses incurred as the result of a donative promise. Now the doctrine of promissory estoppel, or detrimental reliance as it is sometimes called, can be used to make some gift promises enforceable. **Promissory estoppel** is a theory that allows a plaintiff like Sister Antillico to defeat the argument that she has not given a promise supported by consideration.

The name *promissory estoppel* refers to a widely used principle in the law: the estoppel theory. The word *estoppel* comes from Old English and means "prevent." Thus, the **estoppel theory** means a party should be prevented ("estopped") from denying certain facts when his own conduct makes it unfair to allow him to deny those facts to gain an advantage. There are all kinds of estoppel arguments in law. In *promissory estoppel*, the estoppel argument works to let a plaintiff like Sister Antillico assert that the promisor should be prevented ("estopped") from asserting lack of consideration as grounds not to enforce his promise.

If Sister Antillico were to file her lawsuit today, she might achieve justice after all these years. To do this, she would have to show that she relied on the gift promise of her brother-in-law and that this damaged her. Today Sister Antillico could assert that her brother-in-law should be prevented from using her lack of consideration as an argument against enforcement because he misled and damaged her with his donative promises.

Contract law now views some gift promises as irrevocable and enforceable under the doctrine of promissory estoppel. The earliest use of promissory estoppel treated losses suffered in reliance on a gift promise as a *substitute for consideration*. Thus, under early use of promissory estoppel, a contract might be created. Some early opinions about detrimental reliance even said the losses were a substitute for all elements of a contract: offer and acceptance, as well as consideration. Later opinions have developed the idea that no contract need be created. The more modern view of promissory estoppel is that it provides an alternative way to enforce some promises even without a

Promissory estoppel An estoppel argument or theory that allows a plaintiff to enforce the promisor's promise although she has not given a promise supported by consideration. The promisor is prevented from using lack of consideration as an argument to defeat enforceability of his own promise.

Estoppel theory A legal theory used in many areas of law. Under estoppel theory, a party is prevented ("estopped") from denying certain facts when his own conduct makes it unfair to allow him to deny those facts to gain an advantage.

contract. The promise to make what would otherwise be a gift can become irrevocable if the promisee relies on it and this reliance causes losses to the promisee.

How Loss Is Measured Under Promissory Estoppel

Not all losses suffered in reliance on a gift promise will make the promise enforceable. The courts have developed tests to define the kind and amount of loss a gift recipient has to suffer to make a promise enforceable under the theory of promissory estoppel. The earliest test said this loss had to fulfill all of the following requirements in order for the promisee to enforce the gift promise:

- The reliance must have been foreseeable to the promisor of the gift.
- The intended recipient of the gift must actually have relied on the promise of the gift.
- The reliance must have caused loss or detriment.
- The promisee's reliance on the gift promise must have been reasonable under the circumstances.
- The promisee must be able to show she would suffer *substantial* economic loss if the giver were allowed to retract his promise.
- It must be shown that the only way to avoid the injustice caused by retraction is to enforce the gift promise and not to allow retraction.

A later test abandoned the requirement that reliance on the promise must be "substantial." Many states use this more recent test and allow recovery for any amount of reliance if the other requirements of promissory estoppel are met. The Restatement (Second) § 90 summarizes this view as follows:

> A promise which the promisor should reasonably expect to induce action or forbearance on the part of the promisee or a third person and which does induce such action or forbearance is binding if injustice can be avoided only by enforcement of the promise.

The § 90 view is also notable because it indicates an expansion of the theory of promissory estoppel. Under this view, the original promise need not even have been a promise to make a gift. Here, any promise that induces the required kind of reliance may be enforceable under the promissory estoppel theory. Thus, § 90 extends the doctrine of promissory estoppel and reflects the modern view: where *any promise* reasonably and foreseeably causes reliance and harm, it can be enforced in order to recover losses. Under modern law, the doctrine of promissory estoppel is used to recover losses suffered because of other noncontractual promises, not just donative promises. This idea is covered in more detail in Chapter 12.

Recovery Under Promissory Estoppel

Although detrimental reliance on a promise can make the promise enforceable under any theory of promissory estoppel, the theory chosen can affect the amount of recovery a successful plaintiff obtains. If a jurisdiction uses the theory that detrimental reliance substitutes for one or more elements of a *contract,* recovery is usually based on some idea of a *contract price.* In Sister

Antillico's case, for example, she might recover the full extent of what the brother-in-law promised: the money equivalent of a home and a living for the rest of her life.

In jurisdictions using the theory that detrimental reliance does not create a contract, there is no contract price by which to measure recovery. In that case, recovery under promissory estoppel will be based on the amount of actual loss the plaintiff suffered in reliance on the promise. In Sister Antillico's case, this would probably be much less than the full money equivalent of a home and living for the rest of her life. It would probably be her out-of-pocket losses: her costs of moving herself and her family, extra living or other expenses she incurred because of the move, and perhaps something for the value of the leasehold she gave up.

Some courts even blend theories of recovery and say that even if technically a contract was formed, recovery should be only the amount necessary to give the plaintiff fair compensation for losses suffered in reliance on the promise. Differences in recovery under the contract price and under the alternative theory of "reliance" are explored further in Chapter 12.

Chapter Review Questions

1. How may consideration for a contract be defined?
2. How does consideration differ in unilateral and bilateral contracts?
3. What is an illusory promise, and why are such promises not considered legally adequate consideration?
4. Under what circumstances do promises to confer gifts become irrevocable? How is recovery measured if a gift promise is enforced?
5. Under what circumstances are promises where the promisor has a moral obligation to perform legally enforceable?
6. What is the preexisting duty rule, and how does it affect promises to discharge a greater debt for a lesser sum?
7. When is promising to give up a legal right or claim good consideration for a contract?

Key Terms

Accord and satisfaction, 89
Bargained-for-exchange, 76
Benefit theory of consideration, 75
Covenant, 79
Detriment, 75
Detriment theory of consideration, 75
Donative promise, 80
Estoppel theory, 94

Illusory promise, 78
Liquidated debt, 89
Modification, 86
Nominal consideration, 90
Preexisting duty rule, 85
Promisee, 74
Promisor, 74
Promissory estoppel, 94
Release, 91
Unliquidated debt, 89

Notes

1. For a case with similar facts, see *Watkins & Son v. Carrig,* 91 N. H. 459; 21 A.2d 591; 138 A.L.R. 131 (1941).

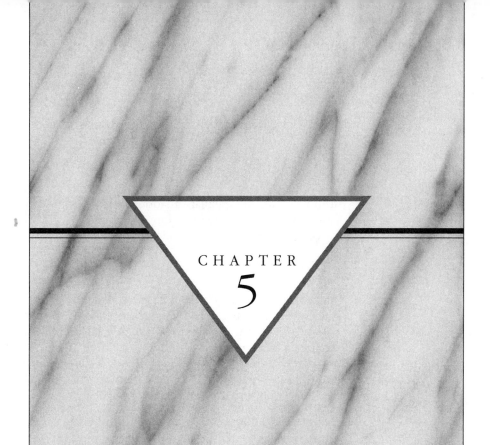

CHAPTER

5

Determining and Interpreting the Terms of the Contract

LEARNING OBJECTIVES FOR THIS CHAPTER:
WHAT YOU SHOULD KNOW!

❑ General methods of contract interpretation.

❑ The definition of parol evidence.

❑ The definition of the parol evidence rule.

❑ The types of parol or extrinsic evidence.

❑ How parol evidence may be used at trial.

❑ When parol evidence issues can be raised.

❑ What an integration clause is.

❑ What a fully integrated contract is.

❑ What a partially integrated contract is.

❑ How parol evidence relates to modification.

❑ The effect omitted terms have on a contract.

Introduction

Why do problems of interpretation arise after a contract is formed? Often such problems occur because words may have more than one meaning or be less precise than the parties envisioned. Sometimes parties have different assumptions about the meaning of contract terms or fail to spell out what they mean, and these problems do not come to light until after formation has occurred. Although most contractual situations probably do not end up in litigation, many differences in interpretation can arise even after the formation process is complete. Consider the following situation.

EXAMPLE **5.1**

George and Sally have a contract that requires George to deliver fresh pastries to "Sally's Cafe" every morning. The contract states there "shall be no extra charges for delivery." Sally receives her first monthly bill and notices George included a mileage allowance for his delivery driver. Sally thinks the provision quoted above means George has to pay gas mileage as part of his costs under the contract. George thinks mileage is not an "extra" charge, but a normal charge. He says an "extra" charge is a charge for handling or packaging pastries.

This disagreement between Sally and George involves a problem of contract interpretation. Although formation of the contract and some performance have taken place, the parties have discovered they do not agree on what the contract means. If the contract is oral rather than written, the parties might not even remember exactly the same wording. Such problems are common, and when they arise, litigation may ensue if the parties cannot resolve the dispute between themselves. In that case, a court may be required to interpret the contract.

If litigation is filed, how should a court seek to resolve problems of interpretation? The methods used to interpret contracts are complex, but in general, courts use the following approaches:

1. Under the *plain meaning rule,* words or phrases in a contract are normally given their clear, ordinary, objective, or "plain" meaning.

2. Where the meaning is ambiguous, a court will normally allow the parties to submit evidence about what they intended the term to mean.

   (a) Terms can be interpreted to have a meaning that is widely used in a particular industry if the contract is made by parties connected to this industry. This is interpretation based on *trade usage.*
   (b) If the parties submit evidence of the meaning of a term in a contract and this evidence shows conflicting interpretations, the conflict is resolved against the drafter and in favor of the other party. Thus, the party who did not draft the contract usually gets the benefit of the doubt.
   (c) In choosing among possible reasonable meanings for a term, a meaning that serves the public interest is preferred.

3. If the contract itself gives a specific definition of a term, the term is interpreted according to the meaning given.

4. Contracts are normally read as a whole. Thus, it is assumed that all provisions are meant to be consistent with one another.
5. It is assumed that each term means the same thing wherever it appears throughout a contract unless different meanings are clearly indicated.
6. If the contract is made up of several different documents, the documents are all interpreted together as part of one whole and interpreted to be reasonably consistent with one another.
7. Circumstances existing at the time of contract formation may be considered to help resolve ambiguities in a contract.

An interesting and famous case involving interpretation of a contract arose in New York when two contracting parties made an agreement to sell "chickens." The European buyer and the American seller eventually found they had different ideas of what a "chicken" was. Note how the parties attempted to argue their positions and how the court applied various rules of interpretation.

A CASE FOR STUDY

Frigaliment Importing Co. v. B.N.S. International Sales Corp.

190 F. Supp. 116 (S.D.N.Y. 1960)

FRIENDLY, Circuit Judge. The issue is, what is chicken? Plaintiff says "chicken" means a young chicken, suitable for broiling and frying. Defendant says "chicken" means any bird of that genus that meets contract specifications on weight and quality, including what it calls "stewing chicken" and plaintiff pejoratively terms "fowl." Dictionaries give both meanings, as well as some others not relevant here. To support its [position] plaintiff sends a number of volleys over the net; defendant essays to return them and adds a few serves of its own. Assuming that both parties were acting in good faith, the case nicely illustrates Holmes' remark "that the making of a contract depends not on the agreement of two minds in one intention, but on the agreement of two sets of external signs—not on the parties' having meant the same thing but on their having said the same thing." The Path of the Law, in Collected Legal Papers, p. 178. I have concluded that plaintiff has not sustained its burden of persuasion that the contract used "chicken" in the narrower sense.

The action is for breach of the warranty that goods sold shall correspond to the description, New York Personal Property Law, McKinney's Consol. Laws, c. 41, § 95. Two contracts are in suit. In the first, dated May 2, 1957, defendant,

a New York sales corporation, confirmed the sale to plaintiff, a Swiss corporation, of:

> US Fresh Frozen Chicken, Grade A, Government Inspected, Eviscerated 2½–3 lbs. and 1½–2 lbs. each all chicken individually wrapped in cryovac, packed in secured fiber cartons or wooden boxes, suitable for export
> 75,000 lbs. 2½–3 lbs . . @$33.00
> 25,000 lbs. 1½–2 lbs . . . @$36.50 per 100 lbs.
> FAS New York
> scheduled May 10, 1957 pursuant to instructions from Penson & Co., New York.

The second contract, also dated May 2, 1957, was identical save that only 50,000 lbs. of the heavier "chicken" were called for, the price of the smaller birds was $37 per 100 lbs., and shipment was scheduled for May 30. The initial shipment under the first contract was short but the balance was shipped on May 17. When the initial shipment arrived in Switzerland, plaintiff found, on May 28, that the 2½–3 lbs. birds were not young chicken suitable for broiling and frying but stewing chicken or "fowl"; indeed, many of the cartons and bags plainly so indicated. Protests ensued. Nevertheless, shipment under the second contract was made on

May 29, the 2½–3 lbs. birds again being stewing chicken. Defendant stopped the transportation of these at Rotterdam. This action followed. [The judge agreed with the parties that New York law governs this case.]

Since the word "chicken" standing alone is ambiguous, I turn first to see whether the contract itself offers any aid to its interpretation. Plaintiff says the 1½–2 lbs. birds necessarily had to be young chicken since the older birds do not come in that size, hence the 2½–3 lbs. birds must likewise be young. This is unpersuasive—a contract for "apples" of two different sizes could be filled with different kinds of apples even though only one species came in both sizes. Defendant notes that the contract called not simply for chicken but for "US Fresh Frozen Chicken, Grade A, Government Inspected." It says the contract thereby incorporated by reference the Department of Agriculture's regulations, which favor its interpretation; I shall return to this after reviewing plaintiff's other contentions.

The first hinges on an exchange of cablegrams which preceded execution of the formal contracts. The negotiations leading up to the contracts were conducted in New York between defendant's secretary, Ernest R. Bauer, and a Mr. Stovicek, who was in New York for the Czechoslovak government at the World Trade Fair. A few days after meeting Bauer at the fair, Stovicek telephoned and inquired whether defendant would be interested in exporting poultry to Switzerland. Bauer then met with Stovicek, who showed him a cable from plaintiff dated April 26, 1957, announcing that they "are buyer" of 25,000 lbs. of chicken 2½–3 lbs. weight, Cryovac packed, grade A Government inspected, at a price up to 33 cents per pound, for shipment on May 10, to be confirmed by the following morning, and were interested in further offerings. After testing the market for price, Bauer accepted, and Stovicek sent a confirmation that evening. Plaintiff stresses that, although these and subsequent cables between plaintiff and defendant, which laid the basis for the additional quantities under the first and for all of the second contract, were predominantly in German, they used the English word "chicken"; it claims this was done because it understood "chicken" meant young chicken whereas the German word, "Huhn,"

included both "Brathuhn" (broilers) and "Suppenhuhn" (stewing chicken), and that defendant, whose officers were thoroughly conversant with German, should have realized this. Whatever force this argument might otherwise have is largely drained away by Bauer's testimony that he asked Stovicek what kind of chickens were wanted, received the answer "any kind of chickens," and then, in German, asked whether the cable meant "Huhn" and received an affirmative response. . . .

Plaintiff's next contention is that there was a definite trade usage that "chicken" meant "young chicken." Defendant showed that it was only beginning in the poultry trade in 1957, thereby bringing itself within the principle that "when one of the parties is not a member of the trade or other circle, his acceptance of the standard must be made to appear" by proving either that he had actual knowledge of the usage or that the usage is "so generally known in the community that his actual individual knowledge of it may be inferred." 9 Wigmore, Evidence (3d ed. § 1940) 2464. Here there was no proof of actual knowledge of the alleged usage; indeed, it is quite plain that defendant's belief was to the contrary. In order to meet the alternative requirement, the law of New York demands a showing that "the usage is of so long continuance, so well established, so notorious, so universal and so reasonable in itself, as that the presumption is violent that the parties contracted with reference to it, and made it a part of their agreement." Walls v. Bailey, 1872, 49 N.Y. 464, 472–473.

Plaintiff endeavored to establish such a usage by the testimony of three witnesses and certain other evidence. Strasser, resident buyer in New York for a large chain of Swiss cooperatives, testified that "on chicken I would definitely understand a broiler." However, the force of this testimony was considerably weakened by the fact that in his own transactions the witness, a careful businessman, protected himself by using "broiler" when that was what he wanted and "fowl" when he wished older birds. . . . a witness' consistent failure to rely on the alleged usage deprives his opinion testimony of much of its effect. Niesielowski, an officer of one of the companies that had furnished the stewing chicken to defendant, testified that "chicken" meant "the male species of the poultry industry.

That could be a broiler, a fryer or a roaster," but not a stewing chicken; however, he also testified that upon receiving defendant's inquiry for "chickens," he asked whether the desire was for "fowl or frying chickens" and, in fact, supplied fowl, although taking the precaution of asking defendant, a day or two after plaintiff's acceptance of the contracts in suit, to change its confirmation of its order from "chickens," as defendant had originally prepared it, to "stewing chickens." Dates, an employee of Urner-Barry Company, which publishes a daily market report on the poultry trade, gave it as his view that the trade meaning of "chicken" was "broilers and fryers." In addition to this opinion testimony, plaintiff relied on the fact that the Urner-Barry service, the Journal of Commerce, and Weinberg Bros. & Co. of Chicago, a large supplier of poultry, published quotations in a manner which, in one way or another, distinguish between "chicken," comprising broilers, fryers and certain other categories, and "fowl," which, Bauer acknowledged, included stewing chickens. This material would be impressive if there were nothing to the contrary. However, there was, as will now be seen.

Defendant's witness Weininger, who operates a chicken eviscerating plant in New Jersey, testified "Chicken is everything except a goose, a duck, and a turkey. Everything is a chicken, but then you have to say, you have to specify which category you want or that you are talking about." Its witness Fox said that in the trade "chicken" would encompass all the various classifications. Sadina, who conducts a food inspection service, testified that he would consider any bird coming within the classes of "chicken" in the Department of Agriculture's regulations to be a chicken. The specifications approved by the General Services Administration include fowl as well as broilers and fryers under the classification "chickens." Statistics of the Institute of American Poultry Industries use the phrases "Young chickens" and "Mature chickens," under the general heading "Total chickens" and the Department of Agriculture's daily and weekly price reports avoid use of the word "chicken" without specification.

Defendant advances several other points which it claims affirmatively support its construction. Primary among these is the regulation of the Department of Agriculture, 7 C.F.R.

§ 70.300–70.370, entitled, "Grading and Inspection of Poultry and Edible Products Thereof" and in particular 70.301 which recited:

"Chickens. The following are the various classes of chickens:
(a) Broiler or fryer . . .
(b) Roaster . . .
(c) Capon . . .
(d) Stag . . .
(e) Hen or stewing chicken or fowl . . .
(f) Cock or old rooster . . .

Defendant argues, as previously noted, that the contract incorporated these regulations by reference. Plaintiff answers that the contract provision related simply to grade and Government inspection and did not incorporate the Government definition of "chicken," and also that the definition in the Regulations is ignored in the trade. However, the latter contention was contradicted by Weininger and Sadina; and there is force in defendant's argument that the contract made the regulations a dictionary, particularly since the reference to Government grading was already in plaintiff's initial cable to Stovicek.

Defendant makes a further argument based on the impossibility of its obtaining broilers and fryers at the 33 cents price offered by plaintiff for the 2½–3 lbs. birds. There is no substantial dispute that, in late April, 1957, the price for 2½–3 lbs. broilers was between 35 and 37 cents per pound, and that when defendant entered into the contracts, it was well aware of this and intended to fill them by supplying fowl in these weights. It claims that plaintiff must likewise have known the market since plaintiff had reserved shipping space on April 23, three days before plaintiff's cable to Stovicek, or, at least, that Stovicek was chargeable with such knowledge. It is scarcely an answer to say, as plaintiff does in its brief, that the 33 cents price offered by the 2½–3 lbs. "chickens" was closer to the prevailing 35 cents price for broilers than to the 30 cents at which defendant procured fowl. Plaintiff must have expected defendant to make some profit—certainly it could not have expected defendant deliberately to incur a loss. . . .

When all the evidence is reviewed, it is clear that defendant believed it could comply with the contracts by delivering stewing chicken in the 2½–3 lbs. size. Defendant's subjective intent would not be significant if this did not coincide with an objective meaning of "chicken." Here it did coincide with one of the dictionary meanings, with the definition in the Department of Agriculture Regulations to which the contract made at least oblique reference, with at least some usage in the trade, with the realities of the market, and with what plaintiff's spokesman had said. Plaintiff asserts it to be equally plain that plaintiff's own subjective intent was to obtain broilers and fryers; the only evidence against this is the material as to market prices and this may not have been sufficiently brought home. In any event it is unnecessary to determine that issue. For plaintiff has the burden of showing that "chicken" was used in the narrower rather than in the broader sense, and this it has not sustained.

Judgment shall be entered dismissing the complaint with costs.

Questions to Consider

1. How did the seller interpret the word "chicken"? How did the buyer interpret the word "chicken"? Whose interpretation did the court favor?
2. What kinds of evidence did the parties introduce to try to support their interpretations?
3. How might the contract have been worded to avoid confusion concerning the meaning of the word "chicken"?
4. Would commercial parties like these ever deliberately cause confusion over the meaning of the term "chicken"? If so, why?
5. What evidence is there in the opinion that the court used the objective theory of contracts to guide its interpretation rather than the subjective theory of contracts?
6. What methods of contract interpretation did the court use?

The Parol Evidence Rule and Contract Interpretation

Some problems of contract interpretation involve a rather unwieldy set of concepts collectively referred to as the parol evidence rule. To understand the parol evidence rule, it is helpful to accept an idea that may seem somewhat suspect to the contemporary mind. This is the belief that written agreements are somehow more reliable and more sacred than oral agreements.

This belief in the importance and reliability of written agreements may stem, at least in part, from the awe with which earlier peoples viewed the ability to write. In the ancient and medieval worlds, most people could not write. The ability to write and the written product itself were generally looked upon with reverence. The modern mind is accustomed to allegations of false advertising, elaborate written securities scams, and outlandish tabloid news reports. Thus, written documents do not always appear reliable or truthful. In fact, contemporary Americans may well believe that the written word can be used for fraudulent purposes as easily as for truthful ones.

Profound skepticism about the veracity of writing is a modern phenomenon. The parol evidence rule arose at a time when there was more trust in the written word. Thus, where parties to a contract reduced their final agreement to a writing and that writing appeared to be complete, courts generally did not allow any additions or contradictions to the contract to be introduced as evidence. This was and is the **parol evidence rule.** The nature of problems under the rule can be seen in the following example.

Parol evidence rule
A collection of concepts concerning the sanctity of written contracts where they represent final and complete agreement of the parties. When parties to a contract reduce their final agreement to a writing and the writing is complete, courts cannot allow any additions or contradictions to the contract to be introduced as evidence.

EXAMPLE **5.2**

Crop Duster v. Farmer John
(The Case of the Omitted Fields)

Last winter Crop Duster and Farmer John spent several days negotiating a crop-dusting contract. Under this contract, Crop Duster agreed to spray all of Farmer John's fields that were ready for chemical treatment as of June 15. When it came time to write up their deal, Crop Duster used a copy of his own standard form contract, which he always uses for his crop-dusting agreements. Both parties signed and dated the contract. Crop Duster has come to the office you work for because he now wants to sue Farmer John for breach of their agreement.

You review the contract on behalf of the attorney you work for and brief the attorney on what it says. You find the contract states that ten fields will be sprayed for a price of $20,000. Crop Duster, however, says that there was more to their deal than what is in the written contract. He says Farmer John told him that by June 15 more fields might be ready for spraying. Crop Duster claims they agreed that Farmer John would let him know by telephone, at least one week in advance, if additional fields needed spraying.

Under Crop Duster's version of the facts, the farmer did telephone him and ask for four additional fields to be sprayed. Crop Duster claims he sprayed the fields and then billed Farmer John an additional $8,000 for the extra fields, for a total price of $28,000. Farmer John has now refused to pay anything but the $20,000 stated in their written contract. Farmer John claims that no matter how many fields were sprayed, they agreed the maximum price would be $20,000.

In addition to the signed form contract, Crop Duster brings to the attorney's office a copy of the final bill for $28,000 that he sent Farmer John. Unfortunately, the only indication he has that Farmer John agreed to pay extra for additional fields is some notes he made in his "day timer" while he was negotiating the contract with Farmer John. Crop Duster says he made notes in his day timer to remind himself of their agreement, but did not think it was necessary to put this additional information in the printed contract.

Questions to Consider

1. Who is telling the truth, Farmer John or Crop Duster?
2. Which documents should the court look at to determine who is telling the truth: Crop Duster's form contract, the bill for services, the handwritten notes Crop Duster made, or all three?
3. Was Crop Duster's form contract as executed by the parties a complete version of their actual agreement?
4. What is the best evidence of the complete contract?

The parol evidence rule developed to answer the question of who was telling the truth in a situation where the parties have a written agreement and one or both parties seek to introduce evidence that does not appear in the agreement. The rule attempts to do this by controlling the evidence the parties can use to prove the terms of a written agreement. Combining many years of legal history and many court decisions and scholarly critiques, we can summarize the parol evidence rule approach as follows:

If the crop duster's standard form contract really does represent everything the parties actually agreed to, then it is their *complete and final agreement,* and the crop duster's handwritten notes must be fraudulent or mistaken. Since fraudulent or mistaken evidence is not a reliable means of arriving at the truth, it should be kept out of evidence.

Thus, the parol evidence rule is intended to prevent a party from introducing into evidence any information that was not really part of the contract. Evidence that is not in the main contract in a case like that of the crop duster and the farmer is called parol evidence. *Parol* is from the French for "word." Here **parol evidence** means written or oral evidence that is outside the written agreement of the parties. For this reason, parol evidence is also called **extrinsic evidence.** Restated in general terms, the parol evidence rule states:

> No extrinsic evidence is admissible to add to or change the terms of a contract if the contract is the final and complete agreement of the parties.

Methods courts use to determine whether a written contract actually represents the final and complete agreement of the parties are further discussed later in the chapter.

Is the Parol Evidence Rule Really a Rule of Evidence?

Much has been written about whether the parol evidence rule is primarily an evidentiary rule or whether it has a purely substantive function. At a basic level, a rule of evidence controls what evidence is admissible at trial. A substantive rule tends to be simply a statement of a legal principle. While the more modern approach views the parol evidence rule as substantive rather than evidentiary, it can actually serve either function. For example, if the parol evidence rule is viewed as excluding any evidence offered at trial that is not contained in a final, complete, written contract, this makes it a rule of evidence. If the parol evidence rule is viewed more as the idea that later agreements take precedence over earlier ones when the later agreements are written down, then it has a substantive function.

From a paralegal point of view, the main importance of the debate over the nature of the parol evidence rule is *timing.* If the parol evidence rule is viewed as a rule of evidence in the applicable jurisdiction, then all relevant parol evidence problems should be raised at trial. Where the rule is regarded as evidentiary, failure of the attorney to raise timely objections at trial may mean these objections have been waived and cannot be raised later. **Objections** are arguments that attorneys raise at trial to prevent information (e.g., witness testimony and documents) from being introduced and used as evidence. If an attorney successfully raises an objection to the introduction of evidence, the evidence stays out of the trial record, and neither the judge nor the jury can use it to decide the case.

Although some cases show that the parol evidence rule does not always foreclose raising parol evidence problems for the first time on appeal, a well-prepared paralegal would not want to take a chance. The paralegal

Parol evidence
Written or oral evidence that is outside the written agreement of the parties; also called **extrinsic evidence.**

Objections Arguments that attorneys raise at trial to prevent information from being introduced and used as evidence.

should bring parol evidence problems to the attorney's attention as soon as they are discovered during trial preparation. A paralegal helping an attorney to prepare for trial needs to know whether the attorney wishes to cover parol evidence problems during the trial. Normally, the attorney would not want to risk waiving any parol evidence issues on appeal.

If the parol evidence rule is regarded as a substantive rule of law in the applicable jurisdiction, these problems can usually be raised on appeal even if they were not raised at trial. If the attorney is handling the case for the first time on appeal, the paralegal should bring any unaddressed parol evidence rule problems to the attorney's attention so the attorney can choose whether to raise these issues on appeal. Even in jurisdictions regarding the parol evidence rule as substantive, however, if the attorney is handling the case at the pretrial stage, the paralegal should still bring these problems to the attorney's attention immediately. Then, the attorney can choose whether to raise them at trial or on appeal. Usually, an attorney would choose to deal with all viable arguments initially.

Policies Behind the Parol Evidence Rule

There are probably several rationales behind the parol evidence rule. One is the belief in the sanctity of written contracts. Another is the idea that terms not in the main contract were probably excluded during final negotiation and were not intended to survive the writing process. A third rationale is the belief that all parties should be encouraged to act diligently to put their full agreement into the writing. If not, they risk losing the benefit of a term they may care about. It is often thought that encouraging parties to "put it all in writing" will promote business stability.

Literally thousands of pages have been written about whether the rationales for the parol evidence rule are right and about whether the rule even works to promote these rationales. The rule itself has been the subject of much criticism and confusion. To some extent, the rule has even been eroded in modern times.[1] The modern tendency has been to disfavor rules that can be used to *automatically* exclude evidence in civil cases.

The reason the parol evidence rule runs contrary to much modern thinking can be seen in Example 5.2. If the standard form contract the crop duster used is found to be complete and final, then his handwritten notes could be automatically excluded from evidence even though he is telling the truth about why this additional information is not in the form contract. Despite such difficulties, however, in general the rule is still alive and well in American courts. Thus, a paralegal preparing for trial or supporting attorneys at trial needs to know how to deal with evidence that raises parol evidence rule problems.

Integration or "Merger" Clauses

Many contracts contain a provision that states that the contract is "the entire agreement" of the parties. Putting in this clause means the contract is the complete and final agreement of the parties. A contract that represents the complete and final agreement of the parties is said to be an **integrated contract.**

Integrated contract
A contract that represents the final and complete agreement of the parties.

Inserting such a clause into a contract brings the parol evidence rule into play. The clause serves to keep out any evidence at trial that would change or add to the contract. A typical example of such a clause in a contract might read:

INTEGRATION

This contract represents the entire agreement of the parties and it shall exclusively determine their rights and obligations. No prior course of dealing between the parties, custom or usage of trade, course of performance, or other evidence shall be admissible to add to, explain, or vary this contract.

Integration clause or provision A contract provision expressly stating that the contract is the complete and final ("entire") agreement of the parties; also called a **merger clause** or an **entire agreement clause.**

Conclusive presumption An assertion that cannot be refuted by offering additional evidence. As it pertains to contract integration, the presence of a valid integration clause is a conclusive presumption the contract is the complete and final agreement of the parties.

In most jurisdictions, this is called an **integration clause,** a **merger clause,** or an **entire agreement clause.** Such a clause is generally considered to be entitled to a conclusive presumption that the contract is a complete and final statement of the terms to which the parties agreed. Full discussion of evidentiary presumptions is best left to a course specifically on the rules of evidence. In general, however, a **conclusive presumption** is an assertion that cannot be refuted by offering additional evidence. An integration clause is regarded as a conclusive presumption about a contract. Thus, the clause (1) means the contract is assumed to be complete and final and (2) prevents either party from introducing any evidence outside the agreement that would supplement or change the contract in any way. The contract is conclusively presumed to be complete and final because that is what the clause says.

Without such a provision, there is usually no presumption that the contract is integrated. Without such a clause, a court may need to make its own finding about whether the contract is complete and final. Such a finding is made if one or both parties request it or if one or both parties assert that the contract is integrated. The outcome of this decision determines what evidence the parties will then be able to submit. Though a paralegal should not automatically assume the attorney wants an integration clause in every contract, it is a common practice. Thus, the paralegal should obtain the attorney's recommendation on each contract she is helping to draft. Further, the paralegal should be aware of the consequences of such a clause (or its absence) when preparing for trial or appeal.

Assignment

1. Note that the language of the integration clause presented above can be easily adapted to a variety of contracts. If the attorney wants the paralegal to include such a clause in a rental agreement, how might the language be adapted?
2. How might the language be adapted for use in a contract to buy and sell floor lamps? An employment contract?

Exhibit 5.1 summarizes the approach used in handling parol evidence rule problems.

EXHIBIT 5.1

A Summary Approach for Handling Parol Evidence Rule Problems

1. Does the rule apply?

    - The parol evidence rule applies only when the contract is written. It does not apply to oral agreements.
    - The parol evidence rule applies only when the written contract represents the complete and final agreement of the parties.

2. How do courts decide whether the contract is the complete and final agreement of the parties?

    - Courts usually use one of two tests to determine whether a written contract introduced into evidence is complete.
    - The **four corners of the document test** (also called the *face of the document test*) is used in some jurisdictions. With this test, the court uses only what is written in the contract to decide whether the parties intended it to be their complete and final agreement.
    - A more modern approach courts use is the **all relevant evidence test.** With this test, the court looks not only at the written contract, but at any evidence that is helpful in revealing whether the contract contains complete and final information about the parties' agreement.
    - If the contract is complete and final, it is referred to as *integrated*.

3. If the contract is integrated, are all parts of it complete, or is some of it incomplete?

    - If a court decides the whole contract is complete, then it is referred to as completely integrated or fully integrated.
    - If a court decides some parts of the contract are complete and some parts of it are not, then it is referred to as only partially integrated.

4. What special vocabulary terms apply to evidence outside the contract?

    - All evidence that is not part of the document or documents initially determined to be the actual agreement of the parties is called parol or extrinsic evidence.
    - There are three possible kinds of extrinsic evidence, depending on the time at which the evidence came into existence:
        - *Prior extrinsic evidence* came into existence before contract formation.
        - *Contemporaneous extrinsic evidence* came into existence at the time of formation.
        - *Subsequent extrinsic evidence* came into existence after contract formation.

Four corners of the document test The older method of deciding whether a contract is integrated. A court considers only what is written in the contract to decide whether the parties intended it to be their complete and final agreement. Also called the **face of the document test.**

All relevant evidence test The modern method of deciding whether a contract is integrated. A court looks not only at the written contract, but also at any evidence helpful in revealing whether the contract contains complete and final information about the parties' agreement.

continued

EXHIBIT 5.1 (CONT.)

A Summary Approach for Handling Parol Evidence Rule Problems

5. What evidence can be introduced to challenge terms in a completely integrated contract?

    • In most courts, oral or written evidence that existed *before* the contract was made or around *the same time* as formation cannot be introduced into evidence if doing so would change or add to the contract terms.
    • Evidence that came into existence *after* the contract was made can be admitted unless a statute prohibits it, because this evidence might indicate the parties modified the contract.

6. What evidence can be introduced to challenge terms in a partially integrated contract?

    • For provisions of the contract found to be complete and final, the same rules apply as for fully integrated contracts.
    • For provisions of the contract found not to be complete and final, all evidence admissible under applicable evidentiary rules can be admitted to add to or change the contract terms if the evidence is shown to reflect the parties' agreement.

7. Even if the contract is completely integrated, can extrinsic evidence be offered for other purposes that the parol evidence rule does not bar?

    • Although only subsequent extrinsic evidence is admissible to add to or change terms in a fully integrated contract, all forms of extrinsic evidence are admissible to *interpret* contract terms, unless the contract itself prohibits this.
    • All forms of extrinsic evidence are admissible to attack the formation of the contract. Thus, extrinsic evidence is admissible, for example, to show the contract was obtained through fraud or mutual mistake of the parties. This cannot be prohibited by language in the contract.

A Further Word About Modification and Parol Evidence

In General

As previously noted, the parol evidence rule does not prohibit admission of evidence if the evidence came into existence *after* the contract was made. The reason is that such evidence may, in fact, be evidence the parties modified the contract. This idea makes sense in terms of general human behavior. If a party negotiated for a particular term to be part of the contract, but the term is not contained in the written agreement, this is probably because the other side refused to accept the term. Thus, it looks suspicious to argue that a prior or contemporaneous term is part of the contract, when the term is not in the final written version.

The probabilities are different, however, if the term a party seeks to introduce into evidence was not in existence during negotiation or was not discussed at that time. With evidence that arises *after* negotiation, it is possible that there was a *modification* of the contract terms in the written agreement. A **modification** is a change in contract terms made by mutual agreement after formation of the contract. Evidence that came into existence after formation could therefore be evidence that the parties mutually changed the contract terms after agreement was reached. To know whether a modification occurred, a court would at least have to look at this subsequent, extrinsic evidence.

Modification A change in contract terms made by mutual agreement of the parties after formation of the contract. The common law requires additional consideration for a modification; the UCC does not.

Common-Law Contract Modifications

The common law generally requires the parties to a contract to give additional consideration for a contract modification. Thus, where common law applies, a party who seeks to introduce subsequent extrinsic evidence to add to or change the terms of an integrated agreement may have other problems in addition to the parol evidence rule. While the rule does not exclude subsequent extrinsic evidence, this evidence alone would not be enough to establish a modification. As noted previously, to show a valid contract modification, the party alleging the modification must show there was some additional consideration for it. The only help the parol evidence rule provides for that party is that the extrinsic evidence needed to show the terms of the modification is not automatically excluded.

UCC Contract Modifications

Consideration is not required for effective modification of UCC contracts. UCC § 2-209 states: "An agreement modifying a contract within this Article needs no consideration to be binding." Thus, for contracts governed by the UCC, the subsequent extrinsic evidence exception to the parol evidence rule is more helpful. Here the extent, clarity, and reliability of the subsequent extrinsic evidence would determine whether an effective modification could be shown.

Assignment

Review Example 5.2 involving Crop Duster and Farmer John. Then answer the following questions:

1. Assume you are a paralegal whose office represents the crop duster in his lawsuit against the farmer. Also assume that you want to help your client prove the farmer agreed to pay extra for spraying the additional four fields. If you were organizing evidence for trial, what piece of evidence would you consider crucial for helping your client to prove this?
2. Will the parol evidence rule affect your ability to use this piece of evidence? How? What if the form contract contains an integration clause? What if it does not?
3. Are there any exceptions to the parol evidence rule that might help you to have this evidence admitted?

4. What is the farmer's best argument to keep this evidence from being admitted?
5. Evidence to be introduced at trial can be classified as documentary, testimonial, or physical. Which kinds of evidence do you think you would be introducing here?

Contract Interpretation and Omitted Terms

Disputes over contracts can arise not only when the parties disagree about what specific contract provisions mean, but also when information is simply left out of the contract. The problem can be illustrated with the following example:

EXAMPLE 5.3

In 1992, Acme Widgets makes a contract to deliver "all of its highest quality Super Widgets produced each month" to Wonder Widget Brokers, Inc. The contract is to run for five years.

In 1996, with one year to go on the contract, Acme starts manufacturing a completely new type of "Super Widget." A revolutionary new chemical process unknown in 1992 makes the new widget possible.

Due to the new chemical process, the new Super Widgets are superior to any widgets on the market and can therefore be sold for $4 per widget. Under the contract, the price of the old Super Widgets is $2.

Naturally, Acme prefers to interpret the contract as not covering the new Super Widgets at all. Wonder Widget Brokers, of course, prefers to interpret the contract provision as requiring sale of the new Super Widgets to them.

In the situation in Example 5.3, what is the buyer's best argument for obtaining the new Super Widgets? The best argument probably is that the contract provision requiring delivery of "highest quality Super Widgets produced each month" should be interpreted to include any and all Super Widgets produced during the life of the contract. The widget seller is sure to argue that this would be unfair, however. Since the chemical process necessary to make the new Super Widgets was unknown when the contract was formed, the seller will surely argue that sale of any completely new and uncontemplated types of Super Widgets could not have been included in the contract. Thus, to get what it wants, the buyer may argue that this dispute is simply a question of contract interpretation. To get what it wants, the seller will argue that this is not a question of contract interpretation at all. Instead, the seller will argue that a term was completely left out because neither party thought of it. The seller will certainly not want the court to read into the contract any term requiring it to sell the new Super Widgets to the buyer for $2.

If a court decides that the question is not one of contract interpretation and that the new Super Widgets were simply not covered in the agreement, then the rules of contract interpretation would not apply. Information omitted from a contract is not subject to rules on interpretation of contracts.

The source of the confusion in Example 5.3, of course, is that it is not clear whether a contract term should be interpreted to include a particular subject or whether that subject was never contemplated by the parties.

Assignment

1. You are a paralegal whose supervising attorney asks you to review the "Super Widget" file. What arguments could you help the attorney formulate to show:

   • That the contract should be interpreted to cover the new Super Widgets
   • That the new Super Widgets were omitted and are not covered at all in the contract

2. Are there any particular documents or other evidence you would like to see in the file to help support these arguments? List the documents of which you think the supervising attorney should be aware.

Extensive or Material Omitted Terms and Their Effect on Interpretation

The omission of some terms has relatively little impact on the contract while the omission of others has substantial impact. A term that appears to have little impact on the contract is referred to as a **minor term.** A term that appears to have greater impact on the contract may be referred to as a **material** or **essential term.** For example, if a painting contract for a multimillion dollar hotel failed to specify what color should be used inside the bathroom cabinets, this would probably be omission of a minor term. If the painting contract failed to specify all exterior colors for the hotel, however, this omission would probably be material.

Omission of essential or material terms can lead to the conclusion that no contract was ever formed. The same result can follow if an extensive number of minor terms are omitted. Sometimes omission of just a few seemingly minor terms can show a contract was not formed if they turn out to be crucial to the contract in some way.

Again, the idea that a contract might not have been formed if too much information is missing is a practical one. If people manage to conclude a deal and reach mutual agreement, they will usually try to cover everything of real importance. If crucial matters are not worked out to their satisfaction, most people will not voluntarily agree to a deal. Thus, the absence of many minor terms, or even one material term, may mean the parties never really reached agreement, and a contract was not formed.

As discussed in Chapters 2 and 8, courts will imply some terms into a contract. They generally refuse, however, to remake a contract for the parties or to form a contract where the parties themselves did not do so. As previously discussed, the UCC is more liberal than common law because it allows formation with fewer specific terms. Additionally, it contains the gap-filler provisions that can be used to supply omitted information if it appears the parties made a contract and if the provisions would be consistent with their reasonable expectations. Under either the UCC or the common law, however, absence of too many important terms may be evidence that a contract was never formed.

Minor term A term that appears to have relatively little impact on the contract, or one that does not have key relevance for it. A minor term may be important but is not crucial.

Material term A term that appears to have a great or important impact or relevance for a contract; a crucial term. Also called an **essential term.**

Chapter Review Questions

1. What methods might a court use to interpret an ambiguous term in a contract? Explain each method.
2. What is the parol evidence rule, and to which contracts does it apply? To which kinds of extrinsic evidence does the rule apply?
3. How might issues involving the parol evidence rule arise in litigation?
4. What is the effect on litigation if the parol evidence rule is characterized as a rule of evidence rather than a substantive rule of law?
5. What are the differences between the common-law and the UCC requirements for modification?
6. What is the difference between contract interpretation and the process of implication?

Key Terms

All relevant evidence test, 107
Conclusive presumption, 106
Four corners of the document test, 107
Integrated contract, 105
Integration clause or provision, 106

Material term, 111
Minor term, 111
Modification, 109
Objections, 104
Parol evidence, 104
Parol evidence rule, 102

Notes

1. Wallach, "The Declining 'Sanctity' of Written Contracts—Impact of the Uniform Commercial Code on the Parol Evidence Rule," 44 Mo. L. Rev. 651, 653 (1979)

PART

II

Contract Performance

CHAPTER
6

Performance and Breach of Contracts

Introduction to Performance Problems in Contracts

P art II of this text shifts the focus from the *formation* of a contract to its *performance*. The discussions in Part II assume that a valid contract exists. Even with a valid contract, however, once the parties begin to do what their agreement calls for, many problems can arise for several reasons. First, many contemporary contracts are made long before actual performance is to begin. Complex modern contracts often require binding agreements to be formed long before the parties will actually render the bulk of their performances. Such agreements are common in projects such as building a shopping mall or highway or procuring crude oil for jet fuel. Many difficulties between the parties can arise during the period after the agreement is made, but before actual performance begins.

Another source of problems is that performance of a contract may extend over a long period of time. Some modern contractual relationships can last five, ten, twenty years, or more. Obviously, such contracts are subject to many changes in circumstances, market conditions, and attitudes of the parties. Even the identity of the parties can change during a long contract performance. Long-term contractual relationships lead to many difficulties that contract law must address.

Even when performance is to follow quickly after formation or will take only a short time, other performance problems can arise. The parties may have a disagreement at any time after performance begins, or one or both may try to back out of the deal. The parties may have disputes about the meaning of contract terms, the timing of performance or deadlines, or the amount of work to be done. Then, they may demand assurances, threaten to stop performing, or actually cease performing altogether. Unfortunately, formation of an agreement is not a guarantee the agreement is clear and complete or that the parties will work well together.

If difficulties arise during the preparation stage of a contract, one or both parties may be reluctant to go forward with performance. If trouble is already brewing on the horizon, one of the parties may cease preparations, pressure the other party to begin performance early, threaten not to perform when the time comes, or try to back out of the contract.

If difficulties arise between the parties after the contract is formed, the mere fact that formation has taken place is not much practical use in determining the rights and duties of the parties. Thus, the law of contracts has developed a number of doctrines to help clarify and determine contract rights and duties at the preparation and performance stages. Exhibit 6.1 presents a broad overview of these doctrines.

Part II is organized around the broad areas of contract law suggested by Exhibit 6.1. Chapter 6 covers the use of conditions in contracts and the nature of contract breach. Chapter 7 covers excuse and discharge of contract performance. Chapter 8 covers defenses to allegations of contract breach and explains how these same ideas can be used as claims that sometimes will allow a party to get out of a contract.

EXHIBIT 6.1

Determining the Rights and Duties of the Parties to a Contract

---

At what point does each party's duty to perform actually arise?

- Does the party have a conditional or an absolute duty to perform?
- Are any excusing conditions present under the circumstances?

When performance is due, what degree of performance is required?

- Is some performance enough, or does performance have to be perfect?
- If some performance is enough, how much is enough?
- If the performance is insufficient, what can the complaining party do about it?

Even if performance is due, can it be excused or discharged in some way?

- Should performance be required if it is impossible?
- Should performance be required if the purpose for which the contract was formed has been frustrated?
- Can the parties themselves voluntarily agree not to require performance?

If full performance is due and not discharged or excused, but is not given, can either party get out of the contract?

- When can lack of contractual capacity be a claim or defense?
- When can failure to write down the contract be used as a claim or defense?
- When can "bad" or dishonest conduct and words be used as a claim or defense?
- When can mistakes made by the parties be used as claims or defenses?
- When can illegality of the contract be used as a claim or defense?
- When can arguments based on public policy be used as claims or defenses?
- When can failure of consideration be used as a claim or defense?
- When can unclear or incomplete terms in a contract be used as claims or defenses?

Contract Litigation Under the UCC or Common Law as a Context for the Legal Concepts

Considering the vast numbers of contracts made in the modern world, it is perhaps surprising that relatively few contracts end up in litigation. For the most part, contracting parties get what they need from the deals they negotiate and go their way sufficiently satisfied not to sue. The contracts we read about in the newspapers or in **reporters** (collections of case opinions written by judges) are the exceptions where the parties were unable to resolve their differences. Nevertheless, paralegals will often handle contracts that end up in litigation. Therefore, you should understand why contract litigation occurs as well as how contract performance and breach concepts operate in litigation.

Reporters Collections of case opinions written by judges.

The most common reason for contract litigation is the belief of one or both parties that the other party has given defective or incomplete performance. If a party believes performance is incomplete or defective, that party may file a lawsuit alleging the other party has breached the contract. A contract **breach** is a failure to render adequate performance when and where performance is due. The document used to file a lawsuit is usually called a complaint. In a **complaint,** the plaintiff sets out her grievances against the other party and asks the court to grant remedies for these grievances.

The other contract party usually responds to the complaint by denying the breach or denying responsibility for it. The document used to respond to the complaint is usually called an **answer.** In it the defendant sets out various reasons why he believes there is no merit to the complaint. In some cases, the party answering the complaint may also file a **countersuit,** alleging the other party is in the wrong. Different jurisdictions refer to countersuits by various names such as *counterclaim.*

The contract party who is suing for breach of contract is the **plaintiff** in the case, and the party being sued is the **defendant.** If one contracting party files a lawsuit and the other files a countersuit, each party is the plaintiff in its own suit and the defendant in the other party's suit.

The typical complaint in a breach of contract action asserts that a contract was formed, notes what performance was to be rendered, and states what was done and what was not done. In other words, the complaint explains that there was a contract and why there was a breach. Then, the complaint requests that the court force the defendant to give certain types of relief (remedies) to make up for the breach. In many cases, more than one remedy is requested and can be given. Contract remedies are covered in detail in Chapter 10.

Breach A failure to render adequate performance when and where performance is due.

Complaint The document in which the plaintiff sets out her grievances against the other party and asks the court to grant remedies for these grievances.

Answer The document used to respond to the complaint.

Countersuit A lawsuit filed by the defendant in opposition to or deduction from the claims filed by the plaintiff in the complaint.

Plaintiff The contract party who files the complaint.

Defendant The party being sued.

The Use of Conditions in Contracts under the Common Law or the UCC

Doctrines involving the use of contract conditions originally developed under the common law but now apply to contracts governed by the UCC. The UCC contains relatively few provisions that specifically discuss conditions, but its drafters appear to have assumed that basic contract doctrines on the use and effect of conditions would apply to these contracts. Thus, the law on conditions presented here also applies to contracts governed by the UCC unless otherwise indicated.

At What Point does the Duty to Perform Actually Arise?

If one of the contracting parties wishes to sue for breach of contract, it must be clear the other party had a duty to perform and then failed to do so. Thus, it is important to determine when the duty to perform arises under a contract. The layperson probably thinks the duty to perform under a contract arises once the contract is made and the date for performance arrives. Actually, this is quite true for many contractual promises. In the case of some promises, however, contract law adds another requirement. To understand this additional requirement, consider the following examples and discuss their differences.

▶ **REMEMBER**   *To breach a contract, a party must have failed to perform when and where the performance was due.*

EXAMPLE **6.1**

Lawncutter promises to mow Homeowner's lawn for $25 "tomorrow morning at 9:00 A.M." Lawncutter will use electric cutting tools. Homeowner promises to pay the $25 when the job is finished.

When tomorrow comes, it is raining. Fearing serious injury if she uses her cutting tools in the rain, Lawncutter fails to mow the lawn at 9:00 A.M. It rains all day, and Lawncutter never cuts Homeowner's lawn.

EXAMPLE **6.2**

Lawncutter promises to mow Homeowner's lawn for $25 "tomorrow morning at 9:00 A.M., weather permitting." Lawncutter uses electric cutting tools. Homeowner promises to pay the $25 when the job is finished.

When tomorrow comes, it is raining. Fearing serious injury if she uses her cutting tools in the rain, Lawncutter fails to mow the lawn at 9:00 A.M. It rains all day, and Lawncutter never cuts Homeowner's lawn.

Questions to Consider

1. In which example would the Homeowner have a better argument that Lawncutter breached their contract?
2. Why would Homeowner's argument be better in one example than in the other?
3. Why would parties include the words "weather permitting" in the contract in Example 2?

Absolute promise
Where the parties have undertaken their respective duties without any qualifications. The duty to perform arises on the date or at the time set by the contract. Also known as a *covenant*.

Covenant   A synonym for an absolute promise. The duty to perform arises on the date or at the time set by the contract.

Conditional promise
A promise in which the parties have agreed the duty to perform will arise or not arise depending upon whether a certain event or events occur.

These are very simple examples, but they illustrate a fundamental difference in when the duty to perform arises. In Example 6.1 there is an **absolute promise;** that is, the parties have undertaken their respective duties without any qualifications. Under an absolute promise, the duty to perform arises on the date or at the time set by the contract. An absolute promise is also sometimes referred to as a **covenant.** In Example 2 there is a **conditional promise;** that is, the parties have agreed to a qualification of Lawncutter's duty to cut. This qualification is that Lawncutter has an obligation to cut *only if* the weather is such that the work can be safely done with electrical equipment. In formal contract vocabulary, Lawncutter's duty to perform arises only if the condition of safe weather is satisfied. The condition is satisfied only if the weather permits safe cutting.

These two kinds of promises, absolute and conditional, control whether a duty to perform ever arises. The Homeowner in Example 6.2 would be ill-advised to sue for breach although he received no performance from Lawncutter. The reason is that placing a condition before the duty to cut prevented that duty to perform from arising if the condition was not met. If the weather prevented cutting, no duty to cut arose. That is the essence of a conditional promise: it helps to control when a party's duty to perform comes about, depending on what happens with the condition.

On the other hand, in Example 6.1, where Lawncutter assumed an absolute duty to perform, the Homeowner might have a better argument that a breach occurred. Failure to perform an absolute promise when the time for performance arrives is normally a breach.

Note that this discussion of conditions relates primarily to bilateral contracts, where conditional promises serve a useful function. As a practical matter, why should someone like Lawncutter make an absolute promise to work with electric cutting tools and then have to choose between serious injury or possibly being sued for breach? Contract law recognizes that in many, far more complex situations, the parties need to hedge their bets, so to speak. They can do this by making promises that need only be kept if the right circumstances occur. This is what the doctrine of conditions is all about.

Classification of Conditions According to the Manner in Which They Were Placed in the Contract

One way to categorize conditions placed in contractual promises is to *describe them according to their origins*. Conditions can be defined by whether the parties themselves or the law placed them in the contract. Under this system of classification, there are three different kinds of conditions:

1. **Express conditions.** These are stated in the contract.

   EXAMPLE 6.3 A contract reads: "Seller will ship 400 pounds of confetti by the 15th of each month provided Seller's confetti production is at seasonal normal by the 5th of each month."

   The parties themselves have explicitly made conditional the Seller's duty to deliver 400 pounds of confetti. They have explicitly stated a condition in the contract so that this duty to deliver depends on the adequacy of the Seller's production capacity.

2. **Implied conditions.** These are not stated in the contract but are placed there by the law either because (1) the parties must have assumed they were part of the bargain (**implied-in-fact conditions**) or because (2) it is good public policy (**implied-in-law conditions**).

   EXAMPLE 6.4 A contract reads: "Seller agrees all confetti delivered will be marketable and will be delivered to Buyer's loading dock. Buyer shall promptly inspect all confetti as to marketability."

   Here there is an express condition that the confetti need only be accepted if it is "marketable." In addition, the contract includes some implied conditions. First, there is an implied condition that the loading dock exists and will be accessible for delivery of the goods. This provision is implied to be included even if the parties did not expressly include it. The rationale is that although they did not expressly say so, they must have assumed the Buyer would provide the dock and that the Seller would not have to build it himself in order to make delivery. Second, there is an implied condition of **good faith.** In all modern contracts under the UCC and the common law, there is an implied promise that the parties will act in good faith. The UCC has a specific statement to this effect, and case law or statute places such an implied condition in common law contracts.

Express conditions Conditions stated in the contract.

Implied-in-fact conditions Conditions not stated in the contract but placed in it by the law on the rationale that the parties must have assumed they were a part of the bargain.

Implied-in-law conditions Conditions not stated in the contract but placed in it by the law for reasons of public policy, even if the parties did not think about them at all; also called *constructive conditions*.

Good faith Honesty in fact in the conduct or transaction concerned. In all modern contracts under the UCC and the common law, there is an implied promise that the parties will act in good faith.

The implied condition of good faith means both parties are promising to act in good faith even if they do not say so in the contract. Thus, in example 6.4 above, the Buyer is implicitly promising to act in good faith when she examines the confetti and decides whether it is "marketable." To state this idea in the terminology of conditions: the Buyer has the right to reject delivery of the confetti *only if* a good faith exercise of judgment shows it is not marketable.

EXAMPLE 6.5   Seller agrees to sell and deliver to Buyer 100 bushels of wheat. Buyer agrees to pay $50 per bushel.

Although neither party has made his promise expressly conditional, modern contract law views the Buyer's promise as subject to an implied condition that the Seller must first perform by delivering the wheat. *Only if* this is done does the Buyer have a duty to pay.

The Seller's promise could be viewed as subject to an implied condition as well. It could be said that the Seller is promising to deliver *only if* the Buyer does not back out of his promise to pay.

The public policy involved in interpreting the parties' promises as conditional is probably one of fairness. It would be most unfair (and impractical in a commercial society) to say the Buyer had made an absolute promise to pay whether or not the Seller actually delivered any wheat. Similarly, it would be unfair to the Seller to assume he had a duty to deliver wheat irrespective of whether the Buyer intended to or did pay.

The terminology of conditions suggests the distinction between express and implied conditions is always clear, but this is not always the case. Although sometimes a condition is clearly either express or implied, at other times the distinction is blurred. In that case, the courts try to make a fair and reasonable interpretation of the contract language. Sometimes it is not even clear whether the promise is conditional or absolute. In such cases, the courts have a tendency to view the promise as absolute.

 A Note on the Duty of Good Faith

Although virtually all modern contracts would be construed to include implied conditions of good faith, it is not always clear what constitutes *good faith*. Perhaps one of the best definitions is the one given in UCC § 1-201(19), which defines good faith as "honesty in fact in the conduct or transaction concerned." For *merchants* dealing in sales of goods, UCC § 2-103(1)(b) goes even further and says good faith is *also* "the observance of reasonable commercial standards of fair dealing in the trade." A well-known comment to § 205 of the Restatement (Second) provides a more complete definition: "Good faith performance or enforcement of the contract emphasizes faithfulness to an agreed common purpose and consistency with the justified expectations of the other party; it excludes a variety of types of conduct characterized as involving 'bad faith' because they violate community standards of decency, fairness, or reasonableness."

Assignment

Since the study of conditions is very abstract, it is helpful to keep asking yourself the basic questions:

- Is the relevant promise absolute or conditional?
- If the promise is conditional, what kind of condition is it?
- How does the condition affect performance?
- Whose performance does the condition affect first or affect most?
- Has the condition been satisfied?

Consider these questions as you read the following problem:

George the General Contractor agrees to remodel Harriet Homeowner's house. Their contract calls for George to use several subcontractors to do the plumbing, electrical work, dry wall, wooden floors, and so on. The contract says the subcontractors will be paid ". . . when General Contractor receives payment from Harriet Homeowner." Harriet has a dispute with George and refuses to make further payment. The subcontractors have not been paid for their work. They claim George must pay them whether Harriet has paid him or not and then resolve his own difficulties with Harriet. George, who is worried about cash flow, claims the contract language means he has to pay the subcontractors only if Harriet pays him.

1. What do you think? Has George made a conditional or an absolute promise to pay his subcontractors? If the promise to pay is conditional and the condition has not been satisfied, then George's duty to pay has not yet arisen, and the subcontractors must wait for their money.
2. Will the economic effect on society be any different if George's promise to pay his subcontractors is interpreted to be absolute rather than conditional?
3. Rewrite the relevant provision in this contract so that (a) George's duty to pay is *clearly conditional* and (b) George's duty to pay is *clearly absolute.*

Classification of Conditions According to Time

Conditions can also be classified according to when the event involved in the condition is to occur. In other words, conditions can be classified based on time. To understand this system of classification, consider the following examples:

EXAMPLE 6.6

Joan promises to pay Sheep Farmer $30.00 per pound for wool on June 1 only if the price of wool on the Chicago Commodities Exchange rises to at least $29.90 per pound before May 28. Otherwise, she will pay $28.00 per pound.

Condition precedent
A promise in which an event or events must occur before performance can become due. If the condition does not occur, the performance does not become due.

In this case, the condition is to occur *before* Joan's duty to perform by paying $30.00 per pound even arises. This type of condition is called a **condition precedent** because it must occur *before* performance can become due. If the condition does not occur, the performance does not become due.

EXAMPLE 6.7

Charlie promises to provide gourmet lettuce to Chez Snob Restaurant at 40 heads per day, so long as the growing season permits this yield.

Condition subsequent A promise involving an event or events that may occur after performance is begun. If the condition occurs, it cuts off the duty to perform.

This type of condition is called a **condition subsequent** because it is to occur after performance has begun. If the condition does occur, it cuts off the duty to perform. If the condition occurs (the growing season no longer permits the yield of at least 40 heads per day), Charlie's obligation ends.

EXAMPLE 6.8

Albert agrees to sell his World Series ticket to Annie if she pays him $100 for it.

Condition concurrent Occurs where both parties have made promises that are dependent on each other and the conditions or performances are to occur at the same time.

In this case, the performances are to occur essentially *simultaneously.* Thus, it could be said that Albert must hand over his ticket or Annie need not pay. It is equally true that Annie must pay or Albert need not hand over the ticket. Performance of each party's promise is a condition of the other's performance. Yet someone must go first, or nothing will ever come of this contract. In this case, contract law says each party's performance is a **condition concurrent** of the other party's performance. Most often conditions of performance are concurrent where both parties have made promises that are dependent on each other and the performances are to occur at the same time. If no conditions are specifically mentioned but the performances are to occur close together, the law often presumes concurrent conditions in the contract, because this evens out the risks of the parties.

▶ **REMEMBER** *Under this system of classification by time, conditions may be one of three kinds:*
   1. *Conditions precedent*
   2. *Conditions subsequent*
   3. *Conditions concurrent*

The two systems of classifying conditions can also be combined. Thus, we could call the condition in Example 6.6 not only a condition precedent, but an *express condition precedent.* The conditions in Examples 6.7 and 6.8 are examples of an *express condition subsequent* and *express and implied conditions concurrent.* For an example of a possible *implied condition precedent,* look back at the General Contractor case in the Assignment. What is the possible implied condition precedent there?

Excuse of Conditions

In a way, placing a condition in a promise can be seen as protection for one (and sometimes both) of the parties. Placing conditions in a contract is a legitimate way for parties to avoid or minimize risk. Review the Lawncutter and Homeowner situation in Example 6.2. The condition in the Lawncutter's promise can be viewed, at least in part, as her attempt to avoid risk. To avoid having to work with electric cutting equipment in the rain, Lawncutter puts in a condition: the necessity to have *safe cutting weather before her duty to perform arises*. She avoids risk by ensuring that if the event does not happen—the weather does not permit safe cutting—she does not have a contractual duty to cut. She need not risk injury to avoid a breach. This condition also protects Homeowner, who does not want Lawncutter to be seriously injured or killed on his property. Thus, by agreeing to make Lawncutter's promise subject to a condition, both parties receive some protection, although the primary benefit goes to Lawncutter.

Although conditions are a legitimate way to reduce or eliminate risk, they can be misused. This most often happens when the party to be primarily protected by the condition has control over its satisfaction. The express condition precedent in Lawncutter's promise cannot be manipulated because it has a characteristic not possessed by all conditional promises: neither party can control the condition because neither party can affect the weather. If the promisor whose promise is conditional has the power to control the condition, however, difficulties may occur. In that case, the promisor may wrongfully manipulate a condition to which his promise is subject to make sure the duty to perform does not arise because the condition has not been satisfied. Wrongful manipulation of a condition can cause satisfaction or occurrence of the condition to be *excused*.

EXAMPLE **6.9**

Suppose you have just inherited a large amount of money from your rich Aunt Agatha. You decide to purchase that little red Mercedes convertible you have always wanted but could not afford. You go to your local Mercedes dealer and order the car of your dreams, which is to cost you $80,000. The dealer tells you that red is not a popular color, however, and that he may have trouble obtaining the convertible in red. To protect himself from breach if his supplier does not have such a car, the dealer promises you the car "only if my supplier can deliver the car to these premises by 5:00 P.M. this coming Friday." You leave the dealership eager for Friday to arrive.

Fifteen minutes later, another customer walks into the dealership and orders the very same car you ordered. However, this customer is willing to pay $85,000. Alas, human nature being what it is, the dealer prefers the second customer to you. The dealer then telephones his supplier who says she can deliver the required red Mercedes next Friday *morning*. The supplier also says that only one such car is currently available. The dealer thinks over his two contracts and tells the supplier, "Oh no, I don't want that car delivered until Saturday morning. Hold off delivery until then."

On Friday at 4:00 P.M., you stop by the dealer's showroom hoping to pick up your brand new, red Mercedes. The dealer tells you the car will not arrive by 5:00 P.M. and says that he therefore has no obligation to sell it to you.

Questions to Consider

1. Under the doctrine of conditions, has the dealer's duty to perform (sell the car to you for $80,000) arisen?

2. If the dealer's duty to perform has not arisen, why not? Is something wrong with this picture?

3. If the dealer's duty to perform has not arisen, can you successfully sue for breach of the contract? Why or why not?

4. Does this result seem fair or unfair? Why?

A party who controls satisfaction of a condition and then dishonestly misuses that control should not receive legal protection for this misuse. This argument is among those used to justify the idea that sometimes a condition in a promise should be **excused** from happening. As we have seen, there is normally no duty to perform a contractual promise unless the relevant express and implied conditions have been satisfied. If a condition favors, or primarily favors, a particular party and this party wrongfully prevents or hinders satisfaction of the condition, the condition will be excused. In that case, the condition need not be satisfied for the duty to perform to arise. Thus, the badly behaving party will not be allowed to gain an advantage from his own bad conduct. This type of excuse of condition is called **prevention,** which refers to the actions of the party who prevents a condition from being satisfied. To excuse a condition on the grounds of prevention, the conduct must involve wrongful behavior or conduct on the part of the contracting party favored by the condition.

In addition to excuse of condition on the grounds of prevention, there are other circumstances in which conditional promises may bring about the duty to perform even though the condition involved in the promise has not been satisfied. The following are the main circumstances in which this may occur:

Excuse of condition Removal of the requirement of satisfaction of a condition in a promise. If a condition is excused, the duty to perform becomes due even though the condition has not been satisfied.

Prevention Where a party deliberately prevents a condition or the other party's performance from occurring. To excuse a condition on the grounds of prevention, the conduct must involve wrongful behavior or conduct by the contracting party favored by the condition.

Waiver Voluntarily and intentionally giving up a known legal right or rights.

1. **Waiver.** To waive means to voluntarily and intentionally give up a known legal right or rights. A condition in a promise may be excused where the party protected by the condition has waived the right to insist the condition be satisfied.

   EXAMPLE 6.10   Homeowner agrees to make final payment to General Contractor "only if my Architect gives you a Certificate of Completion." Architect refuses to give the certificate because General Contractor has failed to complete some minor parts of the building. Homeowner says to General Contractor: "I will pay you off because I can easily have the defects corrected and overall you have done a great job."

   Homeowner has waived the right to issuance of the Architect's certificate as a condition precedent to his duty to pay the contractor. Thus, the owner's waiver excuses the condition of a Certificate of Completion. Provided this was an effective waiver, Homeowner cannot later try to reinstate the condition and refuse payment to the contractor.

Forfeiture An unreasonable or unjustified loss.

2. **Forfeiture.** A forfeiture is an unreasonable or unjustified loss. If nonsatisfaction of a condition in a promise would cause an *unwarranted loss* to the affected party and satisfaction of the condition was *not material* to the other party's part of the contract, the condition will be excused.

   EXAMPLE 6.11   Seller and Buyer have a contract under which Seller will deliver and store lumber at his auxiliary warehouse in Buyer's hometown. Once the lumber is delivered, Buyer is to examine it at the warehouse and, in writing, notify Seller of her acceptance. The written notification to Seller must be made within five working days. The contract price is $500,000 for the lumber.

Seller delivers the lumber to the warehouse. Buyer immediately examines it and lets Seller know by telephone that she will take the lumber because it is completely acceptable and she has her own buyer waiting under contract. Buyer does not get around to notifying Seller in writing for one week. When Seller receives the notification, he tells Buyer that the condition of notification within five working days was not met. Although he has not been inconvenienced, Seller maintains he has no duty to sell the lumber to Buyer.

Here a court would probably hold that precise compliance with the five-day-notice requirement was not material to the contract. Seller has not been harmed by Buyer's failure to comply precisely with the condition of written notice within five working days.

As to hardships involved, here Buyer would stand to lose a $500,000 deal because of a two-day delay in written notice. This seems unfair since Buyer immediately gave actual, oral notice in the parties' telephone conversation. Also, letting Seller insist on satisfaction of the condition would cause additional forfeiture. Buyer might be forced to breach the contract with her own buyer if she could find no timely replacement for Seller's lumber.

When an express condition has not been complied with, courts usually "balance the equities," or determine what would be fair to both parties. A court would look at the relative importance of the condition to obtaining full performance under the contract, the behavior of the parties, the losses each would suffer, and the benefits each would enjoy if the condition is excused or not excused. If noncompliance with an express condition has a material effect on the contract, however, it will not be excused even if some forfeiture is involved.

3. **Impossibility.** If it is impossible to comply with a condition, a party may be excused from doing so as long as fulfillment of the condition is not a material part of the other party's contract expectations.

EXAMPLE 6.12 Insured's automobile breaks down in the middle of the Mojave Desert. Insured's automobile insurance requires use of one of five "approved," nationwide towing companies. Because of the isolated location and extreme heat of the desert, Insured is forced to rely on the help of a motorist passing by on the highway. When this motorist reaches the nearest town, she arranges for a private towing company to come back for Insured. There is no "approved" towing company within 500 miles. This private company charges a standard rate that is comparable to any of the five "approved" towing companies. Insured accepts the tow from the private company and promptly notifies Insurer when they reach town.

Here, the difference in cost of using an unapproved company is insignificant. Furthermore, it was highly impracticable to remain stranded in the Mojave Desert with the closest approved tower 500 miles away. Thus, the condition of using only an "approved" towing company would be excused. Under the contract, Insured can still make a claim for towing reimbursement.

Impossibility The situation where certain acts required under the contract have become objectively impossible. Satisfaction of a condition may be excused if its fulfillment is not a material part of the other party's contract expectations.

The Nature of Contract Breach

How a Breach Occurs

As previously noted, a contract breach occurs whenever a party has a present duty to perform and fails to do so. All absolute promises must be performed at the date and time when performance is specified in the contract. Conditional promises need only be performed when the condition has been satisfied or excused. Once the condition has occurred or been excused, however, a conditional promise is treated the same as an absolute promise in regard to whether performance is due. Thus, contract breaches occur in the same manner whether a promise is absolute or conditional: if the time for performance arrives and performance is due, nonperformance is a breach. Conditions control whether the performance is due at all. To summarize, performance is due in any of the following situations and nonperformance is a breach:

- The promise to perform is absolute, and the date and time for performance arrive.
- The promise to perform is conditional, the condition is satisfied, and the date and time for performance arrive.
- The promise to perform is conditional, the condition is excused, and the date and time for performance arrive.

Effect of the Seriousness of the Breach

Defining the Breach by the Degree of Nonperformance

Material breach A breach where so little performance has occurred that a significant part of what the nonbreaching party had achieved by obtaining the contract is seriously threatened, interfered with, or destroyed.

Minor breach A breach that does not cause significant interference with what the nonbreaching party bargained for.

Partial breach A minor breach of a contract.

Total breach A breach that is so large and significant that the whole contract is unperformed, interfered with or destroyed.

A breach may be either *material* or *minor*. All material and minor breaches give the nonbreaching party the right to sue for relief. No specific formula is available for deciding whether a breach is minor or material; the difference is one of degree. Theoretically, a **material breach** occurs where there has been so little performance that a significant part of what the nonbreaching party had achieved by obtaining the contract is seriously threatened, interfered with, or destroyed. To some extent, then, a **minor breach** is characterized by default: a breach is minor if it does not cause significant interference with what the nonbreaching party bargained for. Some courts and some experts use the terms **partial breach** and **total breach** instead of minor breach and major breach. This language occurs in the Restatement (Second).

One advantage of using the terms *partial* and *total breach* is that they seem more consistent with the right to file litigation and the right of the nonbreaching party to stop performance. Whether the breach is partial (minor) or total (material), the nonbreaching party has the right to file litigation, but *only if* the breach is total (material) does the nonbreaching party *also* have the legal right to stop performance. This result makes some sense: where a contract has been only *partially* breached, why shouldn't the nonbreaching party have to go forward with the rest of the contract? Similarly, where the breach is so large and significant that it is a *total* breach of the contract, it would seem unfair and unproductive to require the nonbreaching party to continue to give performance.

At the same time, the terms *total* and *partial breach* can give a somewhat unrealistic picture of what happens in cases of contract breach. Often a breach may have such a serious impact on expectations under the contract that it is "material" even though it is not really "total" because the breaching party has not stopped doing everything it is required to do. The authors of the Restatement appear to have recognized this. They preserved the term *material* for a breach that is very serious, but does not give the nonbreaching party the legal right to stop performance. Under this vocabulary, only total breaches justify the nonbreaching party in stopping performance. This system of three categories of breach—partial, material, and total—is practical because it takes into account the complex situations that can arise in contract disputes. Not all jurisdictions define the degree of breach in the same way, however. Paralegals should be aware of how courts in a relevant jurisdiction use vocabulary and concepts concerning the seriousness of a breach. Some research into applicable state or federal law may be required.

Defining the Breach by the Degree of Performance

Another way that courts look at contract breaches and their effect on the duty to perform is to focus on what the allegedly breaching party did *right,* rather than on what was done *wrong.* In other words, the courts focus on how much performance has been rendered and its quality. Under this view, if a party's performance is at least *substantial,* any breach he has committed is only *minor.* If there has been no performance at all or the performance is not at least substantial, then the breach may be *material.*

As with materiality of breaches, no specific formula exists to determine when a party has rendered substantial performance. Basically, if a party's performance has been enough to give the other party the essence of what was bargained for, the performance is substantial. Thus, substantial performance need not be complete or perfect. It need only give to the nonbreaching party the major portion of what that party was bargaining for under the contract.

▶ **REMEMBER**   *Whether breaches are defined by how much or how little perfor-mance has occurred, they all entitle the wronged, or nonbreaching, party to sue. Generally, the lawsuit may be filed immediately after the breach is committed. Whether the wronged, or nonbreaching, party also has the right to stop its own performance under the contract requires a further decision about how significant the breach is in view of the performance that was to be obtained through the contract.*

Whether a contracting party actually does sue immediately (or at all) for minor breaches depends more on practicality than on theory. Often a contracting party will decide that it is not cost-effective, desirable, or even affordable to pursue a lawsuit, even though there has been an acknowledged small breach. Simply having the legal right to sue, however, can help the nonbreaching party obtain some kind of relief without litigation. If the breaching party acknowledges there has been a breach, knows there is a right to sue, and is operating in good faith, this party may be more inclined to make an adjustment in the contract price or in the amount of performance the other party still owes. Knowing that a breach can be shown may make the breaching party more willing to remedy defects in performance without litigation. This can save a client attorney's fees and court time.

Election Where There is a Material Breach

Election A choice between two alternatives.

A party has a *right* to cease performance and sue immediately where a material or total breach has occurred. This right does not mean the nonbreaching party has a *duty* to do these things, however. Even in the case of a material or total breach, the nonbreaching party has an **election** to continue with the contract and sue for a partial breach, or she may choose not to sue at all. A material or total breach by one contracting party essentially gives the other contracting party a legal right to do any of the following:

1. Sue for a material breach and cease performance;
2. Sue for a minor breach and keep performing, or
3. Not sue at all and keep performing.

Having this choice is called *having an election*. Exercising this choice is called *making an election*.

If the aggrieved party does try to go forward with the contract, she should be careful. The party who elects to continue with a contract in which there has been a material or total breach should not indicate by language or conduct that she has waived the right to sue for damages or object to the breach. Remember that a *waiver* can occur where there is voluntary relinquishment of a known legal right.

Exercise

▶ Drafting

Suppose you are a paralegal with the City Attorney of Columbia City, State of Columbia. One of the staff attorneys you work for wants to write a letter to a party the city believes has breached its contract. The attorney has asked you to help her write the first draft of a paragraph in the letter. The attorney will review and rewrite what you have written, and the correspondence will go out under the name of the City Attorney. However, your staff attorney wants you to get a start on the paragraph. Your paragraph should make clear that (1) the City Attorney's office believes there has been a material breach; (2) Columbia City does not want to cancel the contract, but wants the other party to continue performing and remedy the breach; and (3) the City does not intend to waive any of its legal rights, including the right to sue for damages if the breach is not remedied. You review the case file, and the factual situation appears to be as follows:

Last fall, Columbia City made a contract with Reliable Construction, Inc., to repair 100 miles of highway surface and the suspension bridge on Columbia Interstate Highway 100. The project was to begin in April, weather permitting, and be completed by the following winter. It snows in Columbia, and construction cannot be effectively completed during the winter months. Although the weather was excellent in April, Reliable did not begin the job until May 15. Since Reliable did not put on any extra crew or work overtime, the project is now at least six weeks behind schedule. In addition, Columbia City inspectors have examined the work completed on the highway and claim it is defective. The City inspectors say the work will have to be completely redone because the wrong paving materials and chemicals were used. They doubt that this work can be completed before winter because repair of the suspension bridge should begin in a week if it is to be finished before winter. If the paving project is completed too close to winter, the surface will not have time to cure and may crack in the subfreezing temperatures. The City believes Reliable should add as many crew and work as much overtime as necessary to complete the project on time and properly perform.

The UCC Perfect Tender Rule

The doctrine of substantial performance, discussed earlier in the chapter, is widely followed by common law courts. The drafters of the UCC, however, rejected this doctrine in favor of what is referred to as the *perfect tender rule*. **Tender** means *readiness* to perform or, sometimes, the performance itself. In contracts for sale of goods, the "tender" must conform to the contract in every way; that is, performance and the readiness to perform must be perfect. If the buyer has ordered two hundred red widgets with thingamajigs on top to be shipped air freight in green boxes, then that is exactly what must be done to conform to the contract. If the widgets arrive from the seller in blue boxes, the buyer is entitled to reject them.

The UCC perfect tender rule has been criticized.[1] Why should the buyer be entitled to reject goods that conform completely to the contract just because the packing, which will probably be thrown out, is not as ordered? Nevertheless, the UCC retains the perfect tender rule. UCC § 2-601 states:

Tender Readiness to perform or, sometimes, the performance itself.

> **Buyer's Rights on Improper Deliver**
> Subject to the provisions of this Article on breach in installment contracts (§ 2-612) and unless otherwise agreed under the sections on contractual limitations of remedy (§§ 2-718 and 2-719), if the goods or the tender of delivery fail in any respect to conform to the contract, the buyer may:
> (a) reject the whole; or
> (b) accept the whole; or
> (c) accept any commercial unit or units and reject the rest.

▶ **REMEMBER** *Under UCC § 2-602 rejection of goods must always occur within a "reasonable" time after their delivery or tender.*

Historically, before the UCC was enacted, many jurisdictions followed the perfect tender rule for sales of goods. When the UCC's drafters adapted the rule for the UCC, they apparently took some of the criticisms into account and put some limitations on the rule to make it fairer and more workable. The main limitations on the right to reject when the performance is not "perfect" relate to the buyer's obligation to give the seller the right to **cure,** or do whatever is necessary to render the required contract performance as it should have been done in the first place.

The seller may *cure* the defect in tender or performance in two situations:

Cure Doing whatever is necessary to render the required contract performance as it should have been done in the first place.

1. A seller may cure when the time for performance stated in the contract has not actually expired.

2. A seller may cure when the time for performance *has* expired, but the seller reasonably believes the buyer will accept a cure, either with or without a price adjustment. In this case, the seller must "seasonably" notify the buyer of the intent to cure and must then actually cure within a reasonable time after notification.

The Seller and the UCC Perfect Tender Rule

Although the UCC's wording is not entirely clear, the *limitations* on the perfect tender rule appear to apply only to the buyer, not the seller. Both the seller and the buyer are bound to give perfect tender. Only the *buyer* must give an opportunity to cure, however; the seller need not give the buyer any opportunity to cure. Thus, if the buyer does not give "perfect tender" by paying the seller's bill in the amount and at the time due, then the rule simply does not apply. If nonpayment by the buyer is significant enough, it is a material breach, and the seller may sue. The seller may also sue if the buyer refuses to accept perfectly conforming goods, even though the time for the buyer's performance has not expired. That is, the seller need not allow the buyer to cure by leaving the rejected goods on the buyer's premises and waiting to see if the buyer changes his mind. Nor is the seller obligated to keep trying to deliver goods after the buyer has clearly indicated he will not accept them.

Installment Contracts Under the UCC

Installment contract A contract in which performance occurs in separate parts or goods are shipped in separate lots, and each part or lot is to be paid for separately.

As the quotation from UCC § 2-601 indicates, the perfect tender rule does not apply to installment contracts. An **installment contract** for goods is a contract under which goods are to be shipped in separate lots and each lot will be paid for separately. In installment contracts for the sale of goods, the buyer must accept even nonconforming goods unless the nature of a shipment substantially impairs the value of the contract as a whole. Where delivery of a nonconforming installment does not substantially impair the value of the contract, the buyer must accept the goods and allow the seller to cure if the seller gives adequate assurances that she will do so.

Anticipatory Breach or Repudiation

Thus far, a breach has been defined as a failure to perform under the contract when and where performance is due. What if a contracting party indicates ahead of time that he has no intention of performing when the time comes? Must the other party wait to see if the threat of nonperformance is real? Can this party cease her preparations because of the threat of nonperformance, or can she demand some reassurance? And what if the threatening party changes his mind and decides to perform after all—must the other party accept this performance? These questions are the subject of the doctrine of *anticipatory repudiation*.

Anticipatory repudiation Occurs if either party repudiates the contract before the time for performance arrives; also referred to as *anticipatory breach*.

Repudiation A clear indication in advance of an intention not to perform contractual duties arising in the future.

Anticipatory repudiation occurs if either party repudiates the contract before the time for performance arrives. Anticipatory repudiation is also sometimes referred to as *anticipatory breach*. The term *repudiation* is probably more appropriate here, however, because a breach is best understood as failure to perform a *present* contract duty. **Repudiation** is advance indication of an intention not to perform contractual duties arising in the future.

An anticipatory repudiation by one contracting party excuses the other party's duty to hold himself ready to perform the contract. The aggrieved party may also bring an immediate lawsuit for the entire contract, just as if the refusal to perform were an ordinary breach occurring after the date performance was due.

A repudiation can occur through the words of a contracting party, through conduct, or through some combination of these. However, the repudiation must be very clear. It must be an affirmative and unconditional refusal to perform as promised when the time for performance arrives. Both the common law and the UCC give the repudiating party an opportunity to change her mind and withdraw the repudiation any time before the date set for her performance. This right to withdraw a repudiation is called a right to *retract*. The right to retract a repudiation may be exercised by the repudiating party unless the repudiation has damaged the other party or the other party has clearly accepted it.

Both the UCC and the Restatement (Second) take the position that a contracting party who *reasonably* fears repudiation by the other party may ask for reassurance. This is called the right to demand adequate **assurance of performance.** The nonrepudiating party has a right to demand adequate assurance of performance whether the repudiation is voluntary or involuntary. Although this doctrine is more specifically developed in the UCC, many courts follow the doctrine where common law applies to a contract. Thus, a paralegal should be aware of how the law in a relevant jurisdiction treats the right to adequate assurance of performance whether a contract is governed by common law or the UCC. A failure to give adequate assurance of performance in a timely manner normally entitles the aggrieved party to treat the contract as repudiated. Under UCC § 2-609, the assurance must be demanded in writing and must be given within thirty days. Restatement (Second) § 251 reflects the common-law viewpoint, which is that reassurance must be given within a "reasonable time."

Assurance of performance A contracting party who reasonably fears repudiation by the other party may ask for reassurance.

Consider the following case synopsis and then apply the case to the fact pattern in the Assignment.

A CASE FOR STUDY

Unique Systems, Inc. v. Zotos International, Inc.

622 F.2d 373 (8th Cir. 1980)

Lilja was the holder of a patent on a multistation hair-spray system intended for use in beauty salons. Unique Systems was to help Lilja develop, manufacture, and place in inventory hair-spray systems. Zotos was a major manufacturer and distributor to the professional beauty field of such items as shampoos, permanents, and setting lotions. The parties had no experience in the manufacture of hair-spray systems or any other type of beauty-salon equipment. Under the contract that was subject of the litigation Zotos was to purchase the hair-spray systems for resale through its nationwide system of wholesale distributors. The contract called for a two-year period during which Zotos would buy 15,000 systems with an option to buy at least 7,500 systems in years three and four. The parties later amended the contract to require distribution of the systems in "month one." "Month one" was defined as a "mutually agreed date in the year 1974." Sometime after the modification and before the date for performance, Zotos began to fear the market for the hair-spray systems was deteriorating. It then

---

A CASE FOR STUDY

Unique Systems, Inc. v. Zotos International, Inc.

622 F.2d 373 (8th Cir. 1980)

indicated it would not proceed unless Lilja agreed to a market test of the completed hair-spray systems. This Lilja refused to do, and Zotos then refused to proceed with the contract. Lilja decided Zotos's refusal to proceed was anticipatory repudiation and filed suit on the contract. In holding that Lilja was in the right and could recover, the court remarked:

If a party to a contract demands of the other party a performance to which he has no right

under the contract and states definitely that, unless his demand is complied with, he will not render his promised performance, an anticipatory repudiation has been committed. . . . When Zotos told Lilja in August of 1975 that it would not proceed until market tests were performed with the results subject to Zotos's approval, Zotos repudiated the contract and was in total breach. No market tests were required by the contract, a fact that Zotos admits that it knew.

Assignment

You are a paralegal for a law firm that represents small businesses. SlimPen, one of your clients, has come to the attorney you work for with the following problem. The attorney has asked you to review the case and give her a preliminary idea of the client's legal position. To do this, you should state the legal issues involved in this case in view of what you know about anticipatory repudiation and the rule in *Unique Systems, Inc. v. Zotos International, Inc.* Then, state how you think each legal issue could be resolved.

SlimPen, Inc., manufactures ballpoint pens and has entered into a contract with a distributor of office supplies, DistribCo., Inc. The contract calls for SlimPen to make twelve deliveries of ballpoint pens to DistribCo. during the next calendar year, beginning in January. All deliveries are to be made in the first week of each month, and DistribCo. is to distribute the pens to stationery and office supply stores by the fifteenth of every month. These stores will send all money from the sale of the pens to DistribCo., which will retain 10 percent and send the other 90 percent to SlimPen.

The contract was executed in September of the previous year. In October, SlimPen realizes it could have purchased cheaper distribution services from another company, Finder, Inc. Finder is a rival of DistribCo., and the two companies have often been in direct competition. Finder courts SlimPen and also indicates to SlimPen that DistribCo. is widely reputed to be in financial trouble. Finder guarantees SlimPen that it will undertake distribution for 8 percent. In view of this information, SlimPen's CEO telephones DisbtribCo. On November 5 and demands that DistribCo. provide written proof of its financial stability. On December 6, having heard nothing from DistribCo., SlimPen notifies DistribCo. that it is terminating the contract. SlimPen immediately negotiates and executes a contract for distribution services with Finder for an 8 percent fee. DistribCo. has filed suit against SlimPen for breach of contract.

Chapter Review Questions

1. What are the differences between an absolute promise and a conditional promise?
2. What is the difference between a condition precedent and a condition subsequent?
3. If a promise is subject to a condition precedent, what must occur before contract performance becomes due?
4. If a promise is subject to a condition subsequent, how does that affect the contract performance that is due?
5. What are the differences between express and implied conditions?
6. If a promise is subject to a condition and this condition is not satisfied, is there any other way performance can become due?
7. When will a breach be characterized as material? Minor?
8. What are the differences between the doctrine of substantial performance and the perfect tender rule?
9. What are the differences between a present breach and an anticipatory breach?

Key Terms

Absolute promise, 118
Answer, 118
Anticipatory repudiation, 130
Assurance of performance, 131
Breach, 117
Complaint, 117
Condition concurrent, 122
Condition precedent, 122
Condition subsequent, 122
Conditional promise, 118
Countersuit, 117
Covenant, 118
Cure, 129
Defendant, 117
Election, 128
Excuse of condition, 124
Express conditions, 119

Forfeiture, 124
Good faith, 119
Implied-in-fact conditions, 119
Implied-in-law conditions, 119
Impossibility, 125
Installment contract, 130
Material breach, 126
Minor breach, 126
Partial breach, 126
Plaintiff, 117
Prevention, 124
Reporters, 116
Repudiation, 130
Tender, 129
Total breach, 126
Waiver, 124

Notes

1. Honnold, "Buyer's Right of Rejection," 97 U. Pa. L. Rev. 457 (1949). See also Sebert, "Rejection, Revocation and Cure under Article 2 of the Uniform Commercial Code: Some Modest Proposals," 84 Nw. L. Rev. 375 (1990).

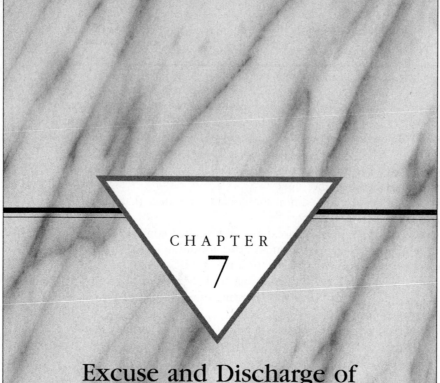

C H A P T E R

7

Excuse and Discharge of Contractual Obligations

Introduction

Even where contractual performances are currently due under a valid contract, those performances may be discharged in many ways. This chapter deals with four general methods by which the performances of contracting parties may be **excused** or **discharged:**

- By agreement of the parties themselves
- By operation of law
- By impossibility
- By frustration of the purpose of the contract

Although the parties sometimes use these methods of discharge between themselves, the methods are also often used as defenses in breach of contract actions. If the defendant can show his performance is legally excused or discharged, the plaintiff will not be successful in suing for breach of contract concerning that performance.

Note that the words *excuse* and *discharge* are used differently here from the way they are used when referring to conditions. Properly speaking, conditions are not "discharged" at all. They may be "excused" from *occurring* under many of the circumstances discussed in the previous chapter. This "excuse of condition" has the effect of making a performance come due. In this chapter, the word *excuse* is used to refer to the next stage of contract life. Here it means that no matter how a performance has become due, there are some circumstances under which the party who is to perform can be legally excused or discharged from having to do so.

Discharge by Agreement of the Parties

Discharge by Mutual Rescission

Where the parties have a bilateral contract and no performance has yet taken place, the parties may mutually agree to *rescind* the contract. A **rescission** is a cancellation of the contract. One way a rescission can occur is through the voluntary agreement of the parties. If one party wishes a rescission and the other refuses, the party who wishes to rescind can file litigation to try to obtain it. If the party who is suing for rescission wins the lawsuit, the judge can grant rescission in the form of a court order.

To discharge a contract through rescission, the contract must be *bilateral,* and no performance can have been rendered by either party. The rule that mutual rescission is no longer available once there has been some performance may seem arbitrary. Why shouldn't the parties be able to rescind if they both agree, even where one party has rendered performance? Under these circumstances, perhaps the performing party could be accommodated by payment for services rendered. Although the reasons for this rule are not entirely clear, it may be related to how consideration is viewed in the case of a rescission. Normally, each party to a mutual rescission agreement is seen as supporting its promise to rescind with the surrender of the future right to receive performance under the contract. A party that has already *received* performance has nothing to surrender, at least to the extent of performance received. Thus, if parties make a mutual rescission agreement after performance has taken place, the rescission is usually viewed as ineffective.

Excuse/discharge of performance The various doctrines under which a contracting party who is to perform can be legally excused from having to do so.

Rescission Cancellation of the contract by mutual agreement.

The Vocabulary of Rescission

Executory contract
A contract under
which no performance
has yet taken place.

A contract under which no performance has yet taken place is referred to as **executory.** Discharge by rescission is not effective unless the contract is fully executory. This vocabulary can be confusing as it means the opposite of what it appears to mean: an executory contract is one under which neither party has given performance. To refer to the opposite situation—a contract where some performance *has* taken place—contract law generally uses the term **executed.** Thus, a *fully executory contract* is one under which no performances at all have occurred. A *partially executory contract* and a *partially executed contract* are the same: a contract under which *some* performance has taken place. A *fully executed contract* is one under which all performances have taken place. The word *executed* is also sometimes used for the formal agreement to, or signing of, a contract. Thus, the paralegal should look carefully to see how the term *executed* is used in a particular situation.

Executed contract
A contract under
which all performances
have taken place.

Discharge by Release

In some ways, a release is related to a rescission. As noted earlier in the chapter, if parties want to discharge their duties under a contract, but one or both have given some performance, they cannot effectively rescind the agreement. However, they can make an agreement called a *release,* which accomplishes the same thing as a rescission since it discharges a specified performance under the contract. In contract law, a **release** can be defined as an agreement in which a contracting party voluntarily gives up some or all of his contractual rights.

Release An agree-
ment in which a con-
tracting party volun-
tarily gives up some or
all of his contractual
rights.

Traditionally, a release required consideration that was separate from (in addition to) the consideration for the contract. This is probably still the rule in the majority of states. Some states, however, have passed statutes that substitute a writing for independent consideration; that is, if the parties execute a written release, no extra consideration is necessary.[1] Under UCC § 1-107, the drafters also chose to follow the rule that written releases need not be supported by independent consideration. A written release is effective as long as it is signed and delivered by the aggrieved party.

Why would contracting parties be willing to execute a release? Suppose we return to a very simple factual setting—the Lawncutter and the Homeowner.

EXAMPLE 7.1

Suppose Lawncutter has agreed to cut Homeowner's front yard and back yard for $25 each. Thus, the total contract price is $50. After cutting the front yard, Lawncutter gets a contract to mow the lawn at Country Club for $500. Country Club wants its lawn cut immediately, and Lawncutter cannot handle both jobs at once. Thus, Lawncutter informs Homeowner that she definitely will not finish his job. This, of course, is a breach. Under the contract, Homeowner has a legal right to insist on performance and to receive it. If Lawncutter does not repent and finish cutting, Homeowner has the right to file a lawsuit. Will this step necessarily bring about the performance, however? Will filing and pursuing a lawsuit necessarily be the best solution for Homeowner's life generally?

In this instance, Lawncutter is unlikely to fulfill her obligation to Homeowner because the Country Club contract appears much more attractive. Existence of the legal right to receive performance is no guarantee the performance will ever be rendered. Lawncutter's second contract with Country Club probably makes it cost-effective for her to breach the first contract and let the chips fall where they may. One solution in a situation like this is to allow the parties to execute a release. In return for having Homeowner release her from any further obligation to cut the back lawn, Lawncutter could make some accommodations to Homeowner. For example, to motivate Homeowner, Lawncutter could agree to charge nothing for the front lawn or to charge only a minimal amount. Homeowner might be persuaded to give up the right to sue and the right to insist on full performance in return for paying Lawncutter only $5 for cutting the front lawn. If Homeowner pays another cutter $25 (or even $30) for the back lawn, he is still $15 or $20 to the good overall.

If Homeowner and Lawncutter do make a release agreement along these lines, the result is a reasonable compromise. Lawncutter is free to pursue a bigger, commercially profitable job; Homeowner has saved some money overall. This simple example realistically illustrates why contracting parties are interested in obtaining releases in many situations. In the real world, people under contract do not always do what they are supposed to do. In many such cases, compromise is sometimes more tolerable, less expensive, and less time-consuming than a lawsuit. Allowing contract obligations to be discharged under a release is thus practical and useful.

The Vocabulary of Release

In Example 7.1, Homeowner would be referred to as the releasor, while Lawncutter would be the releasee. The **releasor** is the party who is giving up the rights, and the **releasee** is the party who is being discharged from liability for nonperformance. Sometimes the parties execute a **mutual release** in which each party discharges the other party's remaining duties of performance and excuses liability for nonperformance. A mutual release would be appropriate where both parties have rendered some performance but still have some performance owed to them.

Generally, a release is not an admission of liability or fault. The language of releases usually refers simply to the compromise positions of the parties and avoids statements that might imply there was wrongdoing or inadequacy of performance. For example, a release executed in Example 7.1 might contain the following statement:

> This Release shall not be construed for any purpose as an admission of liability, but represents solely a compromise and settlement of Homeowner's claims against Lawncutter.

Releases are also used in connection with settling litigation. In many cases, parties who are already involved in litigation decide to execute a release instead of continuing to litigate. In such a release, a party gives up his rights to pursue the claims in return for some payment or performance from the other party. Releases are also widely used in the settlement of cases in which litigation has

Releasor Under a release, the party giving up some or all of her contractual rights.
Releasee Under a release, the party who is being discharged from liability for nonperformance.
Mutual release A release in which each party discharges the other party's remaining duties of performance and excuses liability for nonperformance.

not been filed, but is likely. Insurance companies, for example, often obtain releases from their own insureds or the victims of their insureds before paying out on a claim. In a typical insurance claim involving bodily or property injuries, the injured party giving the release gives up the right to sue on these injury claims. In return, the insurance company pays out money for injuries or damage to property. In this situation, the injured person is the releasor, and the insurance company is the releasee.

Discharge by Novation

In some situations where one or both contracting parties do not want to go forward with performance, they make a novation. Courts and legal scholars use the term *novation* to describe a number of arrangements in which a new party is substituted for one of the original contracting parties. Although some commentators question whether it is useful or accurate to describe these substituted arrangements as novations, most American jurisdictions still recognize such agreements and use this vocabulary. Thus, the paralegal is likely to encounter the term and should be familiar with it.

Novation An arrangement in which two contracting parties bring in a third party as a substitute for one of them. A new contract is formed between the remaining original party and the substitute.

Here, the term **novation** is used to refer to a substituted contractual arrangement under which the two original contracting parties bring in a third party as a complete substitute for one of them. Thus, if P_1 has a contract with O under which P_1 is to paint O's home, P_1 and O can agree to substitute another painter, P_2, who will now have the obligation to paint O's home and will be entitled to the payment. This arrangement is similar to other arrangements mentioned elsewhere in this text (such as delegation of duties and accord and satisfaction). The following factors distinguish a novation from these other arrangements:

1. All three parties intended P_1's liability to cease immediately upon execution of the substituted agreement.
2. A new duty of P_2 to paint O's house is created immediately upon execution of the substituted agreement.
3. P_2 is not one of the original contracting parties.
4. P_2 now has the sole right to receive payment under the contract (P_1 has no right to payment).

Thus, a novation is a substituted contract in which the parties agree that one of the original contracting parties will be completely substituted out and a new party will be completely substituted in. The new party now has all the contractual liability and benefits, and the old party has none. The legal result of this arrangement is that O can look only to P_2 for the paint job. If P_2 fails to perform, O does not have a cause of action against P_1. O can sue only P_2. A novation requires the mutual agreement of all three parties concerned. It is a way for the original contracting party who is "leaving" the contract to be voluntarily discharged from the duty to perform.

Discharge by Accord and Satisfaction

Another way for a party to be discharged from the duty to perform, whether or not some performance has taken place, is for the two contracting parties to make a different kind of substituted contract: an *accord and satisfaction*. Under this arrangement, no new *party* is substituted in; instead discharge of performance occurs because the parties set up a substituted *performance*.

EXAMPLE 7.2

Suppose B agreed to purchase S's used car. Under their contract, B is to pay $4,000 to S over a four-month period with an added 10 percent "straight" interest. Straight interest here means simply 10 percent of $4,000, or $400. To purchase the car, B thus agreed to pay S $1,100 per month for four consecutive months: $1,000 for the purchase price plus $100 for the interest. Suppose that B takes the car and the pink slip and makes payments for two months. Thus, S has received $2,200 of the $4,400 owed to him. Then, B gets into serious financial trouble and cannot pay the remaining $2,200 in two payments as the parties agreed.

Of course, S could sue and try to take back the car, refunding some of the purchase price. Alternatively, B could return the car voluntarily and negotiate for the return of the purchase price. Suppose, though, that B wants to keep the car and S does not want it back. Besides S has already spent the payments B gave him.

In this case, the parties could work out an alternative arrangement acceptable to both that might come closer to what each wants. For example, B has a matured savings bond in the amount of $1,800 that he is willing to cash in for payment on the car, if S will agree to make that the final payment. The total payments would be $400 less than S is actually entitled to receive under the contract, but since S does not want the car back and realizes that he might otherwise have to wait a long time for his money or not get it at all, given B's financial troubles, this arrangement might be acceptable.

If the parties in Example 7.2 wanted to make an accord and satisfaction under these circumstances, they could. The accord and the satisfaction are actually two different transactions that together form the new agreement. First, if the parties agree the cashed-in savings bond will completely pay off B's debt on the car, this is the *accord*. Once the accord is *performed* and B actually turns the money over to S, this is the *satisfaction*. In other words, the **accord** is the agreement for a substituted performance, and the **satisfaction** is the performance of the accord.

Another common use of the accord and satisfaction is in the settlement of debts where the amount owed is in dispute. Such disputes often arise in connection with service or construction contracts.

Accord The agreement that a different performance will be substituted for the performance due under a contract.

Satisfaction The performance of an accord.

EXAMPLE 7.3

Contractor bills Homeowner a total of $50,000 for a renovation of Homeowner's summer home. Homeowner has paid Contractor $30,000 so far, and Contractor believes $20,000 more is owed. Homeowner believes there is an error in the bill and refuses to pay more than a total of $45,000. Homeowner thus believes only $15,000 is still owed. Contractor can, of course, choose to sue Homeowner, but he may not consider this the best option, particularly if Homeowner has some good arguments to support her position or if litigating over $5,000 seems too expensive. Instead Contractor and Homeowner could make an accord and satisfaction. For example, the parties could compromise and split the difference by agreeing that Homeowner only owes Contractor $17,500 more. Thus, under the accord, each party has given up half the disputed amount. When the final payment of $17,500 to Contractor is made, the satisfaction has taken place.

American jurisdictions have traditionally viewed the legal effect of an accord in two different ways. Some jurisdictions view the accord as a complete discharge of the promisor's duty under the original contract. Under this view, once the parties agree to a substitute transaction, they give up the right ever to insist or sue on the original transaction. Under this view of the accord, if a party fails to follow through with the satisfaction, the other party can only insist or sue on the arrangement involved in the accord. Other jurisdictions do not discharge a party's original contract debts or duties until the satisfaction is performed. A paralegal should research the law of the applicable jurisdiction to determine whether the accord or the satisfaction discharges the original contract performance.

Effect of Checks Marked "Payment in Full"

Unliquidated Debt
An uncertain or disputed amount of money owed.

Traditionally, a party who owed a disputed or undetermined amount of money (an **unliquidated debt**) could bring about an accord and satisfaction through use of a *full-payment check*. In other words, if one contracting party owed a disputed amount to the other contracting party, the debtor could send a check for *less than* the creditor was demanding. If the check bore the words "payment in full," the greater debt was discharged when the creditor cashed or deposited the check. This is considered to be a form of accord and satisfaction. Here the check is viewed as the offer for the accord, and depositing or cashing it as the acceptance and performance of the accord.

In modern law, this full-payment check rule for unliquidated debts has come under criticism. One problem is that a creditor who has pressing financial needs may be forced to cash or deposit the check, even if it is not a fair settlement of the debt. The creditor in these situations is between a rock and a hard place. If the creditor needs money badly, she will feel pressure to accept the lesser payment because at least some money will be immediately available. If the creditor accepts the payment, however, she risks waiving her right to the remainder of what she believes she is owed. To avoid harsh results, some courts now consider words such as "payment in full" to be only one of several factors to be used in determining what the parties intended. For example, the exact wording "payment in full" is not as important as whether the words and the situation reasonably appear to indicate an offer for an accord has been made.

Liquidated debt A certain or undisputed amount of money owed.

Where a debt is **liquidated**—that is, it involves a certain or undisputed amount—the courts are more reluctant to recognize an accord and satisfaction in full-payment check situations. Some courts hold that an accord and satisfaction takes place just as it would with an unliquidated debt. Many other courts, however, hold that an accord and satisfaction has not occurred, even though the creditor cashes or deposits the check. Thus, in many jurisdictions the full amount of the original debt is still owed after the creditor cashes or deposits the check, and there is no discharge of the duty to perform or pay the original amount owed.

Under the UCC, the rule about whether full-payment checks will discharge a contractual obligation is not so clear. UCC § 1-207 states:

(1) A party who with explicit reservation of rights performs or promises performance or assents to performance in a manner demanded or offered by the other party does not thereby prejudice the rights reserved. Such words as "without prejudice," "under protest" or the like are sufficient.

(2) Subsection (1) does not apply to an accord and satisfaction.

Because this section does not refer specifically to full-payment checks, the courts have struggled with whether § 1-207 applies to such checks. The meaning of the section is particularly mysterious in view of § 1-207(2), which exempts accord and satisfaction. As noted before, the common law treats full-payment checks as a form of accord and satisfaction. Some courts interpret § 1-207 to mean the creditor can prevent the entire debt from being discharged by writing specific words of reservation on the check. Other courts interpret § 1-207 to mean that the creditor cannot prevent the discharge of the entire debt if the check is cashed or deposited, even if he writes words of reservation on the check. In a particular case, a paralegal should be aware of the need to research how § 1-207 is applied in the relevant jurisdiction.

Discharge by Modification

A **modification** occurs when the parties to a contract mutually agree to change its terms in some way. Modifications can be viewed as a form of "discharge" because they often mean that duties of performance under the original terms of agreement are no longer required. Many legal issues may arise with regard to modifications. One concern is whether to require independent or additional consideration for the modification.

Modification An agreement between two contracting parties in which they mutually agree to change terms in the contract.

The requirement of independent consideration is thought to discourage forced modifications. A forced modification can occur if one contracting party is in a much stronger position than the other. By threatening the weaker party in various ways, the stronger party may be able to institute an involuntary modification of the contract to its own unfair advantage. This concern is the same one discussed with the preexisting duty rule. It is feared that the stronger party will extort more performance from the other party without doing any more in return. To discourage this, courts and legal scholars have long felt that requiring additional consideration was necessary. This, they feel, will force the stronger party to pay more if it wants more.

The following example illustrates some of the problems involved in modification.

EXAMPLE 7.4

Buyer and Seller of crude oil have a contract that requires Buyer to pay $10 per barrel. Seller produces the crude oil from lands entirely within the continental United States. Then, the OPEC countries decide to shut down oil production for a year. As a result, crude oil prices rise enormously. Although Seller can produce oil at exactly the same cost as before the production shutdown, it now wants the international market price, which is $50 a barrel. Seller still has a contractual obligation to sell to Buyer for $10 a barrel, however. Among the options Seller may consider is a form of what might be viewed as extortion in a contract context. Seller may simply threaten to deliver no more oil to Buyer until Buyer agrees to "modify" the contract to pay at least $40 per barrel.[2]

If Seller extracts such a "modification" from Buyer and the courts are willing to enforce it, stronger bargaining power will always undercut contractual arrangements in such circumstances. For this reason, the common law requires independent consideration for an effective modification. How would such independent consideration be given? In this case, the parties might agree that although Buyer will now pay $40 per barrel, the following terms will also be given to Buyer:

1. The oil will be of a better grade.
2. Seller will pay all shipping costs.
3. Buyer will have an irrevocable option to renew the contract on more favorable terms if the market price of crude oil drops below $25 per barrel.

Through these terms, Seller may be giving up something "additional" in return for Buyer's duty to pay the higher price. Thus, a court may find the modification is enforceable because both parties gave the necessary additional consideration.

To some degree, legal fictions can be involved in many situations in which independent consideration for a modification is found to be present. In Example 7.4, Buyer may not really be better off after the modification. A buyer who can obtain crude oil for $10 per barrel when everyone else has to pay $50 is in a position that is hard to improve. In addition, it may be difficult to evaluate whether the additional arrangements Seller is making are really worth $30 per barrel. Nevertheless, the courts are inclined to find the necessary independent or additional consideration in such cases. The reason probably has more to do with social policy concerns and economics than with contract theory. Allowing parties to adapt their agreements to changing markets and changing circumstances serves a useful commercial purpose. Without this flexibility, one or both parties may refuse to perform, and they may end up in litigation that could have been avoided by compromise. Thus, without this flexibility, parties might be unable to make long-term contracts, and this would have a profoundly dampening effect on commerce.

Under modern law, both the UCC and many state statutes now allow modifications to be effective without independent or additional consideration, if the parties make the modification in writing. This means that in UCC contracts and common-law contracts governed by such statutes, the preexisting duty rule and independent consideration requirements no longer provide protection from coerced modification. In these cases, other methods must be used to prevent contracting parties from seeking bad faith modification of contracts. The doctrines of duress and unconscionability, discussed elsewhere in this text, may both be available to help recover in coerced modification situations.

Discharge by Operation of Law

Discharge by Bankruptcy

Contractual debts can be discharged when a person declares bankruptcy. The right to declare bankruptcy and the effects are now controlled by federal law. Under the Federal Bankruptcy Act,[3] most kinds of contractual debts can be discharged. A full and specific explanation of which contractual debts are discharged is the topic of a course on bankruptcy. If a party to a contract declares bankruptcy, however, the paralegal should consider the possibility that debts owed under the contract are discharged. In this case, it would be necessary to explore the applicable bankruptcy rules. Some courts have viewed discharge in the case of bankruptcy as merely a "suspension" or "bar" of the duty to perform, but this distinction hardly matters. The effect is the same: private contractual debts are generally not enforceable against someone after she has declared bankruptcy.

Discharge by Statute of Limitations

A **statute of limitations** is a law that places a time limit on the right to file a lawsuit. There are various kinds of statutes of limitations. Most states have passed statutes that control how long someone has to file a lawsuit on a written or oral contract dispute. For example, § 213(2) of the New York Consolidated Laws provides that the following actions must be commenced within six years: "an action upon a contractual obligation or liability, express or implied. . . ."[4] Under New York law, if the six years mentioned in the statute have passed without the aggrieved party's filing a lawsuit, then the duty to perform on the contract may be discharged.

> **Statute of limitations** A law that places a time limit on the right to file a lawsuit.

Here again, one might debate whether the contractual duty is really being discharged or whether it still exists and is just unenforceable. In any event, the net result is the same. Unless extenuating circumstances exist, the parties usually cannot sue on a contract dispute once a statute of limitations has run.

The paralegal should be aware, however, that if a debtor makes a new promise to pay the debt barred by the statute of limitations, this *new* promise is enforceable. The old debt is still discharged or barred by the statute, but the new promise is enforceable up to the amount involved.

EXAMPLE **7.5**

If D owed C $500 on a contract and the statute of limitations ran without C's filing a lawsuit, the $500 debt is discharged. However, if D then suffers from feelings of remorse and promises to pay C $350, this new amount is enforceable. D would only have a duty to pay $500 if this was the amount stated in D's new promise.

Discharge by Full Performance

To some degree, the parties' full performance of their obligations under the contract can be thought of as a form of discharge; that is, the legal effect of full performance under a particular contract is that it "discharges" further obligation under the contract. In fact, this is probably the most common form of contractual discharge. As previously stated, most contracts do not result in unresolvable disputes that end up in litigation. In the majority of contracts, the parties perform acceptably to each other and go their ways. Sometimes the parties even maintain successful contractual relations for very long periods of time.

Discharge by Impossibility of Performance

Early English common law took a rather harsh view of events that made it impossible for contracting parties to perform. This view is summarized by the Latin phrase *pacta sunt servanda,* meaning that a promise must be kept even if it is impossible to perform. Nevertheless, the law eventually created exceptions to this rule, perhaps because its harshness caused discomfort. Ultimately, it seems unfair to hold someone responsible under a contract that has become impossible for him to perform.

Since the mid-1800s the courts have been struggling with why situations of **impossibility** should discharge contractual obligations. Several theories have been advanced, and many modifications of the theories have occurred. Under modern law, it is generally conceded that where a performance has become truly impossible, it is discharged or excused. The problem, of course, is to decide what is meant by impossibility.

The earliest idea was that to excuse performance, circumstances had to make the performance completely impossible. Furthermore, this impossibility had to be such that no one could complete performance. In other words, impossibility was viewed as objective. It was not enough that the particular promisor was unable to render or complete performance. For discharge to occur through the doctrine of impossibility, circumstances had to be such that no one else would be able to give or complete the performance.

Although it is probably still true that impossibility must be objective, it is no longer true that only complete impossibility excuses performance. Under modern American law, an additional doctrine of *impracticability* or *commercial impracticability* recognizes that performance need not be completely impossible for it to be excused. Under **impracticability,** performance may be excused if it is highly impractical or unreasonably burdensome for a party to render that performance. Circumstances that make it impossible or impracticable to render performance must be very different from those the parties assumed would exist during the life of the contract. Impossibility or impracticability must involve the occurrence of events whose *nonoccurrence* was a basic assumption underlying the contract. A famous example of such circumstances occurred in the following case.

Impossibility The situation where certain acts required under the contract have become objectively impossible.

Impracticability The situation where certain acts required under the contract are not impossible to perform, but can be done only with excessive or unreasonable efforts or costs.

A CASE FOR STUDY
Taylor v. Caldwell
122 Eng. Rep. 309 (1863)

The judgment of the court was now delivered by

BLACKBURN, J.   In this case the plaintiffs and defendants had, on 27th, 1861, entered into a contract by which the defendants agreed to let the plaintiffs have the use of The Surrey Gardens and Music Hall on four days then to come, viz., June 17th, July 15th, August 15th, and August 19th, for the purpose of giving a series of four grand concerts, and day and night fetes, at the Gardens and Hall on those days respectively; and the plaintiffs agreed to take the Gardens and Hall on those days, and pay £100 for each day.

[The court finds this agreement is not a lease arrangement and points out the importance of

the idea that without the use of the Music Hall, the entertainments that were the subject of the agreement could not take place.]

After the making of the agreement, and before the first day on which a concert was to be given, the Hall was destroyed by fire. This destruction, we must take it on the evidence, was without the fault of either party, and was so complete that in consequence the concerts could not be given as intended. And the question we have to decide is whether, under these circumstances, the loss which the plaintiffs have sustained is to fall upon the defendants. The parties when framing their agreement evidently had not present to their minds the possibility of such a disaster and have made no express stipulation with reference to it, so that the answer to the question must depend upon the general rules of law applicable to such a contract.

There seems no doubt that where there is a positive contract to do a thing, not in itself unlawful, the contractor must perform it or pay damages for not doing it, although in consequence of unforeseen accidents, the performance of his contract has become unexpectedly burthensome or even impossible. . . . But this rule is only applicable when the contract is positive and absolute, and not subject to any condition either express or implied; and there are authorities which, as we think, establish the principle that where, from the nature of the contract, it appears that the parties must from the beginning have known that it could not be fulfilled unless when the time for the fulfillment of the contract arrived some particular specified thing continued to exist, so that, when entering into the contract, they must have contemplated such continuing existence as the foundation of what was to be done; there, in the absence of any express or implied warranty that the thing shall exist, the contract is not to be construed as a positive contract, but as subject to an implied condition that the parties shall be excused in case, before breach, performance becomes impossible from the perishing of the thing without default of the contractor.

There seems little doubt that this implication tends to further the great object of making the legal construction such as to fulfill the intention of those who entered into the contract. For in the course of affairs men in making such contracts in general would if it were brought to their minds, say that there should be such a condition. . . .

There is a class of contracts in which a person binds himself to do something which requires to be performed by him in person; and such promises, e.g. promises to marry, or promises to serve for a certain time, are never in practice qualified by an express exception of the death of the party; and therefore in such cases the contract is in terms broken if the promisor dies before fulfillment. Yet it was very early determined that, if the performance is personal, the executors are not liable. . . .

There are instances where the implied con-

dition is of the life of a human being, but there are others in which the same implication is made as to the continued existence of a thing. For example, where a contract of sale is made amounting to a bargain and sale, transferring presently the property in specific chattels, which are to be delivered to the vendor at a future day; there, if the chattels, without the fault of the vendor, perish in the interval, the purchaser must pay the price and the vendor is excused from performing his contract to deliver, which has become impossible. . . .

It may, we think, be safely asserted to be now English law, that in all contracts of loan of chattels or bailments if the performance of the promise of the borrower or bailee to return the things lent or bailed, becomes impossible because it has perished, this impossibility (if not arising from the fault of the borrower or bailee from some risk which he has taken upon himself) excuses the borrower or bailee from the performance of his promise to redeliver the chattel. . . . The principle seems to us to be that, in contracts in which the performance depends upon the continued existence of a given person or thing, a condition is implied that the impossibility of performance arising from the perishing of the person or thing shall excuse the performance.

In none of these cases is the promise in words other than positive, nor is there any express stipulation that the destruction of the person or thing shall excuse the performance; but that excuse is by law implied, because from the nature of the contract it is apparent that the parties contracted on the basis of the continued existence of the particular person or chattel. In the present case, looking at the whole contract, we find that the parties contracted on the basis of the continued existence of the Music Hall at the time when the concerts were to be given, that being essential to their performance.

We think, therefore, that the Music Hall having ceased to exist, without fault of either party, both parties are excused, the plaintiffs from taking the gardens and paying the money, the defendants from performing their promise to give the use of the Hall and Gardens and other things. Consequently the rule must be absolute to enter the verdict for the defendants.

Rule absolute.

Questions to Consider

1. Were any conditional duties involved in this contract? If so, what were they and were the conditions express or implied?
2. What does the court see as the relationship between conditions and excuse of performance based on impossibility?
3. Based on this case, how might impossibility be defined?
4. Could this case also illustrate impracticability? Why or why not?

In a number of specific situations, courts tend to find performance is excused on the grounds of impossibility or impracticability. Remember that in each individual case, it still must be shown that circumstances make it objectively impossible for the promisor to perform, that the promisor has not assumed the risk of the events occurring, and that nonoccurrence of these events was a basic assumption of the contract. In the following circumstances, however, a finding of impossibility or impracticability is likely:

1. Supervening destruction of the subject matter, including failure of the subject matter to come into being.

   EXAMPLE 7.6   Farmer agrees with Supermarket to sell corn from his fields to Supermarket. A fire rages through all of Farmer's fields, destroying all the corn, or the seeds planted are defective and no corn grows. Farmer's performance would be excused as impossible.

2. Supervening illegality or government acts.

   EXAMPLE 7.7   City passes a zoning ordinance that makes it illegal to operate industrial plants in the Elm Street District. Contractor's contract with Property Owner provides that Contractor will build a tomato canning factory on Elm Street. The construction has now become illegal, and thus the parties' performances under the contract are discharged.

3. Failure of a specific and exclusive source of supply.

   EXAMPLE 7.8   Farmer makes a contract with Supermarket. Farmer is to sell to Supermarket "all wheat from the South Field." The South Field becomes polluted from the recycling plant nearby, and no wheat matures in the field. Farmer's duty to perform by selling wheat from the South Field is discharged. (Note: This excuse of performance might also occur on grounds of illegality if the polluted wheat did mature but was illegal to sell.)

4. Destruction of a repair or remodel project.

   EXAMPLE 7.9   Contractor is hired to renovate Restaurant Chez Snob. Chez Snob burns down during the renovation process. Contractor's performance (completion of renovation) is discharged.
   Note that the result is different where the construction project is not renovation, but new construction. *Destruction of new construction usually does not discharge the contractor's duty to perform.*

   EXAMPLE 7.10   School District hires Contractor to build an elementary school. When the project is half completed, it burns down. Contractor must rebuild and complete the project. His duty to perform is not discharged. (His duty to perform *on time* may be discharged, however, because of the fire.)

Under modern law, the differences in when destruction of a construction project discharges performance probably have to do with insurance practices. Generally, the owner is expected to insure a remodel, and its destruction thus relieves the contractor of liability for performance. Contractors are usually expected to insure new projects, however, and therefore they have liability for destruction of the project.

5. Destruction of goods *before* the risk of loss has passed.

EXAMPLE 7.11   Buyer and Seller make a contract in New York to sell four thousand Bentley apple-coring machines. Seller procures such machines from its supplier in Maine. Seller's storage warehouse is struck by lightning, and all machines are ruined. The risk of loss has not yet passed to Buyer, and thus Seller must absorb the loss. Buyer's duty to perform is discharged.

Note that the UCC contains several rules on when the risk of loss passes to the buyer. Destruction of goods must occur *before* the risk of loss passes to the buyer to discharge the buyer's obligations under the contract. To briefly summarize when risk of loss passes to the buyer:

- **Shipped goods generally.** Risk of loss passes when goods are delivered to the carrier or means of transportation.
- **Shipped goods to be delivered to a particular destination.** Risk of loss passes when goods are delivered or tendered to the buyer *at that destination*.
- **No shipment required and seller is a merchant.** Risk of loss passes when the buyer actually receives the goods.
- **No shipment required and seller is not a merchant.** Risk of loss passes when the seller tenders delivery (makes the goods immediately available).

The UCC makes use of a common commercial term, F.O.B., to determine whether the buyer or the seller has this risk of loss. F.O.B. means "free on board" and is a delivery term. For example, if the contract provides that delivery is to be "F.O.B. the place of shipment," the seller must assume the responsibility and the expense of placing the goods in possession of the carrier. Thus, the risk of loss passes to the buyer only when the seller has done this. If the contract provides that delivery is to be "F.O.B. the place of destination," the seller must assume the full responsibility and expense of transporting the goods, or having them transported, to that destination and making them available to the buyer. Here the risk of loss remains with the seller and does not pass to the buyer until the goods are available to the buyer. If the contract provides that delivery is to be "F.O.B. vessel" or "F.O.B. car" (or other vehicle), then the seller must not only arrange and pay for shipping, but must also load the goods on board the vessel or vehicle named by the buyer. Risk of loss passes to the buyer only after the seller loads the goods.

A similar delivery term, F.A.S., means "free alongside" and is often used in reference to shipping arrangements on navigable waters. For example, if the contract provides that delivery is to be "F.A.S. vessel," the seller must deliver the goods alongside the vessel, but has no responsibility to load them. The risk of loss thus passes to the buyer once the goods are delivered and ready to load.

6. Death or severe personal illness of the party who was to render services under a personal services contract.

EXAMPLE 7.12   M is a famous quilt maker. She contracts with Folk Art Museum to design and make a quilt within one year to celebrate Museum's fifty-year anniversary. M has a bad fall and breaks both arms. Her doctors do surgery and say she cannot quilt again for at least eighteen months. M's duty to make the quilt for Museum is discharged.

Temporary and Partial Impossibility or Impracticability

If a particular set of circumstances renders a performance only partially impossible or partially impracticable, then performance is still due to the extent possible or practicable. *Partial impossibility* or *partial impracticability* refers to a situation where part of the contract performance cannot be given, but some performance is still possible or practicable. The portion of the contract performance affected by impossibility or impracticability is excused, but the portion that is still possible or practicable must be given, unless this would be useless or close to it. Stated another way, if the part of the contract performance that is still possible or practicable amounts to at least substantial performance on the contract as a whole, this performance is not excused.

EXAMPLE   7.13

House Painter is to paint Homeowner's house and garage, but the garage unexpectedly (and through no fault of the parties) burns down right after the parties sign the contract and before painter has done anything. The duty to paint the garage would be excused here because it has become impossible. Whether the *entire* painting performance, which includes the house, is discharged depends on whether painting the house alone constitutes substantial performance of the contract. If the garage was a relatively minor part of the job and the house was the main task, House Painter's performance would be only partially discharged (no duty to paint the garage), and the remainder of the performance would still be owed (duty to paint the house).

If the impracticability or impossibility is of a temporary nature, the duty to perform can simply be suspended rather than discharged permanently. Of course, some difficult issues can arise with regard to temporary impracticability or impossibility since contracting parties do not always define "temporary" the same way. If a "temporary" set of circumstances makes performance impossible or impracticable, the parties can have a dispute about whether the "temporary" impossibility is lasting too long to justify keeping the promisor on the hook.

A famous example of this situation occurred in *Autry v. Republic Productions,* 30 Cal. 2d 144, 180 P.2d 888 (1947), a case involving the "singing cowboy," Gene Autry. When Autry was drafted into the army to fight in World War II, he had a contract with Republic Productions to perform in several films. The contract included some renewal options that meant it might run for several more years if Republic exercised the options. Autry was drafted in 1942 and did not return home until 1945. Republic then wanted to reinstate the contract, including the options. Autry claimed his duties under the contract were permanently discharged because three years had gone by and many changes had taken place. Republic claimed Autry's duty to make movies had been only temporarily suspended. The court sided with Autry, finding that so many circumstances had changed while he was in the army that he would be severely disadvantaged if he continued under the contract. The court held that Autry's performance under the contract was permanently discharged.

Courts in this situation often find there is a permanent discharge only if the hardship caused by the delayed performance is substantial. Without such hardship, a contracting party is normally required to resume performance once the impossibility or impracticability is resolved. If the hardship is not too great, the impossibility or impracticability may be characterized as only temporary, and any excuse from performance would be only temporary.

Discharge by Frustration of Purpose

Discharge of a contract through **frustration of purpose** is a relatively modern doctrine in contract law. Essentially, this doctrine allows for discharge of the duty to perform under a contract when the contract itself can no longer be substantially carried out for the purpose for which it was formed. The doctrine differs from impossibility or impracticability in that the disputed performance is usually still possible, but it has become pointless, at least from the aggrieved party's point of view. To successfully argue that frustration of purpose excuses performance, it must be shown that performance has become useless or almost useless. One of the most famous cases to illustrate the doctrine follows.

Frustration of purpose The doctrine under which contractual duties to perform are discharged because changed circumstances demonstrate that the contract can no longer be carried out for its essential purpose.

A CASE FOR STUDY
Krell v. Henry
2 King's Bench 740 (1903)

[Under a written contract made on June 20, 1902, Henry agreed to rent from Krell, a flat on Pall Mall for June 26 and 27. Henry rented the flat because of an official public announcement that the coronation of King Edward VII would take place on those days. The official announcement also described the coronation route as passing along Pall Mall. Henry paid Krell £25 down and agreed to pay him £50 later. However, the king became seriously ill, and the coronation did not take place on June 26 and 27. The written contract made no specific mention of the coronation or any other purpose for which the flat was rented. However, Henry had found out about the flat because several days before the ill-fated coronation, Krell had placed a sign in the flat's windows that advertised good views for the coronation procession. Krell demanded from Henry the remaining £50 of the rent, and Henry declined to pay. Krell then sued. The trial court found for Henry, and Krell, the landlord, appealed.]

Vaughan Williams, L.J. The real question in this case is the extent of the application in English law of the principle of the Roman law which has been adopted and acted on in many English decisions, and notably in the case of Taylor v. Caldwell. . . . I do not think that the principle of the civil law as introduced into the English law is limited to cases in which the event causing the impossibility of performance is the destruction or non-existence of some

A CASE FOR STUDY
Krell v. Henry
2 King's Bench 740 (1903)

thing which is the subject matter of the contract or of some condition or state of things expressly specified as a condition of it. I think that you first have to ascertain, not necessarily from the terms of the contract, but, if required, from necessary inferences, drawn from surrounding circumstances recognized by both contracting parties, what is the substance of the contract, and then to ask the question whether that substantial contract needs for its foundation the assumption of the existence of a particular state of things. If it does, this will limit the operation of the general words, and in such case, if the contract becomes impossible of performance by reason of the non-existence of the state of things assumed by both contracting parties as the foundation of the contract, there will be no breach of the contract thus limited. Now what are the facts of the case. . . . [The court sets out the facts summarized above.]

In my judgment the use of the rooms was let and taken for the purpose of seeing the Royal procession. It was not a demise of the rooms, or even an agreement to let and take the rooms. It is a licence to use rooms for a particular purpose and none other. And in my judgment the taking place of those processions on the days proclaimed along the proclaimed route, which passed 56A, Pall Mall, was regarded by both contracting parties as the foundation of the contract; and I think that it cannot reasonably be supposed to have been in the contemplation of the contracting parties, when the contract was made, that the coronation would not be held on the proclaimed days, or the processions not take place on those days along the proclaimed route; and I think that the words imposing on the defendant the obligation to accept and pay for the use of the rooms for the named days, although general and unconditional, were not used with reference to the possibility of the particular contingency which afterwards occurred.

It was suggested in the course of the argument that if the occurrence, on the proclaimed days, of the coronation and the procession in this case were the foundation of the contract, and if the general words are thereby limited or qualified, so that in the event of the non-occurrence of the coronation and procession along the proclaimed route they would discharge both parties from further performance of the contract, it would follow that if a cabman was engaged to take someone to Epsom on Derby Day at a suitable enhanced price for such a journey, say £10, both parties to the contract would be discharged in the contingency of the race at Epsom for some reason becoming impossible; but I do not think this follows, for I do not think that in the cab case the happening of the race would be the foundation of the contract. No doubt the purpose of the engager would be to go to see the Derby, and the price would be proportionately high; but the cab had no special qualification for this particular occasion. Any other cab would have done as well. . . . Whereas in the case of the coronation, there is not merely the purpose of the hirer to see the coronation procession, but it is the basis of the contract as much for the lessor as the hirer; and I think that if the King, before the coronation day and after the contract, had died, the hirer could not have insisted on having the rooms on the days named. It could not in the cab case be reasonably said that seeing the Derby race was the foundation of the contract, as it was of the licence in this case. Whereas in the present case, where the rooms were offered and taken, by reason of their peculiar suitability from the position of the rooms for a view of the coronation procession, surely the view of the coronation procession was the foundation of the contract, which is a very different thing from the purpose of the man who engaged the cab—namely, to see the race—being held to be the foundation of the contract.

Each case must be judged by its own circumstances. In each case one must ask oneself, first, what, having regard to all the circumstances, was the foundation of the contract? Secondly, was the performance of the contract prevented? Thirdly, was the event which prevented the performance of the contract of such a character that it cannot reasonably be said to have been in the contemplation of the parties at the date of the contract? If all these questions are answered in the affirmative (as I think they should be in this case), I think both parties are discharged from further performance of the contract. . . .

Appeal dismissed.

Questions to Consider

1. Looking at the written contract alone, was the real purpose of the contract clear? Why or why not?
2. If the purpose of a contract is not clear from its express provisions, what part can circumstances surrounding the bargain play in interpreting its meaning?
3. If you were a paralegal for Henry's attorney, what evidence would you have prepared to submit at trial to prove the real purpose of the contract?
4. What facts of the case were most important to the outcome? If you were a paralegal for the attorneys on either side, what evidence would you have prepared to submit at trial to establish these facts?
5. What does the court mean in asserting that the case of the flat rental and the case of the cab rental for Derby Day are different? Explain.
6. Based on this opinion, how might frustration of purpose be defined, and when does it excuse performance?

Consistently with *Krell v. Henry,* it can be seen that frustration discharges performance when there are (1) supervening circumstances not foreseen by the parties, and (2) such circumstances destroy or materially impair the value of the contract, as it was understood by both parties. Note that if there is still substantial value that can be obtained from the contract in the way the parties intended, the performance usually is not discharged.

Assignment

For each of the following hypothetical situations:

1. State which form (or forms) of discharge would most likely be available, if any.
2. Explain why this form (or forms) of discharge is available, or why discharge is not available.

► Hypothetical 1

Joe and Jennie make a contract under which Jennie is to perform part-time marketing services for Joe's landscaping business. Under the contract, Jennie is to receive a weekly increase of $10 per week for every new client she brings in. Her base salary is $100 per week. In the first six months of their arrangement, Jennie brings in six new clients who, in turn, bring Joe $1,000 per week in additional income. Jennie now wishes to change their arrangement so that she will get 10 percent of all gross profits from clients she brings in. Jennie is proving so effective at marketing that two other landscaping firms are seeking her services.

► Hypothetical 2

Dairy Farmer makes a contract with Breeder to purchase fifty Guernsey calves when they are born in the spring. The calves will consist of five bull calves and forty-five heifers. The calves are to be delivered to Dairy Farmer when they are six months old. The provisions of the contract call for Breeder to load all the calves on the train and deliver them to Dairy Farmer's place of business, Happy Dairy Farms. Shortly after the contract is signed, Breeder discovers that all his cows have a form of hoof and mouth disease, which means they will risk producing infected offspring if they get pregnant this season. Breeder's veterinarian is confident all the cows can get pregnant next season. Dairy Farmer is still interested in doing business with Breeder because Breeder's Guernsey cows are exceptionally fine and known to be superior milk producers.

▶ Hypothetical 3

Bart and Sally agree to the sale of Sally's five-acre tract of undeveloped land in Columbia County, State of Columbia. The contract price is $1 million. Bart is to make a down payment of $100,000 within thirty days of the date of execution of the contract. Then, ninety days after execution of the contract, Bart is to pay the first of nine monthly payments of $100,000. Thirty days from the date of the last monthly payment, Bart is to pay 10 percent straight interest on the $1 million purchase price, or $100,000. Thus, the entire transaction is to take one year to complete. Bart hopes to use the land to develop a commercial and industrial complex.

Ten days after the parties sign their contract, however, the Columbia state legislature passes a Master Plan that restricts the area where Sally's tract of land is located to light industrial use. Bart still would like the land, but he has to reconsider his plans for the commercial and industrial park to meet the requirements of the new Master Plan. After consulting with a number of independent real estate appraisers, Bart thinks the change in allowable uses has reduced the overall market value of the land by about one-fourth.

Chapter Review Questions

1. In what ways may contract performance be discharged? Explain each briefly.
2. Which forms of discharge are available if some contract performance has already taken place?
3. What effect does a check marked payment in full have on the duty to pay a debt?
4. What are the requirements for a modification under the common law and under the UCC, and how do they differ?
5. Under the UCC, when would destruction of goods discharge the buyer's contractual obligation to pay for them?
6. What are the similarities and differences between the doctrines of impossibility and impracticability?
7. When does frustration of purpose discharge contract performance?

Key Terms

Accord, 139
Excuse/discharge of performance, 135
Executed contract, 136
Executory contract, 136
Frustration of purpose, 149
Impossibility, 144
Impracticability, 144
Liquidated debt, 140
Modification, 141

Mutual release, 137
Novation, 138
Release, 136
Releasee, 137
Releasor, 137
Rescission, 135
Satisfaction, 139
Statute of limitations, 143
Unliquidated debt, 140

Notes

1. See, e.g., California Civil Code § 1541 (West 1982).
2. *Eastern Airlines, Inc. v. Gulf Oil Corp.,* 415 F.Supp. 429 (S.D. Fla. 1979).
3. See 11 U.S.C.A. §§ 101 et. seq. (West 1993).
4. N.Y. Civ. Prac. L. & R. § 213(2) (Consol. 1988).

PART

III

Contract Defenses

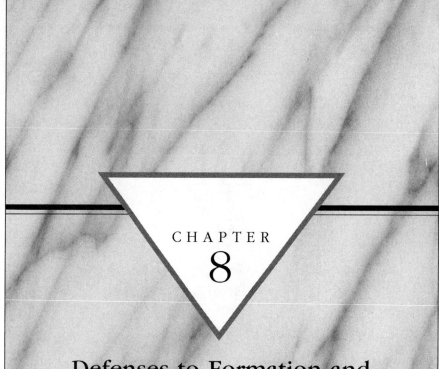

CHAPTER
8

Defenses to Formation and Enforcement

LEARNING OBJECTIVES FOR THIS CHAPTER:
WHAT YOU SHOULD KNOW!

❒ What a defense to formation is.
❒ What a defense to enforcement is.
❒ Differences between claims and defenses.
❒ What is meant by pleading in the alternative.
❒ Definition and use of the defense of indefiniteness.
❒ What is meant by implication and interpretation of contract terms.
❒ How UCC "gap-filler" provisions are used.
❒ Definitions and use of the defenses based on mistake.

Introduction to Contract Defenses

Any argument can be a **defense** if the defendant uses it to assert he does not have liability for the plaintiff's grievances. Some defenses have been used so frequently in contract litigation that they have become well-developed doctrines. Generally, these defenses use one of the following broad theories to deny liability: (1) no contract was formed because the parties never reached agreement, (2) although a contract was formed it is unenforceable, or (3) performance under the contract is not required because it has been discharged or excused. Exhibit 8.1 summarizes these defenses.

The defenses asserting that performance was discharged or excused were discussed in Chapter 7. Remember that if a party believes performance under the contract has been excused or discharged in some way, this can be raised as a defense in a lawsuit. If such a defense is to be successful, the defendant must fulfill the requirements of the particular type of discharge as discussed in Chapter 7.

Discharge and excuse of performance have been briefly reintroduced here as a reminder that these doctrines can be used as contract defenses. The use of discharge and excuse of performance in litigation is similar to the use of the other defenses listed in Exhibit 8.1.

Defense A theory the defendant in a lawsuit uses to assert he does not have liability for the plaintiff's grievances.

EXAMPLE 8.1

Assume Landlord is suing Tenant 1 for the remainder of the rent on a two-year lease. Tenant 1 believes Landlord agreed to a novation, with Tenant 2 taking over the lease and agreeing to pay the rent. If this is true, Tenant 1 might use this novation as a defense against Landlord in the lawsuit. In *Landlord v. Tenant 1,* Tenant 1 will argue that performance under the contract was discharged by novation. Thus, Tenant 1 would not dispute that a contract (the lease) was formed. Instead, Tenant 1 would argue that performance under the original lease was not required because the novation had discharged her duty to perform. As previously noted, to use novation successfully as a defense, Tenant 1 must show that the requirements for a legally enforceable novation were met. If a novation can be shown to have taken place under the law of the relevant jurisdiction and the facts of her case, Tenant 1 can use novation as a defense to deny liability under the contract.

The doctrines of discharge and excuse of performance were covered in Chapter 7 and are not discussed further here. This Chapter and Chapter 9 focus on other classic arguments used as defenses to the formation and enforcement of contracts. One of these defenses, the Statute of Frauds, is the subject of a separate chapter, Chapter 10.

The Shield Versus the Sword

Students sometimes find it difficult to understand that many arguments used as defenses may also be used as *causes of action,* or *claims,* by a plaintiff. As a defense, fraud might be used in the following way.

EXHIBIT 8.1

Contract Defenses

DEFENSES USED TO ARGUE THAT NO FORMATION HAS TAKEN PLACE OR THAT THE CONTRACT IS UNENFORCEABLE

- Indefiniteness
- Duress
- Undue influence
- Fraud, misrepresentation, concealment
- Statue of Frauds
- Lack of capacity to contract
- Illegality
- Unconscionability
- Mistake

DEFENSES USED TO ARGUE NO PERFORMANCE UNDER THE CONTRACT IS REQUIRED BECAUSE IT HAS BEEN DISCHARGED OR EXCUSED

- Performance was subject to a condition.
- The right to performance was waived.
- Performance was excused because of impossibility (or impracticability).
- Performance was discharged because of frustration.
- Performance was discharged on grounds such as modification, novation, or rescission.

EXAMPLE 8.2

A procures a contract with B through fraud. A (the fraudulent party) managed to get a very good deal out of the transaction at the expense of B (the defrauded party). B later realizes how disadvantageous the contract is and suspects A's fraud. B therefore refuses to perform on the contract. Although it was A who committed the fraud, A may sue to enforce their agreement. This result is especially likely because A obtained a good deal and may want to press her advantage. A may be willing to risk that the fraud will come to light or may even deny that the fraud occurred. If A sues B for breach of the contract or sues to enforce the contract, B is entitled to raise A's fraud as a *defense* in the lawsuit.

Cause of action/claim An argument made by the plaintiff in a lawsuit in which the plaintiff alleges that she suffered wrongs because of the other party's words or conduct.

As a claim or cause of action, A's fraud would be used differently. A contract **cause of action,** or **claim,** is an argument made by the plaintiff in which she alleges that she suffered wrongs because of the other contracting party's words or conduct. In some circumstances, the defrauded party may want to beat the other party to the punch and sue for rescission of the contract before being sued for breach or enforcement. Thus, if B in Example 2 sues to rescind the contract, the plaintiff "victim" is using fraud as a cause of action or claim, not as a defense. In that case, B would use the accusation of fraud to try to have the contract rescinded.

This dual use of a theory as a claim or as a defense is sometimes referred to as the "sword" (cause of action, or claim) versus the "shield" (defense). Whether a doctrine is used offensively (as a sword) or defensively (as a shield) may depend on who sues first. In some cases, both parties may use the doctrine in countersuits. The paralegal student should keep in mind that many defenses can also be used as causes of action, or claims. Whether used as a claim, cause of action, or defense, the requirements of the doctrines themselves remain the same.

Pleading "In the Alternative"

If a particular doctrine is used as a defense, it may be used as a defense to formation, to enforcement, or to both. This is because American law recognizes *pleading in the alternative.* **Pleading in the alternative** occurs when a party to a lawsuit advances arguments that conflict with one another. Thus, suppose A, the alleged perpetrator of the fraud in Example 2, sued to enforce the contract with B. The defendant B, the alleged victim of the fraud, could defend against the lawsuit by arguing either (1) that no contract was formed or (2) that although a contract was formed, it is unenforceable. That is what is meant by making alternative arguments. It is logically inconsistent to argue that no contract was formed and then argue that one was formed but should not be enforced. To make the second argument, the party must admit the first one is not true.

A party is permitted to advance inconsistent or "alternative" arguments at the beginning of litigation. Ultimately, though, the party can recover on only one of the inconsistent theories. Thus, B initially advances the inconsistent arguments that *the contract was not formed* and that *the contract was formed but is unenforceable.* One of these arguments must be found valid for B to prevail in his lawsuit or to successfully defend against A in A's lawsuit. If A eventually proves that she did not obtain the contract by fraud and that *formation occurred,* B has a "fallback" argument: he is not liable because the fraud should *prevent contract enforcement.*

Pleading in the alternative is a sensible solution to the realities of litigation. Normally, a party files a lawsuit without having all the information needed to pursue the suit. Sometimes this is because the statute of limitations may run unless the lawsuit is filed. Even without pressure from a statute of limitations, however, parties often need the help of *discovery procedures* to obtain information in the possession of the other party.

Discovery is the official information-gathering stage in litigation and begins after the lawsuit is filed. **Discovery procedures** are often designed to compel, or attempt to compel, the opposing party to disclose relevant information. Because few parties voluntarily disclose incriminating evidence, many discovery procedures are designed to deal with this problem. Pleading in the alternative allows a party to make a plausible argument before he has all the information necessary to substantiate the argument. Then, as more information is acquired during discovery, or even at trial, these arguments can be changed and adapted. Arguments not supported by the facts can be dropped.

Note that making *arguments that are inconsistent with each other* (pleading in the alternative) is not the same thing as making *consistent arguments that advance different grounds for recovery.* For example, B may have other grievances against A arising out of their contract relationship. B's property may have been damaged through A's negligence on the job, or B may believe A's conduct has violated a statute. Most lawsuits involve several different theories of recovery and several different claims arising out of the same set of circumstances or transaction.

Pleading in the alternative The practice in which a party to a lawsuit advances arguments that conflict with one another.

Discovery After a lawsuit is filed, the official information-gathering stage or period of time.

Discovery procedures After a lawsuit is filed, the methods used to obtain information in the possession of the other party or to compel, or attempt to compel, the opposing party to disclose relevant information.

The Defense of Indefiniteness

In General

Indefiniteness The situation in which some necessary information is missing from an alleged contract.

Indefiniteness, which was first discussed in Chapter 2 in connection with formation, means that necessary information is missing from a contract. Because missing contract information can be troublesome, the law requires the parties to exchange sufficient information during the formation process. This is one rationale for the traditional common-law rule that an offer for a contract must not only be communicated and clearly manifest a present contractual intent, but must be "certain and definite." The drafters of the UCC addressed the requirement of definiteness in § 2-204 by providing that a contract for sale of goods cannot be formed unless it is clear "the parties intended to make a contract and there is a reasonably certain basis for giving an appropriate remedy." Where the information in an offer or in the UCC formation process is insufficient, no formation can take place. If one party tries to enforce the alleged contract, the other party can raise the defense that no formation took place because information was missing. In that case, indefiniteness is a defense to formation.

In other contract situations, problems with indefiniteness arise later than the formation stage. In that case, indefiniteness is more likely to be a defense to enforcement. How can parties believe they have formed a contract yet fail to include all the information needed? Such situations have more to do with human nature than with the law. Unfortunately, people do not always spell out their assumptions, or they believe the other party thinks the way they do. Sometimes, in the pressure and hurry of the business world, people simply forget important details. People may not realize information is missing from their agreement until after they finish negotiating. This can occur when the parties try to put together a single written agreement from various forms, or drafts, or from correspondence that went back and forth. Sometimes the missing information becomes apparent only when one party performs and the other claims the performance is incorrect or incomplete. Problems of indefiniteness can also occur where performance is done in stages and difficulties arise in a later stage, or where one party deliberately withheld information in order not to "scare off" the other.

Whether missing information indicates no contract was formed or prevents later enforcement of a contract depends on a number of factors. Generally, the more detail included in the alleged contract between the parties, the more likely a final agreement was reached. Although a high level of detail is not conclusive proof a contract was made, contracting parties generally want to know what they are getting into; they tend to want their own rights and obligations and those of the other party spelled out. When such details are missing, it may be because the negotiating process fell apart before the contract was formed. In that case, information is missing because a complete deal and a complete agreement never took place. In other cases, the technical requirements of formation were met, but it later turns out that crucial information was omitted. Here, indefiniteness is more likely to be a defense to enforcement. Refusing enforcement of an indefinite contract is practical because the parties are unlikely to render satisfactory performance in the absence of crucial information. In that case, it matters little that the contract technically was formed.

The Process of Implication

If it becomes apparent that information is missing from the alleged contract because no formation took place, there can be no contract. If a contract was formed, however, the contract may still be enforceable even though it lacks some information. You should not assume that missing information automatically means a contract is too indefinite for enforcement. Whether enforcement can occur depends on how important the missing information is and on whether it can be reasonably and reliably determined. In theory, certain kinds of missing information could be fairly easily supplied.

EXAMPLE **8.3**

Suppose S agrees to deliver 5,000 red, heart-shaped balloons to B's place of business for the Valentine's Day holiday and the contract price is $2,500. The *time for performance* (delivery date and time of day) are missing from the express terms of the contract, but this omission need not be fatal. The time for delivery could be assumed to be a "reasonable" date and time; that is, S could be required to deliver the balloons during business hours, before Valentine's Day, and in time to be used effectively in B's Valentine's Day sales. Although the parties did not expressly state these terms, the buyer likely wanted the Valentine's Day articles in time to use them for the holiday, not after, and probably expected delivery during normal business hours.

Over the centuries, courts have developed a process for supplying missing but necessary terms in a contract. Called **implication,** this process enables a court to place missing information in a contract. If implication were used for the contract in Example 3, the indefiniteness would presumably not be a valid defense to formation or enforcement. Formation appears to have taken place, and since the time for performance can be implied, the missing information can be supplied. Note in the following case how the court implies some information into the contract but refuses to imply other information.

Implication The process by which a court supplies missing information for a contract according to the parties' intent.

A CASE FOR STUDY
Haines v. New York
41 N.Y.2d, 364 N.E.2d 820 (1977)

GABRIELLI, Judge. In the early 1920's, respondent City of New York and intervenors Town of Hunter of Tannersville embarked upon negotiations for the construction of a sewage system to serve the village and a portion of the town. These negotiations were prompted by the city's need and desire to prevent the discharge of untreated sewage by residents of the area into Gooseberry Creek, a stream which fed a reservoir of the city's water supply system in the Schoharie watershed.

In 1923, the Legislature enacted enabling legislation authorizing the city to enter into contracts with municipalities in the watershed area "for the purpose of providing, maintaining [and] operating systems and plants for the collection and disposal of sewage" . . . . The statute further provided that any such contracts would be subject to the approval of the New York City Board of Estimate and Apportionment.

The negotiations culminated in an agreement in 1924 between the city and intervenors. By this agreement, the city assumed the obligation of constructing a sewage system consisting of a sewage disposal plant and sewer mains and laterals, and agreed that "all costs of construction and subsequent operation, maintenance and repair of said sewage system with the house connections thereof and said disposal works shall be at the expense" of the city. The agreement also required the city to extend the sewer lines when "necessitated by future growth and building constructions of the respective communities." The village and town were obligated to and did obtain the necessary easements for the construction of the system and sewage lines.

The Board of Estimate, on December 9, 1926, approved the agreement and authorized the issuance of $500,000 of "corporate stock" of the City of New York for construction of the system by appropriate resolution. It is interesting to here note that a modification of the original agreement occurred in 1925 wherein the village agreed to reimburse the city for a specified amount representing the expense of changing the location of certain sewer lines. The plant was completed and commenced operation in 1928. The city has continued to maintain the plant through the ensuing years and in 1958 expended $193,000 to rehabilitate and expand the treatment plant and facilities.

Presently, the average flow of the plant has increased from an initial figure of 118,000 gallons per day to over 600,000 gallons daily and the trial court found that the plant "was operating substantially in excess of design capacity." The city asserts, and it is not disputed by any of the parties in this action, that the system cannot bear any significant additional "loadings" because this would result in inadequate treatment of all the sewage and consequently harm the city's water supply. The instant controversy arose when plaintiff, who is the owner of a tract of unimproved land which he seeks to develop into 50 residential lots, applied to the city for permission to connect houses, which he intends to construct on the lots, to existing sewer lines. The city refused permission on the ground that it had no obligation to further expand the plant, which is presently operating at full capacity, to accommodate this new construction.

Plaintiff then commenced this action for declaratory and injunctive relief, in which intervenors town and village joined as plaintiffs, maintaining that the 1924 agreement is perpetual in duration and obligates the city to expend additional capital funds to enlarge the existing plant or build a new one to accommodate the present and future needs of the municipalities. Both the trial court and the Appellate Division, by a divided court, held in favor of plaintiff and intervenors concluding, that, while the contract did not call for perpetual performance, the city was bound to construct additional facilities to meet increased demand until such time as the village or town is legally obligated to maintain a sewage disposal system. Two members of the court dissented in part stating that the agreement should not be construed as requiring the city to construct new or additional facilities.

We conclude the city is presently obligated to maintain the existing plant but is not required to expand that plant or construct any new facilities to accommodate plaintiff's substantial, or any other, increased demands on the sewage system. The initial problem encountered in ascertaining the nature and extent of the city's obligation pursuant to the 1924 agreement is its duration. We reject, as did the courts below, the plaintiff's contention that the city is perpetually bound under the agreement. The contract did not expressly provide for perpetual performance and both the trial court and the Appellate Division found that the parties did not so intend. Under these circumstances, the law will not imply that a contract calling for continuing performance is perpetual in duration. [Citations]

On the other hand, the city's contention that the contract is terminable at will because it provides for no express duration should also be rejected. In the absence of an express term fixing the duration of a contract, the courts may inquire into the intent of the parties and supply the missing term if a duration may be fairly and reasonably fixed by the surrounding circumstances and the parties' intent [Citations].

While we have not previously had occasion to apply it, the weight of authority supports the related rule that where the parties have not clearly expressed the duration of a contract, the courts will imply that they intended performance to continue for a reasonable time [Citations]. For compelling policy reasons, this rule has not been, and should not be, applied to contracts of employment or exclusive agency, distributorship, or requirements contracts which have been analogized to employment contracts. . . . The considerations relevant to such contracts do not obtain here.

Thus, we hold that it is reasonable to infer from the circumstances of the 1924 agreement that the parties intended the city to maintain the sewage disposal facility until such time as the city no longer needed or desired the water, the purity of which the plant was designed to insure. The city argues that it is no longer obligated to maintain the plant because State law now prohibits persons from discharging raw sewage into streams such as Gooseberry Creek. However, the parties did not contemplate the passage of environmental control laws which would prohibit individuals or municipalities from discharging raw, untreated sewage into certain streams. Thus, the city agreed to assume the obligation of assuring that its water supply remained unpolluted and it may not now avoid that obligation for reasons not contemplated by the parties when the agreement was executed, and not within the purview of their intent, expressed or implied.

Having determined the duration of the city's obligation, the scope of its duty remains to be defined. By the agreement, the city obligated itself to build a specifically described disposal facility and to extend the lines of that facility to meet future increased demand. At the present time, the extension of those lines would result in the overloading of the system. Plaintiff claims that the city is required to build a new plant or expand the existing facility to overcome the problem. We disagree. The city should not be required to extend the lines to plaintiffs' property if to do so would overload the system and result in its inability to properly treat sewage. In providing for the extension of sewer lines, the contract does not obligate the city to provide sewage disposal services for properties in areas of the municipalities not presently served or even to new properties in areas which are presently served where to do so could reasonably be expected to significantly increase the demand on present plant facilities.

Thus, those paragraphs of the judgment which provide that the city is obligated to construct any additional facilities required to meet increased demand and that plaintiff is entitled to full use of the sewer lines should be stricken.

Accordingly, the order of the Appellate Division should be modified and the case remitted to Supreme Court, Greene County, for the entry of judgment in accordance with the opinion herein, and, as so modified, affirmed, with costs to appellants against plaintiffs-respondents only. . . . Order modified. . . .

Questions to Consider

1. What was the nature of the contract being disputed in this case? What had the parties agreed to do under the contract? Was there any question that the contract had been formed?
2. What term was missing from the contract? How long had the parties performed under the contract despite the missing term? Why might the parties have left out the disputed term?
3. What terms did the court refuse to imply into the contract? Why? What term did the court imply into the contract? Why? After the court modified the contract to include this term, is it clear how long the contract should last? Why or why not?
4. Why did the court say that a contract term of "reasonable duration" should not be implied into employment contracts and other contracts analogous to them? What do such analogous contracts have in common with employment agreements? Could other missing information be implied into such contracts? Why or why not?
5. What is the guiding principle under which the court supplies missing information for a contract?
6. If you were a paralegal for the city attorney's staff, what evidence would you prepare to submit at trial to prove the city's claims? If you were a paralegal for the intervenors' attorneys, what evidence would you prepare to submit at trial to prove their claims?

However practical implying missing information might be, implication has limits. Otherwise, a court might be able to supply more information for the contract than the parties did. For this reason, missing information is fatal indefiniteness under some circumstances.

EXAMPLE **8.4**

Suppose B agrees to build a small hotel of fifty rooms for $5 million. The contract does not specify how many double, single, or multiperson suites the hotel is to have. Here, a "reasonable number," or even a "standard number," of the various suites cannot be determined. There is no such thing. Such requirements are highly individual with hotels and their owners and depend on such things as location, clientele, and construction budget. Unless it could be shown that the parties agreed to the number of such rooms in some other way, or unless some other reasonable and objective basis for implying the missing information was available, this contract would be fatally indefinite.

Implication of Contract Terms: Common Law Versus the UCC

The Common Law

The common law has strict rules requiring definiteness in contracts. As *Haines v. New York* demonstrates, however, the fact that a contract does not expressly contain all information the parties need does not automatically mean it is too indefinite for enforcement. There is wide variation in the common-law approach to indefiniteness, and courts are not always consistent in analyzing when a contract is too indefinite for enforcement. Usually, a contract is too indefinite for enforcement if a court cannot "cure" the indefiniteness by implying information into the contract with reasonable accuracy. The *Haines* court apparently felt it could do so.

Even if the contract is indefinite as to some detail that cannot be implied, it will not fail unless this indefiniteness is *material*. Relatively minor omissions from a contract do not render the contract unenforceable. Thus, a $5 million construction contract does not fail for indefiniteness because the owner and contractor forgot to specify the paint color for the closets.

Under modern common law, there are no particular terms that, if omitted, automatically mean the contract is too indefinite for enforcement. For example, even price can be filled in by using reasonable price, or market price, provided there is some indication the parties intended that price. Such things as time for performance and even some terms of performance can be filled in by what would be reasonable under the circumstances or by industry standards and practices. Quantity and subject matter are generally the most problematic terms to imply. Quantity tends to be a personal or individual matter that depends on circumstances. If the buyer, for example, has not specified how much he wants, determining what would be "reasonable" in this case is difficult. Nevertheless, under some circumstances even quantity may be implied. Consider the following situation.

Assignment

Buyer and Seller of machine maintenance services have done business together for several years. Buyer always hires Seller's company to repair and maintain all machines on Buyer's premises. The two contracting parties make year-to-year contracts, and Buyer always grants to Seller the exclusive right to do all maintenance and repair of the machines. For the past three years, this arrangement has resulted in Seller's billing Buyer between $25,000 and $30,000 total per year for repair and maintenance. Buyer has always paid the amount billed. This particular year Seller bills $31,000, and Buyer refuses to pay, saying she did not agree to pay that much under this year's contract. When reviewed, the parties' contract does not specifically state the quantity of maintenance and repair services to be provided.

1. How might a court imply the missing quantity term—that is, how much maintenance and repair service is Buyer obligated to take? Why? Should any limit be placed on the quantity of services under the contract? Why or why not?
2. Can a court accurately estimate the amount of services for which Buyer must pay under the contract? Why or why not? How much discretion does a court have to supply missing information?
3. What indication is there that this problem involves indefiniteness that might affect enforcement, not indefiniteness as to formation?
4. What facts would be most important to the court if the quantity of services is to be implied into the contract?
5. If you were a paralegal helping to prepare this contract dispute for trial, what evidence would you want to provide as proof of the facts most important for implying the quantity of services covered in the contract?

Leaving out the subject matter of a contract can be very problematic. This indefiniteness is fatal if there is no reasonable way to know what the parties were bargaining for. If the parties did not even indicate what the contract is intended to be about, a court may have no reasonable way to fill in this information. Suppose, for example, Buyer orders hardware supplies from Hardware Store Owner. If the parties have not done business together and Buyer does not specify whether he wants nails, hinges, or metal pipe, how can such information be implied? Similarly, if Buyer and Seller on a real estate contract do not indicate what land is involved, there is really no way to fill in "reasonable land."

If one or both parties to a contract have already given some performance at the time the indefiniteness is discovered, a court may use this partial performance to imply the missing information. This method of curing indefiniteness can be used, of course, only where the performance is shown to be relevant to the missing terms. Where the partial performance appears to be related to the missing contract terms, and the other party has accepted it, courts may use the performance to help cure the indefiniteness.

The UCC

The UCC has rather liberal and detailed rules on the implication of terms to cure problems with indefiniteness. As previously noted, § 2-204(3) states:

> (3) Even though one or more terms are left open a contract for sale does not fail for indefiniteness if the parties have intended to make a contract and there is a reasonably certain basis for giving an appropriate remedy.

Several sections of the UCC can be used to fill in "gaps" in contracts by specifying what such terms are if the parties omit them. These UCC

Gap-filler provisions
Sections of the UCC used to fill in information missing from a contract ("gaps") by specifying what the terms should be.

provisions are often collectively referred to as the **gap-filler provisions.** Courts addressing indefiniteness in contracts governed by the UCC consult these provisions to find out what information should be implied. The major "gap fillers" are found in the following sections of the UCC:

1. Time for shipment or delivery of goods—§ 2-309. If not specified, delivery is to be made within a "reasonable time."
2. Place of delivery of goods—§ 2-308. If not specified, the place of delivery is the seller's place of business or, if none, the seller's home. If the goods are known to be located elsewhere, that location is the place of delivery if the parties do not specify otherwise.
3. Price of goods—§ 2-305. The price is a reasonable price if (a) the parties do not specify the price; (b) the price is left to be determined by the parties, and they fail to agree; or (c) the price is to be set by external standards (such as a public price list) or a third person, and this is not done.
4. Time for payment for goods—§ 2-310. If the time for payment is omitted, then payment is due at the time and place at which the buyer is to receive the goods.
5. Duration of a contract for goods—§ 2-309(2). If a contract provides for successive performances but is indefinite about how long the agreement lasts, the agreement lasts a "reasonable time." Unless otherwise agreed, however, either party may terminate the contract by reasonable notification that is received by the other party.

The UCC drafters developed these specific and detailed gap-filler provisions while the common law was still quite strict about requiring essential terms to be spelled out. Since then, modern common law has been influenced by the UCC gap-filler provisions and has increasingly followed the UCC approach. Courts now often use the UCC gap-filler provisions as guidelines to imply missing information in contracts where common law applies. Since much of this modern trend in the common law is state specific, the paralegal should always be aware of the need to research applicable statutes and cases in any given contract case. Generally, however, the common-law trend can be summarized in the words of the Restatement Second, § 33(2): "The terms of a contract are reasonably certain if they provide a basis for determining the existence of a breach and for giving an appropriate remedy."

Where the Evidence Shows the Parties Did Not Reach Agreement

It should be remembered that under both the UCC and the common law, indefiniteness may be a sign no agreement was ever reached. The Restatement (Second), § 33(3) provides: "The fact that one or more terms of a proposed bargain are left open or uncertain may show that a manifestation of intention is not intended to be understood as an offer or as an acceptance." Similarly, UCC § 2-204 (3) has been interpreted to mean that the gap-filler provisions apply only if "the parties have intended to make a contract and there is a reasonably certain basis for giving an appropriate remedy."

A court will not make a contract for the parties. In contracts governed by the UCC or common law, a court will not imply missing information unless both the following requirements are met:

1. It must be shown that the parties actually reached agreement; that is, there must be a contract.
2. There must be a reliable way to determine the missing information. If it is not possible to tell what the parties meant, or the gap-filler provisions do not appear applicable, then terms will not be automatically implied, and the contract may fail for indefiniteness.

Assignment

1. In which (if either) of these cases could the defense of indefiniteness successfully be used? Why?
2. Would the indefiniteness most likely be used as a defense to formation or to enforcement? Why?

▶ Hypothetical 1

S has an agreement with B that B will purchase two tons of "onions" at "30 cents per pound." The agreement does not state the type of onions, although S has two different grades of onions, "standard" and "gourmet." Depending on quantity, supply, and market conditions, both types of onions have sold for between 20 cents and 35 cents per pound during the last year. In the produce industry, "onion" has no special meaning and can be used to refer to any kind of onion. When time for the shipment comes, S delivers standard onions and bills them at 30 cents per pound. B refuses shipment, claiming he is owed "gourmet" onions. S sues on the contract.

▶ Hypothetical 2

Same facts as in HYPOTHETICAL 1, except that the contract calls for the "onions" to be delivered in two different lots. When S makes the first delivery and bills for 30 cents per pound, B accepts the onions and pays. Later, because of customer complaints, B refuses the second delivery of onions, claiming he is owed "gourmet" onions. S sues for the amount of the second bill, which was also billed at 30 cents per pound.

Defenses Involving Mistake

As a defense or as a cause of action, the doctrine of *mistake* really involves five different theories, all related to errors or "mistakes" made in the contract. The theories have different requirements, however, and the remedies available are different, depending upon which particular type of mistake is proven to exist. The defenses based on mistake consist of the following:

- Mistakes made in transmission
- Mistakes made in "transcription" of the contract
- Mutual mistakes
- Unilateral mistakes
- Misunderstandings or "ambiguity"

Mistakes Made in Transmission

Mistake made in transmission A defense based on the situation where an intermediary (such as a telegraph company) conveys a party's offer and makes an error in communicating that offer.

A **mistake made in transmission** occurs where a party chooses an intermediary (such as a telegraph company) to convey her offer and the intermediary makes an error in communicating the offer.

EXAMPLE 8.5

Suppose the offeror intends a telegram to state: "I will sell you 1,000 widgets for $1.10 per widget." The telegram actually sent, however, states: "I will sell you 1,000 widgets for $1.00 per widget." If the offeror does not discover the error and the recipient has no way of detecting the error, the offer may be accepted with the mistake included. If the recipient accepts, the offeror has a contract for $.10 less per widget than he intended. In such a case, the offeror may refuse to sell the widgets for $1.00. On the other hand, the other party may feel a contract was formed and may even sue to enforce it.

In the case of the erroneous telegram offer in Example 8.5, the majority of common-law courts side with the innocent offeree. As long as the offeree had no actual knowledge and no reason to know of the mistake, a contract exists. The terms are those provided in the erroneous telegram. In such a case, if the offeree sues to enforce her agreement, the offeror could not effectively raise the mistake made in transmission as a defense. Nor could the offeror successfully sue to rescind the contract on the grounds of the mistake. The only remedy available to the offeror is a lawsuit against the telegraph company. This remedy is virtually worthless, however, because such intermediaries have their own contract with each customer that usually limits damages to the price of the telegram.

The advent of modern means of communication such as fax and E-mail has greatly reduced the use of telegrams. While it is not yet clear who will be responsible for clerical errors made in communications such as faxes and E-mail, the courts will likely continue to follow the common-law preference. Thus, the party who makes the error will probably be bound by it unless the other party knows or has reason to know of the mistake.

Mistakes Made in Transcription

Mistake made in transcription A defense based on the situation where parties made an oral contract, then put it into a writing that does not accurately summarize the oral agreement.

Reformation The process by which a court corrects ("reforms") a written version of a contract to reflect proven terms of an earlier oral agreement.

The defense of a **mistake made in transcription** relates to the narrow set of circumstances in which the parties make an oral contract, then put it into a writing that does not accurately summarize the oral agreement. A party who believes the subsequent written version of the contract is erroneous may refuse to perform. This is particularly likely where the alleged mistake is significant and affects performance. If the other party does not agree the writing is mistaken, he may sue on the written version of the contract. If so, the party who believes the writing is erroneous can defend on this theory. The party who believes the written version of the contract is erroneous asserts the defense that the demanded performance was not part of the oral contract. If this can be proven, the party has a valid defense. If the earlier oral terms of the contract can be proven with sufficient certainty, the aggrieved party may even be entitled to *reformation*. **Reformation** occurs where the court gives a judgment correcting, ("reforming") the contract to reflect the proven terms of the oral agreement.

In some instances, the party who believes a mistake in transcription occurred may sue.

EXAMPLE 8.6

Buyer and Seller orally agree to the sale and delivery of goods. They specify that Seller will deliver all goods to Buyer's main warehouse in a specific city or to any other comparable destination within a "60-mile radius" of Buyer's main warehouse. When the contract is put into writing, the drafter accidentally states "50-mile radius" instead of "60-mile radius." When the date for delivery comes, Buyer wishes to exercise the alternative delivery option and have Seller deliver the goods to an auxiliary warehouse 55 miles away from the main warehouse. The parties discover the contract says Seller is only required to make alternative deliveries within a 50-mile radius.

If the parties cannot informally agree that a mistake has occurred and Seller refuses to deliver to the auxiliary warehouse, Buyer may sue. A lawsuit would be particularly likely where the contract called for ongoing deliveries over a period of time. In that situation, Buyer would be faced with a written contract that never required delivery to her auxiliary warehouse. To make Seller obligated to deliver to the auxiliary warehouse, Buyer could sue for reformation of the contract. If Buyer could clearly show the 50-mile radius provision was a mistake, a court would reform the contract to reflect their real agreement, which called for delivery within a 60-mile radius.

If reformation was not useful or possible, Buyer might sue instead for rescission or breach of the contract. In those situations, Buyer would still have to prove that there was a mistake in transcription to show why Seller's refusal to deliver was wrongful.

Mutual Mistake

The doctrine of **mutual mistake** is based on the idea that an enforceable contract cannot exist unless the parties reached a common understanding. Where the parties had different basic assumptions about the agreement, this difference may prevent formation of the contract because it robs the parties of a common understanding, or mutual assent. If a true mutual mistake is proven, the party who is harmed by the mistake has the option of rescinding the contract.

Not all differences of opinion about the terms of a contract involve the doctrine of mutual mistake. Like mistakes made in transcription, this doctrine applies to a fairly narrow set of circumstances. All of the following are required to show a mutual mistake:

- An erroneous assumption about the *factual* circumstances of the contract existed.
- Both parties made *the same* erroneous assumption.
- The erroneous assumption occurred *at the time of formation of the contract.*
- The erroneous assumption has a *material effect* on the contract.
- The complaining party *did not assume the risk* of the alleged error or mistake.

Only mistakes of fact made in the formation of a contract satisfy the requirements of the doctrine of mutual mistake. Mistakes of judgment

Mutual mistake A defense based on the argument that the parties had erroneous assumptions about material, factual circumstances surrounding the bargain. Mutual mistake may prevent formation of the contract because it robs the parties of a common understanding, or mutual assent.

normally cannot be used to show a mutual mistake or as grounds to rescind a contract. Distinguishing between an erroneous judgment or opinion and an erroneous assumption of fact is not always easy.

EXAMPLE **8.7**

The sale of a racehorse provides an illustration. Generally, if the buyer of a racehorse later complains she was mistaken about *how fast* the horse was, the complaint involves a mistake in judgment. Suppose, however, that at the moment of contract formation, unknown to both the buyer and seller, the racehorse was dead. Assuming both parties were bargaining for the sale of a live racehorse, they would both have made a mistaken assumption of fact. Specifically, both made the mistaken assumption that the horse was alive.

Note that in Example 8.7, both parties have made the very same erroneous assumption and it has a material effect on the contract. There is no specific test for whether a mistake has a material effect on a contract. Generally, the idea is that contracts should not be rescinded for mutual mistake unless the mistake deprives the aggrieved party of the essence of what she was bargaining for. In the racehorse transaction, the mistake is clearly material since a dead racehorse is useless for the purpose for which it was purchased.

The requirement that the party complaining of mutual mistake did not assume the risk of the mistake can be problematic. Confusion has arisen over the role "assumption of risk" plays in the doctrine of mutual mistake. The idea appears to be that if a party sues to rescind or defends against enforcement of the contract on grounds of mutual mistake, he must not have assumed the risk of what went wrong.

For example, review the racehorse transaction. Could it not be argued that a buyer who later complains the horse is too slow took precisely that risk in making the purchase? Parties exchanging a racehorse cannot predict the horse's speed with complete accuracy. Thus, each party normally takes a calculated risk in deciding whether to go through with the transaction at the specified price. If the horse turns out to be very fast and a real winner, the seller cannot successfully sue to rescind the contract and get back the horse or charge more money. If the horse turns out to be slower than the buyer hoped, the buyer cannot sue to rescind. Both parties, however, would ordinarily believe the horse was *alive* when it was sold. It is unlikely either party would even think to question this fact without a specific reason to do so. Thus, it would be unreasonable to say the buyer assumed the risk the horse was dead. This risk seems to fall outside the scope of what ordinary reasonable parties would think of as a possibility.

The assumption of risk doctrine in mutual mistake can affect whether the mistake is characterized as "fact" or "opinion." Many courts have found there is a relationship between assumption of risk and the nature of the mistake. Simply put, the more likely the complaining party assumed the risk of what went wrong, the more likely a court will characterize the mistake as one of "opinion." Thus, the contract could not be rescinded, or the party raising mutual mistake as a defense would be unsuccessful.

A CASE FOR STUDY
Sherwood v. Walker
66 Mich. 568, 33 N.W. 919 (1887)

MORSE, J.   Replevin for a cow. Suit commenced in justice's court; judgment for plaintiff; appealed to circuit court of Wayne County, and verdict and judgment for plaintiff in that court. The defendant brings error, and sets out 25 assignments of the same.

The main controversy depends upon the construction of a contract for the sale of a cow. The plaintiff claims that the title passed, and bases his action upon such a claim. The defendants contend that the contract was executory, and by its terms no title to the animal was acquired by plaintiff. The defendants reside at Detroit, but are in business at Walkerville, Ontario, and have a farm at Greenfield, in Wayne County, upon which were some blooded cattle supposed to be barren as breeders. The Walkers are importers and breeders of polled Angus cattle. The plaintiff is a banker living at Plymouth, in Wayne County. He called upon the defendants at Walkerville for the purchase of some of their stock, but found none there that suited him. Meeting one of the defendants afterwards, he was informed that they had a few head upon their Greenfield farm. He was asked to go out and look at them, with the statement at the time that they were probably barren, and would not breed. May 5, 1886, plaintiff went out to Greenfield and saw the cattle. A few days thereafter, he called upon one of the defendants with the view of purchasing a cow, known as "Rose 2d of Aberlone." After considerable talk it was agreed that defendants would telephone Sherwood at his home in Plymouth in reference to the price. The second morning after this talk he was called up by telephone, and the terms of the sale were finally agreed upon. He was to pay five and one-half cents per pound, live weight, fifty pounds shrinkage.

[The parties arranged for Rose to be transported and paid for. The sale price for Rose, who weighed 1,420 pounds, was $80. However, when the buyer went to finalize the sale, the seller refused to take the money or deliver the cow. The buyer then sued for replevin to obtain

Rose. During trial, the seller submitted the following evidence.]

The defendants then introduced evidence tending to show that at the time of the alleged sale it was believed by both the plaintiff and themselves that the cow was barren and would not breed; that she cost $850, and if not barren would be worth from $750 to $1,000 . . . that the defendants were informed by said Graham [defendant's agent] that in his judgment the cow was with calf, and therefore they instructed him not to deliver her to plaintiff, and on the twentieth of May, 1886, telegraphed plaintiff what Graham thought about the cow being with calf, and that consequently they could not sell her. The cow had a calf in the month of October following. . . .

It appears from the record that both parties supposed this cow was barren and would not breed, and she was sold by the pound for an insignificant sum as compared with her real value if a breeder. She was evidently sold and purchased on the relation of her value for beef, unless the plaintiff had learned of her true condition, and concealed such knowledge from the defendants. Before the plaintiff secured the possession of the animal, the defendants learned that she was with calf, and therefore of great value, and undertook to rescind the sale by refusing to deliver her. The question arises whether they had a right to do so. The circuit judge ruled that this fact did not avoid the sale and it made no difference whether she was barren or not. I am of the opinion that the court erred in this holding. I know that this is a close question, and the dividing line between the adjudicated cases is not easily discerned. But it must be considered as well settled that a party who has given an apparent consent to a contract of sale may refuse to execute it, or he may avoid it after it has been completed, if the assent was founded, or the contract made upon the mistake of a material fact, such as the subject matter of the sale, the price, or some collateral fact materially inducing the agreement; and this can be done when the mistake is mutual. . . .

It seems to me, however, in the case made by this record, that the mistake or misapprehension of the parties went to the whole substance of the agreement. If the cow was a breeder, she was worth at least $750; if barren, she was worth not over $80. The parties would not have made the contract of sale except upon the understanding and belief that she was incapable of breeding, and of no use as a cow. It is true she is now the identical animal that they thought her to be when the contract was made; there is no mistake as to the identity of the creature. Yet the mistake was not of the mere quality of the animal, but went to the very nature of the thing. A barren cow is substantially a different creature than a breeding one. . . . She was not in fact the animal, or the kind of animal, the defendants intended to sell or the plaintiff to buy. She was not a barren cow, and, if this fact had been known, there would have been no contract. . . . The court should have instructed the jury that if they found that the cow was sold, or contracted to be sold, upon the understanding of both parties that she was barren, and useless for the purpose of breeding, and that in fact she was not barren, but capable of breeding, then the defendants had a right to rescind, and refuse to deliver, and the verdict should be in their favor.

The judgment of the court below must be reversed, and a new trial granted, with costs of this court to defendants.

Questions to Consider

1. Review the requirements of mutual mistake listed at the beginning of this section. Do the facts of the case satisfy these requirements? Why or why not?
2. Should the case come out differently if Rose was believed to be a *poor* "breeder" and then turned out to be a prodigious breeder? Why or why not?
3. How is this case different from the case of a racehorse who turns out to be slower than the buyer hoped?

Unilateral Mistake

Unilateral mistake
A defense based on the argument that one contracting party made a clerical or computational error and should therefore be allowed to rescind the contract.

A **unilateral mistake** in a contract is usually a clerical or computational error made by one contracting party. As with mutual mistake, the error must involve factual assumptions rather than opinions. Under the older common-law view, courts found unilateral errors were grounds neither to rescind the contract nor to successfully defend against enforcement of the contract.

EXAMPLE 8.8

Suppose a subcontractor made an error in calculating his bid and discovered the error only after he had submitted the bid to the general contractor who was bidding on the main job. Under the common-law approach, the subcontractor was bound to the price in his bid.

Traditionally, the only exception to the result in Example 8.8 was if the party in the general contractor's position actually knew, or had reason to know, of the error when he accepted the bid. In that case, the subcontractor's unilateral mistake would be grounds for rescission and could be used successfully to defend against enforcement by the other party. The rationale for this exception was that it would not be good public policy to allow a party to "snap up" a contract offer she knew to be erroneous.

In the modern commercial world, there is a trend to allow contract rescission where a unilateral mistake was made. Some modern courts even allow rescission where the "nonmistaken party" knew nothing of the mistake at the time the contract was made. This trend appears to be based in part on a changed view of the nature of detrimental reliance in cases of unilateral mistake. The traditional common-law view of a unilateral mistake automatically assumed the nonmistaken party (such as the general contractor) had detrimentally relied on the mistaken bid and would therefore be prejudiced by its withdrawal.

The more modern (although still apparently minority) view is that often very little real prejudice results to a party who relies on a mistaken bid or offer. For example, a general contractor who relies on a subcontractor's erroneous bid can often substitute a comparable subcontractor reasonably easily. Some courts even hold that unilateral mistake is grounds for rescission in cases involving actual harm and actual reliance by the nonmistaken party. In such a case, these courts take the view that damages for the harm adequately compensate the nonmistaken party. A party who is the victim of the other party's unilateral error can obtain an accurate contract with someone else and then collect damages for the harm done by the mistake. This approach is practical because it may mean that an unwillingly subcontractor will not be forced to work on a job he believes he has underbid.

Misunderstanding or Ambiguity

Misunderstanding or **ambiguity** involves the situation where the contracting parties have *different,* equally reasonable interpretations of a phrase or provision in a contract and this difference is material to the contract. A genuine misunderstanding about the meaning of words in a contract can be the basis of rescission and can provide a valid defense against enforcement. The rationale is that if the parties had two completely different ideas in mind, they never reached the required consensus, or "meeting of the minds." For misunderstanding or ambiguity to be a valid defense to formation, however, it must materially affect the contract. Misunderstanding or ambiguity as to a minor term is not likely to result in contract rescission.

Different interpretations of contract terms do not necessarily result in rescission even when the difference is material. First, the disputed terms must objectively be capable of at least two different interpretations. Second, the interpretations made by both parties must be reasonable. If one interpretation of the disputed terms is reasonable and the other is not, then the contract will still remain enforceable. The disputed terms will be interpreted according to the meaning given by the party with the reasonable interpretation. In other words, the doctrine of misunderstanding or ambiguity is not intended to allow someone to get out of a contract simply by thinking up a different or "creative" meaning for disputed terms.

What if both parties to a contract have interpretations that are reasonable, but one party's interpretation is *more reasonable?* Here, the doctrine of ambiguity arguably does not even apply. The reality of contract formation and performance is that parties often have somewhat different interpretations of a contract term or terms. Usually, each party prefers an interpretation of a contract term favorable to itself. Such differences are not a basis for rescission on the grounds of ambiguity. A true ambiguity in a contract occurs only where all three of the following requirements are met: (1) the parties have two different interpretations of an *ambiguous* contract term; (2) both these interpretations are equally reasonable; and (3) the difference in interpretation is material to the contract.

Ambiguity/ misunderstanding A doctrine that prevents formation of a contract where the parties had equally reasonable but different interpretations of a material term, phrase, or provision.

Chapter Review Questions

1. What are the differences between using a contract defense as a defense to formation and using it as a defense to enforcement?
2. What are the differences between using fraud as a cause of action in a contract action and using it as a defense in a contract action?
3. What is meant by pleading in the alternative? Give some examples.
4. Make up and explain a fact pattern in which indefiniteness might be used as defense. (You might want to exchange fact patterns with a classmate and see whether you each agree with the other's analysis.)
5. Make up fact patterns for the other defenses to contract formation and enforcement and explain whether or not the defense will be successful in each case.
6. How might a court imply a price term into a contract under the UCC (or a state commercial code)?
7. If A can show her oral contract with B was written down incorrectly, what remedies might she obtain from the court?
8. What is the modern trend on the question of whether a party can obtain rescission of a contract on the grounds of unilateral mistake?

Key Terms

Ambiguity/misunderstanding, 173
Cause of action/claim, 158
Defense, 157
Discovery, 159
Discovery procedures, 159
Gap-filler provisions, 156
Implication, 161
Indefiniteness, 160

Mistake made in transcription, 168
Mistake made in transmission, 168
Mutual mistake, 169
Pleading in the alternative, 159
Reformation, 168
Unilateral mistake, 172

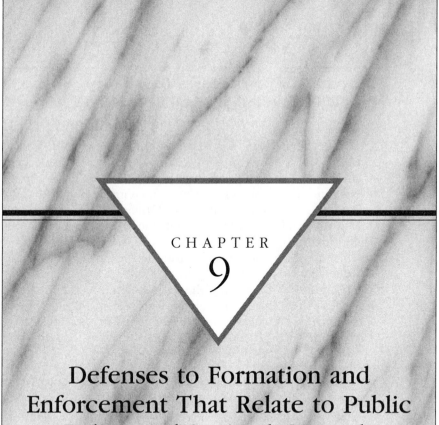

CHAPTER
9

Defenses to Formation and Enforcement That Relate to Public Policy and Societal Controls

LEARNING OBJECTIVES FOR THIS CHAPTER: WHAT YOU SHOULD KNOW!

❒ Definition and use of the defense of duress.

❒ Definition and use of the defense of undue influence.

❒ Definitions and uses of the defenses of fraud, misrepresentation, and concealment.

❒ Definitions and uses of defenses based on lack of contractual capacity.

❒ Definition and use of the defense of illegality.

❒ Definition and use of the defense of unconscionability.

❒ Definition and use of a warranty.

Introduction to Defenses Based on Public Policy and Societal Controls

Many abuses can take place in the contract bargaining process. Some of these abuses are now the subject of state and federal consumer legislation. For example, many statutes now make it safer for the purchaser of stock to make a sale contract with stock sellers by forcing disclosure of relevant financial information. Abuses in contract sales of stock are no longer a matter of pure contract principles.[1] Other abuses may also now be subject to legislative and administrative regulation specific to a certain industry. The banking and insurance industries are examples of highly regulated industries in which most contracts must be made according to guidelines developed by legislation and administrative agencies. Contract law itself, however, has long had many means for abating the various abuses committed in commercial societies in their pursuit of contractual agreements. Scholars such as E. Allan Farnsworth and William Young have referred to these defenses as "policing the bargain."[2] This chapter treats contract defenses that reflect public policy and societal concerns by discouraging, preventing, or curing abuses in the making of contracts.

You may find it helpful to review the material in Chapter 8 on how defenses are used in litigation because the defenses discussed in this chapter are used the same way. Each may also be used as a "sword" or a "shield." However, the defenses of indefiniteness and mistake covered in Chapter 8 arise from concerns about whether parties have actually reached a mutual, clear, and reasonably complete agreement and whether impractical performance situations can be avoided. The defenses covered in this chapter arise from ethical and moral judgments made over centuries of Anglo-American law and are concerned with what types of bargains the law ought or ought not to enforce.

Duress Compelled, or involuntary, consent. Used as a defense, it occurs when one party threatens another to obtain a contract advantage.

Election A choice between or among legal alternatives, or the exercise of this choice. (E.g., the non-breaching party may have an election to sue for a major breach and cease performance, to sue for a minor breach and not cease performance, or not to sue at all.

Economic duress A defense based on the argument that one party forced the other into a contract by creating a situation that so seriously threatened the financial welfare of the other that he had no real choice but to enter a disadvantageous agreement.

The Defense of Duress

In any area of the law, **duress** is compelled, or involuntary, consent. It occurs when one party threatens another to obtain some advantage. The threat can occur through physical threats or through wrongful conduct. In contract law, the use of duress to obtain an agreement may void formation. The reason it "may" have this effect is that contracts induced through duress give the aggrieved party the right to make an **election**, or to choose between two alternatives (election also refers to the actual act of choosing between the alternatives). With regard to duress, the aggrieved party can choose between the alternatives of (1) enforcing the contract or (2) voiding the contract. Thus, as a defense, duress would normally be raised when the party who used duress to procure the contract sues the other party. Establishing duress gives the defendant a choice of voiding or enforcing the contract. As a claim or cause of action, duress can be raised when the aggrieved party wants to have the contract declared void.

In a modern commercial setting, *economic duress* is more likely to be an issue than actual physical duress. **Economic duress** occurs when one party commits wrongful acts that seriously threaten the financial welfare of the other party and that party has no real means to avoid the threat other than to enter into a very disadvantageous agreement. Merely driving up prices, making a commodity scarce, or taking advantage of a party's financial weakness is not economic duress, however. The contract doctrine of economic duress has not proven to be an effective policing device in cases involving cutthroat or borderline commercial practices. To successfully avoid a contract by alleging economic duress requires a strong showing of (1) wrongdoing by the aggressor, (2) economic hardship to the aggrieved party (financial ruin in some cases), and (3) very little choice about entering into the contract. Note the following case.

A CASE FOR STUDY

Chouinard v. Chouinard

568 F.2d 430 (5th Cir. 1978)

[ARC Corporation was owned by Fred Chouinard, Fred's father Al Chouinard, and Fred's twin brother Ed Chouinard. Fred was the president and apparently ran the business. Over the years, the parties were in dispute concerning the precise nature of the ownership interests of Ed and Al. At one point, Ed concluded that he and Al each owned [37.5%] of ARC, and that the value of each of their interests was close to $500,000. These conclusions were not shared by Fred. In 1974, ARC got into substantial financial difficulties due in part to a bad decision by Fred and badly needed new financing. Fred was able to obtain financing from the Heller Company, a commercial lender, but when Heller learned that Ed and Al claimed a stock ownership interest, Heller made it clear that it would not make a loan until the stock-ownership dispute was settled. Fred's attorney drafted a proposed instrument in which all parties would agree that Heller could make the loan but no one acknowledged anyone else's ownership claim. This proposal was apparently never "put on the table," because the attorney for Ed and Al informed Fred's counsel that this was a good occasion to settle the ownership issue. Fred's counsel labeled that approach as "blackmail," but Fred realized that the Heller loan was essential. Accordingly, he agreed to pay Ed and Al $95,000 each, mostly in the form of promissory notes, in exchange for releases by Ed and Al of all their claims to ownership in ARC. Fred then closed the loan with Heller, and ARC obtained the needed funds. Subsequently, Fred brought suit to set the promissory notes aside. Held: for Ed and Al.]

While there is ample evidence of economic necessity and financial peril, neither the "threat of considerable financial loss" nor "impending bankruptcy" establish economic duress. Such economic duress must be attributable to the party against whom duress is alleged. "Mere hard bargaining positions, if lawful, and the press of financial circumstances, not caused by the [party against whom the contract is sought to be voided], will not be deemed duress." [Citation]

The only possible claim of duress is that Ed and Al, recognizing the weakened state of the company, seized that opportunity to settle the long-standing dispute regarding stockownership. Because duress may not be implied merely from the making of a hard bargain, the question becomes whether the conduct of Ed and Al was wrongful. The law in Georgia and other jurisdictions makes clear that it was not, for the two men were merely asserting a legal right, i.e., their right to a certain share of the stock in the company. [Citation] Fred admitted that Ed and Al were stockholders in the company, and the long-standing dispute was over the percentage of the company each owned. Thus, while there is no doubt that Fred was between the proverbial rock and a hard place, it is clear that his own actions put him there and that Ed and Al merely took advantage of the situation to insist upon settlement of the intrafamilial stock squabble. . . .

We conclude, therefore, that there is simply no duress shown on this record, for one crucial element is missing: a wrongful act by the defendants to create and take advantage of an untenable situation. Ed and Al had nothing to do with the financial quagmire in which Fred found himself, and we cannot find duress simply because they refused to throw him a rope free of any "strings."

Questions to Consider

1. Which elements of the test for economic duress were satisfied in *Chouinard v. Chouinard?*

2. Would the case have been decided differently if Al and Ed had gone secretly to Heller and convinced the lender to withhold funds until after they had secured a promise of payment from Fred? Why or why not?

3. Would the case have been decided differently if Al and Ed had been at least partly to blame for ARC's financial difficulties? Why or why not?

Assignment

1. In which (if either) of the following situations could the defense of duress successfully be raised? Why?
2. Would the defense be used as a defense to formation or as a defense to enforcement? Why?

▶ Hypothetical 1

Restaurant Supplier has been on the verge of bankruptcy for two years. Supplier hires Andy Agent to promote its business. Their employment agreement provides that Agent will receive 1 percent of the gross revenues from all business he brings in. Andy Agent arranges a huge supply contract with Posh Hotels, a worldwide chain. Posh has done business with Andy Agent before and is awarding the business to Supplier based mainly on the association with Agent. On the night before the contract is to be signed, Andy Agent refuses to represent Supplier or to close the deal unless Supplier agrees Agent will receive 50 percent of the gross revenues from the Posh Hotel deal. Without the deal, Supplier will be out of business, so Supplier agrees. The deal is signed, but Supplier then refuses to pay Andy anything but 1 percent of the gross revenues from the deal. Andy Agent sues Supplier for breach of the agreement to pay 50 percent of gross revenues.

▶ Hypothetical 2

Killer Chemicals, Inc., is the biggest maker of a pesticide called Titon 12A. Titon 12A is the only truly effective organic pesticide on the market. Its main ingredient is an extract made from the bark of eucalyptus trees. Only five American firms are in the business of making the extract. To ensure its supply of bark extract, Killer obtains six-year contracts with all five extraction firms. These contracts are so large that none of the firms has much production capacity left over with which to make bark extract contracts with Killer's competitors. Soon Killer realizes that the buyers of Titon 12A cannot obtain adequate supplies without purchasing from Killer. Immediately, Killer triples the price of Titon 12A and refuses contracts to its customers unless they pay the new price. Central Farm Industries makes one of these contracts with Killer, which delivers the Titon 12A as called for in the contract. Central Farm Industries then refuses to pay the new price, claiming it is too high. Killer sues for breach of contract.

The Defense of Undue Influence

Undue influence occurs when someone has a confidential or fiduciary relationship with another person, or even another group, and abuses that relationship to obtain an advantageous contract. In a *fiduciary* or *confidential relationship,* one party has an obligation to protect the other. A **fiduciary relationship** can be defined as the existence of a special financial or other relationship in which a more knowledgeable or stronger party has responsibility for the welfare of a less knowledgeable or weaker party. For example, an attorney hired to draft a trust through which a nonprofit foundation hopes to handle contributions would normally have a fiduciary relationship with her client, the foundation. The following are other typical examples of situations in which a fiduciary duty would exist between the parties:

- A trustee and the beneficiaries of a trust
- An executor and the beneficiaries of a will
- An insurance company and its insured
- A bank and its clients or customers
- A corporate board of directors and the shareholders
- An accountant and the client

If someone with a fiduciary or confidential relationship misuses her position to obtain a contract advantage, this may be grounds to defend against formation or enforcement of the contract. Thus, undue influence is procuring a contract through abuse of a position of special trust and confidence. The stereotypical example of undue influence is the hardhearted banker or shady attorney who prevails upon an elderly, infirm, or naive client to sell him property at a ridiculously low price. Such a contract for sale of property would be voidable at the option of the party who was the victim of the undue influence. Thus, the victimized party can choose either to void the contract or to enforce it if, for some reason, he wishes to.

In modern times, there has been some movement to recognize the doctrine of undue influence in cases where a traditional fiduciary or confidential relationship does not exist.[3] The law in this area is changing in some jurisdictions, and the paralegal should be aware of this trend and do state-specific research, if necessary.

The Defenses of Fraud, Misrepresentation, and Concealment

Fraud in contract law is a somewhat loose term for many situations in which contracts are procured by deceit of some kind. In contract law, the doctrine is complicated by the fact that the law of torts has a related and more completely developed doctrine. Adding to the complications is the courts' treatment of contract fraud, which has often been marked by confusion and inconsistency.

Fraud is intentional or unintentional deceit. Used as a contract defense (or cause of action), *fraud* generally requires a showing that the aggrieved party was hurt by actually relying on the fraudulent words or conduct rather than by something else. For example, if A tries to procure a contract by lying about the availability of supply, but B *knows this is a lie,* B cannot later claim to have been defrauded by A's lie.

Undue influence A defense based on the argument that a contracting party with a confidential or fiduciary relationship and duty to another abused that relationship to obtain a contract advantage.

Fiduciary or confidential relationship A legal relationship in which a party with superior knowledge, expertise, or capability has an obligation to protect another less knowledgeable, less expert, or less capable party.

Fraud A defense based on the argument that a contract was procured by, or involves, material deceit of some kind.

EXHIBIT 9.1

Intentional and Unintentional Fraud

INTENTIONAL FRAUD

- Deceitful conduct,
- deliberately engaged in ("intent" to defraud),
- that actually caused harm to the aggrieved party (harm may be presumed), and
- the harm has a material effect on the contract.

UNINTENTIONAL OR NEGLIGENT FRAUD

- Deceitful conduct,
- negligently or unintentionally engaged in,
- that actually caused
- demonstrated harm to the aggrieved party, and
- the harm has a material effect on the contract.

Historically, courts also required the defrauded party to show she suffered some actual harm because of the fraud. In more modern times, courts tend not to require such a showing if the fraud was intentional. Most modern courts would presume the aggrieved party suffered harm if intentional fraud was committed. Where the fraud was unintentional (or "negligent"), most courts would still require the aggrieved party to show she had actually been harmed by the fraud.

There is no fraud if the allegedly fraudulent conduct involves statements of opinion rather than assertions of fact. In other words, if someone clearly identifies information as opinion rather than fact, the recipient of the information has an independent duty to assess its worth and cannot claim to have been defrauded if it later turns out to be untrue. Basic definitions of intentional and unintentional fraud are summarized in Exhibit 9.1. Whether a party uses fraud as a defense or as a cause of action, he must show that these elements of fraud are present.

Misrepresentation, concealment, and nondisclosure are related categories of fraud, in that they all involve specific kinds of deceit. **Misrepresentation** involves intentional or negligent assertions of fact. Therefore, it is primarily committed through written or spoken words that the speaker or writer knows, or should know, are false.

Nondisclosure and *concealment* generally involve withholding information rather than giving out false information. Failure of one party to tell the other contracting party about *material information* to which he has access, but to which the other party has no reasonable access, can be fraudulent nondisclosure or fraudulent concealment.

In general, contracting parties have no obligation to acquaint each other with all relevant information about the contract. In fact, realistically, much contract negotiation is based on each party's trying to get as much as it can out of a deal without saying too much about its own intentions. At some point, however, such "keeping one's own counsel" can become deceitful. That point is reached in the doctrines of concealment and nondisclosure. If the information withheld is material to the contract and a reasonable person would find such information necessary in making a decision, then someone who withholds it may be guilty of nondisclosure or concealment.

Misrepresentation
A defense based on the argument that one contracting party made intentional or negligent assertions of fact that were untrue.

The difference between concealment and nondisclosure is often blurred, but it is related to whether the deceit is active or relatively passive. **Concealment** occurs when one contracting party takes some positive action to cover up information that has a material effect on the contract. **Nondisclosure** is very similar, but may simply involve doing nothing, rather than taking positive steps to cover up material information.

The effect of a *material* fraud, misrepresentation, concealment, or nondisclosure is basically the same. The most common result is that any type of material, deceitful wrongdoing makes a contract voidable by the aggrieved party, who can elect to enforce or rescind the contract. This rule has some exceptions, however, and you should check them while researching the law of the relevant jurisdiction. As with so many "generic" contract law concepts, the specific definition and application of a doctrine depend on cases and statutes in the particular state or under federal law.

Fraud, misrepresentation, concealment, and nondisclosure are also areas of law where many state or federal consumer laws overlap. For example, in the area of residential home sales, common-law doctrines of fraud have frequently been replaced by statutory disclosure requirements aimed at protecting prospective homeowners.[4]

Concealment A defense based on the argument that one contracting party actively withheld information material to the contract or to entering into the contract.

Nondisclosure A defense based on the argument that one contracting party intentionally or negligently failed to reveal material facts concerning the contract.

Assignment

1. Could the defenses of fraud, misrepresentation, concealment, or nondisclosure be raised in the following situations?
2. Which, if any, of these defenses would most likely be successful? Why?

▶ Hypothetical 1

Bruce lives in a trailer park where he owns his own mobile home. The mobile home has been for sale for several weeks for $5,000. Lenny comes to look at the mobile home, intending to purchase it if it is in good condition. Everything seems to check out, but unknown to Lenny, the hookup for the propane gas is faulty. Propane gas is delivered to the mobile home, and tanks are placed outside with hoses running to the inside of the trailer to supply the stove, heating system, and water heater. The faulty propane gas hookup is not dangerous, but it uses one and one-half times the amount of propane it should. Bruce is aware of the problem with the hookup and has noticed that it has been slowly increasing lately. Although the faulty hookup cannot be visually detected, Bruce says nothing about it to Lenny. Lenny purchases the mobile home "as is" for $1,000 down and two successive monthly payments of $2,000 each. A month later, when his propane tanks run out way ahead of time, Lenny discovers the problem and refuses to make any further payment on the mobile home. Bruce sues on the sale contract for the remainder of the price.

▶ Hypothetical 2

Same facts as in Hypothetical 1, except that when Lenny comes to look at the mobile home and asks about the propane system, Bruce says, "Oh it's fine—it's getting a little old now, but it works fine." Bruce also shows Lenny a copy of an inspection receipt from the Columbia Gas & Electric Company that shows the amount of propane used in the last month. Unknown to Lenny, Bruce has falsified the figures on the receipt and photocopied it so the changes are not noticeable.

Contract Defenses Based on Lack of Capacity

The General Rule

Minority A defense to contract formation or enforcement based on the argument that one contracting party is too young to make contracts because she is below the age established by state statute or case law.

Mental incapacity A defense to contract formation or enforcement based on the argument that mentally handicapped persons cannot make contracts that can be enforced against them.

Contract law recognizes two kinds of incapacity: *minority* and *mental incapacity*. Contractual incapacity on the grounds of **minority** means some persons are deemed too young to make contracts. This rule is generally statutory; that is, states usually pass a statute that specifies how old a person must be to enter into legal contracts. The traditional age was twenty-one, but many states today have changed the age to eighteen.

Mental incapacity as a defense to contract formation or enforcement means mentally handicapped persons cannot make contracts. Mental handicap or mental incapacity for contract purposes does not require an official medical or legal finding that a party is mentally unfit. Such a finding can certainly be used as *evidence* of contractual incapacity, but it is not necessary. Although there is no universally accepted definition of mental incapacity, most jurisdictions use roughly the following concept: a person is mentally incapacitated and cannot make a contract if she is unable to understand the nature and extent of each party's rights and responsibilities under the contract. Lack of contractual capacity is a practical concept and does not require a showing of criminal insanity or a psychiatric determination of mental illness. If a person is mentally handicapped to the extent that she does not understand the nature of the agreement being made and cannot carry out or receive performance effectively, she will be considered to have mental incapacity to contract.

Sometimes we state the concept of unenforceability in a misleading way by saying that people who are too young or too mentally handicapped cannot make legally enforceable agreements. This phrasing makes the rule sound harsh toward the incapacitated person, whereas what we really mean is that such contracts cannot be enforced *against* the incapacitated person. The purpose of the rules regarding mental incapacity and minority is to protect those who have the incapacity. The rules on when such contracts are enforceable are intended to be consistent with this purpose.

For example, suppose an unscrupulous (adult) video games salesperson makes a $500 contract with a minor. Although the minor has the incapacity, it is the *adult* who cannot enforce the contract. Furthermore, the minor usually gets a *choice* about whether to enforce. The minor (or, more realistically, the minor's representative) can choose to enforce the contract or rescind it. This rule is usually stated by saying that the contract is voidable at the option of the incapacitated party. There may be two rationales for this rule. First, inability to enforce may be a *deterrent* to people who want to take advantage of the weak or defenseless by making unscrupulous contracts with them. Second, if someone succeeds in taking advantage of an incapacitated person by making a contract with him, the law may be able to *prevent further damage* by refusing to enforce the contract.

The Exception to the Rule

Contracts involving necessities of life, or *necessaries,* are a widely recognized exception to the rule that a contract is voidable at the option of an incapacitated party. Necessities of life are such things as food, shelter, clothing, and medical care. If the subject matter of a contract made with an incapacitated person involves a necessity of life, then the incapacitated party may not be able to rescind the contract even if he (or his representative) wishes to do so. This rule also protects the incapacitated person. The reason for the exception is that people with control over necessities of life may be more inclined to provide them if they can make an enforceable agreement for reimbursement.

EXAMPLE 9.1

Suppose Mr. Niceguy gives food and shelter to a person who is lost and suffering from Alzheimer's disease. If the Alzheimer's sufferer makes Mr. Niceguy a promise of reimbursement, Mr. Niceguy can later enforce this agreement. The amount of the reimbursement would normally be the costs of the food and shelter. The reason Mr. Niceguy's contract is enforceable whereas the video games contract was not is the different subject matter of the agreements. Since video games are not yet considered a necessity of life, the adult cannot enforce in that case. In Mr. Niceguy's case, food and shelter are necessities of life. Thus, Mr. Niceguy can enforce the contract even against the wishes of the Alzheimer's sufferer or his representative.

Contract Defenses Based on Illegality

The General Rule

A contract is **illegal** if either its purpose or the consideration used is illegal. What is not so clear is what we actually mean by the word *illegal*. For the most part, modern courts give the concept of **illegality** a broad interpretation. Among other things, a contract may be illegal if it violates public policy of some kind, if it is unconstitutional or criminal, if it is immoral or unprofessional, or if it violates a statute or administrative regulation.

Generally speaking, the courts will not enforce illegal contracts. However, common sense indicates that this might be a harsh rule in some cases. Suppose, for example, that one party to a contract is ignorant of the illegality and had no reasonable way to discover it or know the other party's purpose. It also might be harsh to deny enforcement if the illegality does not seem to be central to the contract from the point of view of the party asking for enforcement. It might also be harsh to deny enforcement to a party who could show she was relatively innocent in comparison to the other party's degree of illegal conduct. Consider the following situation.

Illegal contract A contract in which the consideration used by one or both parties is illegal, or for which the contract goal or purpose is illegal. An illegal contract may be unenforceable by one or both parties.

Illegality An act that violates public policy, a statute, or an administrative regulation, or that is unconstitutional, criminal, immoral, or unprofessional. An illegality in a contract may provide a defense to formation or enforcement of the contract.

EXAMPLE 9.2

Suppose A makes a contract to rent undeveloped farmland to B. B agrees to pay $1,000 per month to A. B plants his crop and pays the first month's rent of $1,000 to A. Then, B goes on growing his crop but pays no more rent. After four months, A succeeds in evicting B from the land because of nonpayment of rent. A then decides to sue B for the additional unpaid three months' rent, or $3,000. It turns out that, unknown to A, the crop B was growing was illegal marijuana. In the lawsuit against him, B might raise the defense of illegality against A; that is, B argues that A cannot enforce the contract because its purpose (renting land to grow a controlled substance) was illegal.

Should a court refuse to enforce A's contract claim for rent because B was engaging in illegal conduct? This seems harsh under the circumstances. First, the illegality does not appear to be central to the contract, at least from A's point of view. In fact, A apparently was not aware of B's illegal purpose, although perhaps she should have been. Even if A should have checked into B's purpose for renting the land, B would appear to be the more guilty party since he deliberately engaged in illegal acts. Most courts would not penalize A under these circumstances. This result could be justified under the theory that the illegality was not central to the contract or that A was less guilty than B.

Enforcement of Illegal Contracts

The relative guilt of parties to an illegal contract has long played a role in whether courts will allow any enforcement of such a contract. If the parties appear to be equally at fault in engaging in illegal conduct, courts will usually refuse enforcement to them both. Note that *enforcement* here means the right to go to court and obtain remedies based on the contract. The common law addressed enforcement of illegal contracts under the idea conveyed in the Latin phrase *in pari delicto potior est conditio defendentis*. Literally translated, this phrase means where parties are equally at fault, the condition of the defending party is the better one. In practice, this means that if the parties are equally wrong (**in pari delicto**), the courts will deny enforcement to whichever party requests it.

In pari delicto A Latin phrase meaning that the parties are equally wrong in their conduct related to a contract. Courts will deny enforcement to whichever party requests it.

Malum in se A wrong considered to be so heinous or unacceptable that it is "evil in and of itself."

Malum prohibitum An act that is made illegal by the government or legislature because it involves conduct society wishes to discourage.

If the kind of illegality involved in the contract is very serious or reprehensible, the parties will generally be found to be equally wrong. Common law uses the Latin phrase *malum in se* to describe such illegal acts; that is, some acts are considered to be "evil" (*malum*) in and of themselves (*in se*). **Malum in se** illegalities are acts that civilized human beings universally find abhorrent: murder, rape, torture, and the like. If a contract is illegal and the illegality is malum in se, the parties are considered to be equally wrong, and the courts will not allow either of them to enforce the contract.

Where the illegality involved in a contract is not malum in se, it is usually classified as only *malum prohibitum*. **Malum prohibitum** illegalities are acts made illegal by the government or legislature and involve conduct that society discourages through legislation or regulation. In some sense, these are lesser illegalities, because they are not considered inherently evil. Usually, malum prohibitum acts are discouraged in order to protect the health and welfare of the citizenry or promote the revenue-raising functions of government. If the illegality is malum prohibitum, the parties are not automatically equally wrong. A court will look further to see if there is a difference in the amount of fault that can be attributed to the parties.

In some categories of malum prohibitum illegality, one party is traditionally considered to be less at fault than the other. Contracts made in violation of a licensing statute are an example. Where the purpose of a statute is not just to raise money but also to protect the public health, safety, or welfare, a member of the public will normally be viewed as less at fault than the party who was required to be licensed and failed to comply.

Suppose a particular state legislature has passed a statute requiring all building contractors working within the state to pass a licensing exam before they can deal with the public. Although the statute may be aimed partly at revenue raising, its major purpose is to protect the public by requiring contractors to demonstrate knowledge and expertise before they do construction that might endanger the public. If a contractor disobeys the state licensing requirements, courts in that state might refuse to enforce any contracts the contractor makes.

EXAMPLE **9.3**

Contractor, who is unlicensed, makes a contract with Homeowner for an extensive remodel. Homeowner and Contractor have a disagreement over the scope of the work under the contract, and Contractor claims Homeowner owes her money. Contractor sues.

In the case of *Contractor v. Homeowner*, a court might refuse enforcement to Contractor, but not to Homeowner. The illegality involved is essentially Contractor's failure to comply with state licensing requirements. Of course, Homeowner might also be viewed as having some guilt if he knew Contractor was not licensed. In that case, Homeowner might be considered to have at least encouraged Contractor's illegal behavior. Most courts would view Contractor as being more guilty than Homeowner, however, even if Homeowner knew Contractor was not licensed. The reason for this is that licensing of contractors is required as a matter of public protection. Courts tend to believe that preventing unlicensed contractors from enforcing their contracts promotes this policy by discouraging contractors from engaging in construction work unless they are licensed. Thus, the court would probably not allow Contractor to enforce the contract. Homeowner would be viewed as less guilty because the statute was passed to protect members of the public like Homeowner.

Note how the court addresses degrees of guilt in the following case.

A CASE FOR STUDY

Golberg v. Sanglier

96 Wash. 2d 874, 639 P.2d 1347 (1982)

UTTER, Justice. Petitioners Robert Golberg and Miriam Pierce seek review of the Court of Appeals reversal of the trial court's judgment in their favor and its dismissal of petitioners' claim against their former partners, respondents John D. Sanglier and Nick Carras. Petitioners received an award of damages based on the trial court's finding that the sale of their partnership interest to the remaining partners was induced by fraud. The Court of Appeals reversed the trial court and dismissed petitioners' case with prejudice, finding the partnership agreement was illegal and thus unenforceable. We review that decision here, reversing the Court of Appeals and reinstating the trial court's judgment for petitioners.

Respondent John D. Sanglier applied to General Motors in 1973 for a Cadillac dealership. Sanglier had been general sales manager for Carras Cadillac, Inc., which voluntarily terminated its franchise early in 1974. The Motors Holding and Cadillac divisions of General Motors required Sanglier to provide 25 percent of the franchise capital requirements, $100,000 in unencumbered funds. In return, Motors Holding would provide the remaining 75 percent of the initial capital requirements and become majority stockholder and only voting stockholder.

In March 1974, Sanglier contacted petitioner Golberg, who eventually agreed, along with petitioner Pierce, to put up the $100,000 needed by Sanglier in return for a three-way partnership. In April 1974, the three met in a Tacoma attorney's office to discuss forming a partnership. They agreed that the two investors would each have a 25 percent interest in the partnership and that Sanglier, who was to make no capital investment, would be the dealer and have a 50 percent interest in the partnership. Eventually, Nick Carras also joined the partnership: Carras, Golberg, and Pierce each provided $33,333.33.

The next month the group met at the office of their Tacoma attorney and conferred with his partner. They discussed nondisclosure to Motors Holding and Cadillac of the true source of Sanglier's funds, and that Sanglier had already represented to Cadillac, and would represent to Motors Holding, that the funds were a gift from his mother-in-law. The attorney advised the group that Sanglier's statements might be a misrepresentation.

Motors Holding decided that an Oldsmobile franchise would have to be teamed with the Cadillac franchise which called for a further investment by Sanglier of $25,000. Pierce, Golberg, and Carras each contributed their pro rata share of the $25,000, bringing the total capital investment of each to $41,666.

Motors Holding and Sanglier entered an agreement to buy the Carras Cadillac real property, buildings, and equipment, and in August 1974, Motors Holding formed Sanglier Cadillac-Oldsmobile, Inc., a Delaware corporation. Sanglier acknowledged, as was required by the Cadillac and Motors Holding divisions, that the $125,000 investment was his own money free and clear of any present or future right, claim, or interest of any kind. Motors Holding came up with another $645,000, part of which represented a loan to the dealership. The rest was taken in preferred and common stock. Motors Holding took all the voting stock. Sanglier was retained as president of the dealership.

In December, the four partners—Sanglier, Carras, Pierce and Golberg—executed a document entitled "Partnership Agreement," which provided the partnership should remain undisclosed and that none of the profits would be shared until Motors Holding was paid in full. Sanglier would devote his dividends and one half of his salary bonus to paying Motors Holding, but he could retain his salary. Stock and

notes he purchased would go into escrow for the partnership, to be transferred when Motors Holding was paid in full. From that point, each partner would share 25 percent of the partnership profits and losses.

In the fall of 1975, the partners met to discuss the possible sale of the partnership to another dealer. Late that fall or early the next year, Sanglier told Golberg the deal was off, though he actually continued to negotiate and eventually entered into an option agreement, taking $165,000 in option money. Carras knew about this deal, and with this money Sanglier bought Carras' share of the partnership, paid off some debts to Carras, and used the rest for personal reasons. Carras also agreed to assist Sanglier in buying out the other two partners who were not told about any of these transactions.

Between July and December 1976, Carras attended four partnership meetings, pretending he was still a partner. He told Pierce and Golberg that Sanglier was mismanaging the business, not acting in the best interest of the partnership, drinking and gambling excessively, and that they would be lucky to get their initial investment back.

In mid-December, Sanglier with Carras co-signing, borrowed $85,000 from a bank. On December 20, Sanglier bought out the interests of petitioners Golberg and Pierce by giving each a check for $41,666, the amount of their capital investment. Carras, whose interest had already been purchased by Sanglier, was also given a check which he had agreed in advance to tear up. Golberg and Pierce were not told about the loan that Carras cosigned. The parties signed a document drafted by Carras that purported to "terminate, dissolve and wind up" the partnership created on December 1, 1974.

In March 1978, Golberg and Pierce found out about Sanglier's option agreement to sell the dealership. Sanglier orally offered to let them back into the partnership if each would return the $41,666, pay a pro rata share of his start-up costs and premiums, and sign on the contingent liability of the dealership that he was personally guaranteeing. They declined.

The option agreement was never consummated and Sanglier repaid the $165,000 to the prospective purchaser in May 1978. In March 1978, Golberg and Pierce commenced this action, seeking damages under the partnership agreement based on fraud, breach of the partnership agreement and fiduciary duties, and violation of RCW 21.20.010 of the Washington securities laws. The plaintiffs sought to rescind the sale of their partnership interests or, in the alternative, to be awarded damages.

The trial court held in favor of petitioners, awarding each $261,917.32, their shares of the fair market value of the dealership/partnership as of the date they discovered Sanglier's and Carras's breach of their partnership duties. The Court of Appeals reversed the trial court and dismissed the complaint with prejudice. The appellate court held that the defendants Sanglier and Carras had standing to raise the defense of illegality of the partnership, and that such defense defeated any claims Golberg and Pierce had under the partnership agreement. This court granted Golberg's and Pierce's petition for review.

If a contract is illegal, our courts will leave the parties to that contract where it finds them. The same rule applies if the contract grows immediately out of and is connected with an illegal act. The Court of Appeals refused to entertain petitioners' claim based on the partnership agreement because the agreement had the effect "of deceiving Motors Holding" . . . . We will analyze each of the Court of Appeals findings of illegality.

RCW 21.20.010 (2) states that it is unlawful for any person in connection with the purchase of any security to make any untrue statement of a material fact or to omit to state a material fact necessary in order to make the statements made, in the light of the circumstances under which they are made, not misleading . . . . The Court of Appeals found that Sanglier violated this part of the act in his misrepresentation to Motors Holding that the funds constituting the 25 percent capital investment were his "own funds, free and clear of any present or future right, claim or interest of any kind." Golberg v. Sanglier, supra at 192, 616 P.2d 1239. The Court of Appeals determined these funds were not free and clear but were encumbered in that "(t)he dealer's interest, represented by stock, was required . . . to be placed in escrow . . ." Golberg v. Sanglier, supra at 192, 616 P.2d 1239.

Although we do not doubt that Sanglier's representation as to the status of his funds was "material" to the transaction, we must question the Court of Appeals conclusion that such representation was "untrue." The escrow requirement, upon which the Court of Appeals relied for its finding of untruthfulness, did not relate to the initial capital investment Sanglier was required by Motors Holding to provide. It related only to the profits from the dealership, and Motors Holding did not require that the profits of the dealership be unencumbered. They required only that the 25 percent investment be unencumbered. Thus, the Court of Appeals did not provide a valid basis for reversing the trial court and finding that the capital contribution provided by Sanglier was encumbered. . . .

Although doubt should be resolved in favor of petitioners as to whether Sanglier misrepresented the status of his funds, there is no question that he misrepresented the source of his funds. He told Motors Holding and Cadillac that the funds were a gift from his mother-in-law while the funds were actually provided by the partnership. However, neither the trial court nor the Court of Appeals found that Sanglier's misrepresentation as to the source of his funds was "material" to the transaction, as is required for a violation of section 2 of the act. And it is not clear to us whether such misrepresentation was material to the transaction. In light of both lower courts' findings with respect to Sanglier's misrepresentation as to the source of his funds, we hold that a violation of RCW 21.20.010 (2) is not established.

The Court of Appeals also found that the partnership agreement violated section 3 of RCW 21.20.010, which makes illegal "any act, practice, or course of business which operates or would operate as a fraud or deceit upon any person." We agree that Sanglier's misrepresentation as to the source of his funds and the partnership's agreement to perpetuate this misrepresentation by requiring nondisclosure of its existence did "operate as a fraud or deceit" upon Motors Holding in contravention of section 3. Nonetheless, the extent to which petitioners are culpable must be fully understood. The partnership agreement was designed to give Sanglier the 25 percent capital investment as his own unencumbered funds. There is substantial support in the record to support a finding that the funds were his own and were unencumbered.

His misrepresentation that the funds came from his mother-in-law does not eradicate the partnership's attempt to comply with Motors Holding's and Cadillac's requirements for the transaction and petitioners' belief that what they were doing was legal. While the entire partnership would have been civilly liable for Sanglier's violation of section 3 such liability is not dispositive of the question whether the parties were in pari delicto. The Court of Appeals seems implicitly to have relied on this assumption. Golberg v. Sanglier, supra at 195, 616 P.2d 1239. While both parties may be equally liable to third parties for the illegality of their transaction, they may not necessarily be in pari delicto.

Having determined the extent to which the partnership agreement is unlawful, we must still examine the question whether petitioners were in pari delicto with respondents. The trial court found, in its conclusion of law No. 13, that petitioners were not in pari delicto. The Court of Appeals did not overrule this conclusion of law by the trial court, but stated only: "even if the plaintiffs were not in pari delicto, they would be limited to disaffirming their agreement and recovering the funds they paid under it." Golberg v. Sanglier, supra at 197, 616 P.2d 1239.

Before proceeding to a discussion of the merits of this part of the Court of Appeals holding, we must first reflect upon the purposes of the rule of in pari delicto. The maxim "in pari delicto potior est conditio defendentis" declares that the defendant will prevail when the parties are of equal guilt. Where the parties are not equally culpable, the defense of in pari delicto is not appropriate. Id. Where the conduct of the party who seeks to enlist support of the doctrine outrages public sensibilities more than the conduct of the party against whom the doctrine is sought to be applied, courts will not support application of the rule.

Ultimately, a decision as to whether a party is in pari delicto relies on public policy considerations and not a neat calculus for determining differential fault. The fundamental concern that should guide a court in making its decision is whether the "public good (will be) enhanced." [Citation] Of course, public policy "is a very unruly horse, and when once you get astride it you never know where it will carry you." [Citation]

The key to a determination of this nature is whether our decision will be more likely to prevent such illegal transactions in the future. There are two policy implications of the Court of Appeals holding: first, unwary investors who enter questionably legal transactions are on notice they are subject to fraud and deceit without legal recourse; second, opportunists such as Sanglier are encouraged to draw such unwary persons into questionable investment schemes, return their initial investment under fraudulent pretenses, and dupe them out of their profits, all with full assurance that they will be insulated from legal recourse. These implications are inconsistent with the purposes of the rule of in pari delicto. These rules are intended to prevent the guilty party from reaping the benefit of his wrongful conduct, or to protect the public from the future consequences of an illegal contract. They do not necessarily apply to both parties to the agreement unless both are truly in pari delicto. . . . [T]he courts should not be so enamored with the Latin phrase "in pari delicto" that they blindly extend the rule to every case where illegality appears somewhere in the transaction. The fundamental purpose of the rule must always be kept in mind, and the realities of the situation must be considered. Where, by applying the rule, the public cannot be protected because the transaction has been completed, where no serious moral turpitude is involved, where the defendant is the one guilty of the greatest moral fault, and where to apply the rule will be to permit the defendant to be unjustly enriched at the expense of the plaintiff, the rule should not be applied." [Citation] In order to best effectuate the purposes of the rule, enforcement of the plaintiff's claim may be appropriate: In some cases . . . effective deterrence is best realized by enforcing the plaintiff's claim rather than leaving the defendant in possession of the benefit; or the forfeiture resulting from unenforceability is disproportionately harsh considering the nature of the illegality. In each such case, how the aims of policy can best be achieved depends on the kind of illegality and the particular facts involved. As Mr. Justice Holmes has stated: "But a person does not become an outlaw and lose all rights by doing an illegal act. The right not to be led by fraud to change one's situation is anterior to and independent of the contract." [Citation] The plaintiff's right not to be defrauded is anterior if he or she can demonstrate he or she is not in pari delicto.

In applying these public policy concerns to this case, numerous factors surface that support the trial court's conclusion of law that petitioners were not in pari delicto. First, the trial court found that petitioners "did not at any time intend to enter an illegal contract or to damage Motors Holding or General Motors." Finding of fact No. 12. While petitioners' lack of illegal intent may be irrelevant to finding an act illegal under certain provisions of the state's securities laws, lack of scienter is relevant to determining whether a party is in pari delicto. Even an unreasonable belief that the transaction is legal may provide the basis for finding a party not in pari delicto.

The trial court also found petitioners "had no prior experience in the automobile business, and relied on the experience and knowledge of the defendants" .... It is true that one of the advising attorneys offered that Sanglier's statements to Motors Holding "might be" a misrepresentation. This speculation was apparently resolved in favor of the transaction's legality since both the attorneys and petitioners were under the impression that the partnership agreement was legal when created. In retrospect, we may condemn petitioners' actions, but as one commentator has stated: The careful and the timorous may avoid worries and possible penalties by following such advice as "When the matter is doubtful, don't"; but such a practice may unnecessarily limit his own enterprise and the general prosperity as well.

The trial court's finding that petitioners were not in pari delicto is supported by substantial evidence. Still to be resolved is whether the Court of Appeals correctly concluded that petitioners' relief was limited to "disaffirming their agreement and recovering the funds they paid under it." Golberg v. Sanglier, 27 Wash. App. 179, 197, 616 P.2d 1239 (1980). The rule articulated by Williston seems to support the Court of Appeals position: Probably no more exact principle can be laid down than this, that if a plaintiff although culpable has not been guilty of moral turpitude, and the loss he will suffer by being denied relief is wholly out of

proportion to the requirements either of public policy or of appropriate individual punishment, he may be allowed to recover back the consideration with which he has parted. Recovery of consideration is a restitutionary remedy, and it would appear that Williston's conclusion is based on earlier authority that limited parties not in pari delicto to restitutionary remedies. Unlike Williston, Corbin states that when a party is not in pari delicto he is entitled to some legal remedy and that "[o]ur legal system provides a good variety of legal remedies and they are applied by the courts with a high degree of flexibility." [Citation] Many courts have demonstrated this flexibility in shaping a full range of remedies to parties not in pari delicto. The trial court imposed a restitutionary remedy in finding that Sanglier held the profits of the dealership in constructive trust. A constructive trust is imposed not because of the intention of the parties but because the person holding the title to property would profit by a wrong or would be unjustly enriched if he were permitted to keep the property. The trial court's remedy is exemplary of the kind of flexibility courts need in shaping restitutionary remedies for plaintiffs not in pari delicto. If the trial court were rigidly limited to the remedy discussed in Williston, supra, justice could not be rendered. While recovery of initial consideration will usually be sufficient, it is not adequate as the only available remedy. Respondents' entire scheme to defraud their partners was based on returning petitioners' initial consideration so to deprive them of profits. Sanglier was unjustly enriched with profits and it is that inequity the trial court sought to rectify in providing its remedy.

Public policy is better served by upholding the trial court in this case. The policy implications of our holding are twofold: first, petitioners will be adequately deterred from entering questionable transactions by the scars of this regrettable experience; and second, respondents, who were the primary transgressors of the law with respect to this transaction, will be justly required to disgorge profits accruing to them from their improper behavior. The trend of modern jurisprudence is to get away from the technical or literal application of ancient maxims of the law intended to prevent fraud by refusing audience to a party who in his complaint discloses that he himself is tainted with moral turpitude, when its application in the particular case would prove but a cover and shelter for the scoundrel who by falsehood and deceit inveigled the complainant to trust him with his money. In other words, where the ends of public policy will rather be promoted by giving than refusing relief, courts prefer the former. In short, although the complainant may in some degree be in delicto, yet, unless he is also in pari delicto with the defendant, it does not, and should not, follow that the doors of the temple of justice should be closed against him. [Citation]

The Court of Appeals is reversed and the trial court's judgment is reinstated.

Questions to Consider

1. What was the illegality involved in this case? Was there more than one illegality? Explain.
2. Why did the Washington Supreme Court find that the parties were not in pari delicto?
3. Why did the Washington Supreme Court reinstate the trial verdict in favor of Golberg and Pierce?
4. Can you determine from this case when parties involved in future illegal transactions might or might not be in pari delicto? What factors seem most critical in making such a determination?
5. What factual changes might you make in the case that would cause Golberg and Pierce to be in pari delicto with Sanglier?

Assignment

1. Which, if either, of the following cases involve illegal contracts?
2. In which of the following cases would a court be likely to allow enforcement, and by whom? Why?

▶ Hypothetical 1: The Case of the Historic Preservation Ordinance

On February 1, Contractor makes an agreement with Building Owner to convert Owner's 1925 commercial property from a greeting card shop to a handmade clothing shop. Extensive remodeling will be needed to make room for a small garment-making factory on the premises.

On February 15, City Council passes a zoning ordinance making the location of Owner's building a "Historic Preservation Zone." The ordinance prohibits even light manufacturing in the Historic Zone and requires all "material changes" to buildings more that 30 years old to be approved by the Municipal Planning Commission. Contractor and Owner agree to go ahead with the remodel anyway because, as Owner says, they already had a contract and "who knows what the Municipal Planning Commission might do to our plans."

Contractor begins work, but he and Owner have a falling out and Contractor walks off the job. Owner files a lawsuit against Contractor for breach of contract.

▶ Hypothetical 2: The Case against Toxic Waste

Killer Chemicals, Inc., now manufactures a pesticide called "Glop." Because residues left from the Glop manufacturing process may be toxic, Killer must dispose of them according to the provisions of the Columbia State Toxic Wastes Act. The Act provides: "§ 3A—All toxic waste to be disposed of under this Act must be distributed or sold only to authorized and licensed Columbia State Toxic Waste Disposal Agents. Sale or disposal of toxic waste to unauthorized and/or unlicensed persons is punishable as a crime under § 3B of this Act." Section 3B of the Act describes whether unauthorized sales of toxic waste are felonies or misdemeanors.

Killer has always made contracts with Agent for waste disposal of residues from Glop manufacturing. Agent is licensed and authorized under Columbia State law. Agent's prices have been increasing, however, and Killer has looked for a cheaper way to dispose of the Glop residues. Killer finds an out-of-state agent, Thelma, who will handle and dispose of the residues more cheaply. Thelma is not licensed by Columbia State, although she is licensed in her own state and has an excellent reputation for toxic waste disposal. Killer decides to go with Thelma, and the parties make a one-year contract under which Thelma is to handle transportation and disposal of all toxic wastes from the manufacture of Glop. Thelma handles the transportation and disposal success-fully for six months, but the parties then have a falling out because Thelma wants to raise the contract price to help cover her own increased costs.

Killer refuses to let Thelma raise the contract price, and Thelma refuses to continue performance under the contract. Killer sues Thelma for breach of contract. Thelma raises the defense that Killer cannot enforce the contract because it is illegal. Since the contract involves a very large quantity of toxic waste, if the contract is illegal, disposing of the residues through Thelma would qualify as a felony under § 3B of the Act.

Contract Defenses Based on Unconscionability

Although the traditional common law of contracts recognized a number of related ideas, the modern doctrine of unconscionability in contracts was first developed by the drafters of the UCC. The UCC provides:

> § 2-302 **Unconscionable Contract or Clause.**
> (1) If the court as a matter of law finds the contract or any clause of the contract to have been unconscionable at the time it was made the court may refuse to enforce the contract, or it may enforce the remainder of the contract without the unconscionable clause, or it may so limit the application of any unconscionable clause as to avoid any unconscionable result.

Since this provision was first presented, § 2-302 has had widespread influence, and the doctrine of unconscionability is now part of the common law of contracts, as well as the UCC. Although it is generally accepted, the doctrine of unconscionability is not well defined, possibly because it is still relatively new and under development. Even the drafters of the UCC neglected to include a true definition of unconscionability in § 2-302. Careful reading reveals that § 2-302 is really an announcement of the doctrine and some ideas about how it should operate. The drafters never actually define unconscionability.

Unconscionability Defined

Although there is no universally accepted definition of **unconscionability,** the general meaning of the concept is clear. The doctrine allows a party to

Unconscionability
A defense based on the argument that in light of commercial realities or the circumstances of a particular trade or case, the contract, its language, or the bargaining process was so one-sided as to be extremely unfair.

remove a provision from a contract, or invalidate the contract itself, where the following requirements are met:

- The provision or contract is so one-sided as to be oppressive.
- The one-sided provisions are not what a reasonable person would expect to find in the contract ("unfair surprise").
- The parties were of very unequal bargaining strength.
- The weaker of the two parties had little or no choice about whether to enter into the contract.

The drafters of the UCC stated it this way: "The basic test is whether, in the light of the general commercial background and the commercial needs of the particular trade or case, the clauses involved are so one-sided as to be unconscionable under the circumstances existing at the time of the making of the contract."[5] In other words, if the bargain is grossly unfair to one party, and he was forced into the contract, then the problematic provisions may be unconscionable.

Gross unfairness in a contract provision or in a whole contract is not always easy to measure. The traditional law of contracts favors almost a frontier spirit of negotiation, with each party viewed as equally strong, savvy, and capable. That one party was able to drive a harder bargain than the other was considered an insufficient reason to invalidate a contract. Additionally, contract law tends to treat each party as having full knowledge of all the details in a contract. Each party to a contract is generally bound by all its provisions, even if she has not actually read or fully understood them.

In modern times, however, it has been recognized that not all contracting parties are equally strong, savvy, and capable. In real life, there are many inequalities in bargaining strength and ability. Furthermore, a contract may contain language that one of the parties is not in a position to fully understand or is unable to turn down under the particular circumstances. These factors may result in a contract that disproportionately favors one party and is grossly unfair to the other.

Besides unfairness and inequality of bargaining power, the doctrine of unconscionability is concerned with unfair "surprise" and lack of choice. Unfair surprise concerns the idea that some contracts contain provisions a reasonable person would not expect to find. Where such provisions are so unfair or oppressive that the "surprised" party would not have entered into the contract if he had understood their implication, courts may not enforce these provisions. Lack of choice involves the idea that if a person accepted an oppressive contractual arrangement because she was more or less forced to do so, enforcement of the oppressive provisions (or, possibly, the entire contract) should be refused. No simple formula is available to determine when all four factors will combine to make a contract or its provisions unenforceable because of unconscionability. It is also possible a court would find unconscionability where two or three factors were met in a compelling way.

Three general types of contracts or contract provisions have given rise to much of the litigation concerning unconscionability issues:

- Adhesion contracts
- Exculpatory clauses
- Disclaimers and limitations of warranty

Adhesion Contracts

Many lawsuits involving issues of unconscionability have arisen from what are known as adhesion contracts. **Adhesion contracts** are agreements where one party is so much weaker than the other party that the stronger party essentially forces the weaker one to "adhere" to the contract it provides. Such situations arise most often when individuals are dealing with large and powerful institutions. The following are examples of adhesion contracts:

Adhesion contracts
Agreements in which one party is so much weaker than the other that the stronger party essentially forces the weaker one to "adhere" to the contract it provides.

- Hospital contracts where a patient is refused lifesaving care unless he signs an agreement not to sue the hospital or its doctors in case of malpractice
- Insurance contracts that turn out to exempt from coverage the very type of damage the insured was trying to protect against
- Various kinds of loan or financing agreements written in language so confusing or obscure the average person cannot understand that the loan conditions are extremely unfair and unfavorable

Exculpatory Clauses

Many other lawsuits involving unconscionability arise from contractual arrangements loosely known as exculpatory clauses. **Exculpatory clauses** are provisions in a contract that release a party from liability for injuries caused by its own deliberate wrongdoing or negligence. Most jurisdictions have not permitted parties to contract away liability for deliberate or intentional wrongdoing. However, contract provisions that relieve a party from liability for negligent wrongdoing have been widely enforced. It is these arrangements that have given rise to many cases involving issues of unconscionability.

Exculpatory clauses
Provisions in a contract that release a party from liability for injuries caused by its own wrongdoing or negligence.

EXAMPLE **9.4**

Suppose a couple sign up to take sailboarding lessons from Sun & Fun Sports Company, Inc. Sun & Fun presents the couple with its standard sailboarding contract, which they sign. The contract contains a consent provision that states:

> The undersigned agree they will not hold Sun & Fun Sports Company, Inc., liable for injuries caused by acts of negligence on the part of staff and/or instructors employed by the company and suffered by the undersigned in connection with providing sailboarding lessons.

The couple begin taking lessons, but during a lesson, the sailboarding instructor leaves Husband alone in the water and he is a poor swimmer. As a result, Husband panics, loses control of his sailboard, and falls off because of the extremely rough surf. Husband is hit on the head by the sailboard and almost drowns. Before he is rescued, Husband suffers damage to his lungs, a concussion, two broken fingers, and extreme emotional distress.

Husband then sues Sun & Fun on a negligence theory to obtain compensation for his injuries. Sun & Fun is likely to raise as a defense the fact that Husband signed the contractual consent provision releasing Sun & Fun from liability for negligence. Sun & Fun will claim the consent provision is an enforceable part of its contract. To counter this argument, Husband might claim the consent form is unconscionable and should not be enforced.

Some exculpatory clauses like that in Sun & Fun's standard contract have been found to be *enforceable* even though they release a party from liability for its own negligence. Generally, however, courts do not find such clauses enforceable where enforcement would present a public danger, or where there is some other public interest in preventing release from liability under the circumstances. Thus, to predict the outcome in *Husband v. Sun & Fun,* one would need to know more about case and statutory law in Husband's state and more about the specific facts of Husband's case.

Questions to Consider

1. Can you think of any reasons a court might find a public interest in the case involving Sun & Fun's exculpatory clause?

2. What kind of activity is sailboarding? Should it be considered similar to engaging in amateur or professional boxing? Or is it more like joining an amateur softball team or taking ballet lessons? Should the nature of the activity make a difference in enforcing the exculpatory clause?

3. Is there any argument in *Husband v. Sun & Fun* that more than mere negligence on the part of the instructor was involved? Should this make a difference in enforcing the exculpatory clause?

Disclaimers and Limitations of Warranty

Warranty A guarantee of performance or quality concerning commercial or consumer goods, products, real estate, personal property of all kinds, or services.

Express warranties Guarantees concerning contract performance or quality of goods, services, or subject matter that are explicitly stated in the contract.

Implied warranties Guarantees concerning contract performance or quality of goods, services, or subject matter not explicitly stated in the contract, but which the parties would reasonably have assumed were present in the contract, or which the law construes to be in a contract.

In contract law, a **warranty** is a guarantee concerning commercial or consumer goods, products, real estate, personal property of all kinds, or services. Warranties can be express or implied. **Express warranties** are explicitly stated in the contract. **Implied warranties** are warranties that the parties would reasonably have assumed were present in the contract or that the law construes to be in a contract. The following are examples of some common kinds of warranties:

- A warranty that the contractual item is fit for the specific purpose for which it was purchased
- A warranty that the contractual item is fit for the general, "ordinary" purposes for which such items are used
- A warranty that all representations made by the seller concerning the subject matter of the contract are true
- A warranty that the contractual item will not wear out or break down before a certain time and that if it does, it will be replaced at little or no cost
- A warranty that the seller has "clear title" to the item being sold
- A warranty that any samples or models used to obtain the contract are representative of the actual items being sold

Both the common law and the UCC recognize a wide variety of express and implied warranties in contracts, but both also permit contracting parties to eliminate or alter warranties under many circumstances. When a party succeeds in eliminating or altering a warranty in a way that is overly harsh or unfair, and this has an unexpected result for the other party, the contract may be unconscionable. Consider the following case.

EXAMPLE   **9.5**

Mr. and Mrs. Smith purchase a new car from Car Dealer. The sale contract they sign contains a clause that states:

> The manufacturer of this automobile warrants that all parts of it (except the tires) are free from defect in material or workmanship under normal use. Manufacturer's liability under this warranty is limited to replacement of any part which is or becomes defective within the first 100 days of purchase.

Within two weeks of purchase, the car's brakes fail due to faulty construction. Unfortunately, the failure of the brakes causes the couple to have a serious accident in which they are both gravely injured. Their injuries cost $70,000 in hospital and medical bills, and lost wages. The cost of replacing the defective brakes is $1,000.

If the Smiths (or their insurance company on their behalf) sue the car manufacturer, should the manufacturer's limitation of warranty be enforceable? Why or why not?

Courts have not looked favorably on a car dealer or manufacturer's attempt to limit automobile warranties relating to reliability, safety, and fitness of the car. Attempts to avoid liability for personal injury by placing limitations on an automobile warranty have been found to be unconscionable.[6]

Procedural and Substantive Unconscionability

Many legal scholars and courts make a distinction between two different kinds of unconscionability: procedural unconscionability and substantive unconscionability. In theory, **procedural unconscionability** involves grossly unfair or oppressive procedures or conduct *in the bargaining process*. **Substantive unconscionability** involves unfair or oppressive provisions in the contract terms themselves without regard to the bargaining process by which the terms became part of the contract. Although the distinction between substantive and procedural unconscionability can be useful at times, often the distinction is easier to describe in theory than it is to use in fact. Sometimes both types of unconscionability may be present in the same contract.

The doctrines of procedural and substantive unconscionability both involve the same concerns for unfairness, inequality of bargaining strength, lack of choice, and surprise avoidance of reasonable expectations. They are not really different doctrines, but the same doctrine examined in two different stages of contract life: the negotiation process and the ultimate contractual agreement itself. If a court finds that a contract involved either kind of unconscionability, it may refuse to enforce the contract or may allow enforcement only if the unconscionable provisions are struck out.

Procedural unconscionability Grossly unfair or oppressive conduct by one contracting party during the bargaining process. **Substantive unconscionability** Unfair or oppressive provisions in the actual terms of a contract, without regard to the bargaining process by which the terms became part of the contract.

Assignment

One year, the northern part of the state of Columbia experiences ninety straight days of heavy rain. Northern Columbia has hilly terrain and somewhat unstable soil. As a result of the rain, many homeowners suffer severe damage from mud and slides. One such homeowner, Harry, suffers major damage when his home slides from the top of his hillside lot to the bottom. Harry has held homeowner's insurance with Insurance Company since he purchased his home 25 years ago. During that time, he has paid more than $30,000 for coverage from Insurance Company. Harry wants to make a claim under his homeowner's policy, which states: "*General Coverage E:* In addition to specific types of damage covered by this policy under *Specific Coverage B*, Insurance Company agrees to cover all damage to home caused by flooding or wind, excluding damage to home caused by soil subsidence." Slide damage is not listed as covered under *Specific Coverage B*.

All other insurance companies offering homeowner's insurance in Columbia include the same provision in their policies and will not issue policies without this language even if the individual homeowner disputes the provision or asks that it be changed. Insurance Company has a "take it or leave it" policy about coverage, as do all of the other insurance companies selling policies in Columbia. When Harry puts in a claim, Insurance Company denies coverage, saying *General Coverage E* means the damage to his home is not covered because the damage was the result of soil subsidence.

1. How much choice did Harry (or other homeowners in Columbia) have in selecting insurance coverage for his home? Who has more bargaining power, Harry or Insurance Company? Why?
2. How would a reasonable homeowner be likely to interpret *Specific Coverage B* before the problem with the hillside slide arose? Why?
3. Could you rewrite *General Coverage E* so that it clearly excludes damage of the type Harry's home suffered? Could you rewrite it so that it clearly includes damage of the type Harry's home suffered? Should it make any difference that the policy language seems capable of more than one interpretation or that Insurance Company wrote the language? Why?
4. If the damage to Harry's home is not covered under his policy, does this result seem unfair in any way? Why or why not?
5. If a court wanted to find *General Coverage E* unconscionable, should it characterize this as procedural unconscionability, substantive unconscionability, or both? Why?

Chapter Review Questions

1. What are the differences between economic duress and physical duress used as contract defenses?
2. Assume investment Banker obtains a sale contract from one of Bank's investment clients that involves sale to Bank of Client's land at half-price. Also assume Banker failed to disclose a reassessment of Client's land that would raise its price by 30 percent. If Client later refuses to go through with the contract and Bank sues, what defenses might Client raise, and why?
3. How do the defenses of fraud, misrepresentation, and concealment differ?
4. What does mental incapacity mean in a contract case?
5. What is meant by the defense of minority?

6. What are the various circumstances under which a court will deny enforcement to an illegal contract?
7. What is meant by unconscionability in general, and what is the difference between procedural and substantive unconscionability?

Key Terms

Adhesion contracts, 193
Concealment, 181
Duress, 176
Economic duress, 176
Election, 176
Exculpatory clauses, 193
Express warranties, 194
Fiduciary or confidential
relationship, 179
Fraud, 179
Illegal contract, 183
Illegality, 183
Implied warranties, 194
In pari delicto, 184

Malum in se, 184
Malum prohibitum, 184
Mental incapacity, 182
Minority, 182
Misrepresentation, 180
Nondisclosure, 181
Procedural unconscionability,
195
Substantive unconscionability,
195
Unconscionability, 191
Undue influence, 179
Warranty, 194

Notes

1. The Securities Act of 1933, 15 U.S.C.A. § 77(a) et. seq. (1981) and The Securities Exchange Act of 1934, 15 U.S.C.A. § 78(a) et. seq. (1981). Absence of regulation in contracts for the sale of stock was in large part responsible for the American stock market crash of 1929 and the worldwide depression that followed. The federal securities acts and the state models that follow them all supplant the common law of contracts and are intended to curb abuses in stock sales.

2. See E. Allan Farnsworth and William F. Young, *Contracts,* 5th ed. (1995), "Policing the Bargain" beginning at p. 324.

3. *Odorizzi v. Bloomfield School District,* 246 Cal.App.2d 133, 54 Cal.Rptr. 533 (1966). This case was recently cited in *Tyler v. Children's Home Society,* 29 Cal.App.4th 511 (1994).

4. See, e.g., California Civil Code § 1102 et. seq., especially the disclosure form provisions in § 1102.6.

5. See comments to UCC § 2-302 in *Uniform Laws Annotated,* vol. 1A (St. Paul: West Publishing, 1989), p. 16.

6. For a similar warranty situation, see *Henningsen v. Bloomfield Motors, Inc.,* 161 A.2d 69, 94, 32 N.J. 358, (1960) where the New Jersey Supreme Court found the provision to be unconscionable.

CHAPTER

10

Defenses to Formation and Enforcement: The Statute of Frauds

Introduction

In the ancient English legal system, contractual promises were not enforceable unless they were written down. Gradually, however, the law of England changed, and oral contractual promises became enforceable. That is still the case today in both England and the United States where the law recognizes the enforceability of many oral contracts. Enforcing oral contracts presents a number of difficulties, however. First, people tend to forget over time. If a disagreement arises over an oral contract, by the time a court is asked to resolve the dispute, the parties may have forgotten important information or remember it differently. The second problem is that people are strongly tempted to lie about oral contracts because there is no writing to contradict what they say.

By the seventeenth century, English courts were faced with a crisis in the enforcement of oral contracts because lying about them in litigation had become a widespread practice. To address this problem, the English Parliament enacted what is now referred to as the *Statute of Frauds*.[1] The **Statute of Frauds** was a law *against* the commission of fraud through perjury. **Perjury** is lying after swearing a legal oath to tell the truth. By passing such a law, the English Parliament hoped to prevent lying about oral contracts and their fraudulent enforcement. The English Statute of Frauds came to America with the English settlers and the colonial law courts.

The original English Statute of Frauds covered many documents besides contracts, but it is the coverage of contracts that is relevant to the study of basic contract law. The Statute of Frauds originally required five different types of contracts to be in writing:

1. Contracts in which one party agreed to pay the debts of another party.
2. Contracts for the sale or transfer of an interest in real property.
3. Contracts that could not be completely performed in one year.
4. Contracts made "in consideration of" marriage.
5. Contracts for the sale of goods where the contract price was ten pounds sterling, or above.

The Statute of Frauds also provided that unless the party suing on one of these types of contracts could produce a written memorandum of the agreement, a court would not enforce it.

Today, American law requires these same five types of contracts to be in writing, or a court will not enforce them. Although, of course, many changes have occurred in the details of the Statute of Frauds, the same general scheme laid out by the English Parliament in the seventeenth century is still followed. Most states have passed statutes listing the kinds of contracts that have a writing requirement. These still include the original categories in the English Statute of Frauds as well as others that have been added over the years.

Sometimes beginning students of contract law misunderstand the effect of the Statute of Frauds. The Statute of Frauds did not prohibit oral contracts. In fact, it has had somewhat the opposite effect. Unless a particular kind of contract is specifically required to be in writing by the law of the relevant jurisdiction, the contract need not be written. If the Statute of Frauds requires a contract to be in writing, we say it "falls within the Statute." Modern contract law regards oral contracts as legally enforceable unless they fall within the Statute of Frauds.

Statute of Frauds An English statute passed in 1676 and adopted in modified form throughout the United States; requires some legal documents, including certain kinds of contracts, to be in writing.

Perjury Knowingly giving lying testimony after swearing a legal oath to tell the truth.

What Kind of Writing Is Required by the Statute of Frauds?

State requirements for a sufficient written contract vary somewhat, so you should always check the applicable state law. When dealing with federal jurisdictions, the relevant federal law should be researched. As a general matter, under the common law a writing is usually sufficient to satisfy the Statute of Frauds if it meets certain "traditional" requirements, which can be summarized as follows:

Party to be charged
The party sought to be held liable on a contract.

1. The written memorandum must be signed by the party sought to be held liable on the contract. This party is sometimes called the **party to be charged.** Suppose, for example, A sues B to enforce a five-year employment contract that A alleges B wrongfully breached. In that case, A must have a written contract with B's signature on it. Generally, preprinted forms with a company or individual name, official letterhead, and typewritten signatures are accepted as satisfying the signature requirement.
2. The writing must show evidence of the essential terms of the contract: the parties, the subject matter of the agreement, the price, quantity, and enough of the terms of the performance to show what was to happen, and when.
3. Some jurisdictions require a formal recital of the specific *consideration* for the contract. The rationale for this requirement is that much of the fraudulent evidence the Statute seeks to prohibit would be admitted if consideration could be proven by evidence not in the writing.

A writing that satisfies the Statute of Frauds can be one document or a series of documents. If it consists of a series of documents, however, the law usually requires a showing that all the documents are "integrated." Here, the word *integrated* means the writings can be shown to belong together and are part of a single whole agreement. If writings were not required to be integrated, it would be relatively easy for one party to obtain a piece of paper with the other party's signature and put it together with many other pieces of paper to fabricate a whole contract or part of a contract.

Problems Where the Writing is Incomplete

Difficulties can arise if a writing that is offered to satisfy the Statute of Frauds is incomplete. This problem relates to the parol evidence rule discussed earlier. If the party who gives evidence of the missing information is lying, then the court is promoting fraud by admitting such evidence. For this reason, oral evidence of missing essential terms is usually not permitted where a contract falls within the Statute of Frauds and a writing exists. However, if the evidence offered is simply needed to explain or clarify a term already included in the writing, it can be admitted, as can evidence that is consistent with what is already in the contract and is just "additional" information.

Like the parol evidence rule, this area of the law has created much confusion and complexity. Specific answers about admitting evidence in specific contract cases must be researched in the relevant jurisdiction. The paralegal should be alert to the problem of introducing into evidence information allegedly missing from a writing offered to satisfy the Statute of Frauds. Even if the omitted information is needed at trial, having it admitted into evidence may be difficult.

Part Performance of a Contract Within the Statute of Frauds

Human nature does not always work the way the law envisions. In many situations, the parties to a contract simply fail to put their agreement in writing in spite of legal requirements to do so. Failure to write down their agreement does not necessarily mean the parties have no contract, but it may mean they have no right to obtain enforcement. The general effect of failure to comply with the Statute of Frauds is twofold: (1) each party may give up the right to obtain enforcement of the contract in court, and (2) each party may give the other a defense of noncompliance with the Statute of Frauds if a lawsuit is brought on the alleged contract.

Under many circumstances, if the defendant raises the Statute of Frauds as a defense, it creates a hardship on the party who wants enforcement. For example, suppose the parties really had a contract and the plaintiff is in the right. Only the failure to "put it in writing" allows the defendant to get off the hook. As noted earlier, even if the plaintiff is telling the truth, courts will deny enforcement of an oral contract that falls within the Statute of Frauds. This result may be harsh, but Anglo-American law apparently considers this to be a fair trade-off against the larger policy of preventing fraud by requiring a written memorandum in the first place.

The situation may be different where a party to an oral agreement that falls within the Statute can show there has been some performance on the alleged contract. Most jurisdictions follow the general rule that **part performance** of an oral contract within the Statute of Frauds provides an exception that allows the contract to be enforced. Part performance occurs when one contracting party renders to the other some portion of the performance due under the alleged agreement. This result makes some sense. The underlying policy reason for requiring a written contract is to prevent fraud. Thus, part performance that appears to be nonfraudulent and to be reliable evidence of the oral contract should be permitted to excuse the writing requirement. The following example and questions illustrate why part performance may show the parties had a contract although they did not write it down.

Part performance
When one or both parties to a contract render some portion of the performance owed. Part performance of an oral contract that falls within the Statute of Frauds may be an exception that allows the contract to be enforced.

EXAMPLE **10.1**

Jack and Jill negotiate for several days for the sale of Whiteacre, a plot of undeveloped land. Jill, the seller, wants $100,000 for Whiteacre because it lies in an area that is partly large country estates and partly small family farms. She thinks the area will maintain its current high real estate prices. Jack, the buyer, wants to pay only $80,000 for the land because it does not have sewer, water, and power hookups. Jack estimates that the improvements will cost in excess of $20,000. He thinks the land will hold its value because of the location.

Eventually, the parties work out a compromise. Jack agrees to take the land, as is, for $88,000. The parties have known each other since they were climbing up and down hills together in grade school, so they agree to seal the deal with a handshake. Jack is to have the immediate right to occupy Whiteacre, and he makes a first payment of $44,000 to Jill. The remaining $44,000 is to be paid within the next 30 days.

Two weeks later, Miss Muffet approaches Jill and offers her $95,000 cash for Whiteacre. Realizing she sold the land too cheaply, Jill goes to Jack and tells him she has changed her mind. Jack says it is too late to change her mind; they had a deal. He reminds Jill of their childhood friendship and points out that he has already paid half the purchase price. Besides, he says, he has already had power and water supplied to the land and is in the process of completing a sewer hookup. He adamantly refuses to rescind their agreement. Jill tells Jack she will never deliver the deed to Whiteacre. As for their childhood together, she tells Jack the way she remembers it, he only carried the water bucket when it was empty. Thus, says Jill, she fully intends to sell to another buyer. Jack then sues Jill for breach of contract. Jill, of course, raises the Statute of Frauds as a defense in the breach of contract action against her.

Questions to Consider

1. Does the sale of Whiteacre fall within the Statute of Frauds? Why?
2. Can Jack supply a written memorandum of their alleged contract?
3. Is there any proof of the *existence* of their agreement that Jack might offer? Is there any proof of what *the terms* of their alleged agreement might be?
4. If Jack tries to prove the contract by using his and Jill's conduct after they allegedly made the deal, is this conduct likely to be reliable evidence? Why, or why not?

Human conduct sometimes gives an indication of what the law ought to be. The use of the doctrine of part performance to take a contract out of the Statute of Frauds is an example. If one party to the alleged contract has given some performance consistent with the agreement, she probably did not do so out of pure generosity. It is far more likely that the performance consistent with an alleged contract was given because she believed in the contract. This is particularly likely where evidence shows the performing party accomplished a significant amount or where the performance benefited the other party. Most people do not make voluntary, free, valuable performances to other people. Such conduct is more likely to indicate a contractual arrangement that the law may wish to enforce.

The same rationale is behind both the part performance exception to the Statute of Frauds and the Statute itself. In both cases, the law aims at keeping out unreliable or untruthful evidence. It does not seek to keep out reliable or truthful evidence. People may well be tempted to lie about oral agreements. If one party has already begun to perform consistently with the alleged agreement, however, and this performance is accepted by the other party, it appears the party who *refutes* the contract is lying. Thus, to allow the Statute of Frauds to bar the contract in a case of relevant, proven part performance would promote fraud.

The amount or type of part performance that excuses the writing requirement is not the same for every kind of contract. The paralegal should be aware that what constitutes part performance may vary. The doctrine of part performance has been particularly well developed in contracts for the sale of land, and the UCC deals specifically with the doctrine in the case of sales of goods. Part performance in land sales and sales of goods contracts is discussed further below.

Estoppel and Noncompliance with the Statute of Frauds

Like part performance, the doctrine of *estoppel* operates to permit enforcement of an oral contract that falls within the Statute of Frauds. Estoppel was previously discussed under the doctrine of *promissory estoppel* in Chapter 4. Promissory estoppel is the modern theory used to make noncontractual promises enforceable if the promisee has reasonably and foreseeably relied on the promise to her detriment. A related but somewhat different idea of estoppel is used in connection with the Statute of Frauds.

Both promissory estoppel and estoppel to assert the Statute of Frauds involve the idea of preventing ("estopping") a party from using a particular argument at trial. With promissory estoppel, a promisor is prevented from denying enforceability of a promise on the grounds that the promisee has given no consideration or that there is no contract. With estoppel to plead the Statute of Frauds, a party is prevented from asserting that lack of a writing bars enforceability of the contract. If a party successfully uses the theory of estoppel to excuse the Statute of Frauds, a contract will be enforceable although it fell within the Statute and should therefore have been in writing. Note how the doctrine of estoppel operates in the following case.

A CASE FOR STUDY

Monarco v. Lo Greco

35 Cal. 2d 621, 220 P.2d 737 (1950)

TRAYNOR, Justice. Natale and Carmela Castiglia were married in 1919 in Colorado. Carmela had three children, John, Rosie and Christie, by a previous marriage. Rosie was married to Nick Norcia. Natale had one grandchild, plaintiff Carmen Monarco, the son of a deceased daughter by a previous marriage. Natale and Carmela moved to California where they invested their assets, amounting to approximately $4,000, in a half interest in agricultural property. Rosie and Nick Norcia acquired the other half interest. Christie, then in his early teens, moved with the family to California. Plaintiff remained in Colorado. In 1926, Christie, then 18 years old, decided to leave the home of his mother and step-father and seek an independent living. Natale and Carmela, however, wanted him to stay with them and participate in the family venture. They made an oral proposal to Christie that if he stayed home and

worked they would keep their property in joint tenancy so that it would pass to the survivor who would leave it to Christie by will except for small devises to John and Rosie. In performance of this agreement Christie remained home and worked diligently in the family venture. He gave up any opportunity for further education or any chance to accumulate property of his own. He received only his room and board and spending money. When he married and suggested the possibility of securing some present interest to support his wife, Natale told him that his wife should move in with the family and that Christie need not worry, for he would receive all the property when Natale and Carmela died. Natale and Carmela placed all of their property in joint tenancy and in 1941 both executed wills leaving all their property to Christie with the exception of small devises to Rosie and John and $500 to plaintiff. Although these wills did not refer to the agreement, their terms were agreed upon by Christie, Natale and Carmela. The venture was successful, so that at the time of Natale's death his and Carmela's interest was worth approximately $100,000. Shortly before his death Natale became dissatisfied with the agreement and determined to leave his half of the joint property to his grandson, the plaintiff. Without informing Christie or Carmela he arranged the necessary conveyances to terminate the joint tenancies and executed a will leaving all of his property to plaintiff. This will was probated and the court entered its decree distributing the property to plaintiff. After the decree of distribution became final, plaintiff brought these actions for partition of the properties and an accounting. By cross-complaint Carmela asked that plaintiff be declared a constructive trustee of the property he received as a result of Natale's breach of his agreement to keep the property in joint tenancy. On the basis of the foregoing facts the trial court gave judgment for defendants and cross-complainant, and plaintiff has appealed.

The controlling question is whether plaintiff is estopped from relying upon the statute of frauds (Civil Code § 1624; Code Civ.Proc. § 1973) to defeat the enforcement of the oral contract. The doctrine of estoppel to assert the statute of frauds has been consistently applied by the courts of this state to prevent fraud that would result from refusal to enforce oral contracts in certain circumstances. Such fraud may inhere in the unconscionable injury that would result from denying enforcement of the contract after one party has been induced by the other seriously to change his position in reliance on the contract, or in the unjust enrichment that would result if a party who has received the benefits of the other's performance were allowed to rely upon the statute. In many cases both elements are present. Thus not only may one party have so seriously changed his position in reliance upon, or in performance of, the contract that he would suffer an unconscionable injury if it were not enforced, but the other may have reaped the benefits of the contract so that he would be unjustly enriched if he could escape its obligations.

In this case both elements are present. In reliance on Natale's repeated assurances that he

would receive the property when Natale and Carmela died, Christie gave up any opportunity to accumulate property of his own and devoted his life to making the family venture a success. That he would be seriously prejudiced by a refusal to enforce the contract is made clear by a comparison of his position with that of Rosie and Nick Norcia. Because the Norcia's were able to make a small investment when the family venture was started, their interest, now worth approximately $100,000, has been protected. Christie, on the other hand, forbore from demanding any present interest in the venture in exchange for his labors on the assurance that Natale's and Carmela's interest would pass to him on their death. Had he invested money instead of labor in the venture on the same oral understanding, a resulting trust would have arisen in his favor. His twenty years of labor should have equal effect. On the other hand, Natale reaped the benefits of the contract. He and his devisees would be unjustly enriched if the statute of frauds could be invoked to relieve him from performance of his own obligations thereunder.

It is contended, however, that an estoppel to plead the statute of frauds can only arise when there have been representations with respect to the requirements of the statute indicating that a writing is not necessary or will be executed or that the statute will not be relied upon as a defense. This element was present in the leading case of Seymour v. Oelrichs, [Citation omitted] and it is not surprising therefore that it has been listed as a requirement of an estoppel in later cases that have held on their facts that there was or was not an estoppel. Those cases, however, that have refused to find an estoppel have been cases where the court found either that no unconscionable injury would result from refusing to enforce the oral contract, or that the remedy of quantum meruit for services rendered was adequate. In those cases, however, where either an unconscionable injury or unjust enrichment would result from refusal to enforce the contract, the doctrine of estoppel has been applied whether or not plaintiff relied upon representations going to the requirements of the statute itself. Likewise in the case of partly performed oral contracts for the sale of land specific enforcement will be decreed whether or not there have been representations going to the requirements of the statute, because its denial would result in a fraud on the plaintiff who has gone into possession or made improvements in reliance on the contract. In reality it is not the representation that the contract will be put in writing or that the statute will not be invoked, but the promise that the contract will be performed that a party relies upon when he changes his position because of it. Moreover, a party who has accepted the benefits of an oral contract will be unjustly enriched if the contract is not enforced whether his representations related to the requirements of the statute or were limited to affirmations that the contract would be performed.

It is settled that neither the remedy of an action at law for damages for breach of contract nor the quasi-contractual remedy for the value of services rendered is adequate for the breach of a contract to leave property by will in exchange for services of a peculiar nature involving the assumption or continuation of a close family relationship. The facts of this case clearly bring it within the foregoing rule.

It is contended, however, that since Christie is not a party to this action, his change of position in reliance on Natale's promises will not support Carmela's efforts to secure the benefits of the contract due to her. In this respect, plaintiff contends that defendants did not plead a contract for Christie's benefit but only one whereby Carmela was entitled to ownership as the surviving joint tenant. When the action was commenced, however, Carmela was the person entitled to the property under the terms of the contract. It was therefore appropriate that she should be the one to seek its enforcement. To the extent that Natale's promise to keep the property in joint tenancy with Carmela was supported by the consideration of Christie's services, Carmela was a third party beneficiary of the agreement between Christie and Natale. She was entitled to rely upon the elements of estoppel provided by Christie's change of position in reliance on the contract and Natale's acceptance of the benefits. "(I)t is the change of position of the contracting parties, and not the beneficiaries of the contract, that forms the estoppel to rely upon the statute

of frauds." Ryan v. Welte. [Citation] In this respect the present case is governed by Notten v. Mensing. [Citation] In the Notten case a childless couple made an oral agreement that each would leave all his property to the other on the condition that the survivor would leave it equally to the heirs of both. The husband died first leaving a will in accordance with the agreement. The wife accepted the benefits thereby accruing to her. In breach of her agreement, however, she left all her property to her own heirs. In an action by the husband's heirs to impress a constructive trust on the amount due them under the agreement it was held that the wife's heirs were estopped to plead the statute of frauds. The basis of the estoppel was not anything done by the husband's heirs, but the husband's change in position in dying without providing for his own heirs, a change in position made irrevocable by the wife's acceptance of the benefits of the agreement. Likewise, Christie in reliance on the contract contributed his services for over twenty years to make the family venture a success, and Natale accepted the benefits thereof. Plaintiff is thus estopped because of these facts just as were the wife's heirs in the Notten case. The judgments are affirmed.

Questions to Consider

1. What was the agreement between Christie and the Castiglias? Why did that agreement require a writing?
2. How long did this agreement remain in effect? Did the parties perform under the agreement? Who performed and how much performance was given?
3. How did the grandson of Natale Castiglia come to have an interest in the California property that Carmela (and ultimately Christie) claimed?
4. Which party does the California Supreme Court favor, Carmela (and Christie) or Natale's grandson? Why?
5. What remedy does the court grant to Carmela? Why? How critical to the remedy granted was Christie's reliance on Natale's promise?
6. What rule concerning the Statute of Frauds and estoppel comes from this case?

The Effect of Noncompliance With the Statute of Frauds

The law does not view a contract as void solely because it fails to comply with the Statute of Frauds. Most courts find noncompliance with the Statute makes the contract voidable, rather than void. If no problems arise, oral contracts within the Statute of Frauds are generally enforceable as to the parties themselves. Thus, if the parties perform the contract and no disputes require litigation, the contract cannot later be invalidated just because it was not in writing. Noncompliance with the Statute of Frauds does mean, however, that the contract cannot be used to obtain legal rights *in court* unless there is some form of part performance or a basis for estoppel to excuse the Statute. Thus, where a contract is established through full or part performance, or where one party is estopped to plead noncompliance with the Statute of Frauds, there is no defense to formation.

If performance or estoppel cannot be used to excuse noncompliance with the Statute of Frauds, there may be a defense to enforcement even if the contract was technically formed. Furthermore, if evidence shows there is no written memorandum of the contract because the parties never reached agreement at all, the Statute is a defense to formation. Thus, where a contract falls within the Statute of Frauds and the writing requirement is not satisfied, the evidence must be explored to establish what really happened. One may be able to prove that the parties reached agreement and formed the contract, but the lack of a writing may also mean the parties failed to reach agreement.

Specific Contracts that Fall Within the Statute of Frauds

As previously noted, not all jurisdictions use the same wording for their Statutes of Frauds, so you must always be aware of the specific law in the relevant state or federal jurisdiction. Usually, though, modern law requires at least the five contracts mentioned in the original English Statute of Frauds to be in writing and sometimes includes additional kinds of contracts as well. The five "traditional" categories of contracts that fall within the Statute have received centuries of attention from courts and scholars, and the law concerning them is well-developed. Thus, these contracts require some further discussion.

Contracts for the Sale or Transfer of an Interest in Land

Easement The right to use the property of another, particularly another's land. Ownership of an easement is considered ownership of an interest in land.

Although sale of real property of any kind is the transaction that fits most clearly within this category, most jurisdictions also consider *rental* of real property to be in this category. In some jurisdictions, only real property rental leases for longer than one year fall within the Statute of Frauds, and shorter leases, though oral, are enforceable. Contracts that grant rights in *easements* are also interests in real property. An **easement** is the right to use land, but ownership of the easement itself is considered ownership of an interest in land.

Sometimes it is difficult to tell whether the contract interest being transferred is an "interest in land." An example of an "interest" that is hard to categorize is a contract to do strip-mining. Strip-mining removes minerals from the land, but so severely damages the land in the process that it may become unusable. Should this be considered a transfer of an "interest in land"? The short answer is that contract law usually looks to the law of real property in the relevant jurisdiction to determine what is an interest in land. If the paralegal needs to know whether a particular interest is considered to be land for the purpose of complying with the Statute of Frauds, real property law as well as contract law should be researched in the governing jurisdiction.

Part performance on a contract for the sale of land can generally be shown in two or three ways. The *buyer's* part performance may be shown where he has either (1) paid at least part of the purchase price and taken possession of the land or (2) made valuable improvements to the land. The *seller's* part performance may be shown where she has done what is necessary to convey an ownership interest to the buyer. For example, the delivery of the deed to the buyer by the seller would usually be evidence of sufficient part performance on the seller's part, and failure to have a written contract could be excused if the buyer sues.

Contracts Made in Consideration of Marriage

Today very little is left of this category of unenforceable oral contracts. Two main types of marital contracts are now required to be in writing: *prenuptial agreements* and property settlements made in connection with divorce. **Prenuptial agreements** are contracts concerning the private and joint property rights of people who plan to marry. Divorce settlements are contracts concerning the division of property in connection with the legal dissolution of a marriage. The child custody and child support issues connected to a divorce proceeding are no longer purely a matter of private contract. Although private contracts can sometimes be made in connection with these issues, family law courts must approve such arrangements. Modern family law now has more to say about child custody and support than traditional contract law does.

As late as the early twentieth century, some promises to marry were treated as contractual and were required to be in writing. There was even a cause of action based on breach of the promise to marry. Generally, modern law does not treat promises to marry as contracts, but there are some exceptions where the marriage is truly the consideration for the promise.[2] Thus, you should be aware that in certain rare situations, promises to marry are treated as contracts. They are usually required to be in writing to be enforceable.

Another modern arrangement that raises contract and Statute of Frauds issues is the contract between unmarried cohabitants. In some cases, a couple live together as married people but do not go through a legally recognized ceremony. If they make a contractual agreement to share earnings or other property, issues may arise concerning the enforceability of the agreement. It is not clear that such agreements are "in consideration of marriage" or that they must always be in writing. Some courts have held that unmarried cohabitants can orally agree to pool their earnings and property as long as the consideration was not the performance of sexual services.[3] You should recognize that this is a developing area of the law. Additionally, you should be aware that to date courts generally have not required *express* contracts

Prenuptial agreements Contracts concerning the separate and joint property rights of people who plan to marry.

between unmarried cohabitants to be in writing. Such contracts are enforceable although oral.

Promises to Answer for the Debt of Another

Many legal arrangements in the commercial world involve the responsibility of one party to pay a creditor on behalf of another party. Such arrangements sometimes arise as the result of administering an estate or trust, through private agreement, or from requirements of lending institutions.

All agreements in which one party agrees to undertake payment of another party's debts are broadly referred to as **suretyship agreements,** or guarantee agreements. The party who has agreed to pay is referred to as the **surety,** or **guarantor.** Laypeople often refer to such arrangements simply as *co-signing* because lending institutions require a second person to co-sign a debt for a borrower with insufficient credit or income. Actually, suretyship agreements encompass many kinds of arrangements, of which co-signing is only one example. Nevertheless, the same general idea exists in all true suretyship agreements: one party has undertaken to pay a debt that is not his own, for another party, out of his own resources.

Generally, any agreement by a party to pay the debts of another must be put into writing, or it is not enforceable.

Suretyship agreements A contract under which one party has undertaken to pay a debt that is not his own, for another party, out of his own resources.

Surety or guarantor A party who has agreed to pay the debt of another. Laypeople often refer to this arrangement as co-signing.

EXAMPLE 10.2

Suppose A agrees to perform a service for B that A will begin and finish within one week, and C agrees to pay A on B's behalf. C's promise to pay A falls within the Statute of Frauds. Note that it is *the promise to pay on someone else's behalf* that must be in writing to be enforceable. A need not have a written contract with B because this contract is for services, not goods or land, and it can be performed in less than one year. However, to enforce C's promise to pay B's debt after the service is performed, A must have C's promise in writing.

One rationale behind requiring suretyship agreements to be in writing is clear: if it were too easy to claim someone else was responsible for our debts, we would all be tempted to do so. Every time a creditor came after a debtor, the debtor might insist someone else had agreed to be responsible for the debt. Thus, if someone has truly agreed to be responsible for the debt of another, the law requires the creditor to have the promise to pay in writing. Of course, the writing must also be signed by the surety, who is the party to be charged in this case.

Contracts that Cannot Be Performed in Less Than One Year

Saying that contracts that cannot be performed in less than one year fall within the Statute of Frauds is somewhat misleading. Actually, the requirement means that the contract must be in writing only if there is *no possibility* of full performance within one year. The rule has a rather theoretical application. A contract to care for someone "for the rest of her life" need not be written down because theoretically the person could die tomorrow. A contract to care for the same person "for five years," however, is clearly within the Statute of Frauds and must be in writing to be enforceable. A contract to care for someone for a five-year period theoretically can be fully performed only in five years. The test of whether a contract falls within this category of the Statute of Frauds is whether the performance can *theoretically be completed in less than a year,* as viewed at the time of formation. If so, the contract is enforceable even if it is oral. If not, then the contract must be written to be enforceable.

The rationale for this section of the Statute of Frauds is obscure. The most common rationale advanced is that with long-term contracts, it is better not to trust merely to the memories of the parties involved. Thus, contracts taking more than a year to perform are required to be written. Unfortunately, this rationale ignores the whole problem of how long a dispute takes to get into court even when the contract "life" was relatively short. Once parties do get into litigation, they can forget many things even if the contract performance itself occurred in a short time.

Because no one has succeeded in offering a completely convincing rationale for this rule, courts have tended to be liberal in construing it. They have tended to find a contract did *not* come within the rule and thus is enforceable, although oral. The party trying to enforce the contract must, of course, still present reliable evidence of the oral agreement, but at least he will not be automatically out of court because of noncompliance with the Statute of Frauds. In spite of the rule's unpopularity with the courts, most states still carry such a provision in their Statute of Frauds. Hence, the paralegal should understand how contracts "not to be performed within one year" are treated.

Contracts for the Sale of Goods Over "Ten Pounds Sterling"

The Basic Rule under the UCC

Although, of course, the amount is no longer measured in sterling, modern American law still requires written contracts for the sale of goods over a specific amount. Since the UCC applies to these contracts, in a specific case the paralegal should normally consult the applicable version of the state commercial code. Section 2-201(1) of the UCC currently provides:

> (1) Except as otherwise provided in this section a contract for the sale of goods for the price of $500 or more is not enforceable by way of action or defense unless there is some writing sufficient to indicate that a contract for sale has been made between the parties and signed by the party against whom enforcement is sought or by his authorized agent or broker. A writing is not insufficient because it omits or incorrectly states a term agreed upon but the contract is not enforceable under this paragraph beyond the quantity of goods shown in such writing.

The language of § 2-201 appears to be a relaxation of the common-law requirements of a writing. Under the UCC, a contract for the sale of goods over $500 can be memorialized in any writing that is "sufficient to indicate that a contract for sale has been made between the parties," as long as it is signed "by the party against whom enforcement is sought or by his authorized agent or broker."

Part performance can take a contract for goods out of the Statute of Frauds if the buyer has made payment for the goods. In that case, the oral contract is enforceable up to the quantity of goods for which the payment has been made. Part performance on a sale of goods contract can also occur where a buyer has ordered "specially manufactured" goods and it can be shown that the manufacturer has made a substantial beginning on the manufacturing process. Specially manufactured goods are goods that are unique in some way and are not suitable for sale to another buyer in the ordinary course of the seller's business.

EXAMPLE 10.3

Suppose that Buyer verbally ordered 2,000 individualized calendars with her business name and telephone number printed on them at a total cost of $1,000. After Seller prints these calendars, Buyer cancels the order. Seller might argue that the calendars are specially manufactured goods because there is no general market for personalized calendars. If Buyer defaults on the contract, Seller cannot turn around and recoup the loss by reselling to another buyer. In this case, Seller's printing of the calendars would probably be enough to show substantial "manufacture." Seller could use this to argue that he has made part performance sufficient to take the contract out of the Statute of Frauds. Thus, the contract would be enforceable although it was oral and the amount involved exceeded $500.

The Special UCC Merchant's Rule

As mentioned earlier, under the common-law rule a writing does not satisfy the requirements of the Statute of Frauds unless it is signed by the party to be charged. Thus, if A sues B for breach of contract and the Statute applies, A must have a written document or documents signed by B in order to have a sufficient writing. The drafters of the UCC preserved this rule for sales of goods unless *both* parties to the contract are merchants. If both parties to the contract are merchants, UCC § 2-201(2) provides:

> (2) Between merchants if within a reasonable time a writing in confirmation of the contract and sufficient against the sender is received and the party receiving it has reason to know its contents, it satisfies the requirements of subsection (1) against such party unless written notice of objection to its contents is given within 10 days after it is received.

As previously noted, UCC § 2-201(1) provides that a writing (between any parties other than two merchants) is sufficient if it indicates a contract for sale of goods has been made and has been signed by the party to be charged.

Taken together, UCC § 2-201(1) and § 2-201(2) indicate the special *merchant's rule* for the UCC Statute of Frauds. One merchant can send to another merchant a memorandum confirming the contract, and this writing signed only by the sender satisfies the Statute of Frauds if the following requirements are also met:

1. The other merchant receives the memo.
2. The other merchant knows or has reason to know the contents of the memo.
3. The memo is sufficient to indicate that a contract for sale of goods was made.
4. The recipient of the memo does not object to the memo within ten days after receipt.

The UCC Writing Requirement

A writing sufficient to satisfy the UCC Statute of Frauds need not be as complete as a writing that satisfies the Statute in cases where common law applies. Under the UCC, a "writing" sufficient to satisfy the Statute can be one document or several integrated documents. As indicated by the wording of UCC § 2-201(1), however, the document or documents need only show that a contract for sale has been made between the parties, be signed by the appropriate party, and indicate what quantity was contracted for. Other necessary terms can often be supplied by using UCC gap-filler provisions, industry standards, any history the parties have of working together on this or previous agreements, and any relevant part performance on the contract.

For a general summary of the Statute of Frauds, see Exhibit 10.1.

E X H I B I T 10.1

A Summary of the Statute of Frauds

- Contracts that must be in writing:
  - Contracts made in connection with marriage.
  - Contracts involving a sale or transfer of real estate.
  - Contracts to pay another's debts.
  - Contracts that cannot be completed in a year.
  - Contracts for the sale of goods over $500.
- A writing that satisfies the Statute may be either:
  - One written document.
  - A series of written documents shown to be integrated.
- A writing satisfies the Statute if it does the following:
  - Common law:

    Indicates the parties to the contract.

    Indicates the subject matter of the agreement.

    Indicates the necessary terms of performance.

    Indicates the price to be paid and the payment terms.

    Indicates the quantity contracted for.

    Is signed by the party to be charged.

    Recites the consideration (some jurisdictions).
  - UCC:

    Indicates a contract for sale was made.

    Is signed by the appropriate party.

    Indicates the quantity contracted for.
- The legal effect if there is no writing or if it is insufficient:
  - The contract cannot be enforced in court.
  - The parties can voluntarily choose to enforce the contract.
  - Full performance of an oral contract that falls within the Statute of Frauds is final (the contract cannot later be attacked for noncompliance with the Statute).
- Two major exceptions excuse noncompliance with the Statute of Frauds:
  - If a contract is partly performed, a court may use this part performance to excuse the writing requirement.
  - If a party can show she reasonably relied on the other party's words or conduct in connection with failure to obtain a writing, a court may allow estoppel to plead the Statute of Frauds.

KRAM, District Judge. On October 12, 1984 I issued my decision in the above-captioned matter. It has come to my attention that certain modifications of this Order are necessary. Such modifications are reflected in this amended opinion.

This case was tried in a one-day trial before the bench. In the intervening months, counsel for both sides have prepared and submitted post-trial memoranda. After careful consideration of the evidence adduced at trial and the arguments put forth in the post-trial briefs, and for the reasons set out below, the Court finds for plaintiff in the amount of $250,000.

Plaintiff Enrique Foster Gittes ("Gittes") is a businessman and financial consultant. In 1981, his services as a consultant were retained by an English company, NNC Energy plc ("NCC"), of which he was also a director. NCC's principal business was as a holding company, investing its capital in other businesses in return for a stake in those businesses. Gittes' activities for NCC were not made clear at trial; however, NCC believed his services to be useful and worthwhile, and compensated him at the rate of $100,000 per year for his consultancy work.

One of NCC's investments was a substantial holding of the shares of an American company, Simplicity Pattern, Co. ("Simplicity"). For reasons which are not relevant here, Gittes' contract to perform consulting services for NCC was assigned to Simplicity. Prior to that assignment, Gittes was elected to the Board of Directors of Simplicity. It is this dual relationship between Gittes and Simplicity which led to this lawsuit.

In April, 1982, NCC found itself in difficult financial condition and decided to sell its holdings in Simplicity as a means of realizing badly needed cash. To that end, NCC began a search for a purchaser of the Simplicity shares, in which search Gittes was an active participant. The search led to offers to buy from at least two sources, one in New York and one in Europe. NCC apparently decided to accept the offer from the New York purchaser, while holding the European offer in reserve in the event the

New York purchaser withdrew or otherwise failed to close the sale.

The sale by NCC of its Simplicity stock was apparently made more urgent shortly before the agreement to sell the shares was to be consummated, by the threat of various financial sources to call outstanding debt, thereby forcing NCC into receivership. On May 7, 1982, the sale of the shares to the New York purchaser was scheduled to take place in the offices of the law firm Debevoise & Plimpton. Gittes and the individual defendant, Edward W. Cook, arrived together. At some point after the closing began, it came to Gittes' attention that the purchaser apparently required the resignation of the four directors of Simplicity who had been elected by NCC as a shareholder of Simplicity. These directors included Gittes and three other directors of NCC; of the four, only Gittes had failed to tender his resignation prior to the closing. Apparently, in fact, only Gittes had not been informed that these resignations were considered a necessary prerequisite to consummation of the purchase of the shares by the New York purchaser. When informed of this fact, Gittes initially flatly refused to tender his resignation from the Simplicity board. There is significant divergence, both of opinion and in the evidence adduced at trial, as to Gittes' motivation for refusing to resign. His motivation, however, is not relevant here.

Gittes' refusal to resign created serious problems, jeopardizing the closing. Clearly, some accommodation needed to be made, and eventually one was agreed upon; Gittes would resign from his position on the Simplicity board and his consultancy with Simplicity in return for a five year, $50,000 per year, consultancy contract with Cook International, Inc. ("Cook International"). Cook International, headed by Edward W. Cook and the largest shareholder of NCC, stood to be the greatest loser if the sale of the Simplicity shares failed to occur and resulted in NCC's going into receivership. Cook International, through its chairman Edward W. Cook, offered to employ Gittes as a financial consultant, an offer which Gittes accepted. Subsequently, however, Gittes was given no responsibilities and was never paid, and on October 12, 1982, Cook International repudiated the contract by letter to Gittes. Shortly thereafter, Gittes commenced this action.

The issues in this case tend to overlap. Plaintiff claims that Cook's offer to employ him as a consultant was accepted by him and was sufficiently definite to constitute a contract. Defendants, in response, claim that any alleged contract based on the undisputed facts fails to satisfy the Statute of Frauds because it was never reduced to a writing signed by the party to be charged. Furthermore, defendants argue that the contract, assuming there was one, was made under duress and is therefore voidable. In reply, plaintiff points to several subsequent writings issuing from defendants in which reference is made to the consultancy agreement between Cook International and Gittes, and that these writings satisfy the Statute of Frauds. Furthermore, plaintiff claims that any pressure which Gittes exerted on Cook and Cook International did not rise to the level of duress within the meaning of contract law and that any duty which Gittes owed NCC to facilitate the sale of the Simplicity shares as a means of relieving NCC's financial difficulty is not assertable by Cook International either independently or as a shareholder of NCC.

The logical starting place in this analysis is with the question whether there ever was a contract between Cook International and Gittes. It is undisputed that Edward W. Cook acting in his capacity as chairman of Cook International, offered Gittes a consultancy contract with Cook International for a five-year term at an annual compensation of $50,000, and that Gittes accepted the offer. Cook testified that he never intended to honor the offer, and that he had been advised by one of his attorneys, a partner at Debevoise & Plimpton, that such an agreement would be unenforceable in any event. Cook's lack of intent to honor his offer is relevant on two points: whether there was some fraudulent inducement to Gittes in entering the contract, and whether some element of promissory estoppel is present in Gittes' resigning the directorship and the consultancy which he held with Simplicity in reliance on Cook's offer of work with Cook International. The fraud issue we put aside for the moment. With respect to promissory estoppel, Gittes clearly relied on

Cook's promise when he resigned from his positions at Simplicity. Furthermore, given the situation, his reliance was reasonable since Gittes had no reason to doubt the sincerity of Cook's offer. Finally, Gittes' reasonable reliance was obviously detrimental, entailing as it did the surrender of positions at Simplicity which provided Gittes with compensation in excess of $100,000 per year. Thus far, then, we have offer, acceptance and reasonable detrimental reliance.

The next point in this contract analysis concerns the degree to which the agreement between Gittes and Cook International was, or needed to be, reduced to writing to satisfy the Statute of Frauds. In New York, the applicable Statute of Frauds is General Obligations Law § 5-701, which states in relevant part that "Every agreement, promise or undertaking is void unless it or some note or memorandum thereof be in writing, and subscribed by the party to be charged therewith, or by his lawful agent, if such agreement, promise or undertaking . . . [b]y its terms is not to be performed within one year from the making thereof or the performance of which is not to be completed before the end of a lifetime. . . ." The agreement in question here falls within this section of New York GOL since it was "not to be performed within one year [of its] making." From this conclusion the issue becomes whether there was a sufficient writing or memorandum of the agreement and whether it was subscribed by the party to be charged.

Both parties agree that, notwithstanding Cook's assent to Gittes' suggestion that the agreement be reduced to a written contract, and Gittes' submission to Cook of a form consulting contract, there was never executed a document which would serve as a formal agreement between the parties. This fact is only the beginning of the inquiry, however. As case law demonstrates, several writings other than a formal contract can suffice to satisfy the requirement of the Statute of Frauds. In the instant case, plaintiff proposes that at least two other writings promulgated by the defendant fill this requirement: a Prospectus issued by Cook International, the text of which was approved by Cook and refers to Cook's agreement to employ Gittes as a consultant for five years at an annual compensation of $50,000 per year; and a memorandum signed by Cook which contains substantially the same terms and states flatly that

Cook agreed to them as a necessary condition to Gittes' resignation from the Simplicity Board of Directors. Defendant contends that these documents do not satisfy the threshold requirements of the New York Statute of Frauds, that a writing must contain the essential terms of the agreement. "The concept of essentiality is relative. A term is "essential," and must thus appear in the "memorandum," if it seriously affects the rights and obligations of the parties and there is a significant evidentiary dispute as to its content.

In the instant case, the writings each contain the duration of the agreement (five years) and the annual compensation (fifty thousand dollars). The Cook International Prospectus makes further reference to employment of Gittes "as a consultant to Cook. . . ." Two of these terms, duration and compensation, are essential within the requirements of the Statute of Frauds because they seriously affect the rights and obligations of the parties.

Defendants agree that duration and compensation are essential and acknowledge that these terms are contained in the proffered writings. The defendants do, however, take issue with whether the nature of the plaintiff's duties under the alleged contract are an essential term and if so whether those duties are adequately described or are sufficiently determinable by reference to existing external facts as to eliminate any significant evidentiary dispute as to that term of the contract.

Plaintiff argues that his duties under the agreement are not essential terms of a contract within the context of this lawsuit because the significant evidentiary issue is not whether plaintiff performed adequately but rather whether the parties were obligated to perform at all. This argument is well taken and I hold that plaintiff's duties are not an essential term and therefore need not be reduced to writing. My holding is closely linked to the posture of this case. If defendants had awaited a tender of performance from plaintiff and then rejected it as inadequate and refused to compensate plaintiff, the nature of plaintiff's duties would clearly be the subject of a significant evidentiary dispute in a suit brought by plaintiff for breach. That is not this case, however, because defendants apparently choose to repudiate any agreement prior to a tender of performance, the precise nature of the required performance is not properly raised.

Furthermore, were the nature of plaintiff's duties properly before this Court, it appears from the aforementioned writings and a third document introduced at trial . . . that both parties had a clear idea as to plaintiff's skills and abilities and the work for which he held himself out as equipped. Defendants' disclaimers of such knowledge, and their further argument that these duties were not ascertainable by reference to external facts are disingenuous. "Consultant" is a term with significant baggage in this society and especially in the context of business and financial dealings.

Finally, it bears noting that defendants used the term to describe plaintiff and were fully aware at that time of his background and the nature of the services he had rendered to his previous employers. In sum, then, there are no missing material terms from the writings memorializing the agreement in question. The writings are either subscribed to or signed by the parties to be charged, to wit, Edward Cook, individually and Cook International, Inc., by Edward Cook, its chairman. The agreement therefore satisfies the Statute of Frauds. . . .

It is my holding that . . . since these defendants have no defense to the existence of the consultancy agreement, and all the essential elements of that agreement are present, Cook International is liable for the full value of the agreement, Two Hundred Fifty Thousand Dollars ($250,000).

Questions to Consider

1. Was the agreement between Gittes and Cook International required to be in writing? Why?
2. What did Gittes argue should be used as the "writing" that summarized his consultancy contract? Did the court agree? Why or why not?
3. What terms did the court feel were most important in this contract?
4. As to the terms of Gittes's employment, how essential was it that the contract contain a specific description of his duties? Did the court find that the contract contained an adequate description of Gittes's duties? Why or why not?
5. What does the court mean by the phrase, "The concept of essentiality is relative"?

Chapter Review Questions

1. What does it mean to say that a contract "falls within the Statute of Frauds"?
2. What kinds of contracts fall within the Statute of Frauds? Explain each requirement.
3. What differences are there between the common-law and the UCC Statutes of Frauds?
4. What role can part performance or estoppel play with regard to the Statute of Frauds?
5. If a contract falls within the Statute of Frauds and there is no writing, what might this indicate?

Key Terms

Easement, 206
Part performance, 201
Party to be charged, 200
Perjury, 199
Prenuptial agreements, 207
Statute of Frauds, 199
Surety or guarantor, 208
Suretyship agreements, 208

Notes

1. The original Statute of Frauds is part of An Act for the Prevention of Frauds and Perjuries, 29 Charles II, Chapter 3, Section 4, (1676). See also 72 Am. Jur. 2d, Statute of Frauds, Section 1 et. seq.
2. See, e.g., *Byers v. Byers,* 618 P.2d 930 (Okla. 1980).
3. See, e.g., *Marvin v. Marvin,* 18 Cal.3d 660; 134 Cal. Rptr. 815; 557 P.2d 106 (1976).

Contract Remedies

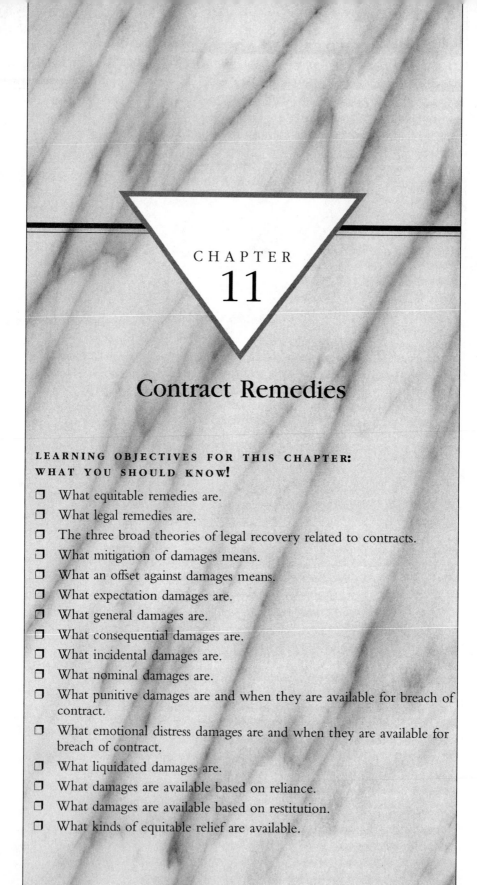

CHAPTER

11

Contract Remedies

Introduction

When attorneys and legal scholars speak of remedies, including contract remedies, they are generally referring to the results of a successful lawsuit or to what a successful lawsuit might achieve. If a party wins a lawsuit or part of a lawsuit, she is awarded certain remedies to rectify the wrongs for which she sued. In Anglo-American law, there are two broad categories of remedies: equitable remedies and legal remedies. **Equitable remedies** involve a variety of actions a court can order the parties to undertake to make up for the wrongs suffered by the successful party in the lawsuit. **Legal remedies** involve giving money to the successful party in litigation as a substitute for performance or to make up for wrongs suffered. Money awarded as a legal remedy is called **damages.**

Historically, Anglo-American courts were divided into Courts of Equity and Courts of Law, which were empowered to give equitable remedies and legal remedies, respectively. Under a doctrine known as equitable clean-up, Courts of Equity also had limited authority to hear legal claims and award damages if a party had legal claims related to his equitable claims. Courts of Law, however, could not give equitable remedies at all.[1] On the other hand, the right to a jury trial existed only in Courts of Law; Courts of Equity could not hold jury trials. Equitable claims were heard and decided by judges, not by juries.

When law and equity courts were separate, a party who wanted to file a lawsuit had to decide the main purpose of the action and file in the appropriate court. If the main purpose of the action was to obtain an equitable remedy, the party had to file in a Court of Equity. If the main purpose of the action was to obtain the legal remedy of damages, the party had to file in a Court of Law. Failure to assess the main purpose of the action correctly and to file in the right court could have serious consequences under the old system. Someone who mistakenly filed in the wrong court might have the action dismissed and then be foreclosed from bringing the action again in the proper court if the applicable statute of limitations had run out.

Today, in the United States, the Courts of Equity and Courts of Law are joined in the same system. Thus, whether a party is filing in state or federal court, she can pursue her entire action in one court and can ask for both legal and equitable remedies in the same action. It is still generally true, however, that parties can obtain a jury trial only on the legal claims. There is no right to a jury trial on equitable claims although many equitable courts have authority to convene an advisory jury.[2] A judge or panel of judges decides equitable claims.

Equitable remedies Remedies which do not involve money damages as the primary benefit. Equitable remedies usually involve court orders for the losing party to take certain actions to make up for wrongs suffered by the prevailing party.

Legal remedies Remedies which involve money damages as the primary benefit.

Damages Money which a court orders the losing party in litigation to pay to the successful party in order to make up for wrongs suffered. Contract damages are often viewed as a substitute for performance.

Legal Remedies in Contract Law in General

Three basic legal remedies are available in connection with contract law. All three involve obtaining damages under a particular broad theory. First, a party may bring an action based on the contract. If one party breaches a valid and enforceable contract, the nonbreaching party can sue for recovery of damages. If successful, this party receives damages based on the monetary amount it takes to place her in the same economic position she would have been in had the contract been performed. Such damages are often referred to as *expectation damages*. Expectation damages are discussed more fully later in the chapter.

Second, even if the contract is not valid or enforceable for some reason, a party may be able to sue for damages under one of two alternatives to contract recovery called *restitution* and *reliance*. They also are discussed later in the chapter.[3]

The Duty to Mitigate Damages

Duty to mitigate damages The responsibility of each contracting party to minimize damages as much as reasonably possible if there is a breach of the contract.

Whether damages are awarded on the contract or under the restitution or reliance theories, each party must make reasonable efforts to avoid running up the amount of damages. This is referred to as the **duty to mitigate damages.** To mitigate damages means to minimize them. Each party, at all times, is obligated to do what it can to avoid costs that can reasonably be avoided. When a breach occurs, each party must make decisions about how to act, and these decisions have financial consequences. Some of these consequences can be avoided and some cannot. Suppose, for example, a buyer and seller of steel rails find themselves in the following situation, and the buyer is the breaching party.

EXAMPLE   11.1

Buyer of steel rails defaults on his contract with a steel rail manufacturer. At the time of Buyer's default, Seller has already shipped a large quantity of rails. When Buyer refuses delivery, Seller is faced with a dilemma. Seller can look for another buyer in the vicinity where the rails are located or ship them back 2,000 miles to their point of origin. Suppose Seller has another business location 500 miles away and could ship the rails to that location. Additionally, Seller may have to determine where and how to store the rails while deciding what to do with them.

Questions to Consider

1. What might be the respective costs attached to the various alternatives Seller has?
2. What would be the most sensible and economic course of action for Seller under these circumstances? Why?

The other party may also have to make decisions that have financial consequences. Suppose Example 11.1 were changed to the following situation.

EXAMPLE   11.2

Buyer believes Seller knowingly sent the wrong steel rails hoping Buyer would be pressured into taking them. Buyer feels he is justified in refusing delivery of the rails. In fact, Buyer thinks Seller defaulted on the contract by deliberately sending the wrong rails. Buyer did not discover the rails were the wrong ones, however, until after Seller had completed delivery. Buyer must now decide what to do with the rails. He could leave them where Seller delivered them, take them to another destination for storage, or ship them back at his own cost to Seller.

Questions to Consider

1. What might be the costs of the various alternatives?
2. What would be the most sensible and economic course of action for Buyer under these circumstances? Why?

The doctrine of mitigation of damages addresses issues that arise concerning decisions contracting parties must make if a breach occurs. There are few absolute rules for minimizing damages. With few exceptions, there are no specific requirements for handling a contract breach. Considering the wide variety of facts and circumstances occurring in human relations, having specific rules would be impractical. Rather, each party must use common sense and a reasonable approach to doing things economically. This does not necessarily mean that each party must always choose the cheapest way. A decision can be reasonable even though it is not the cheapest under the circumstances. The general rule on mitigation of damages might be stated as follows:

> If particular costs could have been avoided and a reasonable person would have done so under the circumstances after considering all relevant facts, then these costs cannot be collected as damages from the other party.

From a practical point of view, the paralegal should understand how a failure to mitigate damages relates to the claims made by parties in a lawsuit. If a party wins on a particular claim and a court awards damages, any costs that party should have mitigated are subtracted from the damages awarded on the claim. Stated somewhat differently: if a winning party is found not to have avoided costs that should have been avoided, these costs will not be awarded as damages. Often a court does this by what is called an offset. Based on evidence the parties submit, a court first calculates the total amount of damages for the winning party on a particular claim. Then, any amounts found to be the result of failure to mitigate are subtracted from the damages. Subtraction of amounts a party should have mitigated from damages awarded is referred to as an **offset** against damages.

Damages Based on the Contract Price

The modern theory of contract damages is that the nonbreaching party should be able to recover the benefit of his bargain, or expectation interest. Contract law has been struggling for several centuries to explain what this means, so any simple explanation is bound to be incomplete. Nevertheless, the general idea of **expectation damages** is that when a party enters into a contract, he has certain "expectations" about the outcome of the relationship. By this, we usually mean expectations concerning performance and profitability. When there is a breach, damages are meant to reimburse the nonbreaching party for the breaching party's failure to meet expectations under the agreement.

In modern contract actions, expectation damages are measured using three different categories of damages: general damages, consequential damages, and incidental damages. If these types of damages are added together, the theory is that they will reimburse the nonbreaching party for all losses resulting from the breach. This is thought of as returning to the nonbreaching party the benefit of his bargain, or his expectation interest in the contract.

Offset Generally, any amount of money deducted from a party's damages and credited to the other party. In a contract action, an offset may be made against the prevailing party's damages for amounts that party failed to mitigate or amounts that party should have paid to the losing party.

Expectation damages Damages based on the contract under the theory that they are compensation for the breaching party's failure to meet the aggrieved party's expectations concerning performance and profitability.

General Damages

General damages are calculated by applying a standardized method or formula that awards losses considered to flow naturally from the type of breach involved. Sometimes general damages are called **standardized damages** because they are awarded by these standard methods or formulas. Many different general damages formulas have developed to award damages in the various kinds of contract cases. All of these formulas, however, have the same theoretical basis: they attempt to return to the nonbreaching party the profits he expected to make if the contract had been fully performed, plus any additional out-of-pocket losses. The idea is that out-of-pocket losses and lost profits are typical losses a party suffers in case of a breach. To see how general damages might be measured in a particular case, consider the following example.

EXAMPLE 11.3

Seller of commercial paper supplies makes a sale and delivery contract with Customer. Customer is to pay $25,000 for the supplies. Out of this $25,000, Seller must pay $17,500 to obtain the supplies and $2,500 toward her business overhead; she plans to keep $5,000 as net profit. Customer wrongfully refuses delivery of the paper supplies, and Seller is forced to sell the supplies elsewhere. In the substitute sale, Seller receives only $20,000 for the paper supplies.

Questions to Consider

1. Is Seller short of what she anticipated getting under the original contract?
2. By how much and what does the loss represent?
3. With this loss can Seller still make a profit on the transaction?

Sellers of goods who can resell in the event of the buyer's breach may still suffer a loss based on the difference between the original contract price and the lesser price received in the second sale. In that case, the resale loss is thought of as natural, or typical, under such circumstances and is used to provide a basic theory of general damages in this type of breach of contract case.

To see what the buyer's damages might be like and how general damages might be determined where the seller breaches, consider the following example.

EXAMPLE 11.4

Suppose Seller in Example 11.3 breaches the contract by refusing to deliver the paper supplies to Customer. Customer still needs the supplies, so he must find comparable goods elsewhere. Customer buys substitute paper supplies, but must pay a total of $27,000 for the same supplies he was to have purchased from Seller for $25,000.

Questions to Consider

1. What is the amount of loss suffered by Customer?
2. What does the loss come from?

The buyer's damages in Example 11.4 are thought of as arising naturally from the breach because they are characteristic under the circumstances. When a seller of goods defaults, the buyer often is able to obtain substitute goods elsewhere. Obtaining substitute goods to replace goods that were to be purchased under a contract is called **cover.** The price the buyer must pay for the substitute goods under a new contract is called the **cover price.** If the cover price is higher than the contract price, the buyer's losses stem from the difference between the two prices. This fact is used to formulate the general damages theory for this kind of case.

Most cases of contract breach involve some kind of loss, but, the idea has persisted that specific sorts of losses typically occur in particular kinds of contract breaches. Many of these ideas about standardized losses involve assumptions about how people behave, about right and wrong, and about how the marketplace works, among other things. These assumptions are not always explicitly stated and not always true. Nevertheless, the idea that breach of contract losses can be standardized remains and is the basis for calculating general damages in particular types of contract cases.

Exhibit 11.1 shows three of the best-known methods of determining general damages in specific types of contract cases. Note that the formulas or

Cover When an aggrieved buyer successfully obtains substitute goods to replace those not supplied by the defaulting seller.

Cover price The price an aggrieved buyer pays for the substitute goods to replace those not supplied by the defaulting seller.

EXHIBIT 11.1		
General Damages Formulas		
Type of Contract	**Breaching Party**	**General Damages Formula**
Employment (or services)	Employer	Unpaid wages for the remainder of the contract term minus wages received from substitute employment (or minus wages that ought to have been earned by substitute employment).
Employment (or services)	Employee	The difference between the breaching employee's wages and the replacement employee's wages, plus any other costs of replacement such as advertising or employment agency fees.
Real Property	Seller	Buyer is reimbursed for out-of-pocket expenses, unless the breach was in bad faith. If the breach was in bad faith, buyer gets the difference between the contract price and the fair market value of the property.
Real Property	Buyer	Seller gets the difference between the contract price and the fair market value of the property.

EXHIBIT 11.1 *(continued)*		
General Damages Formulas		
Type of Contract	**Breaching Party**	**General Damages Formula**
Construction	Contractor	*Material breach:* all costs of hiring a substitute contractor to complete the job, including additional materials. *Minor breach:* **cost of completion** (the cost of having minor aspects of the job completed), *or* the difference between the job under the contract and the job as is.★
Construction	Owner	*Performance has begun:* Contractor recovers the full contract price minus any expenses that will not be incurred because of the breach and minus any payments owner has already made. *Performance has not begun:* Contractor recovers lost profits on the contract plus any out-of-pocket losses minus any payments owner has already made.

Cost-of-completion For a construction contract, the price the owner must pay to have the project completed as a result of the builder's minor breach.

Diminution in value For a construction contract, a general damages award based on the difference between the project as it should have been under the contract and the project as built. Where there is a minor breach, diminution in value is substituted for cost of completion if awarding cost of completion involves unjustified waste.

★*In cases where the contractor commits a minor breach of a construction contract, courts have been reluctant to award the owner general damages based on the cost of completing the project if doing so would cause waste. Perhaps the most famous situation of this kind is found in Jacob & Youngs v. Kent, 230 N.Y. 239, 129 N.E. 889 (1920). In that case, the contractor built a country residence using a different, although completely adequate, type of pipe from that called for in the contract. When the owner discovered this, he wanted the entire house pulled down and rebuilt with the right pipe. The court held that doing this would amount to waste under the circumstances and therefore refused to award the owner damages measured by cost of completion. The court awarded damages measured by the reduced value of the house with the substitute type of pipe. This measure of damages is referred to as **diminution in value** and is used when awarding the cost of completion would involve too much waste under the circumstances of the case.*

methods differ depending on which party breached the contract. Since the UCC now governs general damages in sales of goods contracts, these are discussed later in the chapter.

General Damages in Sales of Goods Contracts

The UCC rules now governing contracts for the sale of goods also include remedies for breach of these contracts. The UCC contains fairly detailed provisions on general damages for breach of contracts involving goods. For the most part, the rules on general damages are divided into damages available to the seller when the buyer breaches and damages available to the buyer when the seller breaches.

The general damages formulas take into account the reality that if possible (1) an aggrieved buyer will usually try to obtain substitute goods elsewhere, and (2) an aggrieved seller will usually try to resell the goods the buyer refused to take. Of course, contract breach can involve many other problems such as defective or inferior goods, partial performance, impossibility of resale or cover because of market conditions, and price changes that affect the parties' conduct. Such problems also influence the UCC damages formulas.

Whether the buyer or the seller has breached, the general UCC duty to behave in a commercially reasonable manner and to mitigate damages applies. Thus, both buyer and seller must conduct themselves as reasonable parties would under similar circumstances whether they are the breaching or the nonbreaching party. If a buyer or a seller does not behave in a commercially reasonable manner, the other party may be entitled to an offset against damages owed. In deciding how to handle a breach, each party runs a risk if it does not behave in a commercially reasonable way. This duty to behave with commercial reasonableness can affect a wide array of actions such as obtaining substitute goods; reselling, storing, or transporting goods involved in a breach; or deciding how long to wait before taking various actions.

As with the duty to mitigate damages, there is no specific test for when a party has failed to behave in a commercially reasonable manner. The facts and circumstances of the individual case help to determine this, as do relevant industry or trade practices and plain common sense. What a reasonable person would have done under similar circumstances is also relevant in determining commercial reasonableness. As with the duty to mitigate damages, someone need not always take the very best or cheapest action to satisfy the test for commercial reasonableness. Just because a party's decisions were not the best under the circumstances does not automatically mean they were commercially unreasonable. Similarly, if a party's judgment later turns out to be wrong, this does not necessarily mean it was commercially unreasonable. Commercially reasonable essentially means that conduct and decisions should be sensible at the time under the totality of the circumstances known or reasonably foreseeable at the time.

The Buyer's General Damages

If the seller breaches in a sale of goods contract, the method of determining the buyer's general damages depends on what the seller has done to commit the breach. The general damages available to the buyer may be summarized as follows:

1. If the seller breaches by failing to deliver the goods:

   - The buyer may obtain substitute goods (cover) and get damages based on the difference between the contract price and the cover price.
   - The buyer may choose not to cover and simply recover the difference between the contract price and the market price in effect at the time of the breach, considered to be the time at which the buyer could have covered. (Note: If the buyer chooses not to cover, this might constitute a failure to mitigate under some circumstances.)

2. If the seller breaches by delivering the wrong goods or if the goods are defective in some way:

- The buyer may choose to accept the nonconforming goods. Then, the buyer can get damages based on the difference between the value of the nonconforming goods and the value of the proper goods.
- The buyer may choose not to accept the nonconforming goods. Then, the buyer can reject the goods, cover, and get damages based on the difference between the contract price and the cover price.
- If buyer chooses not to accept the nonconforming goods and rejects them, but cannot cover, then the buyer can get the difference between the contract price and the market price in effect at the time of the breach.

The Seller's General Damages

If the buyer breaches in a sale of goods contract, the seller also has a choice about what to do and how to measure general damages. No matter how the buyer has breached the contract, the seller may try to resell the goods in question. If the seller possesses the goods, the seller simply undertakes the resale. If the buyer has the goods, the seller "identifies" the equivalent of the contract goods and then undertakes resale. Thus, the seller has the same general damages remedies available whether the buyer refuses to accept the goods, repudiates the contract before time for delivery, or fails to make payment after receiving the goods. The methods for determining the seller's general damages may be summarized as follows:

1. If the buyer has wrongfully rejected the goods and the seller is able to resell them:

- The seller may get damages based on the difference between the resale price and the contract price.
- If the general damages under the preceding method do not fully compensate the seller, the seller may get damages based on the profit he expected under the contract if the buyer had fully performed. The seller may include in this profit the reasonable overhead he expected to make under the contract.

2. The seller may choose not to resell the goods and get damages based on the difference between the contract price and the market price of the goods at the time and place they were to be delivered to the buyer.

Consequential (special) damages
Those damages not assumed to flow naturally from the type of breach involved but caused by special circumstances of the individual case or breach.

Consequential Damages

Consequential damages are damages caused by specific circumstances of the individual case and typically do not occur every time the particular type of contract is breached. These damages are also called **special damages** because they arise under special circumstances. Consequential or special damages are also known as *Hadley v. Baxendale* damages, based on the famous case presented later in this section. This category of contract damages arose because in many instances of contract breach, general damages do not fully compensate the nonbreaching party.

To understand why general damages might not always fully compensate the nonbreaching party for loss, consider the following example.

EXAMPLE 11.5

Suppose a chemicals seller makes a chemical sales contract with a buyer. The contract price is $10,000. Seller breaches the contract by failing to deliver any chemicals, and Buyer diligently tries to cover but cannot do so. Because Buyer does not have the expected chemicals on hand, he cannot perform on two resale contracts for the chemicals he has already made with crop dusting companies. Buyer expected to make $10,000 profit on each of these resale contracts and planned to pay for the purchase of the chemicals with $5,000 from each contract. The remaining $5,000 on each contract would be overhead and profit.

The losses the buyer suffers from not being able to go through with his own resale contracts do not always occur in breaches of chemical sales contracts or other sale of goods contracts. Not all breaches of sale of goods contracts involve situations in which the buyer plans to resell the goods purchased. In Example 11.5, the chemicals buyer had already arranged such contracts. Under the circumstances of this particular case, the buyer has suffered extra losses that cannot be compensated by simply awarding general damages.

To see why general damages would not compensate for the buyer's losses on resale contracts, recall how general damages are measured. Since chemicals are goods, general damages would be calculated under the UCC sale of goods formula for the buyer where the seller fails to deliver. Since the buyer was not able to cover, he would normally be entitled to general damages based on the difference between the contract price and the market price at the time he learned of the breach. That amount, however, would only compensate the buyer for losses under the main contract, not losses on the resale contracts.

Although lost profit on resale contracts does not occur in every breach of contract for sale of goods, when it does occur the buyer usually suffers additional financial loss. Normally, this loss would not occur *but for the breach*. This extra loss is the type of loss that has come to be known as consequential or special damages. Special or consequential damages are given for extra losses that are caused by the breach but not compensated under the applicable general damages formula.

To be liable for consequential damages, the breaching party must have been able to foresee such loss at the time the contract was made. The defendant must pay consequential damages flowing from special circumstances of the contract only if she knew of these special circumstances at the time of formation. Consider the following famous case, which provides a good factual setting for understanding why a party who received only general damages might not be fully compensated.

At the trial before *Crompton, J.,* at the last Glouc-ester Assizes, it appeared that the plaintiffs carried on an extensive business as millers at Gloucester; and that, on the 11th of May, their mill was stopped by a breakage of the crank shaft by which the mill was worked. The steam-engine was manufactured by Messrs. Joyce & Co, the engi-neers, at Greenwich, and it became necessary to send the shaft as a pattern for a new one to Greenwich. The fracture was discovered on the 12th, and on the 13th the plaintiffs sent one of their servants to the office of the defendants, who are the well-known carriers trading under the name of Pickford & Co., for the purpose of having the shaft carried to Greenwich. The plaintiffs' servant told the clerk that the shaft must be sent immediately; and in answer to the inquiry when the shaft would be taken, the an-swer was, that if it was sent up by twelve o'clock any day, it would be delivered at Greenwich on the following day. On the following day the shaft was taken by the defendants, before noon, for the purpose of being conveyed to Greenwich, and the sum of $2\pounds$ 4s. was paid for its carriage for the whole distance; at the same time the defendants' clerk was told that a special entry, if required, should be made to hasten its delivery. The de-livery of the shaft at Greenwich was delayed by some neglect; and the consequence was, that the plaintiffs did not receive the new shaft for several days after they would otherwise have done, and the working of their mill was thereby delayed, and they thereby lost the profits they would otherwise have received.

On the part of the defendants, it was ob-jected that these damages were too remote, and that the defendants were not liable with respect to them. The learned Judge left the case gener-ally to the jury, who found a verdict with $25\pounds$ damages beyond the amount paid into court.

Whateley, in the last Michaelmas Term, ob-tained a rule *nisi* for a new trial, on the ground of misdirection.

[The arguments made by counsel are omit-ted.]

The judgment of the court was now deliv-ered by

ALDERSON, B.—We think that there ought to be a new trial in this case; but, in so doing, we deem it to be expedient and necessary to state explicitly the rule which the Judge, at the next trial, ought, in our opinion, to direct the jury to be governed by when they estimate the damages.

It is, indeed, of the last importance that we should do this; for, if the jury are left without any definite rule to guide them, it will, in such cases as these, manifestly lead to the greatest injustice. The Courts have done this on several occasions; and in *Blake v. Midland Railway Com-pany (a),* the Court granted a new trial on this very ground, that the rule had not been defi-nitely laid down to the jury by the learned Judge at *Nisi Prius.*

"There are certain established rules," this Court says, in *Alder v. Keighly (b),* "according to which the jury ought to find." And the Court, in that case, adds: "and here there is a clear rule, that the amount which would have been re-ceived if the contract had been kept, is the measure of damages if the contract is broken."

Now we think the proper rule in such a case as the present is this:—Where two parties have made a contract which one of them has broken, the damages which the other party ought to receive in respect of such breach of contract should be such as may fairly and reasonably be considered either arising naturally, i.e., accord-ing to the usual course of things, from such breach of contract itself, or such as may reason-ably be supposed to have been in the contem-plation of both parties, at the time they made the contract, as the probable result of the breach of it. Now, if the special circumstances under which the contract was actually made were communicated by the plaintiffs to the defen-dants, and thus known to both parties, the damages resulting from the breach of such con-tract, which they would reasonably contem-plate, would be the amount of injury which would ordinarily follow from a breach of con-tract under these special circumstances so known and communicated. But, on the other hand, if these special circumstances were wholly unknown to the party breaking the contract, he, at the most, could only be supposed to have had in his contemplation the amount of injury which would arise generally, and in the great multitude of cases not affected by any special circumstances, from such a breach of contract. For, had the special circumstances been known, the parties might have specially provided for the breach of contract by special terms as to the damages in that case; and of this advantage it would be very unjust to deprive them. Now the above principles are those by which we think the jury ought to be guided in estimating the damages arising out of any breach of contract. It is said, that other cases, such as breaches of contract in the non-payment of money, or in the not making a good title to land, are to be treated as exceptions from this, and as governed by a conventional rule. But as, in such cases, both parties must be supposed to be cognizant of that well-known rule, these cases may, we think, be more properly classed under the rule above enunciated as to cases under known special circumstances, because there both parties may reasonably be presumed to contemplate the estimation of the amount of damages according to the conventional rule. Now, in the present case, if we are to apply the principles above laid down, we find that the only circumstances here communicated by the plaintiffs to the defendants at the time the contract was made, were, that the article to be carried was the broken shaft of a mill, and that the plaintiffs were the millers of that mill. But how do these circumstances show reasonably that the profits of the mill must be stopped by an unreasonable delay in the delivery of the broken shaft by the carrier to the third person? Suppose the plaintiffs had another shaft in their possession put up or putting up at the time, and that they only wished to send back the broken shaft to the engineer who made it; it is clear that this would be quite consistent with the above circumstances, and yet the unreasonable delay in the delivery would have no effect upon the intermediate profits of the mill. Or, again, suppose that, at the time of the delivery to the carrier, the machinery of the mill had been in other respects defective, then, also, the same results would follow. Here it is true that the shaft was actually sent back to serve as a model for a new one, and that the want of a new one was the only cause of the stoppage of the mill, and that the loss of profits really arose from the delay in delivering the broken one to serve as a model. But it is obvious that, in the great multitude of cases of millers sending off broken shafts to third persons by a carrier under ordinary circumstances, such consequences would not, in all probability, have occurred; and these special circumstances were here never communicated by the plaintiffs to the defendants. It follows, therefore, that the loss of profits here cannot reasonably be considered such a consequence of the breach of contract as could have been fairly and reasonably contemplated by both the parties when they made this contract. For such loss would neither have flowed naturally from the breach of this contract in the great multitude of such cases occurring under ordinary circumstances, nor were the special circumstances, which, perhaps, would have made it a reasonable and natural consequence of such breach of contract, communicated to or known by the defendants. The Judge ought, therefore, to have told the jury that, upon the facts then before them, they ought not to take the loss of profits into consideration at all in estimating the damages. There must therefore be a new trial in this case. Rule absolute.

Questions to Consider

1. Which contract did the plaintiff mill owners claim was breached? What was the contract price for this contract? How did the defendant breach this contract?
2. How would general damages be calculated for the defendant's breach of contract? Does the court think such general damages are available in this case?
3. Would this general damages award compensate the plaintiff for the loss of income from the mill? Why or why not?
4. Why does the court say that it would not be good policy to make the defendant pay for harm caused by "special circumstances" it did not know about? What "special circumstances" is the plaintiff asserting existed in this case?
5. Based on the facts given in the case, do you think the court was right in deciding the defendant did not know of the special circumstances the plaintiff says existed? Why or why not?

Incidental Damages

Incidental damages in breach of contract cases are given to reimburse a party for relatively small costs of administering the breach.

EXAMPLE 11.6

If Seller delivers nonconforming goods, this is a breach, and Buyer is entitled to reject the goods. Suppose, however, that Seller assures Buyer she will immediately ship the proper goods and asks Buyer to store the nonconforming goods for a few days. Buyer will probably want reimbursement for storage of these goods. Such storage costs would typically be classified as incidental damages.

Other kinds of losses often characterized as incidental damages are shipping or insurance costs associated with handling a breach, costs of transportation, costs of advertising, and the like.

Incidental damages and consequential damages are similar in that they both are outside the general damages formula. The difference is not always clear and is partly one of degree in many cases. Incidental damages are relatively small amounts that are reasonably necessary to administer or efficiently handle a breach. They are always deemed to be foreseeable by reasonable people. Larger amounts tend to fall into the category of consequential damages and are not really mere costs of administering the breach. Consequential damages are not deemed to be automatically foreseeable. As the court in *Hadley v. Baxendale* said, the party who claims consequential damages must show that the other party knew or ought to have known about special circumstances that would cause such losses in the event of a breach.

Nominal Damages

Nominal damages are a token award of damages in a very small amount, such as one dollar. Under traditional common law, it was thought that the right to file a lawsuit should be available even if the plaintiff could show no real economic injury. Thus, a plaintiff could sue on a matter of principle that was important to her, demand nominal damages, and try to get a court judgment to vindicate her rights. According to the theory, the demand for nominal damages justified such a lawsuit and protected people's right to sue on a matter of principle even though they had not suffered a financial loss.

While the traditional rationale for nominal damages may still be valid, the modern reality is that few can afford to sue for nominal damages. Today a more common practice is for a party to sue for *declaratory relief* if he wants to vindicate or establish certain contract rights. Declaratory relief is discussed further under Equitable Remedies later in this chapter.

Another use of nominal damages is still practical in today's contract litigation. In almost all cases, a plaintiff files a contract claim believing a significant amount of damages is available. It may turn out, however, that these damages are not available because the plaintiff cannot show any real economic loss or because his case is weak. The following example illustrates this point.

EXAMPLE **11.7**

A goods buyer whose supplier has refused to deliver sues the defaulting seller for general, consequential, and incidental damages. The parties had a written contract that contained the following provision awarding attorney's fees to the "prevailing party":

Attorney's Fees

If either party to this agreement files litigation, the prevailing party shall be entitled to all reasonable attorney's fees and all reasonable costs as awarded by a court of competent jurisdiction.

The case comes to trial, and Buyer is able to establish that Seller breached the contract. In addition to general, consequential, and incidental damages, Buyer would expect to recover his attorney's fees if he won in the litigation because he would be the prevailing party.

For a variety of reasons, however, Buyer is unable to establish that he suffered actual financial damage. Thus, general and consequential damages would not be available, even if Buyer could show some incidental damages. Because the court could award nominal damages, however, Buyer would be able to obtain attorney's fees as the winning party. An award of nominal damages can be used to justify an award of attorney's fees to the prevailing party in litigation even if that party did not prove financial loss.

Punitive Damages in Breach of Contract Cases

The basis for an award of punitive damages is punishment and deterrence. Such damages have been awarded in personal injury cases and, in fact, are currently the subject of national debate. In theory, **punitive damages** (also called **exemplary damages**) are noncompensatory damages and are not awarded to reimburse actual losses. They are awarded in cases where the defendant has behaved in a malicious or reprehensible way and deserves punishment. Punitive damages awards are often related to the financial condition of the defendant. When defendants are wealthy, a jury may believe a higher punitive damages award is necessary to punish them financially. Another rationale is that high awards will deter similar conduct in the future both by the defendant and by other potential wrongdoers.

Traditionally, punitive damages awards have not been available in contract litigation. One reason for this is that in Anglo-American contract law, breach does not necessarily involve moral fault. A party who has an enforceable contract really has two choices: perform, or breach and pay. Both are acceptable. For the most part, if a party chooses to breach and pay, contract law is not concerned with whether this behavior is morally right or wrong. Even malicious or intentional contract breaches involving bad conduct on the defendant's part traditionally have not resulted in awards of punitive damages. Some judges and commentators have even argued that freedom to breach is efficient and economically beneficial to society.[4]

Despite this general rule, punitive damages are allowed in certain situations:

1. Punitive damages are available where the conduct involved in the contract breach also constitutes a tort. A **tort** is an injury to one's person or

Exemplary (punitive) damages Damages awarded to a prevailing party which are not based on compensation for actual losses and are intended to punish and deter the bad conduct involved.

Tort A legally recognized injury to one's person or property.

property. Fraud is a type of tort. If, for example, the defendant commits the tort of fraud when breaching a contract, many courts would award punitive damages for the conduct involved in the fraud. Such courts, however, have usually required the tort to be committed wantonly, maliciously, or intentionally. Punitive damages are not imposed for a tort committed in breaching a contract where the tortious conduct was merely negligent.

2. Punitive damages are also available where a breach of a contract involves a fiduciary duty of one party to the other. As previously noted, a **fiduciary duty** is a special responsibility to take care of another in some way. It involves more than the minimal duty of care that ordinary people owe to each other. A fiduciary duty generally exists where there is a special relationship such as between a lawyer and her client; a bank and its depositors; a trustee and the beneficiaries of the trust; a corporate director and the shareholders of the corporation; or an insurance company and its insureds. If someone with a fiduciary duty breaches a contract made with the party to whom this duty is owed, punitive damages may be allowed. Again, this breach of fiduciary duty will not give rise to a punitive damages award unless the breach is malicious or intentional. However, the breach need not also constitute an independent tort. Punitive damages may be available for malicious breaches of fiduciary duty under a contract even where the breach does not amount to a tort.

3. Punitive damages are now available to an insured who successfully shows that her insurance company breached the implied covenant (promise) of good faith in refusing to settle a claim. This is a fairly recent development in the law of contracts.

Fiduciary duty   A special responsibility of one party to care for the interests of another party which exists between such parties as an attorney and her client or, a trustee and beneficiaries of the trust.

EXAMPLE   **11.8**

Insured's automobile is badly damaged in an accident. The automobile is two years old and was in excellent condition before the accident. Insured wants it repaired and has obtained several estimates indicating this is possible. The insurance company refuses to consider the estimates and insists the car is not repairable. It refuses to pay more than low bluebook value for the car and threatens to cancel all coverage on a new vehicle if Insured does not agree to a low settlement amount. If the insurance company's conduct is found to be a breach of the promise of good faith implied into the insurance contract, Insured may be entitled to recover punitive damages in a breach of contract action against the insurer.

For a number of years, one state, California, indicated that a breach of the implied covenant of good faith might be the basis for an award of punitive damages in *any contract. See, e.g., Seaman's Direct Buying Service v. Standard Oil Co. of California,* 36 Cal. 3d 752, 686 P.2d 1158, 206 Cal. Rptr. 354 (1984). Recently, however, *Seaman's* was overruled, and Montana is currently the sole state to recognize the "tort of bad faith in typical arm's length commercial contracts. . ." *Freeman & Mills, Inc. v. Belcher Oil Co.,* 11 Cal. 4th 85, 900 P.2d 669, 44 Cal. Rptr. 2d 420, 428 (1995).

Some states have statutes affecting awards of punitive damages, so you should check your own state statutes in cases involving punitive damages. It is also possible in some cases that federal statutes or cases could affect the availability of punitive damages.

Damages for Emotional Distress in Breach of Contract Cases

Emotional distress damages are money awarded for mental suffering of various kinds. Although emotional distress damages are common in tort law, they are rarely awarded in contract cases. Generally, contract law has paid little attention to whether breach of a contract causes mental suffering in the aggrieved party. There are some traditional exceptions to the general rule, however. Damages for emotional distress are available in breach of contract cases where the contract is of an intensely personal nature, such as a contract for burial of a family member. Where the contract is found to be of a kind that would be likely to produce great mental anguish if not carried out properly, punitive damages have sometimes been awarded.[5] Sometimes damages are awarded for emotional distress in cases where a breach of contract has caused physical, bodily harm.

Emotional distress damages Damages awarded as compensation for mental suffering of various kinds.

Liquidated Damages

Sometimes the parties think ahead to the circumstances that might exist if one of them breaches. For a variety of reasons, the parties may wish to include a contract provision that essentially sets the amount of damages ahead of time or establishes a method for calculating the amount. Such damages are called **liquidated damages,** and the contract provision is called a **liquidated damages clause.** The following are examples of liquidated damages clauses:

Liquidated Damages

In the event either party should breach this contract, the parties agree that the breaching party shall pay to the other party the sum of _____dollars as liquidated damages.

Liquidated Damages

In the event Contractor completes construction after the date herein agreed for issuance of the final certificate, Owner shall be entitled to collect from Contractor $100 per day for every day after the date agreed for issuance of the final certificate until the day of actual issuance of such certificate.

If one of the parties later breaches, the liquidated damages clause is used to calculate the amount of damages instead of adding up the amount of actual damages. The amount based on the liquidated damages clause substitutes for general, consequential, and incidental damages.

Liquidated damages clauses are very common in modern contracts, although traditionally courts have often been reluctant to enforce such clauses because they may involve a penalty against the paying party. A provision in a contract designed purely to deter a breach and punish a party who breaches is usually interpreted as a penalty and not as a valid liquidated damages clause. A contract provision that is a penalty is not enforceable. The idea that private parties cannot enforce penalties against each other through the use of a contract actually began in the Courts of Equity many centuries ago. Eventually, the law courts adopted this viewpoint. In spite of the usefulness of liquidated damages clauses, disapproval of possible penalties has persisted.

Liquidated damages Damages awards which are agreed upon prior to a breach in which the parties try to predict reasonable compensation in the event of a breach. The amount of the liquidated damages, or a formula for calculating them, is usually summarized in the contract.

Liquidated damages clause The provision in a contract which states the amount of liquidated damages to be paid, or a formula for calculating them.

Distinguishing between a valid liquidated damages clause and a clause that is actually a penalty and therefore invalid is sometimes difficult. Courts have generally looked at three factors when considering whether an alleged liquidated damages clause is really a penalty:

1. The intention of the parties
2. Whether actual damages are difficult to prove
3. Whether the amount of damages under the clause is reasonable in light of the actual losses that occurred.

The intention of the parties is probably the least important factor. Even if the parties say the clause is for liquidated damages, a court may hold differently if the other two requirements are not satisfied.

Traditionally, courts have been more likely to hold that a contested clause is a valid liquidated damages clause if the party trying to enforce it can show actual damages were difficult to calculate at the time the contract was made. Usually, this means the party trying to enforce the provision must show that at the time the contract was formed, actual loss in the event of a breach appeared difficult or impossible to calculate. The calculations could be difficult for a variety of reasons: because proof of loss would be hard to obtain, because it would not be clear which losses were caused by the breach and which by other factors, or because no standardized formula was available that would give full compensation in case of a breach.

Applying the difficulty of calculation factor involves the use of some mind-bending fictions. If damages could not be calculated at the time of contract making, on what basis can the amount of liquidated damages be figured when a breach occurs? Nevertheless, liquidated damages clauses have been enforced where the parties can show that at the time of formation, they would have had a difficult or impossible task assessing actual losses in the event of an actual breach. Probably, the real reason for upholding liquidated damages clauses is that they are commercially useful: they tend to prevent litigation, reduce attorney's fees, and provide clarity about reimbursement for losses.

Courts have also been more inclined to hold that a liquidated damages clause is valid and enforceable if the amount of damages provided in the clause bears a reasonable relationship to actual loss. The common law assesses the relationship between liquidated and actual loss as of the time of contract formation. Under common law, a liquidated damages clause is valid if the amount provided is comparable to actual losses insofar as they could be predicted when the contract was made. The UCC views the relationship between actual and liquidated loss as best determined when the breach occurs. Under the UCC, a liquidated damages clause is valid if the parties provided an amount that is comparable to actual losses occurring at the time of the breach.

Contract Damages Based on Reliance

In most contract situations, an aggrieved party will be adequately compensated by receiving the expectation measure of damages as determined by general, consequential, and incidental damages. In a number of situations, however, expectation damages are not adequate or are not available. In these situations, reliance damages may be given. **Reliance damages** are normally measured by calculating all of a party's out-of-pocket losses. All losses caused by the plaintiff's reliance are reimbursed. Since reliance damages are not based on a contract price, the usual measures of expectation damages do not apply. If reliance damages are given, the court uses out-of-pocket losses as a complete substitute for general, consequential, and incidental damages.

Reliance damages may be available in the following situations:

1. *There is no contract, but a gift was intended, and reasonable reliance on the gift has caused a loss to the donee.* The reliance measure of damages is commonly used when a plaintiff recovers for a revoked gift promise under the theory of promissory estoppel. A common problem with reliance recovery under this theory is the extent to which the promise in question should be enforced.

   Recall that promissory estoppel is a doctrine under which donative, or gift, promises can become enforceable.

Reliance damages
Damages awarded as an alternative to recovery on a contract which are measured by calculating a party's out-of-pocket losses.

EXAMPLE 11.9

Janice promises her daughter Ali that she will give Greyacre to her as a gift. Ali gives up her apartment in the city, moves onto the land, and improves it by building a house. Then Janice changes her mind and wants to take back the land. The promise Ali would want to enforce in this case is the promise to give her Greyacre. Since this is a pure gift promise, some choices must be made about recovery under reliance. If Ali successfully establishes a claim to the land under the doctrine of promissory estoppel, a court could simply award her the out-of-pocket losses she suffered. These would include the cost of giving up her apartment, the cost of building the house, possibly moving expenses, and so on. If the court chose to enforce the entire promise, then Ali would get the land with the house on it.

In cases of a gift of land where the donee has moved onto the land and made improvements, most courts have awarded specific performance of the promise (the land with the house), even though the oral promise to make a gift of land violates the Statute of Frauds.

In other cases, the promise relied on may be enforced only up to the amount of out-of-pocket losses caused by the reliance.

EXAMPLE 11.10

A promises B a gift of $30,000 so B can quit working for a year and stay home to write a novel. Then A backs out after B has taken a year's unpaid leave from her job, stayed off the job for two months, and lost $2,000 per month. If B can get back her job, and sue A under promissory estoppel, most courts would probably not enforce A's promise to the full extent of the $30,000. Most courts would probably give B her out-of-pocket losses, or $4,000.

---

2. *There is no contract, but preliminary negotiations have taken place, and as a result, one party has suffered reasonable and foreseeable losses in reliance on the contract.* Promises made in negotiations that do not result in a contract are now

enforceable under the doctrine of promissory estoppel. As mentioned earlier, under modern law, promissory estoppel has expanded to be available in any situation where there is no consideration and the promisee reasonably and detrimentally relies on a promise. It is important to remember that recovery under the expanded doctrine of promissory estoppel or reliance now has broad applicability. The parties often make use of this expanded theory in situations involving losses suffered in negotiation.

Precontractual liability refers to liability for losses suffered because of changes in position in response to promises make during the contract negotiation period. Precontractual liability can occur when parties negotiate for a contract and one of them misleads the other into thinking she has, or will shortly have, a deal. Sometimes one or both parties believe they have a deal, but the deal falls apart before formation actually takes place.

A party may try to recover reliance damages for losses suffered as a result of precontractual negotiation. In this situation, the plaintiff must satisfy the same elements required for enforcement of donative promises: reasonable and foreseeable reliance. Here, however, the reliance is on obtaining a contract rather than on receiving a gift. The plaintiff must show her losses were actually caused by this reliance and not by other factors.

> **Precontractual liability** Losses caused in the negotiating phase of a contract and before it is formed.

EXAMPLE 11.11

Jack O'Lantern, a chain of children's toy stores, promises it will sell a franchise to Paul. To obtain the franchise, Paul performs a number of acts at the request of Jack O'Lantern. Among other things, he turns over $10,000 to Jack O'Lantern and then pays another $15,000 down on a property where he plans to locate his toy store. At this point, Jack O'Lantern backs out and refuses to sell the franchise to Paul. If Paul were to sue and the court decided the parties had no contract, he might be entitled to recover under the doctrine of promissory estoppel. Paul would probably recover his out-of-pocket losses: the $10,000 paid to Jack O'Lantern and the $15,000 down on the land, plus any other losses caused by his reliance on the promise of the franchise.[6]

---

3. *There is a contract, but the breaching party is suing. If this party has rendered performance under the contract for which he has not been compensated, he may sue for reliance damages.* In all American jurisdictions, the breaching party is normally foreclosed from suing on the contract price even if he has suffered losses in partly performing the contract. Historically, the breaching party had no remedy at all for uncompensated losses suffered in performing on a contract. Under modern law, the breaching party may at least have a cause of action for reliance damages in the form of out-of-pocket losses. (Restitution damages are another possibility, as noted later in the chapter.)

4. *There is a contract, the nonbreaching party is suing, and recovery on the contract price would not give adequate compensation.* In this case, modern courts will often allow the plaintiff an election not to sue on the contract. Instead, the nonbreaching party (the plaintiff) can elect to sue for reliance damages.

This situation can arise in a variety of factual settings. Sometimes, for example, a party will discover his costs under the contract have unexpectedly risen and decreased the contract profit margin or destroyed it altogether. Sometimes a party will discover he has dramatically underbid a job.

If the other party breaches a contract that has become a losing one for the nonbreaching party, a suit on the contract price will not result in adequate compensation for the innocent party. Because all general damages formulas are based in large part on return of expected profits under a contract, such formulas do not result in adequate compensation where the profit margin is reduced or destroyed. Many courts will now allow the nonbreaching party on a losing contract to elect to sue for reliance damages. (Restitution damages are another possiblity, as discussed later.) Here the measure of damages includes all out-of-pocket costs the nonbreaching party expended in performing or relying on the contract.

Contract Damages Based on Restitution

Like reliance damages, restitution damages are available in many situations where the contract measure of damages will not adequately compensate the nonbreaching party, or where there is no contract but one of the parties has suffered a loss. Although there are forms of equitable restitution, restitution is normally a legal remedy in breach of contract actions or actions in which restitution is a substitute for contract damages.

Unlike reliance, **restitution** focuses mainly on whether the party suffering the loss has also conferred a benefit on the other party in the process. If so, and if it would be unfair to allow the other party to retain this benefit, restitution damages are available. The restitutionary measure of recovery is the return of the value of the benefit conferred to the party who bestowed it. As the Restatement notes, "A person who has been unjustly enriched at the expense of another is required to make restitution to the other."[7]

> **Restitution** An award of damages not based on the contract and calculated by determining the money equivalent of all benefits the aggrieved party has conferred on the other.

Currently, the idea of restitution as the return of a benefit conferred is a flexible concept. In cases where an actual financial benefit has clearly been conferred on the defendant, restitution damages are readily justified. In other cases the courts have not consistently interpreted the meaning of enrichment or benefit conferred. Some courts have awarded restitution damages where only a theoretical value was bestowed on the defendant. Other courts have fictionally labeled losses sustained by the plaintiff as benefits conferred upon the defendant. Thus, the requirement of unfairness appears to be the most consistent idea in modern cases of restitution. If the plaintiff can show losses and some arguable benefit to the defendant, and it appears *unfair* for the plaintiff to go uncompensated, a court may award restitution damages.

Like reliance damages, restitution damages are a complete substitute for damages based on a contract price. If a court awards restitution damages, they are given in place of general, consequential, and incidental damages. The majority of courts, however, will allow evidence of the contract price to be used to determine the possible value of the benefit conferred.

Restitution damages may be available in the following situations:

1. *There has been a total or material breach of a contract, and the nonbreaching party is suing. In that case, the nonbreaching party may elect to sue for contract damages*

or cancel the contract and sue for restitution damages. (Restitution damages are not available for a partial or minor breach of a contract.) Though expectation damages normally provide a better measure of recovery, if the contract is a losing one, the plaintiff will often elect to sue in restitution. This election is not available if the plaintiff has fully performed and all the defendant must do is pay the price. In that case, most courts confine the plaintiff to expectation damages and do not allow her to elect restitution.

Where the nonbreaching party is suing, a few courts use the contract price as an upper limit of what can be recovered under restitution damages. Most American courts do not place this limitation on restitutionary recovery, however, unless, as noted below, the breaching party is suing.

The nonbreaching plaintiff who successfully recovers in restitution receives the reasonable value of services or goods conferred on the defendant, or the reasonable value of property transferred to the defendant, or the reasonable value of improvements made to the defendant's property. In other words, the plaintiff recovers the reasonable value of her performance to the defendant. Where a particularly clear case of injustice can be made out, but a benefit was not clearly conferred, courts have even characterized the value of the losses as the value of the benefit.[8]

2. *A contract has been formed, but it is unenforceable. Either party may recover the value of benefits conferred under the contract.* Such situations arise where parties have made a contract that failed to comply with the Statute of Frauds, where there was a mutual mistake, or where contract performance is excused because of impossibility or frustration of purpose. Return of benefits conferred on the other party is common in these situations. This list is not exhaustive because restitutionary recovery may be available in almost any situation where the contract is unenforceable unless there is a public policy reason to deny recovery. A public policy reason to deny recovery would be found, for example, with a completely illegal contract such as a contract to commit murder, to ship firearms illegally, or to engage in prostitution. Such a contract would be unenforceable by either party, and restitution would not be available to either party.

3. *The breaching party is suing. In this situation, the plaintiff is often referred to as the defaulting plaintiff. The defaulting plaintiff may be allowed to recover in restitution for the value of the benefits conferred on the nonbreaching defendant. Damages caused to the defendant by the plaintiff's breach are offset against any amount the breaching plaintiff recovers in restitution.* Here courts usually limit the defaulting plaintiff's recovery to the contract price even if the reasonable value of the performance exceeds this amount. Virtually all American courts have followed the rule that a defaulting plaintiff cannot obtain a larger recovery under restitution than he would have had under the contract.

Since a breaching party who has at least *substantially performed* can bring an action for the contract price, restitution damages typically would be sought when the breaching party has given something less than substantial performance. Traditionally, American courts also restricted recovery in restitution to breaching parties who did not commit the contract breach deliberately. Modern American courts, however, appear increasingly willing to allow even a party who commits a deliberate contract breach to sue for restitution.

Assignment

Consider the following hypotheticals and determine what recovery, if any, the winning party could obtain under the reliance or restitution theory.

▶ Hypothetical 1

Aunt Tillie promises her favorite nephew, George, that she will pay for his college tuition, books, rent, and utilities if he will quit his full-time job and go back to school for at least two years. She says that she will give him enough money every month so that he can work part-time and spend the rest of his time studying. Since Aunt Tillie has always been good to George financially and is very fond of him, George decides to do as she requests. He quits his full-time job where his salary is $20,000 per year and moves to Columbia City where he rents an apartment for $500 per month. George pays the first and last month's rent before moving in and also pays moving costs of $1,000. His utilities are $50 per month. George enrolls in Columbia Junior College and pays one quarter's tuition of $150 and $200 for books. He finds a part-time job on campus where he will earn $8,000 per year. Since he lives close to campus and works there, he sells his car for $5,000 and plans to use public transportation.

All goes well for one month; then George asks Aunt Tillie for reimbursement for the expenses he has paid. She refuses. George sues on a theory of promissory estoppel and wins. What should his recovery be?

▶ Hypothetical 2

Mighty Maids, Inc., is an all-women carpentry business. Mighty Maids obtains a contract with the City of Tranquillity to remodel and reconstruct all cabinetwork in the Tranquillity City Hall. The total contract price City will pay Mighty Maids is $300,000. Two events occur shortly after Mighty Maids begins work. First, Mighty Maids discovers the price of the maple to be used for the cabinets has soared. This means the 20 percent profit margin Mighty Maids expected to make on the contract will be reduced to 10 percent. Second, the City of Tranquillity fails to live up to its name and has a bitter dispute over spending money on new cabinets. The Tranquillity City Council votes to revoke the contract as an unauthorized expenditure of public funds. Up to this date, Mighty Maids has expended $100,000 on labor and materials for the cabinets. The materials are all installed and cannot be reused. Assuming the City Council is not justified in revoking the contract and this is a breach, what recovery would be best for Mighty Maids, and why?

Equitable Remedies in Contract Actions

The most common remedies in contract actions are probably legal remedies involving awards of damages. In some cases, however, money cannot adequately compensate an injured party for the harm suffered. Where damages cannot adequately compensate an injured party, equitable remedies may be available. All American jurisdictions require a showing of the inadequacy of legal remedies as a prerequisite to granting equitable relief. Thus, where equitable remedies are requested, the paralegal should verify that no adequate legal remedies are available.

Specific Performance

In some contract situations, damages will not provide adequate relief to the aggrieved party. Such situations tend to occur where (1) the subject matter of the contract is unique or irreplaceable, (2) the damages cannot be calculated with reasonable accuracy, or (3) the winning party may not be able to collect the damages award from the loser. In any of these situations, a party may wish to sue for specific performance of the contract. Specific performance is the primary form of equitable relief used in contract cases.

Specific performance
In contract cases, a form of equitable relief in which the court orders one or both parties to perform according to the contract.

Specific performance is very different from the legal remedy of damages because damages substitute money for the bargained-for performance. If a court orders **specific performance**, the plaintiff receives the bargained-for performance. A contracting party who successfully sues for specific performance obtains a court order that requires the other party to perform the contract.

Granting specific performance means the contracting parties must perform to each other although they are involved in a dispute and are probably not on amicable terms. Thus, specific performance raises a number of practical problems, which are usually considered under the requirement that a court must determine that specific performance is feasible before granting it.

The requirement that specific performance must be feasible means a variety of things. First, it must be possible under the circumstances to carry out the court-ordered performance. Here the court considers practical questions such as the availability of supplies and whether the promised performance will still be effective. There is little point in ordering a performance that is impossible to carry out. Second, the degree of continued court supervision necessary to carry out performance must not be too great. There is no precise formula for this requirement, but generally courts do not grant specific performance of private contracts where intense and continued court involvement will be required to accomplish the contract performance.[9]

Particular kinds of contracts tend to raise problems that affect the likelihood that specific performance will be granted or denied. Typically, the following problems arise with requests for specific performance:

1. *The buyer in a contract for the sale of goods cannot get specific performance unless the goods are "unique" or "in other proper circumstances." UCC §2 2-716 covers the availability of specific performance to the buyer. Essentially, it provides that the buyer can get specific performance only if the goods are of a type that cannot be replaced because no comparable goods are on the market. The meaning of "in the proper circumstances" is not entirely clear but it probably includes situations in which the buyer cannot cover and the goods indicated in the contract existed at the time of formation or have since been identified to the contract.*
2. *The seller in a contract for the sale of goods can get specific performance in the form of an action for the price.* An action for the contract price differs from an action for damages for breach in that the court does not award general, consequential, or incidental damages. Instead, the seller simply sues for full payment under the contract. This usually occurs where the goods delivered (or to be delivered) to the buyer are unique, such as goods imprinted with the buyer's name or logo, or are goods that only a particular buyer can use. In that case, the seller cannot resell the goods even if he still has them. The seller can bring an action for full payment of the contract price.

3. *Employment contracts are rarely enforceable through specific performance. Neither the employee nor the employer can ordinarily get specific performance.* The rationale for this rule is probably an aversion to involuntary servitude where it is the employer who seeks specific performance. As to an employee who seeks specific performance, the rationale may simply be one of practicality: there is little point in forcing an employer to hire someone she does not wish to employ.

One exception to specific performance in the case of employment agreements is enforcement of covenants not to compete. A **covenant not to compete** is either a provision in an employment contract or a separate contract, in which an employee promises not to leave his current employment and start a business that competes with the employer's business. Covenants not to compete are common in industries where there is danger of employees obtaining trade secrets, client and customer lists, or special expertise that would permit them to start or join a rival company. To prevent future competition, the employer commonly requires prospective employees to sign a covenant not to compete. Such a covenant might be worded as follows:

Covenant-not-to-compete A provision in a contract, or a separate contract, in which a party promises not to leave his current employer and start a business which competes with the employer's business.

Noncompetition

If employment is terminated for any cause, employee shall not, for a period of ___years after leaving the employment, engage directly or indirectly, either personally or in any other capacity, in the _____business within the area of _____; nor shall employee solicit business from any customers of employer according to the above terms for himself or others.

If there is an enforceable covenant not to compete, the employer can obtain specific performance of the covenant. This is usually done in the form of an injunction. An injunction is an equitable remedy that is not limited to contract actions, but is widely used in all areas of the law. An **injunction** is a court order that requires a party to litigation to take some action or prohibits a party from taking some action. A court order for specific performance of a covenant not to compete is accomplished by issuing an injunction barring the employee from engaging in business that competes with the former employer. A court grants the injunction on the ground that the employee's competition is a violation of the covenant not to compete.

Injunction A form of equitable relief in which the court orders a party to litigation to take some action or to refrain from taking some action.

The law concerning enforceability of covenants not to compete is extensive. A paralegal should always check applicable cases and statutes in particular cases. As a general matter, covenants not to compete are enforceable if they are *reasonable* as to (1) the geographic area in which competition is prohibited and (2) the length of time the competition is prohibited. The Restatement (Second) takes the position that courts should also consider whether enforcing the covenant will leave the employee without the means of making a living or will compel some form of involuntary servitude.

4. *Courts rarely grant specific performance of construction contracts.* The rationale for this rule is probably that too much court supervision is required in a court-ordered building project where the parties are in dispute. Additionally, there is an adequate remedy at law in most situations where a party

breaches a construction contract: an action for damages based on the contract. Damages almost always provide an adequate remedy for breach of a construction contract.

5. *Specific performance of a real estate contract can be obtained by either the buyer or the seller.* Anglo-American law and philosophy have long prized the possession of land, and each piece of land is viewed as unique. If the buyer sues, damages may be an inadequate remedy because the buyer will be deprived of the special piece of property he has chosen, which is seen as different from any other. This is generally true even in cases of sales of tract homes. These assumptions involve Western cultural biases about the commercial and emotional importance of land. Nevertheless, it is relatively common for the buyer to be able to obtain specific performance of a land sale contract on the theory that all land is unique and that money cannot fully substitute for its loss.

Although it is probably not common for the seller to obtain specific performance, it is possible. Here the rationale for specific performance appears to be the ability of the seller to clear title to the land. A land seller's action for specific performance usually takes the form of a court order under which the buyer must pay the purchase price by a certain date or lose all rights to the property. Once this date passes, the seller either receives the money or, if the buyer fails to pay, receives back clear title to the property and can resell it. Then the seller can file litigation against the buyer to make up the deficiency. Here a **deficiency action** is an action to make up the difference between the resale contract price for the land and the original contract price the first buyer was to pay.

Declaratory Judgement

If a party wishes a judicial determination of rights and responsibilities under a contract, an action for declaratory relief or declaratory judgment is available. **Declaratory judgment** asks the court to determine whatever rights and responsibilities of the parties to the contract are at issue in their dispute. Once a court renders a judgment in the action, this conclusively determines the rights and duties as to the parties and the rights litigated.

Actions for declaratory relief have been available since the early years of the twentieth century and are established by federal and state law.[10] Declaratory relief is a modern equitable remedy that is usually a better alternative than suing for nominal damages when the parties wish a judicial decision concerning contract rights and responsibilities.

Rescission of a Contract

Rescission may be either an equitable or a legal remedy. Some states (e.g., California) have abolished many of the distinctions between legal and equitable rescission. In most states, however, if a contracting party seeks a judgment rescinding a contract on such grounds as mutual mistake, fraud, illegality, or the like, this is considered an equitable cause of action. Where a party seeks to recover property (or the value of it) conferred on a defendant under a contract voidable for mistake, fraud, illegality, or the like, this is usually a legal action. Any judicial **rescission** of a contract is essentially cancellation of the contract. Sometimes rescission entails returning property

Deficiency action In case of a buyer's breach of a land sales contract, an action filed by the seller to recover the difference between what the breaching buyer was to have paid and what the substitute buyer actually paid.

Declaratory judgment A judgment in which a court determines the rights and responsibilities of parties instead of awarding money damages for violation of those rights or failure to perform the responsibilities.

Rescission A decision by a court, or sometimes by the parties themselves, to cancel a contract between them.

or money expended to the parties, and sometimes it does not. The paralegal should research applicable cases and statutes if the right to a jury trial is important in a contract action that asks for rescission. If the form of rescission sought is characterized as equitable, a jury trial normally is not available.

If the parties themselves rescind the contract, it is irrelevant whether their actions are characterized as legal or equitable in nature. The distinctions between legal and equitable remedies apply to claims filed with courts and remedies requested from them.

Reformation

Reformation is an equitable remedy in which the court makes a written contract conform to the parties' original oral agreement or understanding. Some jurisdictions refer to reformation as rectification or revision. Subject to sufficient proof by the parties, the concept underlying reformation is that a court has the power to make the contract read as it was originally understood or agreed upon.

A court cannot reform a contract where there is insufficient proof an agreement was formed and cannot complete an incomplete contract. A court cannot make the contract for the parties under the guise of reformation. Nor can a court reform a contract to remove an ambiguous term or resolve a mutual mistake. The proper use of reformation as a remedy is limited to situations in which the parties reach at least a substantially complete oral agreement and then fail to accurately reflect this agreement in a later written document. Reformation involves a court decree that corrects the later written document to reflect the earlier oral agreement.

> **Reformation** An equitable remedy in which a court rewrites an inaccurate written contract to conform to what is proven to be the original oral agreement or understanding of the parties.

Chapter Review Questions

1. What are the differences between legal and equitable remedies?
2. What kinds of damages are available in contract actions and under what circumstances?
3. When are restitution and reliance available?
4. In what kinds of cases and under what circumstances is specific performance available for breach of contract?
5. What does mitigation of damages mean, and how does the concept of an offset against damages relate to this duty?
6. What are the standardized measures of damages for breach of contract in the following kinds of cases: construction contract where the builder breaches, employment contract where the employer breaches, land sale contract where the seller breaches, sale of goods contract where the buyer breaches?
7. What are specific performance, declaratory relief, rescission, reformation, and injunctions? How do they relate to contract litigation?
8. What is a liquidated damages provision in a contract and under what circumstances are such clauses enforceable?

Key Terms

Consequential damages, 226
Cost of completion, 224

Covenant not to compete, 241
Cover, 223

Notes

1. Once an equity court had taken jurisdiction to decide equitable issues, the court could decide legal issues in the same case under the "clean-up" doctrine. See Levin, "Equitable Clean-up and the Jury," 100 *U.Pa. L. Rev.* 320 (1951).

2. For the right of an equity court to convene an advisory jury, see Dan R. Dobbs, *Law of Remedies,* 2d ed. (St Paul, Minn.: West Publishing, 1993), § 2.6(2) at p. 105.

3. See Fuller and Perdue, "The Reliance Interest in Contract Damages," 46 *Yale L. J.* 52 (1936) and 46 *Yale L. J.* 373 (1937) for the most renowned source of information on expectation, restitution, and reliance.

4. See, e.g., Judge Posner in *Lake River Corp. v. Carborundum Co.,* 769 F.2d 1284 (7th Cir. 1985).

5. See *Christensen v. Superior Court,* 54 Cal. 3d 868, 2 Cal. Rptr. 2d 79, 820 P.2d 181 (1991); and *Brown v. Matthews Mortuary, Inc.,* 118 Idaho 830, 801 P.2d 37 (1990).

6. See, e.g., *Hoffman v. Red Owl Stores,* 26 Wis.2d 683, 133 N.W.2d 267 (1965).

7. Restatement, Restitution (American Law Institute, 1937), § 1.

8. See Perillo, "Restitution in a Contractual Context," 73 *Colum. L.R.* 1208 (1973).

9. See *Board of Education of Oklahoma v. Dowell,* 498 U.S. 237, 111 S.Ct. 630, 112, L.Ed.2d 715 (1991).

10. Most of the states have enacted their own declaratory judgment statutes. The federal statute is found at 28 U.S.C.A. § 2201 (West, 1994) and is reprinted here:

United States Code Annotated
Title 28. Judiciary and Judicial Procedure
Part VI—Particular Proceedings
Chapter 151—Declaratory Judgments
Current through P.L. 104-8, approved 4-17-95 § 2201. Creation of remedy

(a) In a case of actual controversy within its jurisdiction, except with respect to Federal taxes other than actions brought under section 7428 of the Internal Revenue Code of 1986, a proceeding under section 505 or 1146 of title 11, or in any civil action involving an antidumping or countervailing duty proceeding regarding a class or kind of merchandise of a free trade area country (as defined in section 516A (f) (10) of the Tariff Act of 1930), as determined by the administering authority, any court of the United States, upon the filing of an appropriate pleading, may declare the rights and other legal relations of any interested party seeking such declaration, whether or not further relief is or could be sought. Any such declaration shall have the force and effect of a final judgment or decree and shall be reviewable as such.

(b) For limitations on actions brought with respect to drug patents see section 505 or 512 of the Federal Food, Drug, and Cosmetic Act.

PART

V

Third-Party Rights

CHAPTER

12

Assignment and Delegation

Third-Party Rights and Obligations Generally

Up to now, we have been concerned primarily with the rights and obligations of the parties who negotiated the contract. This chapter and the next focus on rights and obligations acquired by a **third party**, an outsider to the contract. A third party who is not one of the parties to the contract nevertheless acquires rights or obligations under it in two main situations. One situation involves transfers of contract rights and obligations under the theories of assignment and delegation. Assignment and delegation are covered in this chapter. The other situation involves creation of what are called third-party beneficiary contracts. These are covered in Chapter 13.

Through either assignment or the creation of a third-party beneficiary contract, a new party becomes part of the contractual arrangement. One primary difference in how these two arrangements are created is a matter of timing. Assignment and delegation of contract rights involve a transfer of the rights *after* the contract is formed. A third-party beneficiary contract is created at the time the contract is formed. Both third-party arrangements extend rights to an outsider who is not one of the contracting parties. Once created, the effect of either of these arrangements is to give rights and/or obligations to this new third party under a contract negotiated by two other parties. Both arrangements are common commercial tools. The whole field of assignment is particularly useful in the modern commercial world because it is the basis for much commercial financing.

Though assignments and delegations and third-party beneficiary contracts have common characteristics, the two areas have separate sets of rules. Many rules apply to one area and not to the other. Thus, it is useful to examine these areas separately.

Third party A party who is not one of the parties to a contract but nevertheless acquires rights or obligations under it.

Assignment of Rights

An **assignment** of contract rights occurs when one party to the contract transfers some or all of his *rights* under the agreement. In a typical commercial assignment, a large department store might transfer its right to receive payment from charge account customers to its bank. Often this is done to obtain a commercial line of credit. The bank agrees to give the department store access to a line of credit on which the store can obtain cash, and the store gives the bank the right to receive payment from the store's charge accounts. These charge accounts, of course, are contracts between the department store and its own customers. The right being transferred is the right to receive payments from the charge accounts when customers purchase goods. These payments would normally go to the department store. Under an effective assignment, they will go to the bank.

Assignment A transfer of some or all of a party's contract rights.

Assignment of Rights and Delegation of Duties

Although the general substantive area is referred to as "assignment," sometimes the assignment actually includes a delegation. A **delegation** is a transfer of contract *duties* to a third party who will perform these duties.[1] Whereas assignment is a transfer of contract rights, delegation occurs when one of the contracting parties seeks to transfer its *obligations* to perform under the contract.

Delegation A transfer of contract duties; the appointment of someone else to perform one's own contract duties.

EXAMPLE 12.1

Luis, a plumber has several commercial contracts and cannot do all of this work, so he finds another plumber to handle some of the contracts. Luis makes a delegation of his duty to do plumbing work to the substitute plumber. The substitute plumber does the work for the other contracting party who hired Luis.

An assignment may also be taking place in Example 12.1; that is, Luis could transfer to the substitute plumber not only the obligation to do work under the contract, but also the right to receive payment for the work. Assignment and delegation can occur together, or each can occur separately.

EXAMPLE 12.2

As it happens, the substitute plumber owes Luis some money. Since the substitute plumber is "cash short," she accepts transfer of the contractual duty to perform plumbing work without the right to get paid for the work. Meanwhile Luis retains the right to receive payment. Through delegation of duties without an assignment of the right to payment, the substitute plumber's debt to Luis can be discharged or reduced.

Sometimes when people speak of "assignment," they really mean both an assignment and a delegation of duties. Thus, you should always examine the transaction closely. Even if a transaction is referred to as an "assignment," it may include a delegation. Probably, the most common form of pure assignment in today's commercial world is assignment of the right to receive payment under a contract.

Vocabulary of Assignment and Delegation

A special vocabulary is used to describe the parties involved in an assignment or a delegation. These terms are listed in Exhibit 12.1. Note what each term means and to whom it refers.

Effect of Valid Assignments and Delegations

The effect of a valid assignment is to set up the rights transferred exclusively in the assignee and to extinguish these rights in the assignor. Thus, as to rights transferred, the assignor generally loses the right to enforce the contract performance. Once the assignment is effective, the assignor cannot obtain the benefit of the rights transferred. Only the assignee can obtain the benefits assigned.

The effect of a valid delegation is different. Even where the delegant has transferred the obligation to perform, she remains secondarily liable to the obligee. The obligee must look first to the delegatee for contract performance of the transferred duties. If the performance is not forthcoming, the obligee can look to the delegant/obligor to perform. In delegation arrangements, the delegant remains a kind of surety for performance on the contract.

EXHIBIT 12.1

Assignment and Delegation Terms

Assignments

• **Assignor.**	The contracting party who makes the transfer of contractual rights.
• **Assignee**.	The third party who receives the transfer of rights.
• **Obligor.**	The other original contracting party who remains obligated to render performance to the assignee.

Delegation

• **Delegant/obligor.**	The contracting party who makes the transfer of contractual duties to perform.
• **Delegatee.**	The third party who receives the transfer of contractual duties to perform.
• **Obligee.**	The other original contracting party to whom the delegated duty is still owed.

Enforceability of Assignments

Enforceability of Assignments in General

To some degree, the law looks more favorably on assignment of rights than on delegation of duties. One reason is that delegation tends to materially affect the other remaining contracting party more than assignment does. This is particularly true where the assignment involves only the right to receive payment. For an example of a transfer that is purely an assignment, consider the following.

EXAMPLE 12.3

CompCo is a construction company that needs cash to run its business. CompCo has many construction contracts already negotiated and signed, but it needs money to pay start-up costs on these contracts such as salaries, materials, and other expenses. From time to time, CompCo also needs money so that it can keep looking for more work during periods of low cash flow. Under the construction contracts, payments from clients are sometimes delayed until a certain percentage of work is completed or are temporarily insufficient to pay CompCo's various costs. To obtain financing, CompCo approaches Columbia Savings & Loan, a commercial lender. The bank agrees to advance a credit line of $800,000, provided CompCo agrees to assign Columbia Savings & Loan a percentage of its payments on the construction contracts.

In this transfer of rights, the assignee Columbia Savings & Loan is receiving only the right to receive payment from the construction contracts. It has no duty to perform any of CompCo's work under the construction contracts. This is a pure assignment of rights.

In the situation in Example 12.3, the law views the assignment arrangement as not substantially changing the performance still owed to the other party to each construction contract. On such a contract, the other party is likely to be a property owner or developer who has negotiated the construction contracts with CompCo. Before the assignment, it was CompCo that would do the work for the property owners or developers. After the assignment, it is still CompCo that will do the work. The main change is that now the owners or developers will pay the bank something when the work is performed rather than paying CompCo only.

Actually, even "pure" assignment arrangements like these do make some changes in the situation of the obligor. Traditionally, contract law characterizes this change as not material. In fact, if all goes well, it makes very little difference to the owners or developers in Example 12.3 whether they pay CompCo or the bank. As will be seen later, however, if all does not go well and the owners or developers refuse to make payments under the contract, the situation may become more complicated. In that case, the bank may sue the property owner or developer, and this party must defend against the bank. Thus, the situation is more complicated than it would have been had the construction company not assigned the contract. Nevertheless, the law continues to view pure assignments as not making material changes regarding the performance due to the obligor. The real rationale for this approach may be that assignment is such a necessary commercial tool the legal system has worked hard to justify it.

In some situations, an assignment may, in fact, significantly change the contract performance still owed by the obligor. The following are some obvious examples of these situations:

- Insurance contracts
- Extensions of personal credit
- Personal services contracts
- Requirements and output contracts
- Assignments materially increasing the obligor's risk
- Assignments materially changing contract terms

Assignment

In each of the following hypotheticals, identify the rights being assigned. Then discuss the following question: If assignment were allowed without limitation in each situation, would it bring about material changes in the performance owed by the obligor? From this discussion you should be able to see why parties sometimes try to prevent assignment of their contracts and why some contracts are not assignable.

▶ Hypothetical 1

Rock of Gibraltar, Inc., is an insurance company that handles mainly casualty insurance for small businesses. Rock receives an application for casualty insurance from Acme, a successful tool and die manufacturing business. Acme has been in business for fifty years. It has had two previous insurers during this time and has submitted only three claims. Two claims were in connection with damage caused by flooding in the geographical area. One claim was for a fire that the police proved was arson by a disgruntled employee. The employee was later found to be mentally unstable and was given long-term medical care. Since the fire, Acme's business has been operated in a steel-frame, concrete building in the warehouse section of town.

Rock investigates Acme's history and finds it has had two late insurance payments in the last twenty years. Both payments were promptly made up, and Acme paid a late fee. Rock decides to insure Acme for casualty. Once the policy is in force, however, Acme transfers its right to be insured to its subsidiary, Nadir, Inc. Nadir is located on separate premises in an old wood building in the warehouse section of town. It is a five-year-old company that makes cotton and hemp industrial rope. Nadir has had one previous insurer and has had no late payments and made no claims.

▶ Hypothetical 2

CleanCo is a janitorial business that services commercial enterprises. CleanCo maintains the premises for the businesses it services in return for a year-to-year written contract. It charges its customers an individualized monthly fee based on the size and difficulty of the cleaning job. CleanCo takes on a new customer, Giant Enterprises, and obtains a very favorable contract with Giant. The monthly fee from Giant on the one-year contract will be $2,000. Once the contract with Giant is written and executed, CleanCo assigns the whole $2,000 monthly fee to its bank. CleanCo's bank then notifies Giant that it should pay its monthly janitorial fee to the bank, rather than to CleanCo.

▶ Hypothetical 3

CleanCo, the janitorial business described in Hypothetical 2, decides to purchase the newest and best industrial vacuums for all its cleaning work. These vacuums, called "Super Suckers," are produced by only one company in the United States, Superior Manufacturing. Because the Super Sucker is in such high demand, Superior's orders are backed up. Once the vacuums are delivered, however, Superior permits the buyer to pay in four equal monthly installments with interest and a $250 processing fee. Superior lines up its contracts in advance, with the payment arrangements included, so that vacuums can be delivered as quickly as they come off the assembly line.

CleanCo makes a written contract with Superior for twelve Super Suckers and agrees to pay off the vacuums in four installments after they are delivered. The interest rate on the unpaid balance is 8 percent until the vacuums are paid for. Two months later, a competitor of CleanCo's offers to pay CleanCo $4,000 if CleanCo will assign its right to receive the Super Suckers to the competitor. CleanCo promptly does this because it wants the $4,000 and feels it can wait longer for the vacuums without seriously decreasing the quality of its janitorial services. The competitor now contacts Superior and claims it has the right to receive twelve Super Suckers under the contract extended to CleanCo, including the four installment payments and 8 percent interest.

▶ Hypothetical 4

Gourmet Gardens is a vegetarian restaurant that specializes in the luncheon trade. It is very successful because it provides high-quality, low-fat, vegetarian food for business people working in the local industrial complex. To ensure that it can obtain enough good lettuce in several varieties, Gourmet Gardens makes

a written contract with Fanny the Farmer. Fanny the Farmer is a large agricul-
tural grower that supplies many fine restaurants with lettuce and other produce.
Gourmet agrees to take all the lettuce it can use for its restaurant from Fanny the
Farmer. Gourmet buys lettuce from Fanny the Farmer for several months under
the contract. Then Gourmet finds high-quality lettuce for a cheaper price at Joe's
Market Supply Company. Thus, Gourmet assigns its right to receive lettuce to
Burger Queen Industries, a hamburger business that uses twice the amount of
gourmet lettuce that Gourmet uses. Burger Queen notifies Fanny the Farmer
that it is taking over Gourmet's right to receive lettuce.

Special Rules in Assignment of Insurance Contracts

Assignment of the Right to Be Insured

As can be seen from Hypothetical 1, insurance contracts depend in large part
on the risks associated with the transaction. An insurer generally decides
whether to offer coverage to a person or a company based on its assessment
of the risks associated with that particular person or company. This is true
whether the insurance is for life, casualty, liability, or health. The risk
assumed in insuring one party will rarely be identical to the risk assumed in
insuring another. If the right to be insured were freely transferable, a carrier
might be forced to grant coverage under the assignment when it would not
have granted coverage initially.

All insurers base the cost of their insurance on the expense of doing
business and the profit margin they hope to achieve. In the insurance
industry, both costs and profit margins are affected by the quantity and size of
the claims the insurer must pay. Assignment of the right to be insured could
radically affect these figures. Because the insurance industry is a modern,
commercial necessity, the law tends not to jeopardize its operation by
considering insurance contracts to be assignable.

Assignment of the Right to Receive Insurance Proceeds

Assignability of the right to be insured is distinguished from assignability of
the right to receive proceeds from insurance. Benefits (payment of money on
the policy) are freely assignable. Many insurance policies contain a provision
stating the party to whom payment is to be made if the contingency insured
against occurs. In a life insurance situation, if the insured dies in a way
covered by the policy, the proceeds go to the beneficiary of the policy. The
holder of the insurance can designate herself, or someone else, to receive the
proceeds. This assignment of insurance proceeds is considered not to
materially vary the risk of the insurance company obligor. This is a pure
assignment of the right to receive payment on the policy.

Assignment of the Right to Receive Credit

Extensions of credit are based on issues similar to those found with insurance.
The creditor assesses the risks associated with giving credit to a particular
applicant in much the same way insurance companies assess risk. The risk
assessment is based on the creditor's expected costs, expected profit margin,
and the probabilities of being paid back. One debtor may be considered a
good risk while another is not. Thus, it has been generally accepted that
extensions of credit are personal and cannot be assigned.

Enforceability of Delegations

While the law tends to favor assignment, the same is not true of delegation. One reason for this difference is that delegation is more likely to materially affect the other original contracting party's situation.

EXAMPLE **12.4**

Return to CompCo from Example 12.3, but this time assume that instead of transferring the contractual right to receive payment on its construction contracts, CompCo transfers to another builder the duty to do the building work on one of its construction contracts. If the delegation is effective, the property owner, the other party to the construction contract, must accept performance from an entirely new builder.

This property owner probably had investigated CompCo very carefully and had obtained references, looked at projects CompCo had built, researched any history of litigation or claims against CompCo, and so on. Further, suppose the substitute construction company does not have a very good reputation, has been sued several times for defective performance, has a history of walking off the job, and has less experience. Here delegation of the duty to perform leaves the owner dealing with a company he would not have hired in the first place.

With delegation, there is often the possibility that the party who was originally contracted to perform is preferred or that the delegatee is not satisfactory to the obligee at all.

Because delegation transfers the duty to perform to someone from whom the obligee did not originally plan to accept performance, it can affect the quality of the performance owed. For this reason the law tends to view delegation less favorably than pure assignment. On the other hand, certain kinds of contract performance are fairly standard. Delegation of a standard performance or to a very comparable delegatee may be effective. Under some circumstances, even construction contracts may be delegable as long as the obligee's rights to performance are not impaired.[2] It should be noted that there is no question about whether general contractors can delegate duties to a subcontractor. Such delegations are common and fully enforceable. More problematic delegations occur where a general contractor delegates the entire job and its supervision to another general contractor, or where one subcontractor delegates to another.

Assignment

To determine whether an assignment or delegation is effective, one must look at the real effect of the arrangement. If it is a pure assignment, such as the payment of money owed for performance under the contract, it is normally effective. If the assignment also involves a delegation of duties, or if there is a delegation of duties alone, it may be ineffective if the delegation causes a material change in the performance owed to the obligee. The facts of the individual case make the difference. Return to Hypotheticals 1 through 4 in the *preceding Assignment, and consider (1) whether the attempted transfer of rights also involves a delegation, and, if so, (2) whether the delegation will be effective in view of the performance still owed to the obligee.*

Wage Assignments

Assignments of the right to receive payments under an employment contract are effective. An employee may assign her right to salary payments to be made by the employer in the future. This is true whether the employment contract is terminable at will or whether it is for a specified term such as one year or five years. Most states, however, have decided that wage assignments involve important public policy issues.

EXAMPLE   12.5

Suppose a divorced couple has three children. Wife has physical custody of the children except on weekends. The court hearing the divorce case orders Husband to pay a certain amount of his salary as child support. Husband also has creditors to whom he is obligated to make payments, so he makes a partial assignment of his wages to pay his creditors. This assignment to his creditors will affect the amount of wages Husband has left over to pay the court-ordered child support.

One rationale for limiting wage assignments is that, carried too far, the assignments might deprive a salaried employee like Husband of so much take-home pay that he would require public assistance.

While the policy issues involved in wage assignments are too varied and complex for a basic contract law text, the subject requires at least minimal treatment because such assignments do occur. The paralegal should always check state law. Many states have developed statutory limitations on the right of an employee to make assignments of wages to be earned in the future. Typically, such statutes require the assignment to be in writing and require that the writing be filed with the employer.

Assignment and Delegation Distinguished from Novation

Novation Full substitution of a new party for one of the original parties to the contract. A novation requires consent of both parties to the contract and of the new third party.

There is another arrangement distinct from assignment and delegation that can be made to bring in a new party. This arrangement is called a novation. A **novation** is a full substitution of a new party for one of the original parties to the contract. A novation requires consent of both parties to the contract and consent of the third party. In a novation, the contracting parties agree that one of them will be fully discharged from the contract and that a completely new party will be fully responsible. Where a novation is effective, the party who is discharged from the contract has no further obligations under it; the obligee can look only to the substituted obligor for performance. This situation is very different from a delegation of duties. There, as noted, the original obligor remains liable if the delegatee fails to perform to the obligee.

In general, no writing is required to give effect to a novation. Nevertheless, it is highly recommended that a written agreement be used to avoid future disputes about the rights and obligations of the parties. The paralegal should remember while many oral agreements may be effective, proving them can be difficult should a dispute arise. This is true for novations as well as for most contractual arrangements.

Requirements of a Common-Law Assignment

At common law, there were very few requirements for an effective assignment. Essentially, the common law found a valid assignment where the following simple requirements were met:

- Words indicating a present intent to make an assignment of rights under a contract that can be rightfully assigned
- An adequate description of the rights being assigned
- A writing if the assignment falls within the Statute of Frauds

An assignment is effective if the assignor reliably shows what contract rights he intends to assign, actually possesses such rights under the contract, and intends to transfer those rights immediately and completely. The law does not require the use of any technical vocabulary, and the assignor need not even use the word *assign* or *assignment* so long as similar words make clear the intent to make an immediate transfer of contract rights.

Revocability of Common-Law Assignments

Usually, consideration is not required for an effective assignment at common law. The lack of consideration, however, means an assignment is fully revocable. Revocation can occur through verbal revocation or through the assignor's making a later assignment to someone else. A later or subsequent assignment is effective even though the assignor does not notify the first assignee of the later assignment.

Although notification is not required, failure to notify the first assignee of a subsequent assignment is risky. If the first assignee has reasonably and detrimentally relied on an assignment *before* a subsequent assignment takes place, the first assignment becomes irrevocable. In that case, the assignor is estopped to deny enforceability of the first assignment because of the first assignee's reliance on it. If the subsequent assignment was also effective, the result is to give the first assignee a cause of action for damages to compensate for loss of the assigned rights. The subsequent assignee would actually receive the effective assignment.

Gratuitous assignments may also be revoked in a number of other ways. The following list summarizes the main events that can cause a gratuitous assignment to be revoked:

- The assignor makes a subsequent assignment.
- The assignor dies.
- The assignor goes bankrupt.
- The assignee receives notice of revocation from the assignor.
- The assignor accepts performance from the obligor in spite of the assignment.

Under common law, if an assignee wishes to have an irrevocable assignment, consideration must be given. Provided the assignor accepts the consideration, the assignment then becomes irrevocable. The general rule in all states is that assignments given for consideration are irrevocable.

Common-Law Assignments and the Writing Requirement

Traditionally, no writing was required for an effective assignment at common law unless the assignment fell within the Statute of Frauds. However, lack of a writing made the assignment revocable unless the assignee gave consideration. Traditionally, if an assignment was oral and the assignee did not give consideration, the assignment was normally fully revocable. Most states have now changed this view by passing statutes making *assignments in writing* that are delivered to the assignee irrevocable even if the assignee gives no consideration. These modern statutes essentially substitute the writing and its delivery for a consideration requirement in the case of gratuitous assignments.

EXAMPLE 12.6

Suppose Mary intends to give Joe a gift of some money when she retires. She therefore orally names Joe as beneficiary of her pension plan. Joe gives nothing in return. Mary can revoke this gift. If, however, Mary makes and delivers to Joe a writing summarizing the assignment, in most states today the assignment would become irrevocable.

As previously noted, the exception to effectiveness of oral assignments is an assignment falling within the Statute of Frauds. If an assignment involves a transfer of rights that fall within the Statute, it must be in writing to be effective. In the absence of a Statute of Frauds problem or a special statute requiring a writing, oral assignments are effective though revocable.

Contractual Provisions that Prohibit Assignment

Sometimes the parties to a contract think ahead about the issue of assignment. One or both of them may want to put a provision in the contract that prohibits assigning any contract rights. Such a provision might read:

Nonassignability of Contract
The parties hereby agree this contract and the rights under it shall not be assignable by either party under any circumstances.

Some contracts contain a very simple statement such as one of the following:

Nonassignability
No rights under this contract shall be assignable.

Nonassignability
This contract is not assignable.

A party who makes an assignment when the contract contains a simple nonassignability clause may be liable for a breach of contract, but the assignment itself may be effective. Commercial law strongly favors the freedom to assign contract rights, and courts have often found such "generic" nonassignability clauses ineffective to prevent assignment.

To prevent assignment, the nonassignability clause must be more specific. A paralegal should research applicable law and formbooks to determine how to draft or review an effective nonassignability clause in a particular jurisdiction. As a general matter, such a clause might read:

Nonassignability of Contract

Any assignment of rights or delegation of duties under this contract shall be void. Execution of this contract is specifically conditioned upon nonassignment by the parties.

This type of clause normally prevents effective assignment because it is considered to be conditional. It states one of the preconditions to the whole contract, which is the agreement not to assign. If this agreement is broken, it is construed to be fundamental to the nonassigning party's expectations in entering into the contract, and normally no assignment is effective.

Many problems have arisen with nonassignability clauses because it is not always clear into which category a particular clause falls or what effect it was intended to have. Because the law favors assignment, courts have a tendency to construe unclear nonassignability clauses as being generic or general and, therefore, not a bar to assignment. In many commercial transactions today, such clauses are enforced even though the wording is not completely clear. Thus, it is important to recognize that construing unclear nonassignability clauses may involve complex issues. You should therefore research applicable case law, statutes, and formbooks before deciding the legal effect of an existing clause or what wording is best if a clause is to be drafted.

Partial Assignments

Under early common law, partial assignments were held not to be enforceable. Partial assignments may mean the obligor will have to pay two or more assignees rather than one party, and this was thought to be too great a burden. Modern law changed this view, and partial assignments are now effective. If any of the partial assignments results in litigation, the party filing the lawsuit will probably have to name all partial assignees in the lawsuit unless this joinder of assignees is shown to be impractical and it is fair to proceed in the litigation without them. If the assignor has retained any rights, she also would have to be included in the lawsuit.

Rights of the Parties After Assignment

Rights of the Assignee

An effective assignment means the assignee acquires all right to performance from the obligor as to the rights assigned. If the obligor refuses to perform on the contract rights assigned, the assignee can sue the obligor directly. As for the obligor, once he has knowledge of the assignment, the required performance must be given only to the assignee. An obligor who renders performance to the assignor with knowledge of the assignment runs a great risk. Performance to the assignor after notice of the assignment does not discharge the obligor's duty to perform to the assignee.

Knowledge of the assignment does not require formal notice from the assignee. Giving formal notice to the obligor is, of course, the safest way for the assignee to protect his right to receive performance. In ordinary, prudent business practice, such notice should be given promptly. Even without direct notice from the assignee, if the obligor receives reliable news of the assignment, she is obligated to at least inquire into the circumstances of the alleged assignment.[3]

Rights of the Obligor

In the situation where the assignee decides to sue the obligor, the obligor may have defenses that can be successfully raised in the lawsuit. This is not true where the law considers the obligor to be at fault for rendering performance to the assignor after receiving knowledge of the assignment. However, suppose the situation were considerably different. Consider the following example.

EXAMPLE 12.7

Handy-Person Hardware Store, Inc., assigns payment from two of its largest customer accounts to Heartless Bank, the credit institution that finances Handy's credit line. Handy's two largest customers are building contractors, Customer A and Customer B, who purchase hardware supplies from Handy. Once Handy makes the assignment to Heartless Bank, Heartless notifies both A and B of the assignment. All goes well until several months later when A stops paying Heartless. Upon inquiry, Heartless learns that A is having a dispute with Handy over the quality of hardware supplies. A claims the supplies were defective and unusable. Therefore, A refuses to pay for the supplies and stops payment on her account with Handy.

A's reluctance to pay is understandable in view of its belief that Handy sold defective goods. Assuming for the moment that A has a valid argument and is acting in good faith, A will probably refuse to pay Heartless Bank for the allegedly defective hardware supplies. Since A would have refused to pay Handy for defective supplies if there were no assignment, existence of the assignment is not likely to change A's reluctance to pay. If Handy does not agree that its supplies were defective, the contracting parties may not be able to resolve their dispute. In that case, the assignee, Heartless, may sue the obligor, A, for payments it believes are due under the assignment. If Heartless sues on the assignment, the defenses the obligor can raise against the assignee become a major issue.

Defenses Available to the Obligor Against the Assignee

Under common law, the possible defenses available to obligors like Customer A are divided into two categories: *contract-related defenses* and *defenses unrelated to the contract*. The obligor may raise against the assignee any and all contract-related defenses whether the defense existed before or after the notice of assignment was given. Defenses unrelated to the contract may only be raised if they existed *before* the notice of assignment was given.

Contract-related defenses include the following:

1. Defenses attacking the validity of the contract under which rights were assigned. These defenses include such arguments as lack of consideration for the contract, lack of a valid acceptance, fraudulent procurement of the contract, duress, and the like.
2. Defenses asserting defective performance of the contract. These defenses include such problems as Customer A's complaint that the hardware store's supplies were defective and any other arguments concerning defective, inadequate, incomplete, or late performance.
3. Any other defense that arises out of the contract involved in the assignment.

Defenses unrelated to the contract arise in connection with other relationships between the obligor and the assignor, including previous contracts between the original contracting parties. In the typical situation, the assignor had a preexisting debt to the obligor and did not pay it. The obligor then wants to stop paying the assignor on the contract that has been assigned. The assignee, however, usually still expects payment under the assignment. In fact, the assignee may not even be aware of the debtor-creditor relationship between the assignor and the obligor.

EXAMPLE   **12.8**

Assume such a debtor-creditor relationship existed between Handy and Customer A in Example 12.7. In the case of Customer A and Heartless Bank, A will want to raise her difficulties in collecting from Handy on the other debt as a defense against Heartless. A will argue that she was entitled to stop paying on the hardware goods because Handy stopped paying her on its other debt. Heartless Bank will undoubtedly be displeased with such an argument since Handy's previous debt had nothing to do with Heartless or the assignment. Whether A can raise Handy's nonpayment of the other debt as a defense against Heartless in a lawsuit on the assignment depends on when Handy defaulted on the other debt. If Handy's default came before notice of the assignment, A may be able to use the default as a defense against Heartless. If the default came after notice of the assignment, however, A cannot raise this as a defense against Heartless.

Priority of Competing Assignees Under the Common Law

Problems sometimes arise when a contracting party tries to assign an interest in her rights to two or more assignees. When more than one alleged assignee asserts an interest in the same contract rights, the situation is referred to as a problem of the priority of competing assignees. **Priority of assignees** is the order of preference given to competing assignees.

Priority of assignees
The order of preference given to competing assignees under the common law or the UCC.

Priority Where the First Assignment Was Gratuitous

It should be remembered that all assignments not made for consideration are revocable. Thus, if the first among competing assignees gave no value for the assignment, the next assignee who gave consideration for the assignment will prevail and will obtain the assignment. This rule is widely recognized in all American jurisdictions.

Priority Where the First Assignee Gave Consideration

Under a widely followed rule, if the first assignee gave consideration, a subsequent assignee cannot prevail if she takes the assignment with notice of the first assignment. There is less agreement about who prevails if both the original and the subsequent assignees gave consideration and the subsequent assignees had no notice of a previous assignment. In such situations, American jurisdictions have applied one of three rules:

English rule A common-law rule for deciding priority among competing assignees. The first assignee to give notice of the assignment to the obligor prevails.

New York rule A common-law rule for deciding priority among competing assignees. The assignee who received the earliest assignment prevails; the first in time is the first in right.

Massachusetts rule A common-law rule for deciding priority among competing assignees. The first assignee prevails unless a successive assignee (1) obtains payment from the obligor, (2) recovers a judgment, (3) enters into a new contract with the obligor, or (4) receives delivery of a tangible item representing the rights assigned where such surrender was required by the obligor's contract.

1. Under **English rule,** the first assignee who gives notice of the assignment to the obligor prevails. The obligor must perform to that assignee.

2. Under the **New York rule,** the assignee who received the earliest assignment prevails; the first in time is the first in right. Under this rule, an obligor who mistakenly performs to a successive assignee because this assignee gave notice first discharges his obligation. The first assignee must then sue the second assignee for damages to recover for the performance due under the assignment.

3. Under the **Massachusetts rule,** the first assignee prevails unless a successive assignee (a) obtains payment from the obligor, (b) recovers a judgment, (c) enters into a new contract with the obligor, or (d) receives delivery of a tangible item representing the rights assigned where such surrender was required by the obligor's contract. The Massachusetts rule was adopted in the Restatements. It is also sometimes called the *four horsemen* rule because of the four circumstances under which the first assignee can be deprived of priority.

Assignments Under the UCC

Today, a vast number of assignments are governed by the UCC. Thus far, our study of UCC contract law has dealt with Article 2 which governs the sale of goods and the rights of buyers and sellers of such goods. A different article of the UCC, Article 9 (referred to in Chapter 1), now governs many commercial assignments. Even if a particular type of assignment was originally governed by the common law (like assignments of accounts), it would now be governed by the UCC. As stated in UCC § 9-102, Article 9 covers:

- All assignments of chattel paper
- All assignments of accounts
- All assignments of a security interest in personal property

Assignments involving chattel paper and those involving accounts will be discussed first, followed by assignments of a security interest in personal property. A paralegal needs to have basic knowledge of these assignments because they often occur in connection with contract relations.

Before continuing with assignments covered by the UCC, note that the UCC does *not* cover assignments of the following:

- Assignments of tort claims
- Assignments of money in a bank account
- Assignments of payment on insurance policies
- Assignments of wages
- Assignments of accounts receivable or contract rights when the assignment is made as part of the ordinary sale of a business
- Assignments of a right to receive payment under a contract if the duty to perform is also delegated to the same party
- Assignments made only for the purpose of *collecting a debt*
- Gratuitous assignments (assignments for which no consideration is given)
- Assignment of a single account to a single creditor in order to pay a previous debt either in whole or in part

Assignments of Chattel Paper

A whole area of the commercial law of contracts deals with buying and selling promissory notes. A **promissory note** is a written contract that creates a debt of one party to another party. A promissory note can be thought of as a kind of "IOU." Promissory notes are used in connection with loans of all kinds. The debtor on the promissory note is often referred to as the **maker;** the creditor on the promissory note is often called the **holder.** Promissory notes themselves are often simply called *notes.* Where the promissory note is accompanied by "security" for the debt summarized in the note, it becomes what is known under the UCC as chattel paper. As used here, **security** is property of the debtor in which the creditor acquires rights, including the right to seize and sell the property if the debtor stops paying the loan. In a transaction involving chattel paper, the creditor requires the debtor to pledge some form of goods as a guarantee the loan will be repaid.

Chattel paper is a writing or writings intended to create *both* a debt *and* a security interest or lease for the creditor in specific goods. Assignments of chattel paper are now governed by the UCC. Many installment sales contracts involve the use of chattel paper.

Promissory note A written contract that creates a debt of one party to another party.

Maker The debtor on a promissory note.

Holder Someone who has possession of a negotiable instrument.

Security In a secured transaction, the property of a debtor in which the creditor acquires rights, including the right to seize and sell the property if the debtor stops paying the loan.

Chattel paper A writing or writings intended to create both a debt and a security interest for the creditor in some form of personal property.

EXAMPLE 12.9

If Cal loans Donald $5,000 and the note is unsecured (there is no property securing the note), the note is not chattel paper. If Donald must put up his car as security for the loan of $5,000, the note becomes chattel paper. If Cal were to assign his right to receive payment from Donald on the note, this assignment would be an assignment of chattel paper.

EXAMPLE 12.10

Suppose a farmer purchases a new tractor from a dealer. The parties execute a conditional sales contract under which the farmer will purchase the tractor "on time." The contract contains the farmer's promise to pay the dealer in installments and gives the dealer a security interest in the tractor purchased. Here the dealer is the note holder and retains an interest in the tractor until the buyer pays in full. If the holder assigns (transfers) to someone else his right to receive payment for the tractor, the security interest in the tractor would also transfer. The original purchase of the tractor involves the use of chattel paper, and the transfer of the right to receive payment for the tractor is an assignment of chattel paper.

Assignment of Accounts

Accounts Any right to receive payment for goods delivered or to be delivered, or any right to receive payment for services rendered or to be rendered.

As noted earlier, under § 9-102 of the UCC sales of "accounts" are now governed by Article 9. Transfers of the right to receive payment from accounts are "assignments." **Accounts** are now defined very broadly under Article 9 as (1) any right to receive payments for goods delivered or to be delivered, or (2) any right to receive payment for services rendered or to be rendered. Note that Article 9 applies only to contract rights to receive payment, not to contract rights to receive some other form of performance. For example, when a department store transfers its rights to receive payment from its charge account customers to its bank or another creditor, this is an assignment and a "sale" of an account under Article 9. The charge account customers are often referred to as **account debtors** because they have the obligation to pay on the accounts assigned.

Account debtors Charge account customers who have the obligation to pay on their accounts.

The definition of accounts also includes a wide variety of contract rights that might not seem readily apparent. Under the UCC, *accounts* are defined to include any right to receive payment for a contract performance that has not yet been earned and that is not accompanied by an instrument or chattel paper. Thus, all assignments of a right to receive payment for contract performance are now governed by Article 9 if the payment is not yet earned at the time of the assignment.

The Secured Transaction

Secured transaction Any type of debtor-creditor relationship in which the creditor requires that the debtor put up collateral (property) to guarantee repayment of the debt.

The major subject covered under Article 9 of the UCC is a commercial arrangement known as a secured transaction. A **secured transaction** is any type of debtor-creditor relationship in which the creditor requires that the debtor put up collateral (property) to guarantee repayment of the debt. An **unsecured transaction** or debt is one in which the debt is not guaranteed by property. In a secured transaction, the creditor is referred to as the **secured party.** As previously noted, the property put up to secure the debt is called *collateral* or *security* for the debt. The initial judgment about how much collateral is necessary to secure the debt is a subject of bargaining between the potential debtor and the potential creditor. Sometimes the assets securing a debt are held by the creditor during the life of the secured transaction, and sometimes they are held by the debtor. The arrangement where the creditor holds the collateral is a **possessory security interest.** The arrangement where the debtor holds the collateral is a **nonpossessory security interest.**

Unsecured transaction Any type of debtor-creditor relationship in which the debtor does not guarantee the debt by putting up property.

Secured party The creditor in a secured transaction.

Secured transactions are similar to the use of chattel paper in that both arrangements require the debtor to pledge specific property to protect the creditor's interest in the debt owed. In both arrangements, the creditor has recourse to this specific property if the debtor fails to pay as required. In both secured transactions and the use of chattel paper, if the debtor defaults the creditor can seize the property securing the debt and sell it to repay the debt. Here **default** means failure of the debtor to pay back the creditor in the manner required.

Chattel paper and secured transactions differ with regard to the procedures used to create the debt, however. With chattel paper, the debt and the security arrangement are usually created in the same document or documents, and no further procedures are necessary to make the chattel paper effective. With secured transactions, several documents and additional procedures may be needed for effectiveness, as described later in this chapter.

Like chattel paper, secured transactions are used frequently in modern commerce because they provide a safety net for the creditor. Unsecured debts can be risky for the creditor: if the debtor defaults and refuses to pay, the creditor must sue him and get a judgment. This judgment must be satisfied out of the debtor's personal assets. Thus, the creditor must discover and locate assets of the debtor sufficient to pay the judgment. A debtor's assets may be subject to the competing claims of other creditors or may be insufficient. If the debtor has other creditors, is in poor financial condition, or resists disclosing assets and paying, satisfying the judgment can be a long and costly process. Sometimes the cost exceeds the amount of the debt. There is no guarantee the creditor will ever recover enough to satisfy the outstanding judgment.

Secured transactions improve the creditor's situation in two ways. First, as previously noted, if the debtor defaults, the creditor can use the specific property securing the debt to satisfy it. Provided the debt is secured with sufficient assets, this process is less risky than trying to satisfy a judgment out of the debtor's general assets in the event of default on unsecured debt. With secured transactions, the creditor need not look around for other assets of the debtor; specific assets are already allocated to satisfy the debt.

The second advantage is that secured transactions usually do not require a court action for the creditor to seize property and enforce her rights if the debtor defaults. Hence a secured transaction is sometimes called a "self-help remedy." According to rules stated in Article 9, the creditor acquires the security or the right to dispose of it if she already possesses the property. Where the creditor does not posses the property, Article 9 contains rules for how the creditor must go about seizing the property securing the debt and selling or disposing of it. Article 9 also covers the rights of the debtor concerning these actions. In compliance with these rules, the creditor uses the security to pay back the debt. Most creditors consider it an advantage not to have to go through litigation to be paid in full for an overdue debt.

Assignments of a Secured Interest in Personal Property

Under § 9-102 (2) all assignments transferring or creating a security interest in personal property are brought within Article 9. Often this occurs when a secured party assigns his own rights under a secured transaction involving personal property. This assignment is then governed by the rules in Article 9 of the UCC.

Personal property is defined broadly under Article 9. According to § 9-102, **personal property** includes "goods, documents, instruments, general intangibles, chattel paper or accounts." **Goods** here has the meaning established by UCC § 2-105 or "all things movable at the time of identification to the contract," including the unborn young of animals, growing crops, and other things attached to realty if they can be severed without material harm to the land.

Possessory security interest An arrangement under which the creditor holds the debtor's collateral securing a debt.

Nonpossessory security interest An arrangement under which the debtor holds the collateral securing a debt to a secured party creditor.

Default Failure of a debtor to pay back the creditor in the manner required.

Personal property Anything capable of being owned that is not real estate. Under the UCC, most commonly any form of goods, documents, instruments, general intangibles, chattel paper, or accounts.

Goods All things movable at the time of identification to the contract including the unborn young of animals, growing crops, and other things attached to realty if they can be severed without material harm to the land.

General intangibles
Nonphysical assets; under the UCC, include personal property other than goods, accounts, chattel paper, documents, instruments, and money.

Document Under the UCC, includes a bill of lading (a list of goods delivered or to be delivered), a receipt for goods, an order for delivery of goods, or any other writing showing the possessor has a right to hold and dispose of the goods described in the writing.

Instrument A negotiable instrument (written promise to pay money to its possessor), a certificated security (written right to receive stock dividends or payments), or any other writing that shows the possessor has a right to the payment of money and that is not a security agreement.

Deed of Trust or **Mortgage** A detailed written statement of the contractual debt summarized in a related promissory note and executed in connection with a sale of real property.

According to UCC § 9-106, **general intangibles** are "any personal property . . . other than goods, accounts, chattel paper, documents, instruments, and money." Under UCC § 1-201 (15), **documents** include such things as bills of lading (lists of goods delivered or to be delivered), receipts for goods, orders for delivery of goods, or any other writing showing the possessor has a right to hold and dispose of the goods described in the writing.

Under UCC § 9-105, an **instrument** is a negotiable instrument (written promise to pay money to its possessor); a certificated security (written right to receive stock dividends or payments), or any other writing that shows the possessor has a right to the payment of money and that is not a security agreement.

Taken together, these sections of the UCC indicate that any assignment of a secured interest in goods, general intangibles, documents, instruments, accounts, or chattel paper is covered by Article 9. Such assignments often occur in connection with the transfer of contract rights, such as those represented by promissory notes. When a note holder assigns the right to receive payment on a note secured by any form of personal property, the interest in the property also transfers. To be effective, this assignment must meet the requirements of Article 9.

A Note Concerning Real Estate Sales

Real estate sales commonly take the form of a secured transaction, but these transactions do not fall under the rules of the UCC because they do not come within the scope of Article 9. Today, if a real estate purchaser is to pay off the purchase price over time, she must pledge the property as security for the outstanding balance. Such arrangements are usually done in the form of a **deed of trust** or a **mortgage.** Neither a deed of trust nor a mortgage is a contract. Each is a detailed written statement of the contractual debt summarized in a related promissory note. Along with a promissory note a deed of trust or a mortgage forms part of a secured transaction involving real property. Sometimes these arrangements require a court proceeding in order for the creditor to foreclose; sometimes they do not. Real estate financing methods and real estate secured transactions are the subject of courses in real property. They are discussed here simply to alert the student to the fact that secured transactions involving real property are not governed by the UCC.

UCC Requirements for an Effective Assignment

Essentially, all assignments covered by the UCC must be in writing. Assignments of chattel paper, accounts, and security interests in personal property must be written. Several different UCC provisions establishing writing requirements are studied more thoroughly in courses on commercial transactions. In general, the writing must (1) adequately identify the subject matter of the assignment, (2) indicate a transfer is intended, and (3) be signed by the party to be charged or his agent.

Assignments under the UCC require consideration to be effective. A variety of UCC provisions establish the requirement that value must be given for effective assignments. Unless the parties provide otherwise, assignments under the UCC are irrevocable if given for consideration.

Priority of Competing Assignees Under the UCC

The drafters of the UCC changed the common-law rules governing rights between competing assignees. Article 9 has the effect of making assignments of accounts, contract rights, and nonpossessory security interests effective against competing assignees only when a public record is made of them. This public record occurs when a financing statement is filed. A **financing statement** describes personal property securing a debt, gives the names and addresses of the debtor and the secured party, and must be signed by the debtor. **Filing** occurs when the creditor submits the financing statement to a central authority such as the office of a County Clerk or, more commonly, a central state office such as the Secretary of State.

Filing a financing statement makes a public record of the parties who have an interest in particular personal property. A central filing system allows creditors or potential creditors to determine if someone else already has a competing interest in collateral. Since these filings are a matter of public record, anyone can access the information. Many states and counties have computerized or telephone services that provide information about financing statements.

Properly filing an adequate financing statement is referred to as **perfection of the security interest.** If an assignee receives a perfected security interest, no new filing is necessary, and the assignee's interests are protected to the same extent the assignor's interests were protected.

Financing statement A document signed by the debtor that describes the personal property involved in securing a debt. A financing statement also contains the names and addresses of the secured party and the debtor.

Filing Submission of a financing statement to a central authority such as the office of a County Clerk or Secretary of State.

Perfection of security interest The proper filing of an adequate financing statement.

EXAMPLE 12.11

Suppose a Buyer purchased pressing machines from Seller under an installment sales contract. Buyer gave Seller a security interest in the machines until the purchase price was paid in full. Seller properly filed an adequate financing statement. Seller then transferred to its bank the right to receive payment under the installment sales contract and the security interest in the pressing machines. This assignment to the bank gives the assignee/bank the same perfected security interest in the collateral that Seller had. The bank is protected against subsequent competing assignees who may have an interest in the pressing machines.

If an assignee does not receive a perfected security interest, the assignee must file a financing statement or risk not having a priority interest in the collateral. If several creditors are competing for the same collateral and all gave consideration, the first assignee who files a financing statement prevails.

Effect of Provisions That Prohibit Assignment

To some degree, the drafters of the UCC changed the common-law view of nonassignability clauses. Under UCC § 9-318 (4), any term in a contract between an account debtor and an assignor that prohibits assignment of the account is ineffective. Assignment of accounts normally cannot be prevented even if the contract creating the account contains a nonassignability clause. Remember that the UCC defines *account* very broadly as the right to receive payment for any goods delivered or to be delivered or the right to receive any services rendered or to be rendered. The ineffectiveness of prohibitions against assignment affects many assignments of contract rights.

UCC § 2-210 (2) provides that, unless otherwise agreed, "all rights of either seller or buyer can be assigned except where the assignment would materially change the duty of the other party, or increase materially the burden or risk imposed on him by his contract, or impair materially his chance of obtaining return performance." Additionally, § 2-210 (2) provides: "A right to damages for breach of the whole contract or a right arising out of the assignor's due performance of his entire obligation can be assigned despite agreement otherwise."

Defenses the Obligor Can Raise Against the Assignee

In this area, the drafters of the UCC seem to have preserved the common-law rule. Under UCC § 9-318, the obligor can assert all contract-related defenses against the assignee, whether the defense came into existence before or after notice of the assignment was given. As under the common law, the obligee can only assert defenses that are not contract related if they came into existence before notice of the assignment was given.

There is one major exception to the basic common-law scheme preserved in Article 9. This exception involves the concept of a holder in due course. A *holder* is someone who has possession of a negotiable instrument. A **negotiable instrument** is any document (such as a money order or certified bank check) containing a debtor's promise to pay the party who obtains (holds) the document. A negotiable instrument is not like a contract, which normally contains several promises besides merely a promise to pay. To become a **holder in due course,** the party who holds the negotiable instrument must have given consideration for it and taken it in good faith without knowledge or notice of any defenses the obligor may have. If a negotiable instrument is assigned to a holder in due course, the obligor cannot assert even contract-related defenses against this assignee. The only exceptions to this rule are defenses that attack the very existence of the contract, such as fraud or incapacity. The obligor can assert these defenses.

You should be aware that some state and federal law now limits the rights of holders in due course if the negotiable instrument was created in connection with consumer installment sales. If a negotiable instrument that involves a consumer installment sales contract is assigned, research of applicable state or federal law is necessary to determine what defenses the consumer obligor has available to assert against the holder.

Modification of Assignments: UCC and Common Law

Both the UCC and modern common law essentially follow the same rules on whether the assignor and the obligor can modify any part of a contract affecting an assignment. These rules depend on whether the obligor has received notice of the assignment. If so, the obligor and the assignor can make modifications only if the assignor has not fully performed on her part of the contract. If the assignor has already fully performed on the contract, and the obligor has notice of the assignment, the assignor and the obligor cannot make contract changes affecting the assignment without consent of the assignee. Before the obligor receives notice of the assignment, the assignor and the obligor can make any changes in the contract they wish to make

Negotiable instrument Any document (such as a money order or certified bank check) containing a debtor's promise to pay the party who obtains (holds) the document.

Holder in due course A party who possesses a negotiable instrument, gave consideration for it, and took it in good faith, without knowledge or notice of any defenses the debtor may have.

between them. Both the UCC and the common law essentially view all such changes as subject to a requirement of good faith.

Assignment

Assume you are a paralegal providing litigation support to an attorney in the following contract actions. Try to determine whether (1) common law or the UCC applies to the assignment, (2) there has been an effective assignment of rights under the contract, and (3) any defenses are available to the obligor. Then state what documents or other evidence the attorney will need to support any available defenses of the obligor or any arguments the assignor will make.

▶ Hypothetical 1

Depp ran a small but rapidly growing flower shop. To expand, he took over larger premises from Martha. Martha's landlord was Swank Investments, Inc., which owns the premises Martha transferred to Depp. The lease required Swank's consent to bring in a new tenant. The consent provision states: "Swank shall not unreasonably withhold consent to a new tenant."

Depp and Martha signed a document titled "Assignment of Lease" in which Depp agreed to abide by all the terms and conditions of Martha's original lease with Swank. Martha told Depp she would send the document to Swank's corporate headquarters for the "Consent of Lessor" provision to be completed. During negotiations with Depp, she said she had already contacted Swank and discussed Depp's qualifications as a tenant. She noted that Swank was favorably disposed toward Depp's tenancy and anticipated no problem with approval.

Depp opened his business on Martha's old premises and enjoyed immediate financial success. However, he noted that Swank had not fulfilled a number of its maintenance and repair responsibilities. Apparently, Martha just let these things go although the lease clearly stated that Swank was responsible for them. Depp negotiated with Swank for two months, but Swank refused to complete the repairs and maintenance. In an effort to put some pressure on Swank, Depp stopped paying 25 percent of his rent, which was his honest estimate of what the repairs and maintenance were worth.

Swank then notified Depp that it had never signed the "Consent of Lessor" provision. Swank now claims that: (1) Depp did not receive a valid assignment of the lease, and that (2) even if he did receive a valid assignment, he has breached it by withholding a portion of his rent.

Depp has come to the law office where you are employed. Your attorney has asked you to make an initial review of the file because Depp wishes the attorney to advise him about his legal position.

▶ Hypothetical 2

Sponge Divers, Inc., is a small corporation that employs divers to bring up sponges from the oceans surrounding Florida. After the sponges are cleaned and processed, they are sold to various regular customers on a continuous basis. Each month Sponge Divers bills its customers who must pay within 30 days of billing.

On March 1, Sponge Divers makes an assignment of its accounts with customers Acme, Beta, Chi, and Delta to Heartless Bank. Acme, Beta, Chi, and Delta's contracts with Sponge Divers contain a provision requiring each of them to take a minimum of $2,000 worth of sponges per month. Under the assignment, Sponge Divers transfers the right to receive all payments on these accounts for one year. The transfer is made using Heartless Bank's commercial assignments form.

On March 2, Delta contacts Sponge Divers, and they agree to reduce the minimum requirements to $1,500 per month. The same day, Acme, Beta, and Chi find out about this, and they also make an agreement with Sponge Divers to reduce the required minimum under their contracts to $1,500 per month.

On March 5, Acme, Beta, Chi, and Delta all receive a letter from Heartless telling them their contract payments have been assigned to Heartless, indicating the address to which payments are to be sent, and reminding them that the monthly amount owed will be a minimum of $2,000 per their contracts with Sponge Divers.

In April, the sponges produced by Sponge Divers appear to be affected by a marine blight that weakens them and makes them unsuitable for commercial use. Acme, Beta, Chi, and Delta all choose to take fewer sponges since they can only sell them for the more limited noncommercial use. Each company takes only enough sponges to be billed the $1,500 minimum. They pay this amount.

In May, Acme, Beta, Chi, and Delta all refuse to take any sponges at all, claiming the quality is substandard for either commercial or noncommercial use. They claim the sponges are unsalable, and they jointly arrange to have lab testing done on the sponges. The lab testing reveals the sponges are infected with parasites that have weakened them and indicates the sponges are probably not salable. Acme, Beta, Chi, and Delta all refuse to pay for the May shipments of sponges.

The office where you are employed represents Heartless Bank, which wishes to know what its legal position is with regard to Sponge Divers, Acme, Beta, Chi, and Delta.

Warranties for Assignments: Common Law and UCC

Warranties Guarantees in a contract or in an assignment of a contract. Warranties may be express or implied.

Implied warranty A guarantee not expressly stated by the parties but which the law implies into a contract or an assignment of a contract.

Express warranty A guarantee expressly stated by the parties.

If an assignment at common law is made for value, the assignor is considered to have made certain guarantees or **warranties** concerning the assignment. These warranties need not be expressly stated by the parties, although they can be. If they are stated, they are **express warranties**. If they are not stated, they are considered to be implied with the assignment itself and thus are called **implied warranties.** If the assignment does not live up to its warranties, the assignee has a cause of action against the assignor for breach of implied warranty and can be held liable for damages caused by this breach.

The assignor is generally required to be responsible for the following implied warranties whenever an assignment is made:

- A *warranty* that the contract rights assigned are free from undisclosed claims or defenses that would interfere with the assignee's rights
- A *warranty* that all documents used in connection with the assignment are genuine

- A *warranty* that the assignor will do nothing to interfere with the assignee's rights under the assignment or his exercise of them

Generally, if the assignee makes a subsequent assignment, the implied warranties of the original assignor do not transfer to the successor assignee. However, the original assignee is usually deemed to give such warranties to the successor assignee. Thus, implied warranties of the original assignor apply only to his assignee. Any successor assignee would receive implied warranties only from his immediate assignor.

The drafters of the UCC apparently chose not to deal with implied warranties in an assignment. Under UCC § 1-103, the common law is brought in to deal with implied warranties in cases involving assignment under the UCC.

Chapter Review Questions

1. Define an assignment and a delegation, and identify the similarities and differences between the two.
2. Which assignments are covered by common law, and which are covered by the UCC?
3. What is the legal effect of placing in a contract a clause that prohibits assignment?
4. If the assignee sues the obligor after a valid assignment is made, what defenses may the obligor raise against the assignee?
5. What kinds of contracts are not assignable?
6. What are the requirements of a valid assignment under the common law and under the UCC?
7. Under what circumstances does an assignment become irrevocable?
8. How is priority among competing assignees decided under the common law and under the UCC?

Key Terms

Key Terms

Promissory note, 261
Secured party, 262
Secured transaction, 262
Security, 261

Third party, 247
Unsecured transaction, 262
Warranties, 268

Notes

1. See John D. Calamari and Joseph M. Perillo, *Contracts,* 3d ed. (St. Paul, Minn.: West Publishing, 1987), § 18-1, p. 722.

2. Construction contracts can be delegable because it is contemplated that the actual work will usually be performed by one other than the obligor, such as a subcontractor. See *New England Iron Co. v. Gilbert Electric R.R.,* 91 N.Y. 153 (1883) and cases digested in 4 *Corbin on Contracts,* § 865.

3. Compare *Farmer's Exchange v. Walter M. Lowney Co.,* 95 Vt. 445, 115 A. 507 (1921) [if obligor "had knowledge of sufficient facts . . . to put it on inquiry it must be held to have notice of all such facts as reasonable diligence in prosecuting its inquiry . . . would have brought to its own knowledge] with *Warrington v. Dawson,* 798 F.2d 1533 (5th Cir. 1986) [no notice where debtor was handed letter from bank while working in fields without reading glasses and no copy of notice was left with him].

CHAPTER 13

Third-Party Beneficiaries

LEARNING OBJECTIVES FOR THIS CHAPTER:
WHAT YOU SHOULD KNOW!

❏ What is a third-party-beneficiary contract?

❏ Who is a third-party beneficiary?

❏ Who is an incidental beneficiary?

❏ What are the rights of an incidental beneficiary?

❏ What is a donee beneficiary?

❏ What is a creditor beneficiary?

❏ What defenses can the promisor raise?

❏ Does the promisee have any rights against the promisor?

❏ What is meant by vesting of rights?

❏ When do a beneficiary's rights vest?

❏ When can the promisor and promisee modify or cancel the contract?

Introduction

The traditional view was that only the parties to a contract could assert rights under it, and only the parties had duties because of it. In the nineteenth century, however, a famous case occurred in the state of New York.[1] The case gave rise to a doctrine by which an outsider, a third party, might acquire rights under someone else's contract. As the American Civil War was approaching, a man named Holly owed a debt to another man named Lawrence. The debt was for $300, a sizable amount of money in pre–Civil War America. Another fellow named Fox approached Holly for a loan, and Holly gave it to him in the amount of $300. Holly made it clear to Fox that the loan was given in exchange for Fox's promise to repay Holly's original debt to Lawrence. For a variety of reasons, Fox failed to pay Lawrence Holly's $300. Lawrence sued Fox who defended himself on the theory that he had no contractual agreement with Fox and, thus, owed him no money. Nevertheless, the court permitted Lawrence to recover Holly's $300 from Fox. The theory used to justify such a recovery was that Holly's loan to Fox was made for the benefit of Lawrence: under Fox's loan contract, Holly intended to pay back Lawrence. This arrangement is called a third-party-beneficiary contract.

The whole area of third-party-beneficiary rights, like assignment and delegation, has its own vocabulary. To understand third-party-beneficiary contracts, it is necessary to be clear on this vocabulary. The outsider who is trying to assert rights under the contract made by two other parties is referred to as a **third-party beneficiary,** or sometimes simply the **beneficiary.** The original contracting party from whom the beneficiary expects performance is called the **promisor.** The other original contracting party (typically, the party who intended the third-party arrangement) is called the **promisee.** *Promisor* and *promisee* have the same meaning in third-party-beneficiary arrangements as they have in an ordinary contract setting. The third party is simply trying to enforce a promise made to someone else on her behalf.

Early concerns with third-party beneficiaries centered around the idea of privity. When two parties have a contractual agreement between them, the law describes them as in **privity of contract** with each another. In *Lawrence v. Fox,* Fox's argument that he had no obligation to Lawrence involved the idea that he was not in privity of contract with Lawrence. Following in the wake of *Lawrence v. Fox,* the modern doctrine of third-party-beneficiary arrangements does not require privity of contract between the third party and the other original contracting party who is to perform to the third party.

The earliest formulations of third-party-beneficiary arrangements were influenced by the First Restatement of Contracts. The First Restatement categorized third-party beneficiaries into three types: creditor beneficiaries, donee beneficiaries, and incidental beneficiaries. **Creditor beneficiaries** were those to whom one of the contracting parties owed a debt. In *Lawrence v. Fox,* Lawrence was a creditor beneficiary of Holly. **Donee beneficiaries** were those to whom one of the contracting parties was attempting to make a gift.

Third-party beneficiary An outsider to a contract made by two other parties who acquires rights under it; sometimes called simply the **beneficiary.**

Promisor In third-party-beneficiary contracts the contracting party from whom the beneficiary expects performance.

Promisee In third-party-beneficiary contracts, the contracting party who intended a benefit to run to a third party.

Privity of contract The legal relationship existing between two contracting parties.

Creditor beneficiary A third-party beneficiary to whom one of the contracting parties owes a debt.

Donee beneficiary A third-party beneficiary to whom one of the contracting parties was attempting to make a gift.

EXAMPLE 13.1

Assume the facts in *Lawrence v. Fox* are changed so that instead of owing money to Lawrence, Holly has a daughter to whom he wishes to make a gift of some money. When Fox approaches Holly for a loan, Holly could grant the loan on condition that Fox repay the loan to Holly's daughter instead of to Holly. If Fox does not repay, then Holly's daughter might sue Fox because she did not receive from him the gift her father intended. The daughter would be a *donee beneficiary*.

Incidental beneficiaries were not true beneficiaries at all. **Incidental beneficiaries** were people who received an unintended windfall because of a contract made between two other parties.

EXAMPLE **13.2**

Suppose Julia Morgan, the famous American architect, were still alive and made a contract with a lucky property owner to build a new home on the owner's land. The neighbors would probably be thrilled, thinking their property values would go up with a Julia Morgan home next-door. They might even derive some personal pleasure from seeing the building or living beside it.

If Morgan and the property owner have a falling out and the Morgan house never gets built, the neighbors cannot claim they are anything but incidental beneficiaries. They were just going to get a lucky break from the coincidence of living next-door to a house designed by Julia Morgan. Neither Morgan nor the property owner ever intended to benefit the neighbors.

Incidental beneficiary A person who receives an unintended windfall because of a contract made between two other parties. An incidental beneficiary is not a third-party beneficiary with enforceable legal rights.

The situation in this example is different from the one in *Lawrence v. Fox,* where at least Holly intended a benefit (payment of $300) to run to Lawrence. Incidental beneficiaries have no right to enforce performance under a contract between two other parties. They are not true third-party beneficiaries at all.

As time passed, the vocabulary of the First Restatement of Contracts gave way to a different way of thinking that is reflected in the Restatement (Second) of Contracts. The Restatement (Second) emphasizes that both creditor beneficiaries and donee beneficiaries should be treated the same and characterized as **intended beneficiaries.** The definition of *incidental beneficiaries* as not really beneficiaries at all was preserved, however. Under the thinking of the Restatement (Second), any third party to whom the two contracting parties intended some benefit to run may acquire the right to enforce the contract and obtain these rights.

What is not clear, however, is exactly what the drafters of the Restatement (Second) meant when they said the contracting parties "intended a benefit to run" to a third party. Some courts interpret this to mean both contracting parties must intend benefits to run to the third party. Other courts interpret it to mean that at least one of the contracting parties must so intend.

Intended beneficiary. Under the Restatement (Second), any person to whom the two contracting parties intended some benefit to run; includes both a creditor and a donee beneficiary.

Modern courts sometimes interpret the "intent" required for third-party-beneficiary contracts as not requiring personal or subjective intent at all. These courts examine the contract between two parties to see if its structure had the effect from the beginning of benefiting a third party. If so, this is sufficient to create a third-party-beneficiary contract regardless of the contracting parties' actual motives.

The paralegal should be aware that the type of intent required for third-party-beneficiary contracts is not uniformly interpreted. For this reason, research may be required to determine the law in the relevant jurisdiction before establishing who is a third-party beneficiary.

Modern Third-Party-Beneficiary Law

Traditional concerns about creditors and donee beneficiaries can still be read in scholarly articles and legal opinions. The modern view of third-party-beneficiary arrangements, however, is predominantly that of the Restatement (Second). Section 302 of the Restatement (Second) characterized someone as a third-party beneficiary if "recognition of a right to performance in the beneficiary is appropriate to effectuate the intention of the parties" and either one of two things is true. The performance of the promise must either pay a debt on behalf of one of the contracting parties or make a gift from one of the contracting parties. Without actually saying so, the Restatement (Second) preserves the idea that both creditor and donee beneficiaries have legitimate third-party rights under appropriate circumstances. However, § 302(2) states: "An incidental beneficiary is a beneficiary who is not an intended beneficiary." The traditional and modern view is that only "intended" beneficiaries have enforceable rights.

Under many circumstances, a potential third party might like to enforce the contract made between two other parties. This situation has arisen frequently in the area of public contracts. For example, consider the following case.

A CASE FOR STUDY

H. R. Moch Co., Inc. v. Rensselaer Water Co.
247 N.Y. 160, 159 N.E. 896 (1928)

Court of Appeals of New York. Jan. 10, 1928. Action by the H. R. Moch Company, Inc., against the Rensselaer Water Company. From a judgment of the Appellate Division, reversing an order of the Special Term, and granting defendant's motion for judgment dismissing the complaint for failure to state facts sufficient to constitute a cause of action, plaintiff appeals. Affirmed.

CARDOZO, C. J.   The defendant, a waterworks company under the laws of this state, made a contract with the city of Rensselaer for the supply of water during a term of years. Water was to be furnished to the city for sewer flushing and street sprinkling; for service to schools and public buildings; and for service at fire hydrants, the latter service at the rate of $42.50 a year for each hydrant. Water was to be furnished to private takers within the city at their homes and factories and other industries at reasonable rates, not exceeding a stated schedule. While this contract was in force, a building caught fire. The flames, spreading to the plaintiff's warehouse near by, destroyed it and its

contents. The defendant, according to the complaint, was promptly notified of the fire, 'but omitted and neglected after such notice, to supply or furnish sufficient or adequate quantity of water, with adequate pressure to stay, suppress, or extinguish the fire before it reached the warehouse of the plaintiff, although the pressure and supply which the defendant was equipped to supply and furnish, and had agreed by said contract to supply and furnish, was adequate and sufficient to prevent the spread of the fire to and the destruction of the plaintiff's warehouse and its contents.' By reason of the failure of the defendant to 'fulfill the provisions of the contract between it and the city of Rensselaer,' the plaintiff is said to have suffered damage, for which judgment is demanded. A motion, in the nature of a demurrer, to dismiss the complaint, was denied at Special Term. The Appellate Division reversed by a divided court.

Liability in the plaintiff's argument is placed on one or other of three grounds. The complaint, we are told, is to be viewed as stating: (1) A cause of action for breach of contract within

Lawrence v. Fox, 20 N.Y. 268; (2) a cause of action for a common-law tort; or (3) a cause of action for the breach of a statutory duty. These several grounds of liability will be considered in succession.

(1) We think the action is not maintainable as one for breach of contract.

No legal duty rests upon a city to supply its inhabitants with protection against fire. That being so, a member of the public may not maintain an action under Lawrence v. Fox against one contracting with the city to furnish water at the hydrants, unless an intention appears that the promisor is to be answerable to individual members of the public as well as to the city for any loss ensuing from the failure to fulfill the promise. No such intention is discernible here. On the contrary, the contract is significantly divided into two branches: One a promise to the city for the benefit of the city in its corporate capacity, in which branch is included the service at the hydrants; and the other a promise to the city for the benefit of private takers, in which branch is included the service at their homes and factories. In a broad sense it is true that every city contract, not improvident or wasteful, is for the benefit of the public. More than this, however, must be shown to give a right of action to a member of the public not formally a party. The benefit, as it is sometimes said, must be one that is not merely incidental and secondary. It must be primary and immediate in such a sense and to such a degree as to bespeak the assumption of a duty to make reparation directly to the individual members of the public if the benefit is lost. The field of obligation would be expanded beyond reasonable limits if less than this were to be demanded as a condition of liability. A promisor undertakes to supply fuel for heating a public building. He is not liable for breach of contract to a visitor who finds the building without fuel, and thus contracts a cold. The list of illustrations can be indefinitely extended. The carrier of the mails under contract with the government is not answerable to the merchant who has lost the benefit of a bargain through negligent delay. The householder is without a remedy against manufacturers of hose and engines, though prompt performance of their contracts would have stayed the ravages of fire. 'The law does not spread its protection so far.' So with the case

at hand. By the vast preponderance of authority, a contract between a city and a water company to furnish water at the city hydrants has in view a benefit to the public that is incidental rather than immediate, an assumption of duty to the city and not to its inhabitants. Such is the ruling of the Supreme Court of the United States though the question is still open in this court. Such with few exceptions has been the ruling in other jurisdictions. Williston, Contracts, § 373, and cases there cited. The diligence of counsel has brought together decisions to that effect from 26 states. Typical examples are Alabama; California; Georgia; Connecticut; Kansas; Maine; New Jersey; and Ohio. Only a few states have held otherwise. An intention to assume an obligation of indefinite extension to every member of the public is seen to be the more improbable when we recall the crushing burden that the obligation would impose. The consequences invited would bear no reasonable proportion to those attached by law to defaults not greatly different. A wrongdoer who by negligence sets fire to a building is liable in damages to the owner where the fire has its origin, but not to other owners who are injured when it spreads. The rule in our state is settled to that effect, whether wisely or unwisely. If the plaintiff is to prevail, one who negligently omits to supply sufficient pressure to extinguish a fire started by another assumes an obligation to pay the ensuing damage, though the whole city is laid low. A promisor will not be deemed to have had in mind the assumption of a risk so overwhelming for any trivial reward.

The cases that have applied the rule of Lawrence v. Fox to contracts made by a city for the benefit of the public are not at war with this conclusion. Through them all there runs as a unifying principle the presence of an intention to compensate the individual members of the public in the event of a default. For example, in Pond v. New Rochelle Water Co., the contract with the city fixed a schedule of rates to be supplied, not to public buildings, but to private takers at their homes. In Matter of International R. Co. v. Rann, the contract was by street railroads to carry passengers for a stated fare. In Smyth v. City of New York, covenants were made by contractors upon public works, not merely to indemnify the city, but to assume its liabilities. These and like cases come within the third group stated in the comprehensive opinion in Seaver v. Ransom, The municipality was contracting in behalf of its inhabitants by covenants intended to be enforced by any of them severally as occasion should arise.

(2) We think the action is not maintainable as one for a common-law tort.

"It is ancient learning that one who assumes to act, even though gratuitously, may thereby become subject to the duty of acting carefully, if he acts at all." The plaintiff would bring its case within the orbit of that principle. The hand once set to a task may not always be withdrawn with impunity though liability would fail if it had never been applied at all. A time-honored formula often phrases the distinction as one between misfeasance and nonfeasance. Incomplete the formula is, and so at times misleading. Given a relation involving in its existence a duty of care irrespective of a contract, a tort may result as well from acts of omission as of commission in the fulfillment of the duty thus recognized by law. What we need to know is not so much the conduct to be avoided when the relation and its attendant duty are established as existing. What we need to know is the conduct that engenders the relation. It is here that the formula, however incomplete, has its value and significance. If conduct has gone forward to such a stage that inaction would commonly result, not negatively merely in withholding a benefit, but positively or actively in working an injury, there exists a relation out of which arises a duty to go forward. So the surgeon who operates without pay is liable, though his negligence is in the omission to sterilize his instruments; the engineer, though his fault is in the failure to shut off steam; the maker of automobiles, at the suit of some one other than the buyer, though his negligence is merely in inadequate inspection. The query always is whether the putative wrongdoer has advanced to such a point as to have launched a force or instrument of harm, or has stopped where inaction is at most a refusal to become an instrument for good.

The plaintiff would have us hold that the defendant, when once it entered upon the performance of its contract with the city, was brought into such a relation with every one who might potentially be benefitted through the supply of water at the hydrants as to give to negligent performance, without reasonable notice of a refusal to continue, the quality of a tort. There is a suggestion of this thought in Guardian Trust & Deposit Co. v. Fisher, but the dictum was rejected in a later case decided by the same court when an opportunity was at hand to turn it into law. We are satisfied that liability would be unduly and indeed indefinitely extended by this enlargement of the zone of duty. The dealer in coal who is to supply fuel for a shop must then answer to the customers if fuel is lacking. The manufacturer of goods, who enters upon the performance of his contract, must answer, in that view, not only to the buyer, but to those who to his knowledge are looking to the buyer for their own sources of supply. Every one making a promise having the quality of a contract will be under a duty to the promisee by virtue of the promise, but under another duty, apart from contract, to an indefinite number of potential beneficiaries when performance has begun. The assumption of one relation will mean the involuntary assumption of a series of new relations, inescapably hooked together. Again we may say in the words of the Supreme Court of the United States, 'The law does not spread its protection so far.' We do not need to determine now what remedy, if any, there might be if the defendant had withheld the water or reduced the pressure with a malicious intent to do injury to the plaintiff or another. We put aside also the problem that would arise if there had been reckless and wanton indifference to consequences measured and foreseen. Difficulties would be present even then, but they need not now perplex us. What we are dealing with at this time is a mere negligent omission, unaccompanied by malice or other aggravating elements. The failure in such circumstances to furnish an adequate supply of water is at most the denial of a benefit. It is not the commission of a wrong.

[The court also goes on to find that the defendant is not liable for breach of a statutory duty where an inhabitant of the city suffers indirect or incidental damage through deficient pressure at the hydrants.]

The judgment should be affirmed, with costs.

Questions to Consider

1. What was the basis for the plaintiff's argument that he was a third-party beneficiary of the water contract between the city and the water company?

2. For what reasons did the court hold that the plaintiff was not a third-party beneficiary? Do you agree with these reasons? Why or why not?

3. Why would a party in the warehouse owner's position want to claim to be a third-party beneficiary?

4. How else might the warehouse owner protect himself against loss?

5. Would the result be different if the city of Rensselaer itself had sued the water company? Why or why not?

Private relationships also give rise to potential third-party claims. In a well-known case,[2] a dying wife, Mrs. Beman, asked her husband, Judge Beman, to draw up her will. He did so but failed to leave Mrs. Beman's house to her favorite niece, Marion. Consequently, the wife did not want to sign the will. Judge Beman offered to draw up another will leaving the house to the niece, but Mrs. Beman felt she would not last long enough to sign the will. Therefore, she made an oral agreement with her husband: she would sign the erroneous will if he would agree to give her niece Marion enough from his own will to make up the value of the house. This was about $6,000. Judge Beman promised; Mrs. Beman signed the erroneous will and died shortly thereafter.

At Judge Beman's death, it was found that his will made no provision for his wife's niece. The niece sued—and won—on the theory that she was a third-party beneficiary of the husband's promises to his wife concerning changes to his will. The court stated that "the right of the beneficiary to sue on a contract made expressly for his benefit has been fully recognized in many American jurisdictions, either by judicial decision or by legislation. . . ."[3] (*Note:* In this case, the parties have the following designations: Mrs. Beman was the *promisee;* Judge Beman was the *promisor;* and niece Marion was the *beneficiary.*)

Another private setting in which third-party-beneficiary issues may arise involves an insolvent debtor. Sometimes the creditors of the debtor get together with the debtor, reduce the amount of their individual claims, and collectively extend the time for the debtor to pay. This arrangement is often called a composition. A **composition** is a contract among the creditors of a particular debtor. Under a composition, a creditor may agree to take less than the amount owed under the debtor's original debt. Usually, a composition is made because the creditors fear either that (1) they will not get repaid at all without mutual agreement, or that (2) one of them will be fully repaid and this will deprive the others of any repayment. If any of the creditors later tries to ignore the composition, the debtor can often successfully claim to be a third-party beneficiary of the composition. This allows the debtor to defend against the claims of any backsliding creditor by enforcing the composition.[4]

Unpaid suppliers or subcontractors on general contracts have sometimes successfully asserted third-party-beneficiary rights. Ordinarily, the subcontractors on a construction project are protected by statutory lien rights. A **lien** is obtained by filing (and sometimes publishing) a notice of the right to receive payment. The lien is filed with a public authority such as a County

Composition A contract among the creditors of a particular debtor in which they reduce the amount of the debt and/or extend the time for repayment.

Lien A charge or claim on property as security for work performed or repayment of a debt.

Recorder and acts as security for work performed. Most states now have lien laws that permit subcontractors to file a lien against the property that is the subject of the construction contract. If the owner on a project, or in many cases the general contractor, does not pay, the subcontractor can sue for payment under the lien.

Sometimes, however, the subcontractor has no lien or cannot enforce the lien. This can result from a variety of circumstances including failure to comply with a state's lien laws. Under most state laws, certain procedures must be followed to acquire an effective lien such as filing within a certain time period, publication of the lien notice, notice to the project owner, and the like. If the subcontractor fails to substantially comply with all the procedures, he will not have a valid lien. Sometimes the contractor has a lien, but it will not result in adequate payment. In that case, the subcontractor may be able to argue that he is a third-party beneficiary of the contractual arrangements made by the owner and contractor. Such situations sometimes arise because of a common practice on construction projects: the owner withholds part of the contract price until the project is completed and all relevant authorities have approved it for occupancy. This is usually done by holding back some pre-agreed amount from each periodic payment for work done. The pre-agreed amount withheld is usually referred to as *retainage*. Retainage on a typical construction project might amount to 10 percent of the total contract price. The owner and the contractor negotiate the retainage amount; the subcontractor usually has little say in the matter. One result of the retainage may be that the subcontractor does not get paid promptly for work completed. In this situation, some subcontractors have argued (with varying degrees of success) that they were third-party beneficiaries of the retainage agreement between the owner and the general contractor.

The liability insurance industry often faces issues of third-party beneficiary claims.

EXAMPLE 13.3

Suppose that Company C is sued for depositing toxic wastes on the plaintiff's land. The plaintiff, the injured party, gets a verdict against C. C is insured by AllStar Insurance Company. The plaintiff in this situation is essentially viewed as a third-party beneficiary of C's insurance contract with its own insurer, AllStar.

Thus, if an insured loses a lawsuit to an injured plaintiff, the insured's insurance company usually must pay the losses to the plaintiff.

Defenses the Promisor Has Against the Beneficiary

If a party qualifies as a third-party beneficiary under the relevant law and files a lawsuit, the focus of third-party beneficiary law changes. The focus shifts to whether or not the promisor has some legitimate reason for not performing. The emphasis is on the defenses the promisor may raise when the third party sues him for specific performance or for damages.

The general rule is that the promisor can raise against the beneficiary any defense that could have been raised against the promisee.

EXAMPLE **13.4**

A subcontractor is suing a project owner for part of the retainage on a construction contract. The owner does not want to pay because some aspects of the general contractor's work are deficient or incomplete. If the general contractor–promisee were seeking payment in a lawsuit, the project owner–promisor would surely raise the defects and incomplete work as defenses against the contractor. Where the third party seeks payment from retainage, the project owner can raise these same defenses against the third party.

This result makes sense. Without this protection of preserving defenses against the promisee, the promisor would be vulnerable to third-party claims where he had not actually obtained the promised performance. On the other hand, the unpaid subcontractor beneficiary may be out of luck because the contractor-promisee has not performed completely or adequately. This can be a hardship where the subcontractor's own performance was complete and adequate.

Sometimes the promisor can even assert any defenses the promisee herself would have against the beneficiary.

EXAMPLE **13.5**

Suppose D purchases a home from Owner. In the home is a new heater that has been purchased on the installment plan. In buying the home, D must assume responsibility for paying the outstanding balance on the heater. The heater was purchased from B, and D agrees to finish paying for the heater by making the monthly payments to B. After D moves in, however, the heater malfunctions, and B refuses to repair or replace it. Therefore, D stops making monthly payments to B. B sues D. If D believes the malfunctions in the heater are due to breach of warranties made to Owner when Owner purchased the heater, D will wish to raise Owner's own breach of warranty arguments as defenses against B. B, of course, would be suing as a third-party beneficiary of D's promise to Owner to assume liability for the heater and go on making payments.

For a case that allowed such a defense, see *Rouse v. United States,* 215 F.2d 872 (D.C. Cir. 1954).

Rights of the Beneficiary Against the Promisee

Whether or not the third-party beneficiary has a claim against the promisee (not just against the promisor) depends upon the relationship between the two of them. If the third-party beneficiary is a creditor of the promisee, the third party can always sue on that debt. This would be the case in the situation in *Lawrence v. Fox.* Since Holly, the promisee, already owed money to Lawrence, the beneficiary, Lawrence, could sue Holly on his underlying debt when Fox failed to pay under the agreement with Holly. In other words, by also expecting payment under a third-party beneficiary arrangement with Fox, Lawrence did not give up the right to collect his $300 debt from Holly. Where a third-party beneficiary is already a creditor of the promisee, the arrangement gives the beneficiary an additional mechanism by which to try to satisfy the debt. The third party will only be paid once, but can essentially choose which arrangement to enforce: his own contractual debt against the promisee, or payment from the promisor under the third-party beneficiary arrangement.

If the third-party beneficiary is not a creditor of the promisee, ordinarily she has no enforcement rights against the promisee. This would be the case in the fictional situation in Example 13.1 in which Holly did not owe money to Lawrence, but instead wanted to make a gift to his daughter. Where Holly's daughter was the beneficiary, there was no underlying contractual debt between Holly and his daughter-beneficiary. If Fox refused to implement the gift by paying Holly's daughter, the daughter would have no rights against Holly, the promisee. She could only sue on the third-party-beneficiary arrangement.

Rights of the Promisee Against the Promisor

Sometimes the question arises as to whether the promisee has any claims against the promisor if the promisor fails to perform to the third party. For example, suppose the promisee, Holly, in *Lawrence v. Fox* wanted to sue the promisor, Fox, for failing to pay off the $300 debt to Lawrence. The majority of courts considering this question have found that the promisee does have a cause of action against the promisor if the promisor fails to perform to the beneficiary. This makes sense: the promisee is the original party to whom the promisor made the promise to perform, even if the performance itself was to be made to the beneficiary.

In the case of a creditor beneficiary situation, this rule can lead to some difficulties. Again, consider *Lawrence v. Fox*. If Holly successfully sues Fox because he did not pay Lawrence, Holly collects at least $300 damages from Fox. Then, if Lawrence also successfully sues Fox because Fox did not pay him, he also collects at least $300 damages from Fox. Fox might ultimately be liable for a double recovery. For this reason, some courts considering this problem have held the promisee can recover directly from the promisor only if he can show he has already paid the debt to the beneficiary. Of course, the promisor can protect himself from double payment of the debt by simply performing to the beneficiary before the promisee gets a judgment against him. Additionally, under a merged system of law and equity, some courts have used their equitable authority to make the judgment in favor of the promisee *payable* only to the third-party beneficiary.

Attempts to Modify or Discharge Third-Party-Beneficiary Contracts

In spite of the commercial usefulness of third-party-beneficiary arrangements, there are times when the two contracting parties change their minds or attempt to modify the contract between them. The problem for the third party is that cancellations and modifications of the contract may destroy or devalue the beneficiary's expected performance. In practical terms, the longer the promisor and promisee wait to make such a cancellation or modification, the more likely it is that the beneficiary has relied on the arrangement. There has been general agreement that at some point in time, the promisor and promisee should essentially lose the right to make contract changes that would damage the rights and expectations of the beneficiary. This point in time is described as the moment at which the beneficiary's rights **vest.** Once the beneficiary's rights vest, the promisee and promisor cannot make any contract changes that damage the beneficiary's interests. It is not always clear at what point in time the beneficiary's rights actually do vest, however.

Courts have used several criteria for deciding the point at which the beneficiary's rights vest and after which it is too late for the promisee and promisor to make contract modifications and cancellations. Earlier courts made a distinction between donee and creditor beneficiaries. They felt the donee beneficiary's rights vested at the moment the contract was made. On the other hand, the creditor beneficiary's rights vested only when she *learned of the contract* and agreed to the arrangement, or when she reasonably relied on the arrangement to her detriment. In a way, this rule gave the donee beneficiary superior protections because her rights vested at an earlier time.

As the views of the Restatement (Second) have gained in popularity and eroded the distinction between creditor and donee beneficiaries, differences in vesting requirements have also changed. Consistent with the Restatement (Second), the modern trend is to find that the rights of any *intended* beneficiary vest at the same point, whether the beneficiary is a creditor or a donee. The modern view is that an intended third-party beneficiary's rights vest *when any one of the three following events occurs:*

1. The beneficiary materially changes position in reasonable reliance on the promised performance.
2. The beneficiary finds out about the contract and consents to the arrangement at the request of either the promisee or the promisor.
3. The beneficiary files a lawsuit on the contract to enforce his rights.

The contracting parties themselves may decide when the third party's rights vest. They can either create an immediate, irrevocable right to performance, or they can agree to reserve the right to modify or cancel the contract for any period. The vesting rules described earlier would normally come into play only if the parties themselves had not made enforceable agreements about vesting. Modern life insurance contracts are a common example of this last type of agreement concerning vesting. Almost all life insurance policies permit the insured (the promisee) at any time to change the name of the beneficiary to whom the insurance company (promisor) must perform.

The rules on vesting can affect which defenses the promisor can raise against the third-party beneficiary in a lawsuit. If the defense the promisor wants to use arose under a contract modification made after the beneficiary's rights vested, the beneficiary is not subject to this defense. Thus, a complete rule on defenses the promisor can raise can be stated as follows: the promisor can raise against the beneficiary any defense he could have raised against the promisee except defenses that come from contract changes made after the beneficiary's rights vested.

Vest/vesting of rights A concept fixing the time at which the promisor and promisee lose the right to make contract changes that would damage the rights and expectations of the beneficiary.

Disclaimer Action
or words by an in-
tended third-party
beneficiary indicating
that the beneficiary
refuses the third-party
rights created under
the other two parties'
contract.

Interestingly, most courts have held that an intended third-party beneficiary can also refuse the third-party rights created under two other parties'
contract. Within a reasonable time of learning of the arrangement, the
beneficiary can refuse it. This is usually referred to as a type of **disclaimer.**
Most courts do not allow disclaimers of third-party beneficiary benefits *after*
the third party initially assented to the arrangement.

Third-Party-Beneficiary Arrangements Distinguished from Assignment and Delegation

Both third-party-beneficiary arrangements and assignment and delegation
give rights to someone who was not a party to the contract. Unlike
assignment and delegation, however, third-party beneficiary rights must be
created at the time of formation and are created by the contract itself.
Assignment and delegation do not arise out of the creation of the contract.
They depend upon the actions of one of the parties to the contract who
makes a *transfer* of rights or duties possessed under the contract. These
transfers need not occur at the time of formation; they may occur at any time.
It is probably also true that more formalities are associated with a valid
assignment or delegation than with a third-party-beneficiary arrangement.
This is particularly true for contracts under the UCC and in situations where
the Statute of Frauds applies. Generally, the Statute of Frauds does not apply
to third-party-beneficiary arrangements.

A CASE FOR STUDY
Lucas v. Hamm
56 Cal. 2d 583, 364 P.2d 685, 15 Cal. Rptr. 821 (1961)

Action by beneficiaries under a will against an
attorney who had been engaged by the testator
to prepare the will. The Superior Court, City
and County of San Francisco, Orla St. Clair, J.,
dismissed the complaint and the plaintiffs appealed. The Supreme Court, Gibson, C. J., held
that the attorney, who allegedly drafted the will
so that trust provisions violated rules as to
perpetuities and restraint on alienation was not
liable to beneficiaries, on basis of negligence or
breach of contract. Affirmed.

GIBSON, C. J.   Plaintiffs, who are some of
the beneficiaries under the will of Eugene H.
Emmick, deceased, brought this action for damages against defendant L. S. Hamm, an attorney
at law who had been engaged by the testator to
prepare the will. They have appealed from a
judgment of dismissal entered after an order
sustaining a general demurrer to the second
amended complaint without leave to amend.

The allegations of the first and second causes
of action are summarized as follows: Defendant
agreed with the testator, for a consideration, to
prepare a will and codicils thereto for him by
which plaintiffs were to be designated as beneficiaries of a trust provided for by paragraph
Eighth of the will and were to receive 15% of
the residue as specified in that paragraph. Defendant, in violation of instructions and in
breach of his contract, negligently prepared testamentary instruments containing phraseology
that was invalid by virtue of section 715.2 and
former sections 715.1 and 716 of the Civil Code
relating to restraints on alienation and the rule
against perpetuities. Paragraph Eighth of these
instruments 'transmitted' the residual estate in
trust and provided that the 'trust shall cease and
terminate at 12 o'clock noon on a day five years
after the date upon which the order distributing
the trust property to the trustee is made by the

Court having jurisdiction over the probation of this will.' After the death of the testator the instruments were admitted to probate. Subsequently defendant, as draftsman of the instruments and as counsel of record for the executors, advised plaintiffs in writing that the residual trust provision was invalid and that plaintiffs would be deprived of the entire amount to which they would have been entitled if the provision had been valid unless they made a settlement with the blood relatives of the testator under which plaintiffs would receive a lesser amount than that provided for them by the testator. As the direct and proximate result of the negligence of defendant and his breach of contract in preparing the testamentary instruments and the written advice referred to above, plaintiffs were compelled to enter into a settlement under which they received a share of the estate amounting to $75,000 less than the sum which they would have received pursuant to testamentary instruments drafted in accordance with the directions of the testator.

It was held in Buckley v. Gray, that an attorney who made a mistake in drafting a will was not liable for negligence or breach of contract to a person named in the will who was deprived of benefits as a result of the error. The court stated that an attorney is liable to his client alone with respect to actions based on negligence in the conduct of his professional duties, and it was reasoned that there could be no recovery for mere negligence where there was no privity by contract or otherwise between the defendant and the person injured. The court further concluded that there could be no recovery on the theory of a contract for the benefit of a third person, because the contract with the attorney was not expressly for the plaintiff's benefit and the testatrix only remotely intended the plaintiff to be benefitted as a result of the contract. For the reasons hereinafter stated the case is overruled.

The reasoning underlying the denial of tort liability in the Buckley case, i.e., the stringent privity test, was rejected in Biakanja v. Irving, where we held that a notary public who, although not authorized to practice law, prepared a will but negligently failed to direct proper attestation was liable in tort to an intended beneficiary who was damaged because of the invalidity of the instrument. It was pointed out that since 1895, when Buckley was decided, the rule that in the absence of privity there was no liability for negligence committed in the performance of a contract had been greatly liberalized. In restating the rule it was said that the determination whether in a specific case the defendant will be held liable to a third person not in privity is a matter of policy and involves the balancing of various factors, among which are the extent to which the transaction was intended to affect the plaintiff, the foreseeability of harm to him, the degree of certainty that the plaintiff suffered injury, the closeness of the connection between the defendant's conduct and the injury, and the policy of preventing future harm. The same general principle must be applied in determining whether a beneficiary is entitled to bring an action for negligence in the drafting of a will when the instrument is drafted by an attorney rather than by a person not authorized to practice law.

Many of the factors which led to the conclusion that the notary public involved in Biakanja was liable are equally applicable here. As in Biakanja, one of the main purposes which the transaction between defendant and the testator intended to accomplish was to provide for the transfer of property to plaintiffs; the damage to plaintiffs in the event of invalidity of the bequest was clearly foreseeable; it became certain, upon the death of the testator without change of the will, that plaintiffs would have received the intended benefits but for the asserted negligence of defendant; and if persons such as plaintiffs are not permitted to recover for the loss resulting from negligence of the draftsman, no one would be able to do so, and the policy to prevent future harm would be impaired.

Since defendant was authorized to practice the profession of an attorney, we must consider an additional factor not present in Biakanja, namely, whether the recognition of liability to beneficiaries of wills negligently drawn by attorneys would impose an undue burden on the profession. Although in some situations liability could be large and unpredictable in amount, this is also true of an attorney's liability to his client. We are of the view that the extension of his liability to beneficiaries injured by a negligently drawn will does not place an undue burden on the profession, particularly when we take into consideration that a contrary conclusion would cause the innocent beneficiary to bear the loss. The fact that the notary public involved in Biakanja was guilty of unauthorized practice of the law was only a minor factor in determining that he was liable, and the absence of the factor in the present case does not justify reaching a different result.

It follows that the lack of privity between plaintiffs and defendant does not preclude plaintiffs from maintaining an action in tort against defendant.

Neither do we agree with the holding in Buckley that beneficiaries damaged by an error in the drafting of a will cannot recover from the draftsman on the theory that they are third-party beneficiaries of the contract between him and the testator. Obviously the main purpose of a contract for the drafting of a will is to accomplish the future transfer of the estate of the testator to the beneficiaries named in the will, and therefore it seems improper to hold, as was done in Buckley, that the testator intended only 'remotely' to benefit those persons. It is true that under a contract for the benefit of a third person performance is usually to be rendered directly to the beneficiary, but this is not necessarily the case. For example, where a life insurance policy lapsed because a bank failed to perform its agreement to pay the premiums out of the insured's bank account, it was held that after the insured's death the beneficiaries could recover against the bank as third-party beneficiaries. Persons who had agreed to procure liability insurance for the protection of the promisees but did not do so were also held liable to injured persons who would have been covered by the insurance, the courts stating that all persons who might be injured were third-party beneficiaries of the contracts to procure insurance. Since, in a situation like those presented here and in the Buckley case, the main purpose of the testator in making his agreement with the attorney is to benefit the persons named in his will and this intent can be effectuated, in the event of a breach by the attorney, only by giving the beneficiaries a right of action, we should recognize, as a matter of policy, that they are entitled to recover as third-party beneficiaries.

Section 1559 of the Civil Code, which provides for enforcement by a third person of a contract made 'expressly' for his benefit, does not preclude this result. The effect of the section is to exclude enforcement by persons who are only incidentally or remotely benefitted. As we have seen, a contract for the drafting of a will unmistakably shows the intent of the testator to benefit the persons to be named in the will, and the attorney must necessarily understand this.

Defendant relies on language in Smith v. Anglo-California Trust Co., and Fruitvale Canning Co. v. Cotton, that to permit a third person to bring an action on a contract there must be 'an intent clearly manifested by the promisor' to secure some benefit to the third person. This language, which was not necessary to the decision in either of the cases, is unfortunate. Insofar as intent to benefit a third person is important in determining his right to bring an action under a contract, it is sufficient that the promisor must have understood that the promisee had such intent. No specific manifestation by the promisor of an intent to benefit the third person is required. The language relied on by defendant is disapproved to the extent that it is inconsistent with these views.

We conclude that intended beneficiaries of a will who lose their testamentary rights because of failure of the attorney who drew the will to properly fulfill his obligations under his contract with the testator may recover as third-party beneficiaries.

However, an attorney is not liable either to his client or to a beneficiary under a will for errors of the kind alleged in the first and second causes of action.

[The court goes on to state that the Rule Against Perpetuities is so complicated that even an attorney exercising ordinary competence cannot always avoid its pitfalls. The court states there is something about the Rule that "seems to facilitate error." The court then adds ". . . and there are few lawyers of any practice in drawing wills and settlements who have not at some time either fallen into the net which the Rule spreads for the unwary, or at least shuddered to think how narrowly they have escaped it." Finding that Attorney Hamm used professional skill and diligence, the court ultimately decides he is not guilty of malpractice, and thus not liable to the beneficiaries of the will.]

Questions to Consider

1. Why had California law formerly held that beneficiaries of a will had no claim against an attorney who negligently prepared the will and thereby damaged them?
2. After *Lucas v. Hamm,* can such beneficiaries make a claim against a negligent attorney? Why or why not?
3. Can you state the court's reasoning for finding that beneficiaries under a will are valid third-party claimants?
4. Would this case have come out differently if the attorney's mistake had involved questions concerning personal federal income tax?
5. Would the beneficiaries under this will be classified as donee or creditor beneficiaries? Why?

Chapter Review Questions

1. What are the different types of third-party beneficiaries?
2. How are third-party-beneficiary contracts created, and how do they differ from assignment and delegation?
3. If the promisor fails to perform to the third party and the third party sues the promisor, what defenses can the promisor raise?
4. If the promisor fails to perform to the third party, can the promisee sue the promisor for performance and, if so, under what circumstances?
5. If the promisor fails to perform to the third party, can the beneficiary sue the promisee and, if so, under what circumstances?
6. Under what circumstances can the promisor and promisee modify the contract when there is a valid third-party beneficiary?

Key Terms

Composition, 277
Creditor beneficiary, 272
Disclaimer, 282
Donee beneficiary, 272
Incidental beneficiary, 273
Intended beneficiaries, 273

Lien, 277
Privity of contract, 272
Promisee, 272
Promisor, 272
Third-party beneficiary, 272
Vest/vesting of rights, 281

Notes

1. *Lawrence v. Fox,* 20 N.Y. 268 (1859).
2. *Seaver v. Ransom,* 224 N.Y. 233, 120 N.E. 639 (1918).
3. *Seaver v. Ransom,* 120 N.E. at 640.
4. Sec, e.g., *Massey v. Del-Valley Corp.,* 46 N.J.Super. 400, 134 A.2d 802 (1957).

Glossary

Absolute promise Where the parties have undertaken their respective duties without any qualifications. The duty to perform arises on the date or at the time set by the contract. Also known as a *covenant*.

Acceptance The effective assent to the offer by its recipient; also, the exercise of the power to make the contract conferred on the offeree by the offeror.

Accommodation A shipment of nonconforming goods identified as a substitute for the goods ordered and sent as an acceptance under a unilateral contract.

Accord The agreement that a different performance will be substituted for the performance due under a contract.

Accord and satisfaction An arrangement by which two contracting parties make a mutual agreement to substitute a different contract for the original one. An **accord** is an offer and acceptance of a performance different from the one due under the contract. A **satisfaction** is performance of the accord. Accord and satisfaction differs from modification in that it results in a completely new, substitute contract.

Account debtors Charge account customers who have the obligation to pay on their accounts.

Accounts Any right to receive payment for goods delivered or to be delivered, or any right to receive payment for services rendered or to be rendered.

Adhesion contracts Agreements in which one party is so much weaker than the other that the stronger party essentially forces the weaker one to "adhere" to the contract it provides.

All relevant evidence test The modern method of deciding whether a contract is integrated. A court looks not only at the written contract, but also at any evidence helpful in revealing whether the contract contains complete and final information about the parties' agreement.

Ambiguity/misunderstanding A doctrine that prevents formation of a contract where the parties had equally reasonable but different interpretations of a material term, phrase, or provision.

Ambiguous offer An offer that does not clearly indicate whether the acceptance called for is a performance or a return promise.

Answer The document used to respond to the complaint.

Anticipatory repudiation Occurs if either party repudiates the contract before the time for performance arrives: also referred to as *anticipatory breach*.

Applicable law provision A contract provision in which the parties themselves state which related state law should govern the transaction.

Assignment A transfer of some or all of a party's contract rights.

Assurance of performance A contracting party who reasonably fears repudiation by the other party may ask for reassurance.

Bargained-for-exchange The requirement of consideration that focuses on *mutuality of exchange* rather than on whether the exchanged value represents loss or gain to a particular party.

Benefit theory of consideration The theory of consideration that requires each party's promises to bestow some benefit on the other.

Bilateral acceptance Acceptance of a contract made by giving to the offeror the requested return promise.

Bilateral contract The type of contract resulting from the effective use of a bilateral acceptance.

Breach A failure to render adequate performance when and where performance is due.

Capacity The ability to understand one's own and the other party's rights and duties under the contract because one is old enough and mentally competent enough.

Cause of action/claim   An argument made by the plaintiff in a lawsuit in which the plaintiff alleges that she suffered wrongs because of the other party's words or conduct.

Chattel paper   A writing or writings intended to create both a debt and a security interest for the creditor in some form of personal property.

Common law   The whole body of rules developed in England from ancient times and adopted in the American colonies before the American Revolution.

Common-law firm offer   An offer in which the offeror makes assurances that the offer will remain open, such as "This offer is guaranteed to last until next Wednesday."

Complaint   The document in which the plaintiff sets out her grievances against the other party and asks the court to grant remedies for these grievances.

Composition   A contract among the creditors of a particular debtor in which they reduce the amount of the debt and/or extend the time for repayment.

Concealment   A defense based on the argument that one contracting party actively withheld information material to the contract or to entering into the contract.

Conclusive presumption   An assertion that cannot be refuted by offering additional evidence. As it pertains to contract integration, the presence of a valid integration clause is a conclusive presumption the contract is the complete and final agreement of the parties.

Condition concurrent   Occurs where both parties have made promises that are dependent on each other and the conditions or performances are to occur at the same time.

Condition precedent   A promise in which an event or events must occur before performance can become due. If the condition does not occur, the performance does not become due.

Condition subsequent   A promise involving an event or events that may occur after performance is begun. If the condition occurs, it cuts off the duty to perform.

Conditional promise   A promise in which the parties have agreed the duty to perform will arise or not arise depending upon whether a certain event or events occur.

Consequential (special) damages   Those damages not assumed to flow naturally from the type of breach involved but caused by special circumstances of the individual case or breach.

Consideration   Acts or promises that involve each party's giving up the right to do something he is otherwise entitled to do or becoming obligated to do something he was not previously obligated to do.

Contract   An enforceable agreement reached through voluntary mutual consent; also, the total obligations and rights resulting from a legally enforceable mutual agreement.

Cost-of-completion   For a construction contract, the price the owner must pay to have the project completed as a result of the builder's minor breach.

Countersuit   A lawsuit filed by the defendant in opposition to or deduction from the claims filed by the plaintiff in the complaint.

Covenant-not-to-compete   A provision in a contract, or a separate contract, in which a party promises not to leave his current employer and start a business which competes with the employer's business.

Covenant   A synonym for an absolute promise.

Cover price   The price an aggrieved buyer pays for the substitute goods to replace those not supplied by the defaulting seller.

Cover   When an aggrieved buyer successfully obtains substitute goods to replace those not supplied by the defaulting seller.

Creditor beneficiary   A third-party beneficiary to whom one of the contracting parties owes a debt.

Cure   Doing whatever is necessary to render the required contract performance as it should have been done in the first place.

Damages   Money which a court orders the losing party in litigation to pay to the successful party in order to make up for wrongs suffered. Contract damages are often viewed as a substitute for performance.

Declaratory judgment   A judgment in which a court determines the rights and responsibilities of parties instead of awarding money damages for violation of those rights or failure to perform the responsibilities.

Deed of Trust or **Mortgage**   A detailed written statement of the contractual debt summarized in a related promissory note and executed in connection with a sale of real property.

Default   Failure of a debtor to pay back the creditor in the manner required.

Defendant   The party being sued in a lawsuit.

Defense   A theory the defendant in a lawsuit uses to assert he does not have liability for the plaintiff's grievances.

Deficiency action   In case of a buyer's breach of a land sales contract, an action filed by the seller to recover the difference between what the breaching buyer was to have paid and what the substitute buyer actually paid.

Delegation   A transfer of contract duties; the appointment of someone else to perform one's own contract duties.

Detriment theory of consideration   The more modern theory of consideration that requires contractual promises to represent a detriment or loss to each promisor.

Detriment   The loss a promisor suffers in agreeing to do something she is not already obligated to do or in agreeing not to do something she is otherwise entitled to do.

Diminution in value   For a construction contract, a general damages award based on the difference between the project as it should have been under the contract and the project as built. Where there is a minor breach, diminution in value is substituted for cost of completion if awarding cost of completion involves unjustified waste.

Disclaimer   Action or words by an intended third-party beneficiary indicating that the beneficiary refuses the third-party rights created under the other two parties' contract.

Discovery procedures   After a lawsuit is filed, the methods used to obtain information in the possession of the other party or to compel, or attempt to compel, the opposing party to disclose relevant information.

Discovery   After a lawsuit is filed, the official information-gathering stage or period of time.

Document   Under the UCC, includes a bill of lading (a list of goods delivered or to be delivered), a receipt for goods, an order for delivery of goods, or any other writing showing the possessor has a right to hold and dispose of the goods described in the writing.

Donative promise   A promise to make a gift.

Donee beneficiary   A third-party beneficiary to whom one of the contracting parties was attempting to make a gift.

Duress   Compelled, or involuntary, consent. Used as a defense, it occurs when one party threatens another to obtain a contract advantage.

Duty to mitigate damages   The responsibility of each contracting party to minimize damages as much as reasonably possible if there is a breach of the contract.

Easement   The right to use the property of another, particularly another's land. Ownership of an easement is considered ownership of an interest in land.

Economic duress   A defense based on the argument that one party forced the other into a contract by creating a situation that so seriously threatened the financial welfare of the other that he had no real choice but to enter a disadvantageous agreement.

Election   A choice between or among legal alternatives, or the exercise of this choice. (E.g., the nonbreaching party may have an election to sue for a major breach and cease performance, to sue for a minor breach and not cease performance, or not to sue at all.)

Emotional distress damages   Damages awarded as compensation for mental suffering of various kinds.

English rule   A .common-law rule for deciding priority among competing assignees. The first assignee to give notice of the assignment to the obligor prevails.

Equitable remedies   Remedies which do not involve money damages as the primary benefit. Equitable remedies usually involve court orders for the losing party to take certain actions to make up for wrongs suffered by the prevailing party.

Estoppel theory   A legal theory used in many areas of law. Under estoppel theory, a party is prevented ("estopped") from denying certain facts when his own conduct makes it unfair to allow him to deny those facts to gain an advantage.

Exculpatory clauses   Provisions in a contract that release a party from liability for injuries caused by its own wrongdoing or negligence.

Excuse of condition   Removal of the requirement of satisfaction of a condition in a promise. If a condition is excused, the duty to perform becomes due even though the condition has not been satisfied.

Excuse/discharge of performance The various doctrines under which a contracting party who is to perform can be legally excused from having to do so.

Executed contract A contract under which all performances have taken place.

Executory contract A contract under which no performance has yet taken place.

Exemplary (punitive) damages Damages awarded to a prevailing party which are not based on compensation for actual losses and are intended to punish and deter the bad conduct involved.

Expectation damages Damages based on the contract under the theory that they are compensation for the breaching party's failure to meet the aggrieved party's expectations concerning performance and profitability.

Express conditions Conditions stated in the contract.

Express warranties Guarantees concerning contract performance or quality of goods, services, or subject matter that are explicitly stated in the contract.

Federal preemption The right of the federal government, through the U.S. Congress, to have exclusive control over some aspects of law if Congress validly exercises its authority and enacts legislation in a given area.

Fiduciary duty A special responsibility of one party to care for the interests of another party which exists between such parties as an attorney and her client or, a trustee and beneficiaries of the trust.

Fiduciary or confidential relationship A legal relationship in which a party with superior knowledge, expertise, or capability has an obligation to protect another less knowledgeable, less expert, or less capable party.

Filing Submission of a financing statement to a central authority such as the office of a County Clerk or Secretary of State.

Financing statement A document signed by the debtor that describes the personal property involved in securing a debt. A financing statement also contains the names and addresses of the secured party and the debtor.

Forfeiture An unreasonable or unjustified loss.

Four corners of the document test The older method of deciding whether a contract is integrated. A court considers only what is written in the contract to decide whether the parties intended it to be their complete and final agreement. Also called the **face of the document test.**

Fraud A defense based on the argument that a contract was procured by, or involves, material deceit of some kind.

Frustration of purpose The doctrine under which contractual duties to perform are discharged because changed circumstances demonstrate that the contract can no longer be carried out for its essential purpose.

Gap-filler provisions Under the UCC, standardized ways to fill in information missing from a contract.

General intangibles Nonphysical assets; under the UCC, include personal property other than goods, accounts, chattel paper, documents, instruments, and money.

General (or standardized) damages Contract damages calculated by applying a standardized method or formula that awards losses considered to flow naturally from the type of breach involved. The aim of standardized damages formulas is to award to the aggrieved party lost net profits and out-of-pocket losses.

Goods All things movable at the time of identification to the contract including the unborn young of animals, growing crops, and other things attached to realty if they can be severed without material harm to the land.

Good faith Honesty in fact in the conduct or transaction concerned. In all modern contracts under the UCC and the common law, there is an implied promise that the parties will act in good faith.

Holder Someone who has possession of a negotiable instrument.

Holder in due course A party who possesses a negotiable instrument, gave consideration for it, and took it in good faith, without knowledge or notice of any defenses the debtor may have.

Illegal contract A contract in which the consideration used by one or both parties is illegal, or for which the contract goal or purpose is illegal. An illegal contract may be unenforceable by one or both parties.

Illegality An act that violates public policy, a statute, or an administrative regulation, or that is unconstitutional, criminal, immoral, or unprofessional. An illegality in a contract may provide a defense to formation or enforcement of the contract.

Illusory promise The traditional term for a promise that does not bind the promisor. Such promises are found where the promisor has not really obligated herself to perform the contract.

Implication The process by which a court supplies missing information for a contract according to the parties' intent.

Implied warranties Guarantees concerning contract performance or quality of goods, services, or subject matter not explicitly stated in the contract, but which the parties would reasonably have assumed were present in the contract, or which the law construes to be in a contract.

Implied-in-fact conditions Conditions not stated in the contract but placed in it by the law on the rationale that the parties must have assumed they were a part of the bargain.

Implied-in-law conditions Conditions not stated in the contract but placed in it by the law for reasons of public policy, even if the parties did not think about them at all; also called *constructive conditions*.

Impossibility The situation where certain acts required under the contract have become objectively impossible.

Impracticability The situation where certain acts required under the contract are not impossible to perform, but can be done only with excessive or unreasonable efforts or costs.

In pari delicto A Latin phrase meaning that the parties are equally wrong in their conduct related to a contract. Courts will deny enforcement to whichever party requests it.

Incidental beneficiary A person who receives an unintended windfall because of a contract made between two other parties. An incidental beneficiary is not a third-party beneficiary with enforceable legal rights.

Incidental damages Damages given to reimburse a prevailing party for relatively small out-of-pocket costs of administering a breach. Shipping, storage, advertising, and additional insurance costs caused by a breach are typical examples of incidental damages.

Indefiniteness The situation in which some necessary information is missing from an alleged contract.

Injunction A form of equitable relief in which the court orders a party to litigation to take some action or to refrain from taking some action.

Installment contract A contract in which performance occurs in separate parts or goods are shipped in separate lots, and each part or lot is to be paid for separately.

Intangible property Property that lacks a physical form, but is capable of being owned or of conferring rights. Patents, copyrights, and trademarks are examples of intangible property.

Integrated contract A contract that represents the final and complete agreement of the parties.

Integration clause or provision A contract provision expressly stating that the contract is the complete and final ("entire") agreement of the parties; also called a **merger clause** or an **entire agreement clause.**

Intended beneficiary. Under the Restatement (Second), any person to whom the two contracting parties intended some benefit to run; includes both a creditor and a donee beneficiary.

Instrument A negotiable instrument (written promise to pay money to its possessor), a certificated security (written right to receive stock dividends or payments), or any other writing that shows the possessor has a right to the payment of money and that is not a security agreement.

Legality In a UCC or common-law contract, this means the contract performance, purpose, and consideration exchanged by the parties are all lawful.

Legal remedies Remedies which involve money damages as the primary benefit.

Lien A charge or claim on property as security for work performed or repayment of a debt.

Liquidated damages Damages awards which are agreed upon prior to a breach in which the parties try to predict reasonable compensation in the event of a breach. The amount of the liquidated damages, or a formula for calculating them, is usually summarized in the contract.

Liquidated damages clause   The provision in a contract which states the amount of liquidated damages to be paid, or a formula for calculating them.

Liquidated debt   A debt where the existence of liability and the amount due are not in dispute.

Maker   The debtor on a promissory note.

Massachusetts rule   A common-law rule for deciding priority among competing assignees. The first assignee prevails unless a successive assignee (1) obtains payment from the obligor, (2) recovers a judgment, (3) enters into a new contract with the obligor, or (4) receives delivery of a tangible item representing the rights assigned where such surrender was required by the obligor's contract.

Mailbox rule   The majority rule followed in the United States that an acceptance is effective at the moment it is properly dispatched, and the offeror no longer has the right to revoke the offer.

Malum in se   A wrong considered to be so heinous or unacceptable that it is "evil in and of itself."

Malum prohibitum   An act that is made illegal by the government or legislature because it involves conduct society wishes to discourage.

Material breach   A breach where so little performance has occurred that a significant part of what the nonbreaching party had achieved by obtaining the contract is seriously threatened, interfered with, or destroyed.

Material term   A term that appears to have a great or important impact or relevance for a contract; a crucial term. Also called an **essential term.**

Mental incapacity   A defense to contract formation or enforcement based on the argument that mentally handicapped persons cannot make contracts that can be enforced against them.

Merchant's firm offer   The UCC's version of the common-law option contract concept. When a merchant creates an option contract under § 2-205, it is called a **UCC firm offer.**

Merchant   Someone who regularly deals in goods of the particular kind involved in the contract, who has special knowledge related to these goods, or who employs such a person as an agent.

Minor breach   A breach that does not cause significant interference with what the nonbreaching party bargained for.

Minor term   A term that appears to have relatively little impact on the contract, or one that does not have key relevance for it. A minor term may be important but is not crucial.

Minority   A defense to contract formation or enforcement based on the argument that one contracting party is too young to make contracts because she is below the age established by state statute or case law.

Mirror-image rule   The common-law rule long followed in England and the United States that an effective acceptance must be identical to the terms of the offer proposed.

Misrepresentation   A defense based on the argument that one contracting party made intentional or negligent assertions of fact that were untrue.

Mistake made in transcription   A defense based on the situation where parties made an oral contract, then put it into a writing that does not accurately summarize the oral agreement.

Mistake made in transmission   A defense based on the situation where an intermediary (such as a telegraph company) conveys a party's offer and makes an error in communicating that offer.

Modification   A change in contract terms made by mutual agreement of the parties after formation of the contract. The common law generally requires additional consideration for a modification; the UCC does not.

Mutual mistake   A defense based on the argument that the parties had erroneous assumptions about material, factual circumstances surrounding the bargain. Mutual mistake may prevent formation of the contract because it robs the parties of a common understanding, or mutual assent.

Mutual release   A release in which each party discharges the other party's remaining duties of performance and excuses liability for nonperformance.

Negotiable instrument   Any document (such as a money order or certified bank check) containing a debtor's promise to pay the party who obtains (holds) the document.

New York rule   A common-law rule for deciding priority among competing assignees. The assignee who received the earliest assignment prevails; the first in time is the first in right.

Nominal consideration   Consideration that is extremely small in relation to the other party's.

Promises supported only by nominal consideration are not enforceable.

Nominal damages A token award of damages in a very small amount given where a party prevails but has suffered no actual economic losses.

Nonconforming goods Goods that do not conform to those required by the contract or that do not conform to those the offeror requested where the offer is for a unilateral contract.

Nondisclosure A defense based on the argument that one contracting party intentionally or negligently failed to reveal material facts concerning the contract.

Nonpossessory security interest An arrangement under which the debtor holds the collateral securing a debt to a secured party creditor.

Novation An arrangement in which two contracting parties bring in a third party as a substitute for one of them. A new contract is formed between the remaining original party and the substitute. A novation requires consent of both parties to the contract and of the new third party.

Objections Arguments that attorneys raise at trial to prevent information from being introduced and used as evidence.

Objective theory of contracts The modern theory of contract making under which courts assume parties had the "intentions" their outward behavior and words would convey to a reasonable person. Each contracting party is entitled to judge the other by the reasonable, outward appearance of things.

Offer A showing of intention to act or refrain from acting in a particular way, such that the recipient of the showing is justified in believing her acceptance will form a legally binding agreement.

Offeree The party to whom the offer is made.

Offeror The party who makes an offer.

Offset Generally, any amount of money deducted from a party's damages and credited to the other party. In a contract action, an offset may be made against the prevailing party's damages for amounts that party failed to mitigate or amounts that party should have paid to the losing party.

Open terms Contract terms for which specific information is purposefully omitted and is intended to be filled in later.

Option contract A preliminary contract made expressly for the purpose of holding open an offer.

Options can also be structured to allow one party the "option" to renew an existing contract at a certain time.

Output contract A contract in which the seller promises all or some percentage of its supply of a certain subject matter to the buyer.

Parol evidence rule A collection of concepts concerning the sanctity of written contracts where they represent final and complete agreement of the parties. When parties to a contract reduce their final agreement to a writing and the writing is complete, courts cannot allow any additions or contradictions to the contract to be introduced as evidence.

Parol evidence Written or oral evidence that is outside the written agreement of the parties; also called **extrinsic evidence.**

Part performance When one or both parties to a contract render some portion of the performance owed. Part performance of an oral contract that falls within the Statute of Frauds may be an exception that allows the contract to be enforced.

Partial breach A minor breach of a contract.
Total breach A breach that is so large and significant that the whole contract is unperformed, interfered with or destroyed.

Party to be charged The party sought to be held liable on a contract.

Perfection of security interest The proper filing of an adequate financing statement.

Perjury Knowingly giving lying testimony after swearing a legal oath to tell the truth.

Personal property Includes almost any sort of property in which one can have an ownership interest and that is not classified as real estate. Under the UCC, most commonly any form of goods, documents, instruments, general intangibles, chattel paper, or accounts. Steel rails, balloons, promissory notes and cattle are examples of personal property.

Plaintiff The party who is suing in a lawsuit; the party who has filed the complaint.

Pleading in the alternative The practice in which a party to a lawsuit advances arguments that conflict with one another.

Possessory security interest An arrangement under which the creditor holds the debtor's collateral securing a debt.

Precontractual liability   Losses caused in the negotiating phase of a contract and before it is formed.

Predominant factor test   A method used by courts in doubtful cases, to determine whether a contract is governed by the UCC or the common law. Depending upon whether the main subject matter and purpose of the contract—its thrust—deal with goods or things that are not goods, a court applies either the UCC or the common law, respectively.

Preexisting duty rule   The rule that if a party already has a legal duty to perform some act or acts, a new promise to perform these same acts does not constitute valid consideration.

Prenuptial agreements   Contracts concerning the separate and joint property rights of people who plan to marry.

Prevention   Where a party deliberately prevents a condition or the other party's performance from occurring. To excuse a condition on the grounds of prevention, the conduct must involve wrongful behavior or conduct by the contracting party favored by the condition.

Primary authority   The law in its entirety, encompassing cases, statutes, and administrative rules, regulations, and decisions.

Priority of assignees   The order of preference given to competing assignees under the common law or the UCC.

Privity of contract   The legal relationship existing between two contracting parties.

Procedural unconscionability   Grossly unfair or oppressive conduct by one contracting party during the bargaining process.

Promisee   The recipient of a promise.

Promisor   The maker of a promise.

Promissory estoppel   An estoppel argument or theory that allows a plaintiff to enforce the promisor's promise although she has not given a promise supported by consideration. The promisor is prevented from using lack of consideration as an argument to defeat enforceability of his own promise.

Promissory note   A written contract that creates a debt of one party to another party.

Reformation   An equitable remedy in which a court rewrites an inaccurate written contract to conform to what is proven to be the original oral agreement or understanding of the parties.

Rejection   Conduct or words (or a combination of the two) on the part of the offeree indicating a refusal of the offer. A rejection terminates the offer.

Release   A contract in which a party voluntarily gives up some or all of his rights. Releases are a common way to discharge remaining contractual obligations through mutual agreement. Releases are also used to settle litigation.

Releasee   Under a release, the party who is being discharged from liability for nonperformance.

Releasor   Under a release, the party giving up some or all of her contractual rights.

Reliance damages   Damages awarded as an alternative to recovery on a contract which are measured by calculating a party's out-of-pocket losses.

Reliance   A change in position that occurs when one party is induced to action or forbearance of action because of information contained in a promise.

Reporters   Collections of case opinions written by judges.

Repudiation   A clear indication in advance of an intention not to perform contractual duties arising in the future.

Requirements contract   A contract in which the buyer agrees to obtain from the seller, and the seller agrees to supply, all or some percentage of a particular subject matter as needed.

Rescission   A decision by a court, or sometimes by the parties themselves, to cancel a contract between them.

Restatements   A series of volumes on one topic, such as contract law, that attempt to standardize that topic by describing and defining the law.

Restitution   An award of damages not based on the contract and calculated by determining the money equivalent of all benefits the aggrieved party has conferred on the other.

Revocation   Conduct or words (or a combination of the two) on the part of the offeror indicating the offer has been withdrawn. A revocation terminates the offer and can occur any time before an effective acceptance.

Satisfaction   The performance of all accord.

Secondary authority   All publications that discuss the law or are used as tools to find the law.

Secured party   The creditor in a secured transaction.

Secured transaction   Any type of debtor-creditor relationship in which the creditor requires the debtor to put up collateral (property) to guarantee repayment of the debt.

Security   In a secured transaction, the property of a debtor in which the creditor acquires rights, including the right to seize and sell the property if the debtor stops paying the loan.

Statute of Frauds   An English statute passed in 1676 and adopted in modified form throughout the United States; requires some legal documents, including certain kinds of contracts, to be in writing.

Statute of limitations   A law that places a time limit on the right to file a lawsuit.

Substantive unconscionability   Unfair or oppressive provisions in the actual terms of a contract, without regard to the bargaining process by which the terms became part of the contract.

Surety or guarantor   A party who has agreed to pay the debt of another. Laypeople often refer to this arrangement as co-signing.

Suretyship agreements   A contract under which one party has undertaken to pay a debt that is not his own, for another party, out of his own resources.

Tangible property   Property that possesses some physical form. Steel ingots, exercise machines, and growing crops are examples.

Tender   Readiness to perform or, sometimes, the performance itself.

Thing in action   The right to sue for recovery of personal property.

Third party   A party who is not one of the parties to a contract but nevertheless acquires rights or obligations under it.

Third-party beneficiary   An outsider to a contract made by two other parties who acquires rights under it; sometimes called simply the **beneficiary.**

Specific performance   In contract cases, a form of equitable relief in which the court orders one or both parties to perform according to the contract.

Tort   A legally recognized injury to one's person or property.

Total breach   A breach that is so large and significant that the whole contract is unperformed, interfered with or destroyed.

Treatise   A long, detailed, scholarly study of a particular area of law.

UCC merchant's provisions   The provisions of the UCC that apply only to experts in buying and selling goods.

Unconscionability   A defense based on the argument that in light of commercial realities or the circumstances of a particular trade or case, the contract, its language, or the bargaining process was so one-sided as to be extremely unfair.

Undue influence   A defense based on the argument that a contracting party with a confidential or fiduciary relationship and duty to another abused that relationship to obtain a contract advantage.

Uniform Commercial Code (UCC)   A scholarly attempt, first published in the 1950s, to systematize and summarize several different areas of commercial law in one document.

Unilateral acceptance   Acceptance of a contract made by giving the actual performance requested by the offeror instead of giving a promise to perform.

Unilateral contract   The type of contract resulting from an effective unilateral acceptance.

Unilateral mistake   A defense based on the argument that one contracting party made a clerical or computational error and should therefore be allowed to rescind the contract.

Unliquidated debt   A debt where the parties have a legitimate disagreement as to the existence of liability or the amount due.

Unsecured transaction   Any type of debtor-creditor relationship in which the debtor does not guarantee the debt by putting up property.

Vest/vesting of rights   A concept fixing the time at which the promisor and promisee lose the right to make contract changes that would damage the rights and expectations of the beneficiary.

Waiver   Voluntarily and intentionally giving up a known legal right or rights.

Warranties   Guarantees in a contract or in an assignment of a contract. Warranties may be express or implied.

Index